June 30–July 4, 2014
Marcq-en-Baroeul, France

I0050987

Association for Computing Machinery

Advancing Computing as a Science & Profession

QoSA'14

Proceedings of the 10th International ACM SIGSOFT Conference on

Quality of Software Architectures

(part of CompArch 2014)

Sponsored by:
ACM SIGSOFT

Association for
Computing Machinery

Advancing Computing as a Science & Profession

The Association for Computing Machinery
2 Penn Plaza, Suite 701
New York, New York 10121-0701

Copyright © 2014 by the Association for Computing Machinery, Inc. (ACM). Permission to make digital or hard copies of portions of this work for personal or classroom use is granted without fee provided that copies are not made or distributed for profit or commercial advantage and that copies bear this notice and the full citation on the first page. Copyright for components of this work owned by others than ACM must be honored. Abstracting with credit is permitted. To copy otherwise, to republish, to post on servers or to redistribute to lists, requires prior specific permission and/or a fee. Request permission to republish from: permissions@acm.org or Fax +1 (212) 869-0481.

For other copying of articles that carry a code at the bottom of the first or last page, copying is permitted provided that the per-copy fee indicated in the code is paid through www.copyright.com.

Notice to Past Authors of ACM-Published Articles
ACM intends to create a complete electronic archive of all articles and/or other material previously published by ACM. If you have written a work that has been previously published by ACM in any journal or conference proceedings prior to 1978, or any SIG Newsletter at any time, and you do NOT want this work to appear in the ACM Digital Library, please inform permissions@acm.org, stating the title of the work, the author(s), and where and when published.

ISBN: 978-1-4503-2576-9 (Digital)

ISBN: 978-1-4503-3117-3 (Print)

Additional copies may be ordered prepaid from:

ACM Order Department
PO Box 30777
New York, NY 10087-0777, USA

Phone: 1-800-342-6626 (USA and Canada)
+1-212-626-0500 (Global)
Fax: +1-212-944-1318
E-mail: acmhelp@acm.org
Hours of Operation: 8:30 am – 4:30 pm ET

Printed in the USA

QoSA 2014 Chairs' Welcome

Welcome to th e Ten th International ACM SIGSOFT *Conference on the Quality of Software Architectures* – QoSA 2014. As software takes on more mission-critical and life-critical ro les the qualities pro vided by a software arch itecture b ecome more critical as well. Th is year th e m ain theme o f Qo SA is "Arch itecting for adaptiv ity". W ith th e ad vances i n m obile n etworks an d embedded systems, we see a p roliferation of sy stems that are m eant to im prove human life, increase sa fety, provide e ntertainment, etc. Ex amples of s uch sy stems include s mart hom es, intelligent navigation, emergency coordination, etc. A k ey issue in these systems is th e ability to adapt to a current situation in the physical world, such that outputs provided by the system remain relevant. In safety critical sys tems this is als o connected with retaining dependability in changing or even unanticipated situations.

This year QoSA attracted 47 subm issions of which 15 were acce pted (13 regular papers a nd 2 short pa pers) for a 32% a cceptance rate. The topi cs range from structural qualiti es suc h as modularity to the runtime qualities of reliability and resilience. In addition, the program includes a keynote talk by Bertrand Meyer, Chair of Software Engineering at ETH Zurich.

QoSA is one of t he fe derated eve nts at C ompArch, th is year to gether with "CBSE 2014: 17 th International ACM SI GSOFT Sy mposium on C omponent B ased Software E ngineering," a nd "WCOP 2014: 19th International Doctoral Symposium on Components and Architecture". We are grateful to the organizers of all these events for making CompArch a successful federated event on Component-based Software Engineering and Software Architecture.

As program chairs at a confer ence lik e Qo SA our job i s sim ple – brin g tog ether world-class research papers with a world-class program committee. We would like to thank all who submitted papers. Their high-quality content is the reason QoSA is a reality. Also, we would like to thank the members of t he pr ogram com mittee who worked hard t o en sure that e very paper had 3 re views and was given careful co nsideration. Your har d w ork i s the reas on QoSA is st rong. Thanks t o Lionel Seinturier, University Lille 1, General Chair of CompArch 2014, and his organization team for t heir exce llent wor k i n coor dinating t he federat ed event s an d m aking p ossible a great conference. Special thanks go to L isa To lles, Cind y Edw ards and th eir a ssociates at S heridan Communications for processing t he papers i n a t imely m anner. Fi nally, we t hank t he hosting university and ACM SIGSOFT.

We hope that yo ur ti me at Qo SA will b e profita ble and en joyable and that you will co ntinue to support QoSA in future years with your submissions and attendance. We also encourage attendees to attend th e keynote and invited talk p resentations. Th ese v aluable and in sightful talks can and will guide us to a better understanding of the future:

Tomas Bures
Faculty of Mathematics and Physics
Charles University
Prague, Czech Republic

John D. McGregor
School of Computing
Clemson University
Clemson, USA

Table of Contents

Session 5: Architecture Analysis II
Session Chair: Ivica Crnkovic *(Mälardalen University)*

Tutorials

Author Index

QoSA 2014 Conference Organization

General Chair: Lionel Seinturier (*Université Lille 1, France*)

Program Chairs: Tomas Bures (*Charles University, Czech Republic*)
John D. McGregor (*Clemson University, USA*)

Local Organizing Committee: Laurence Duchien (*Université Lille 1, France*)
Martin Monperrus (*Université Lille 1, France*)

Publicity Chair: Romain Rouvoy (*Université Lille 1, France*)

Program Committee: Mehmet Aksit (*University of Twente, The Netherlands*)
Aldeida Aleti (*Monash University, Australia*)
Muhammad Ali Babar (*IT University of Copenhagen, Denmark*)
Steffen Becker (*University of Paderborn, Germany*)
Jan Bosch (*Chalmers University of Technology, Sweden*)
Barbora Buhnova (*Masaryk University, Czech Republic*)
Vittorio Cortellessa (*Universita of L'Aquila, Italy*)
Ivica Crnkovic (*Mälardalen University, Sweden*)
Antinisca Di Marco (*University of L'Aquila, Italy*)
Peter Feiler (*SEI, USA*)
Aniruddha Gokhale (*Vanderbilt University, USA*)
Vincenzo Grassi (*University of Roma "Tor Vergata", Italy*)
Lars Grunske (*University of Stuttgart, Germany*)
Rich Hilliard (*IEEE, United States*)
Samuel Kounev (*Karlsruhe Institute of Technology, Germany*)
Heiko Koziolek (*ABB Corporate Research, Germany*)
Patricia Lago (*VU University Amsterdam, The Netherlands*)
Marin Litoiu (*York University, Canada*)
José Merseguer (*Universidad de Zaragoza, Spain*)
Raffaela Mirandola (*Politecnico di Milano, Italy*)
Sven Overhage (*University of Bamberg, Germany*)
Claus Pahl (*Dublin City University, Ireland*)
Dorina Petriu (*Carleton University, Canada*)
Alfonso Pierantonio (*University of L'Aquila, Italy*)
Ralf Reussner (*Karlsruhe Institute of Technology, Germany*)
Jose-Raul Romero (*University of Cordoba, Spain*)
Roshanak Roshandel (*Seattle University, USA*)
Antonino Sabetta (*SAP Research Sophia-Antipolis, France*)
Klaus Schmid (*University of Hildesheim, Germany*)
Heinz Schmidt (*Computer Science, RMIT University, Australia*)
Jean-Guy Schneider (*Swinburne University of Technology, Australia*)
Michael Smit (*Dalhousie University, Canada*)
Judith Stafford (*University of Colorado Boulder, USA*)

Program Committee (continued): Clemens Szyperski *(Microsoft Research, USA)*
Bedir Tekinerdogan *(Bilkent University, Turkey)*
Petr Tuma *(Charles University, Czech Republic)*

Additional reviewers:

Aakash Ahmed
Ahmet Arif Aydin
Jan Olaf Blech
Hongyu Pei Breivold
Fabian Brosig
Antonio Filieri
Robert Heinrich
André van Hoorn
Rouven Krebs
Sebastian Lehrig
Rizwan Mian
Tim Miller

Fouad Omri
Ian Peake
Diego Perez
Marie Christin Platenius
Aurora Ramírez
Gaetana Sapienza
Maria Spichkova
Simon Spinner
Misha Strittmatter
Catia Trubiani
Jürgen Walter

Sponsor:

Trust or Verify?

Bertrand Meyer
ETH Zurich & Eiffel Software
Bertrand.Meyer@inf.ethz.ch

Abstract

Software quality should be built in from the start: a priori.

Software quality can only be guaranteed through verification: a posteriori.

It is easy to find arguments for either of these views. Is quality an a priori or a posteriori attribute? Saying "both" does not answer the question, only turns it into a new one: how should we combine the two approaches?

Building on both my experience with the Eiffel method and the verification work at ETH I will try to define what exact doses of, respectively, "correctness by construction" and modern verification techniques can, at a realistic cost, yield the best possible quality.

The ETH work is based on the idea of "Verification As a Matter Of Course": make verification available to all developments, not just the most critical applications. Integrated in the Eiffel Verification Environment (EVE), the approach combines many different forms of verification, some static (proofs, based on Boogie), some dynamic (tests, based on the AutoTest automatic test framework. The talk will include some of the results from the EVE effort to discuss future trends in the production of reliable architectures.

Categories and Subject Descriptors

D.2.4 [Software Engineering]: Software/Program Verification – *Programming by contract*; D.3.2 [Programming Languages]: Language Classifications – *Object-oriented languages*

Keywords

Eiffel, Design by Contract, correctness by construction

Short Bio

Bertrand Meyer is Professor of Software Engineering at ETH Zurich and Chief Architect of Eiffel Software, based in Santa Barbara, California. He is the author of numerous articles and several best-selling textbooks. He designed the Eiffel programming language and originated the ideas of Design by Contract as well as a number of pioneering ideas in object technology and other areas of software engineering.

Permission to make digital or hard copies of part or all of this work for personal or classroom use is granted without fee provided that copies are not made or distributed for profit or commercial advantage, and that copies bear this notice and the full citation on the first page. Copyrights for third-party components of this work must be honored. For all other uses, contact the owner/author(s). Copyright is held by the author/owner(s).

QoSA'14, June 30–July 4, 2014, Marcq-en-Baroeul, France.
ACM 978-1-4503-2576-9/14/06.
http://dx.doi.org/10.1145/2602576.2611460

Automatic Detection of Performance Anti-patterns in Inter-component Communications

Alexander Wert[1], Marius Oehler[2], Christoph Heger[1], Roozbeh Farahbod[2]
[1]Karlsruhe Institute of Technology, Am Fasanengarten 5, Karlsruhe, Germany
[2]SAP AG, Vincenz-Priessnitz-Strasse 1, Karlsruhe, Germany
alexander.wert@kit.edu , marius.oehler@sap.com , christoph.heger@kit.edu ,
roozbeh.farahbod@sap.com

ABSTRACT

Performance problems such as high response times in software applications have a significant effect on the customer's satisfaction. In enterprise applications, performance problems are frequently manifested in inefficient or unnecessary communication patterns between software components originating from poor architectural design or implementation. Due to high manual effort, thorough performance analysis is often neglected, in practice. In order to overcome this problem, automated engineering approaches are required for the detection of performance problems. In this paper, we introduce several heuristics for measurement-based detection of well-known performance anti-patterns in inter-component communications. The detection heuristics comprise load and instrumentation descriptions for performance tests as well as corresponding detection rules. We integrate these heuristics with Dynamic Spotter, a framework for automatic detection of performance problems. We evaluate our heuristics on four evaluation scenarios based on an e-commerce benchmark (TPC-W) where the heuristics detect the expected communication performance anti-patterns and pinpoint their root causes.

1. INTRODUCTION

In today's enterprise software systems, software performance plays a major role as a differentiating factor between competing software vendors and operators. Software performance comprises response times, throughput and resource consumption. Thus, performance of software systems influences not only the total cost of ownership of software systems but may significantly affect customer satisfaction.

As most enterprise software systems are distributed in terms of components and system nodes, inefficient or even unnecessary communication between single components may hurt performance of the overall system. This includes communication via a message oriented middleware (MOM), remote service calls as well as communication between application servers and corresponding database servers. *Communication*

Performance Anti-patterns (CPAs) such as the *Empty Semi Trucks (EST)* anti-pattern [21] or the *Stifle* anti-pattern [5] describe improper, recurrent design or implementation decisions which impair the performance of the corresponding software system through inefficient communication patterns between individual components. Revealing performance anti-patterns requires deep expertise in software performance engineering as well as detailed understanding of the target system. Identifying the root cause of the revealed problems is even more challenging, especially in large-scale systems with millions of lines of code. In order to manage the complexity of these tasks, systematic engineering approaches are needed which support developers and performance analysts in detecting performance problems and their root causes, or even automate the detection process.

Model-based approaches [4, 22, 25] provide means for performance evaluation of the target system during an early development phase when no executable implementation is available. However, their capabilities on revealing performance problems of a target system can only be as good as the detail level of the available information about the final system. Consequently, at this stage only high level performance problems can be detected. Furthermore, it is not unusual that actual realizations of software systems deviate from the initially created architectures [8]. Performance anti-patterns introduced as part of such deviations cannot be detected by model-based approaches as long as the deviations are not applied back to the initial models. On the other hand, though measurement-based approaches can only be applied when runnable artifacts of the target system are available, they provide more accurate results as they investigate the actual realization of the target system, rather than an abstract model. Existing measurement-based approaches which are applied in the testing phase of the development process either apply regression testing [3,6] to reveal performance anomalies without consecutive root cause analysis, or focus on detection of performance bottlenecks [7, 12]. Approaches which automatically detect performance anti-patterns at operation time [14] are helpful to quickly resolve performance problems when they occur, however, resolving performance problems at operation time is very expensive [2]. Furthermore, the approach in

We follow up on the idea of automatically detecting performance problems. In this paper, we introduce five novel heuristics for the detection of *Communication Performance Anti-patterns (CPAs)*. Designed for the testing phase of a development process, the heuristics utilize the principle of systematic, goal-oriented experimentation [11] which allows

Permission to make digital or hard copies of all or part of this work for personal or classroom use is granted without fee provided that copies are not made or distributed for profit or commercial advantage and that copies bear this notice and the full citation on the first page. Copyrights for components of this work owned by others than ACM must be honored. Abstracting with credit is permitted. To copy otherwise, or republish, to post on servers or to redistribute to lists, requires prior specific permission and/or a fee. Request permissions from permissions@acm.org.

QoSA'14, June 30–July 4, 2014, Marcq-en-Baroeul, France.
Copyright 2014 ACM 978-1-4503-2577-6/14/06 ...$15.00.
http://dx.doi.org/10.1145/2602576.2602579.

an efficient and detailed detection of performance problems and their root causes without major distortion of the measurement data. To this end, the heuristics comprise specific instrumentation descriptions for goal-oriented data gathering from the target system, load descriptions for systematic performance tests as well as detection rules which are applied on the gathered data. For an automated execution, we integrate the heuristics with a framework (*Dynamic Spotter*, in [24] referred to as PPD) for measurement-based diagnosis of performance problems. In this work we offer the following contributions:

1) We provide heuristics for measurement-based detection of a selected set of CPAs.
2) We integrate the heuristics with the Dynamic Spotter, which allows a full automation of their execution. In this context, we further evaluate the applicability and extensibility of the Dynamic Spotter approach.
3) We evaluate the heuristics on four scenarios using the TPC-W benchmark [13] as target application. The evaluation shows the applicability of the described heuristics and their integration with Dynamic Spotter.

The remainder of the paper is structured as follows: In Section 2, we give an overview on known CPAs and their symptoms. Section 3 gives an overview on the Dynamic Spotter approach. In Section 4, the detection heuristics are described in detail. The heuristics are evaluated on the TPC-W benchmark in Section 5. An overview on related work is given in Section 6. Finally, Section 7 concludes this paper with an outlook on future work.

2. COMMUNICATION PERFORMANCE ANTI-PATTERNS

Communication Performance Anti-patterns (CPAs) exhibit poor software performance due to improper messaging, service invocation or method calling behaviour. CPAs become particularly expensive with regards to performance, if single communication steps have to overcome latency in form of computational overhead or network distance. Thus, remote service calls, communication over message oriented middleware (MOM), or database invocations are typical contexts where CPAs occur.

In previous work [23, 24] we made the observation that different performance anti-patterns exhibit similar symptoms, which provides a more systematic way to structure performance anti-patterns. While the focus of the performance problem structure in [24] was on performance bottlenecks, in this paper we extend the hierarchy with CPAs. Following this structuring idea, we collected some communication-related performance problems, symptoms and root causes from literature and structured them in a hierarchical way. The result is depicted in Figure 1.

All occurrences of CPAs come with a high communication overhead which results in high response times under a significant load. In the context of messaging systems the overhead comes from message processing through the messaging clients and the messaging server, such as queueing, serialization, etc. Furthermore, in distributed systems messages have to pass a network, entailing latency which directly affects response times. We subsume these overheads under the symptom *Excessive Messaging*. We consider two different performance anti-patterns which cause excessive messaging: The *Blob*

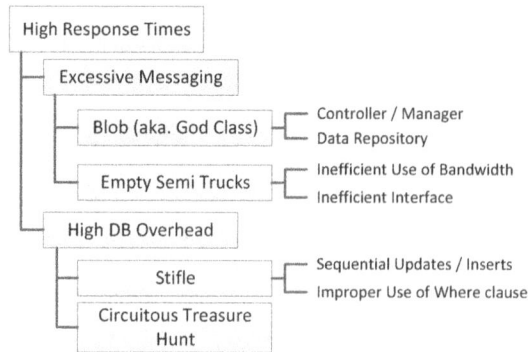

Figure 1: CPA Hierarchy

(aka. *God Class*) [19] and the *Empty Semi Trucks* [21] performance anti-patterns. Both anti-patterns result in an unnecessarily high amount and frequency of messages. A *Blob* is a central component which encapsulates either a big portion of a system's logic and processing code or all the data required for processing. In the former case, the *Blob* serves as a *Controller* or *Manager* collecting data from other components, processing the data on its own, and sending instructions to other components. In the latter case, the *Blob* is a *Data Repository* comprising no, or only little processing logic. Other components store data in the repository and retrieve it from there to perform some data processing. Both manifestations of the *Blob* cause excessive messaging between the *Blob* component and other components. The *Empty Semi Trucks* anti-pattern describes the problem of transmitting too many small messages instead of aggregating messages. As each message comes with a small overhead, taken on the whole, the ratio between the overall messaging overhead and the message payload is way too high, resulting in poor performance. An *Inefficient Interface* which does not allow to aggregate messages or an *Inefficient Use of Bandwidth* are typical root causes for the *Empty Semi Trucks* anti-pattern.

Beside messaging, database queries are another source for the occurrence of CPAs. Each database query entails an overhead for query processing, such as query translation, parsing and optimization. If the database is accessed through a network, network latency adds up to the overhead. Thus, frequent database queries result in a *High DB Overhead (HDBO)*, reducing the performance of the overall system. The *Stifle* [5] and the *Circuitous Treasure Hunt* (CTH) [20] are typical performance anti-patterns causing unnecessarily frequent database requests. The *Stifle* anti-pattern results from an improper use of the database interface. For instance, performing single update or insert statements into the same database table in a loop instead of doing it in a batch results in an unnecessarily high amount of database requests and lower potential for the database to optimize query execution. Not making proper use of the power of WHERE clauses in database queries may result in an unnecessarily high amount of database requests, too. The *CTH* anti-pattern is a result from a bad database schema or query design. *CTH* is similar to the *Stifle*, however, comes with a data dependency between the single queries. For instance, a query requires the result of a previous query as input. The longer the chain of dependencies between individual queries the more the *CTH* anti-pattern hurts performance.

3. THE DYNAMIC SPOTTER APPROACH

In [23, 24] we introduced an extensible framework for automated detection of performance problems (in the following referred to as *Dynamic Spotter*) based on systematic experimentation. The CPA detection heuristics presented in this paper are integrated with the Dynamic Spotter framework. Therefore, in the following, we provide a short summary of the idea behind the Dynamic Spotter. For more information on the Dynamic Spotter approach we refer to [24].

The Dynamic Spotter framework builds on the Performance Problem Diagnostics approach (PPD) introduced in [24] and comprises three main components: (1) a performance problem hierarchy which encapsulates a large set of known performance anti-patterns (as mentioned in Section 2), (2) heuristics to detect each performance anti-pattern in the hierarchy, and (3) an automated systematic experimentation approach that detects performance problems in a system under test (SUT) and identifies their possible root causes.

Measurement-based detection of performance problems requires gathering of measurement data during execution. However, fully detailed instrumentation of the SUT entails a significant measurement overhead which distorts the actual measurement data. Thus, instrumentation of the SUT should be as sparse as possible. On the other hand, executing measurement experiments is time-consuming which means that the number of required experiments should be kept as small as possible. A performance problem hierarchy as mentioned in Section 2 can be utilized to fulfill both requirements while systematically investigating the SUT with respect to existing performance problems. Therefore, the hierarchy is used as a kind of decision tree investigating the SUT gradually from the symptoms of performance problems to the root causes. If a performance problem represented by a node in the performance problem hierarchy has been detected in the SUT, then all the children of that node (more concrete forms of that problem) are investigated in the SUT. If a performance problem could not be found in the SUT, then the whole sub-tree under the corresponding node in the hierarchy is skipped.

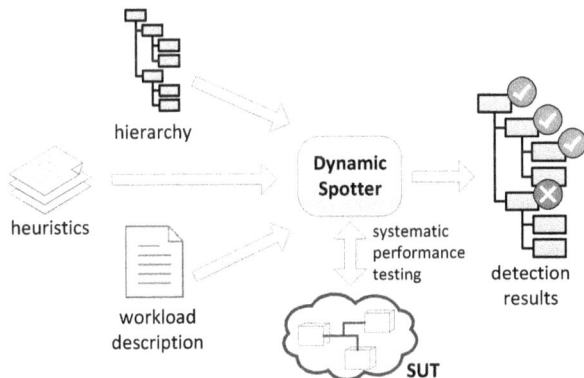

Figure 2: Overview on Dynamic Spotter

Figure 2 gives a schematic overview on Dynamic Spotter. Dynamic Spotter takes as input the described hierarchy of performance problems, for each node of the hierarchy a corresponding detection heuristic and a workload description for load generation. While traversing the hierarchy, Dynamic Spotter executes, for each node of the hierarchy, a set of performance tests according to the load scenarios defined by the corresponding heuristic. To this end, Dynamic Spotter dynamically instruments the SUT specifically for the performance problem under investigation. For load generation, Dynamic Spotter triggers an external load driver using the given workload description. Executing the performance tests yields measurement results for each node of the hierarchy which are analyzed by the detection strategies of corresponding heuristics. A detection strategy processes measurement data and evaluates the corresponding detection rules. Finally, Dynamic Spotter provides a detection result for each node of the hierarchy stating whether the problem represented by the node has been detected in the SUT or not.

Dynamic Spotter is designed as an extensible framework, such that the detection approach can be easily extended with new hierarchies of performance problems, additional detection heuristics as well as plug-ins for further instrumentation and load generation strategies. In this paper we provide an additional performance problem hierarchy and new detection heuristics for CPAs which we integrate with the *Dynamic Spotter* approach for automated execution.

4. DETECTION HEURISTICS

In this section, we introduce five detection heuristics for the CPAs of the hierarchy shown in Figure 1. However, in this paper we do not present a detection heuristic for *Circuitous Treasure Hunt (CTH)*. As described in Section 2, *CTH* implies semantic data dependency between individual database requests. Thus, in order to detect a CTH anti-pattern semantic analysis of the data flow is required, which is beyond the scope of this paper.

For the application of the heuristics described in this section, we assume that we know the following requirements: (1) the maximum load L^{max} the SUT is expected to handle, and (2) a threshold R^{max} for service response times, which defines a violation of performance requirements. This information may come from a domain expert or some service level agreements. We use this information, inter alia, to detect the top-level symptom *High Response Times*. If the average response times of any service of the SUT exceeds R^{max} under the load intensity L^{max}, Dynamic Spotter assumes a *High Response Times* symptom and, thus, descends in the performance problem hierarchy (cf. Figure 1).

In the context of the Dynamic Spotter approach, a detection heuristic[1] for each performance problem comprises three parts: (1) a description of required data to be observed, (2) a description of a series of different load scenarios (in the following referred to as experiments), and (3) a detection strategy applied to the observed data. In the following, we describe the detection heuristics for the remaining nodes of the CPA Hierarchy (cf. Figure 1).

4.1 Detecting Excessive Messaging

As described in Section 2, excessive messaging leads to a high messaging overhead. If the messaging intensity in a SUT is independent of the load, the messaging overhead is a constant which rarely constitutes a performance problem. Let us assume that the messaging intensity directly depends on the system's load. In this case, the scaling behaviour of

---

[1]The results of our detection approach are associated with a degree of uncertainty. Therefore we use the term *heuristic* in this context.

the message throughput with the load is an indicator for excessive messaging. A perfectly scaling system with a minimal messaging overhead shows a proportional growth behaviour between the load committed to the SUT and the throughput of messages. In the case of excessive messaging, the message throughput stops growing linearly before the maximal expected load L^{max} is reached, due to limited passive resources like network bandwidth or message queues. Thus, in order to detect whether messaging in a SUT constitutes a performance problem, we need to evaluate whether the message throughput grows proportionally with the load committed to the SUT. To this end, we develop a detection heuristic for excessive messaging as follows:

Load Description: We define a series of experiments E_i ($i \in \{1, \ldots, n\}$) with increasing loads L_i (number of concurrent users), such that:

$$L_n = L^{max} \wedge \forall i \in \{1, .., n-1\} : L_i < L_{i+1} \qquad (1)$$

Instrumentation Description: For each experiment E_i, this heuristic requires the following metrics to be collected: average throughput T_i of messages passing the MOM, average queue lengths $Q_{i,j}$ ($1 < j < m$) of all m messaging queues as well as the average network utilization $U(nw)_i$.

Detection Analysis: Based on this data, the detection strategy comprises two analysis steps: (1) The experiment E_1 with a load of one user is considered as baseline. As we want to investigate whether the message throughput increases proportionally with the load, the throughput data T_i is normalized with respect to the baseline value T_1: $\widehat{T}_i = \frac{T_i}{T_1}$

(2) On the tuples $(L_i, \widehat{T}_i)$ a linear regression of the form $\widehat{T}(L) = a * L + b$ is applied. As the throughput values have been normalized, we assume a proportional growth of the message throughput, if the slope a of the regression line is close to one. Otherwise, if $a < 0.9$ we assume that the message throughput does not scale properly. If at the same time during any of the experiments E_i, either the network or the CPU of the MOM is utilized to capacity, the heuristic detects an excessive messaging problem which exhausts the resources of the SUT. We consider a CPU as utilized to capacity, if its utilization exceeds 90%. For the capacity limit of the network we use the formula from [10]:

$$N^{max} = R_p * \left(\left\lfloor \frac{S_p}{S_m} \right\rfloor + 1 \right) * \frac{S_m}{2} \qquad (2)$$

Assuming that messaging uses TCP, due to TCP's control flow algorithm the maximal throughput N^{max} is determined by the TCP packet rate R_p, packet size S_p and average message size S_m (cf. Equation 2). If the measured network utilization $U(nw)$ approaches the maximum capacity ($U(nw) > 0.9 * N^{max}$), we consider the network as saturated. In the case that none of the resources are utilized to capacity but at least one message queue length $Q_{i,j}$ grows steadily with the load, the heuristic detects an excessive messaging problem, too. However, in this case message throughput is limited due to long waiting times in the queue.

4.2 Detecting the Blob

In a distributed system, from the communication perspective, a Blob anti-pattern is characterized by a relatively high number of messages transmitted between one single component and all other components. In order to detect a Blob component, the message flow as well as its impact on the performance needs to be analyzed.

Load Description: For the detection of a Blob anti-pattern one experiment is executed, whereby a high load (L^{max}) is applied to make the performance problem visible.

Instrumentation Description: In order to capture the messaging patterns, measurement data from messaging methods is required. Therefore, we utilize the dynamic instrumentation functionality provided by the Dynamic Spotter framework. For this heuristic, measurement probes are dynamically injected into messaging-related methods (like sending and receiving messages, creating connections to the MOM, etc.) capturing the following information:

- *connection-id*: Our assumption is, that each component instance uses its own connection to the MOM. We use the connection id for identification of the component instance.
- *stack trace*: The first time a connection is used, the stack trace is recorded for later root cause localization.
- *message-id*: For each message, a unique message id is transmitted with the message. This id is used to correlate message dispatches with message receptions.
- *timestamp*: Message transmission times are calculated from the timestamps of dispatches and receptions.

Conducting an experiment with the described instrumentation yields a set of records each containing the described information for each sent and received message.

Detection Analysis: Based on this data, the heuristic calculates for each component its contributing part to the overall messaging time. If a component constitutes a significant portion of the overall messaging time, it is considered as a Blob. Therefore, following analysis steps are conducted: First, message dispatches and receptions are correlated using the message-id. Let C be the set of components involved in messaging. Using the connection-id, transmission directions $a \rightarrow b$ ($a, b \in C$) are assigned to each message transmission. Furthermore, for each message transmission a transmission time is calculated using the timestamps. This data processing step yields for each transmission direction a set $T_{a \rightarrow b}$ of message transmission times. For each component $x \in C$, the messaging time contribution p_x^T is derived by comparing the summed messaging time $\overline{t_x}$ excluding component x to the actual total messaging time $\overline{t}$:

$$p_x^T = 1 - \frac{\overline{t_x}}{\overline{t}} \quad , \quad \overline{t_x} = \sum_{\substack{t \in T_{a \rightarrow b} \\ a,b \in C \setminus \{x\}}} t \quad , \quad \overline{t} = \sum_{\substack{t \in T_{a \rightarrow b} \\ a,b \in C}} t \qquad (3)$$

In the same way, for each component $x \in C$ the contribution p_x^N to the overall number of transmitted messages is calculated. If the contribution of component $x \in C$ to the messaging time and the number of messages is much higher than the contributions of other components, x is detected as a Blob component. Hence, inspired by the Three Sigma Rule [18], component $x \in C$ is detected as a Blob if the contribution of x deviates from the mean contribution of other components more than three times the standard deviation:

$$p_x^{T|N} > \operatorname*{mean}_{y \in C \setminus \{x\}} \left(p_y^{T|N} \right) + 3 * \operatorname*{sd}_{y \in C \setminus \{x\}} \left(p_y^{T|N} \right) \qquad (4)$$

Finally, the Blob heuristic correlates the connection-id with the stack trace where it is used to provide detailed information about the root cause to the developer when reporting an occurrence of a Blob anti-pattern.

4.3 Detecting Empty Semi Trucks

An *Empty Semi Trucks (EST)* anti-pattern is characterized by a high amount of small messages transmitted between two components as part of a single user request. However, if a component exhibits a high message transmission rate due to a high load, whereas the frequency of message transmissions per user request is low, we do not consider it an EST. Thus, in order to detect an EST anti-pattern we need to analyze the messaging behaviour of single user requests. The detection heuristic for EST is defined as follows:

Load Description: For the EST heuristic a single-user test is executed to gather the data which is required for the analysis of the messaging behaviour.

Instrumentation Description: In order to capture the flow of messages, similar to the instrumentation of the Blob heuristic (cf. Section 4.2), methods responsible for dispatching and receiving of messages are instrumented with measurement probes collecting the following data:

- *connection-id, stack trace, message-id*: These metrics are used for message correlation and component identification (cf. Section 4.2).
- *message size*: The size of the transmitted message.
- *message payload size*: The size of the transmitted message's payload.

Additionally, in order to determine the context of message dispatches, the EST heuristic includes an instrumentation of all method calls along the paths from entry-points of user requests (e.g. servlets, REST-services, etc.) to message dispatching methods. Thereby, the following information is captured for each method call along the corresponding paths: *thread-id, call depth* and *method timestamps*.

Detection Analysis: The EST heuristic uses the thread-ids, the call depth information and the timestamps to reconstruct a call tree instance for each single user request. Information on the message size and the corresponding payload size are attached to each message dispatching method in the call tree. Call tree instances with the same tree structure are grouped and aggregated with respect to the message size information. Therefore, the average message size S and payload size P are calculated over all call tree instances of a group. Furthermore, repeating sub-trees in the call trees are aggregated to *loops* while counting the number n of executions of the corresponding loop body. The result of these pre-processing steps is a representative call tree, an example of which is depicted in Figure 3.

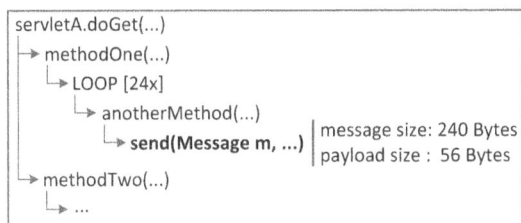

```
servletA.doGet(...)
  → methodOne(...)
    └→ LOOP [24x]
      └→ anotherMethod(...)          ┌─────────────────────────┐
        └→ send(Message m, ...)      │ message size: 240 Bytes │
                                     │ payload size : 56 Bytes │
  → methodTwo(...)                   └─────────────────────────┘
    └→ ...
```

Figure 3: Exemplary Trace

Here, the `send` method (responsible for dispatching of a message) occurs in a branch of the call tree within a `LOOP` which has been iterated 24 times. Messages which are transmitted in a loop are potential candidates for aggregation, hence if small, are possible indicators for an EST anti-pattern.

Based on the aggregated call trees, the EST heuristic calculates for each call m of a dispatch method which has been executed in a loop, the potential p_m for saving inefficient bandwidth usage. Hereby, the assumption is that all messages transmitted within the corresponding loop could be aggregated and transmitted as one message:

$$p_m = (n-1) * (S - P) \qquad (5)$$

where n is the number of loop executions, S is the average message size and P is the average size of the message's payload. Thus, p_m is the amount of bytes transmitted that could have been saved per user request if all messages transmitted within a loop would have been aggregated to one message. If the saving potential is higher than the average payload ($p_m > P$), the EST heuristic reports an occurrence of an EST anti-pattern by pointing to the call path which contains the guilty call m.

4.4 Detecting High DB Overhead

Database overhead which is caused by a high frequency of database requests is manifested either in a high CPU utilization of the database server, or in high locking times of the database requests waiting to be processed. For the High DB Overhead heuristic (*HDBO heuristic*) a sensitivity analysis is conducted between the load and the mentioned metrics, similar to the Excessive Messaging symptom (cf. Section 4.1):

Load Description: Analogously to Excessive Messaging, the HDBO heuristic executes n experiments E_i, while increasing the load L_i from one experiment to the next.

Instrumentation Description: During each experiment E_i, the HDBO heuristic samples the CPU utilization of the database server as well as locking times in the database.

Detection Analysis: First, if during any experiment E_i the mean CPU utilization U_i^{cpu} of the database server exceeds 90%, the HDBO heuristic detects a HDBO symptom. If this is not the case, the HDBO heuristic analyzes the progression of the locks. For each experiment E_i, the measurement data contain a set N_i^{lock} of sampled locking times. Let $\overline{N_i^{lock}}$ be the average of the set N_i^{lock}. Each two consecutive sets (N_i^{lock} and N_{i+1}^{lock}) are compared applying a t-Test. If the t-Test rejects the null hypothesis that the statistical means of N_i^{lock} and N_{i+1}^{lock} are equal and at the same time $\overline{N_{i+1}^{lock}} > \overline{N_i^{lock}}$, then the average locking time during experiment E_{i+1} is significantly higher than during experiment E_i. The HDBO heuristic detects a HDBO symptom, if a j exists, such that for all following experiments E_i ($i > j$) the locking times grow significantly with the load.

4.5 Detecting the Stifle

As described in Section 2, the Stifle anti-pattern is characterized by a significant amount of similar database queries which are executed as part of a single user request to the SUT. As the characteristics of the Stifle anti-pattern are quite similar to the EST anti-pattern, the Stifle detection heuristic is designed in a similar way as the EST heuristic.

Load Description: For the detection of the Stifle anti-pattern a single-user test is executed, as the Stifle heuristic analyzes the relationship between single user requests and corresponding database requests.

Instrumentation Description: For each user request the *name* of the called service (e.g. method-name) as well as the service *timestamps* are collected. Moreover, all methods responsible for execution of database queries are instrumented to provide the *query-timestamp* of the query execution, and the corresponding *query-string*.

Detection Analysis: As only a single-user test is applied for load generation, a sequential processing of the user requests in the SUT is guaranteed. Therefore, the collected timestamps of the service calls and the query-timestamps can be used to correlate service calls with the corresponding database requests. As the same service can be called multiple times during the execution time of the single-user test, for each service call c_i to service s_j we get a set $R_{ij} = \{r_{ij1}, r_{ij2}, \ldots\}$ of corresponding database requests. For each set R_{ij} the database requests r_{ijk} are clustered using the similarity of the corresponding SQL query strings as a distance metric. Two query strings belong to the same cluster if they are equal except for the values of passed parameters. Each cluster is represented by a tuple $\widehat{r}_{ijl} = (q_{ijl}, n_{ijl})$ comprising a representative query string q_{ijl} of the corresponding cluster, and the cluster size n_{ijl} reflecting the number of similar queries which were executed as part of the service call c_i. Aggregating the clusters over all service calls c_i of the same service s_j yields a set $\widehat{R}_j = \{(q_{j1}, \widehat{n}_{j1}), (q_{j2}, \widehat{n}_{j2}), \ldots\}$ of clusters for each service s_j. Here, $\widehat{n}_{jk}$ is the maximum over all cluster sizes belonging to the same query string.

Summing up, the Stifle heuristic provides for each service s_j provided by the SUT and each query string q_{jk} executed as part of that service, the maximum number of database requests containing q_{jk}. If a query q_{jk} is executed more than once ($\widehat{n}_{jk} > 1$), the heuristic reports the query in the context of the corresponding service as the root cause for a Stifle anti-pattern.

5. CASE STUDY

In this section, we present a case study based on TPC-W representing a 3-tier application with inter-component communications over the network layer, thereby evaluating the applicability of the described heuristics and their integration with the Dynamic Spotter. Furthermore, with this case study we provide an additional evaluation of the applicability and extensibility of the Dynamic Spotter approach. In particular, the following research questions are investigated:

RQ-1: Are the described heuristics able to detect the corresponding performance problems in a representative SUT?

RQ-2: How do the combinations of performance problems influence the detection accuracy of the heuristics?

RQ-3: Is the Dynamic Spotter approach with its hierarchical structure of performance problems and the systematic experimentation approach reasonably applicable for the detection of CPAs?

As system under test we use the TPC-W benchmark [13] which emulates an online bookstore providing different services for browsing and buying products. Though TPC-W is deprecated as an e-commerce benchmark, it is still widely used in the scientific community and satisfies our needs for the evaluation of the described detection heuristics. TPC-W represents a typical three tier system with inter-component communications, exhibits a sufficient complexity for meaningful performance problem analysis, and as a former performance benchmark is tailored for high performance.

In order to investigate the described research questions, following the fault injection principle [9] we intentionally inject different instances of the considered performance anti-patterns into the TPC-W application. The result is a set

of different labeled evaluation scenarios. We extended the Dynamic Spotter with the performance problem anti-patterns (cf. Section 2) and the detection heuristics (cf. Section 4), applied the approach to each scenario, and gathered the detection results. These results are compared to the expected results for each labeled scenario providing answers to the described research questions. For the investigation of research question **RQ-1** we consider the detection of each performance problem in isolation. Additionally, we create one scenario containing multiple performance anti-patterns in order to provide answers to question **RQ-2**. An answer to **RQ-3** can be derived from the detection results of all scenarios.

In the following, we describe the experiment design (Section 5.1) and discuss the evaluation results (Section 5.2).

5.1 Experiment Design

Depending on the characteristics of the different performance anti-patterns, different environment setups are required to evaluate their detection. The environment setups and the different evaluation scenarios are described in the following.

5.1.1 Environment Setup

As the Blob and the Empty Semi Trucks (EST) anti-patterns are based on messaging while the Stifle anti-pattern solely concerns database interaction, we consider two fundamentally different environment setups for the evaluation of these scenarios.

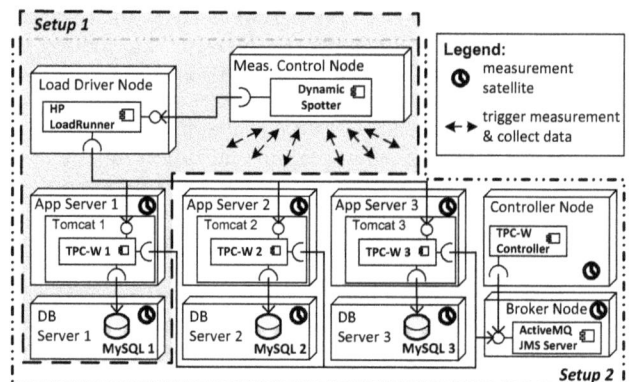

Figure 4: Experiment setup

Setup 1: For the evaluation of the Stifle detection, we use the traditional TPC-W setup (cf. Setup 1 in Figure 4) comprising an application server, a database server and a load driver node. Thereby, the TPC-W application is deployed on an *Apache Tomcat^{TM}7* web server accessing a *MySQL^{TM}5.6* database through a 100 Mbit/s Ethernet. As a load driver, we use *HP LoadRunner^{TM}11.52* which iteratively executes a predefined script for each generated virtual user. Finally, running on a dedicated node, *Dynamic Spotter* encapsulates the automatic detection of the individual performance problems. Therefore, for each series of performance tests to be executed for each single node of the performance problem hierarchy (cf. Figure 1), Dynamic Spotter automatically conducts the following steps: it triggers LoadRunner, instruments the TPC-W application through dedicated *measurement satellites*, gathers measurement data from the satellites and, finally, applies the corresponding detection analysis rules.

Setup 2: In order to evaluate the detection of the Blob and the EST anti-patterns, we need a distributed system comprising communication between individual components. To this end, we extend the classical TPC-W application as illustrated by Setup 2 in Figure 4. We consider a federation of three online shops (TPC-W instances) each comprising its own application server (*App Server 1-3*) and its own database instance (*DB Server 1-3*). In order to provide additional services, the individual TPC-W instances communicate with each other via a dedicated component (*TPC-W Controller*) using Java Message Service (JMS) for message transmission. As messaging service we use *Apache ActiveMQ^{TM} 5.9*. During performance test execution, LoadRunner equally distributes the generated load among the three TPC-W instances. Analogously to Setup 1, Dynamic Spotter automatically triggers load generation, gathers measurement data from all involved nodes, and conducts data analysis.

5.1.2 Evaluation Scenarios

For the case study, we consider the following four evaluation scenarios:

Blob Scenario: Based on Setup 2, we inject a Blob anti-pattern by adapting the architecture of the traditional TPC-W. Assuming that the shopping functionality is equal across all shops within a federation, we move the application logic of all shops to the TPC-W Controller component, while the web servers and the corresponding databases stay with the individual shops. In this way, the TPC-W Controller component constitutes a typical Blob comprising a major part of the processing logic which results in an unnecessarily high amount of messages to be transmitted for each user request between the TPC-W Controller and all TPC-W Instances. Figure 5 illustrates the control flow between the components

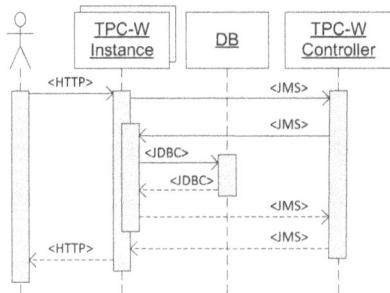

Figure 5: Request processing in the Blob Scenario

for a simple user request. First, each user request is delegated to the TPC-W Controller. As soon as the TPC-W Controller requires data, the controller retrieves the data from the corresponding database via the TPC-W Instance. Thus, for each user request at least four messages are transmitted over JMS.

EST Scenario: Analogously to the Blob Scenario, the EST Scenario is based on Setup 2. However, the application logic of the shopping system is located with the individual TPC-W Instances such that most requests can be processed by the requested TPC-W Instances without the need to communicate with the TPC-W Controller or other TPC-W instances. However, if a search request for a product yields an empty result, the corresponding TPC-W Instance requests the TPC-W Controller to serve the user request by conducting the search request on another TPC-W Instance.

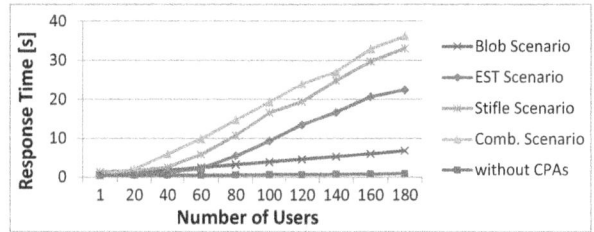

Figure 6: Response times of the evaluation scenarios

In the case that the search request on the second TPC-W Instance has been successful, each found item is transmitted as an individual JMS message, first to the TPC-W Controller and, finally, to the originally requested TPC-W Instance. As the result of a delegated search request is transmitted as a sequence of small massages instead of an aggregated message, it constitutes a typical EST anti-pattern.

Stifle Scenario: As no messaging is required for the isolated evaluation of the Stifle detection, the Stifle Scenario is based on the environment Setup 1. This scenario contains two Stifle instances. First, when a set of books needs to be retrieved from the database, a set of single SELECT-statements is executed in a loop instead of properly using a `WHERE` clause. Second, in TPC-W purchasing an item requires an update on the stock of that item and all items of the corresponding genre. Instead of conducting a batch update on all items, in the Stifle Scenario each item is updated separately.

Combined Scenario: The Combined Scenario contains all introduced anti-patterns: Stifle, Blob and EST. Based on Setup 2, this scenario combines the characteristics of the other three scenarios. The application logic is centralized in the TPC-W Controller, the result of delegated search requests is transmitted as a series of small messages and the two Stifle instances cause frequent database requests.

5.1.3 Information on Performance Tests

For the case study we assume end-to-end response times exceeding 2 seconds as a violation of performance requirements and, thus, as a performance problem. For the generation of load we use a closed workload applying a predefined script which defines a sequence of user requests executed by each generated user. Each single performance test executed in the case study is running 10 minutes in a steady state, plus a warm-up phase of about another 10 minutes.

5.2 Detection Results

We applied Dynamic Spotter with the heuristics presented in this paper on the four evaluation scenarios. As depicted in Figure 6, all scenarios exhibit high response times, which has been detected by Dynamic Spotter. Figure 6 also shows a comparison to the response times of the individual scenarios when resolving the CPAs. Figure 7 gives an overview on the detection results for the complete CPA hierarchy. In the Blob Scenario, the Blob anti-pattern causing Excessive Messaging has been detected. Besides the EST anti-pattern resulting in Excessive Messaging, Dynamic Spotter detected a Blob instance in the EST Scenario, as well. In the third scenario, Dynamic Spotter correctly detected a Stifle anti-pattern causing a HDBO symptom. In the Combined Scenario, Dynamic Spotter detected Excessive Messaging which was caused by

Figure 7: Overview on results: ① **Blob Scen.** ② **EST Scen.** ③ **Stifle Scen.** ④ **Combined Scen.**

component	messaging time [s]	contribution [%]	threshold	result
total	83116	—	—	—
TPC-W 1	24776	29.8	148.5	No Blob
TPC-W 2	29943	36.0	150.9	No Blob
TPC-W 3	28396	34.1	150.4	No Blob
T. Controller	83116	100.0	41.1	Blob

Table 1: Detailed results on Blob detection.

a Blob and an EST. However, the HDBO symptom and the Stifle anti-pattern have not been detected in the Combined Scenario.

In the following, we discuss the results in more detail.

5.2.1 Results for the Blob Scenario

In the Blob scenario, response times exceeded the performance requirement of 2 seconds (cf. Figure 6). As a result of this, Dynamic Spotter triggered the investigation of the symptoms Excessive Messaging and HDBO, according to the hierarchy in Figure 7. Dynamic Spotter did not identify a HDBO symptom as the utilization of all database nodes does not exceed 90% and locking on database tables is negligible. In Figure 8 the results of the heuristic for Excessive

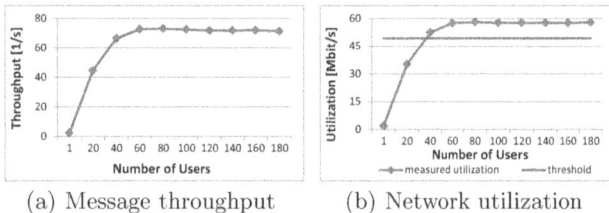

(a) Message throughput   (b) Network utilization

Figure 8: Message throughput and network utilization of the Broker node, (Blob Scenario).

Messaging are depicted. The message throughput of the TPC-W Controller does not scale with the number of users, but stagnates when the load intensity exceeds 60 users. Using Equation 2 to calculate the capacity limit for the network (taking an average message size of 200 Bytes and packet rate of 8561 Hz), we get a threshold of 49 Mbit/s. With a value of 58 Mbit/s, the measured network utilization exceeds the threshold. Hence, Dynamic Spotter detects an Excessive Messaging problem. Consequently, Dynamic Spotter goes deeper into the performance problem hierarchy and investigates the anti-patterns Blob and EST. The EST heuristic did not detect an EST anti-pattern in the Blob Scenario as no message dispatches have been found which were executed in a loop (cf. Section 4.3). However, Dynamic Spotter detected the injected Blob anti-pattern as indicated by the detailed results of the Blob heuristic depicted in Table 1.

The sum over all message transmission times yields a value of 83116 seconds (including parallel transmission of messages). As all messages pass the TPC-W Controller, its contribution to the total messaging time is 100%. Based on Equation 4, the threshold for the Controller component is 41.1. As the messaging time contribution exceeds the threshold, the Blob heuristic detected the TPC-W Controller as a Blob

component. In contrast, the messaging time contributions of the other components are below the corresponding thresholds.

5.2.2 Results for the EST Scenario

The response time performance requirement has been violated (cf. Figure 6). HDBO has not been detected due to low database utilizations and negligible database locking times. The heuristic for Excessive Messaging detected a stagnating message throughput under a load of about 80 users while the network utilization of the messaging server exceeds the threshold of 49 Mbit/s. As a consequence, Dynamic Spotter applied the Blob and EST heuristics. Thereby, the EST heuristic identified two message dispatching methods which were executed in a loop between 64 to 100 times. The identified methods are the methods which are responsible for transmitting the result of the search request from one TPC-W instance via the TPC-W Controller to another TPC-W instance by sending each found item as a single message. The number of loop iterations (64 to 100) corresponds to the number of items found for the search requests. Each message has an average payload of 24 Bytes while exhibiting an additional overhead of 160 Bytes. Thus, 64 messages constitute a network traffic of 11.5 KB. Aggregating these messages to one message yields a saving potential of 9.8 KB (63 times the message overhead of 160 Bytes) which is 85.6% of the network traffic generated by one request. Hence, the EST anti-pattern has been correctly detected. An interesting observation is that the Blob heuristic identified the TPC-W Controller component as a Blob in the EST Scenario. Actually, the detected EST anti-pattern is at the same time a Blob anti-pattern, as all messages pass through the TPC-W Controller, causing a high messaging overhead. Thus, though we preliminary did not expect the Dynamic Spotter to detect a Blob in the EST Scenario, the detection results are indeed correct.

5.2.3 Results for the Stifle Scenario

Dynamic Spotter did not detect the Excessive Messaging symptom in the Stifle Scenario, as in this scenario no messaging has been used. However, a HDBO symptom has been detected. Though, the CPU utilization of the database node is quite low (smaller than 30%), the locking times increase significantly with the load, from 0 seconds to 22.6 seconds. As the HDBO symptom has been detected, Dynamic Spotter resumed with the investigation using the Stifle heuristic. Thereby, two Stifle instances have been found. An **UPDATE** statement in the purchase service of TPC-W, has been executed between 2 and 4299 times (with different parameters) per transaction, depending on how many and which items have been bought. In the product search service, the Stifle heuristic detected a **SELECT** query which has been executed 6 to 2006 times, depending on the search result. Thus, the Stifle heuristic found both Stifle instances which have been injected in the Stifle-Scenario.

5.2.4 *Results for the Combined Scenario*

As expected, in the Combined Scenario, Dynamic Spotter detected the Excessive Messaging symptom, as well as the Blob and the EST anti-patterns as the actual causes for the Excessive Messaging. The detection details on the Blob and the EST are very similar to the Blob and the EST scenarios respectively (cf. sections 5.2.1 and 5.2.2). However, while the Combined Scenario contains the Stifle anti-pattern, the Stifle and its symptom HDBO have not been detected. More precisely, according to the problem hierarchy (cf. Figure 7), Dynamic Spotter did not investigate the Stifle anti-pattern as the symptom HDBO has not been detected. Investigating the measurement data shows that all database utilizations are quite low (below 20%) and database locking times do not increase significantly with the load. Thus, the HDBO symptom did not become visible in the Combined Scenario. The Excessive Messaging caused by the Blob and the EST already throttle the performance of the overall system to a degree that no HDBO could occur. Hence, the Blob and the EST instances hide the Stifle anti-pattern.

5.3 Conclusion on the Case Study

In the isolated scenarios, all CPAs have been detected correctly, which yields a positive answer to research question **RQ-1**. However, in the Combined Scenario, the messaging-related anti-patterns hid the HDBO symptom, preventing Dynamic Spotter from detecting the Stifle anti-pattern.

Considering research question **RQ-2**, we have to conclude from our evaluation results that instances of performance problems may hide other performance problems. Thus, performance problems need to be detected and solved in an iterative approach.

Using the idea of hierarchically structuring performance problems, in our case study, Dynamic Spotter was able to stepwise narrow down the root cause of performance problems from corresponding symptoms. The dynamic, goal-oriented instrumentation approach of Dynamic Spotter kept the measurement overhead low, such that detection results were not impaired by the instrumentation probes. Hence, we can conclude, that the Dynamic Spotter approach is reasonably applicable in the domain of CPAs (cf. **RQ-3**).

5.4 Threats to Validity

In this section, we discuss the threats to validity of our evaluation.

Construct Validity

In general, instrumentation of the SUT may affect the performance of the system and, thus, distort the measurement results. With the instrumentation approach of Dynamic Spotter, we endeavour to intervene the SUT as little as possible. Thus, when measuring performance metrics, we only take high level measurements, however, when details are required to gather structural information for heuristics, we abstain from using performance metrics.

Although the performance problems detected in the case study have been intentionally injected into the SUT, the evaluation results provide important insights on the stated research questions. Moreover, fault injection [9] is an established approach in testing. The system on which we tested our approach is an extension of a widely used benchmark (TPC-W). Though the extensions are designed for evaluation of our heuristics, they neither reduced the complexity of the system, nor introduced changes in the core functionality.

External Validity

TPC-W cannot be compared with a large-scale enterprise system. Nevertheless, it comprises representative components of enterprise systems and comes with a complexity which is sufficient for the first evaluation of our heuristics. Furthermore, for the case study we assumed a fix hardware setup. Therefore, we cannot make any statements about the applicability of the introduced approach on an elastic cloud environment. For future work, we plan to evaluate our approach within SAP's infrastructure on large-scale enterprise systems as well as systems running in cloud environments.

Furthermore, the case study does not provide insights on how our detection approach behaves, if a performance problem results from a set of distributed root causes. Investigating such a scenario is part of future work.

Although the heuristics presented in this paper where realized for certain technologies (e.g. Java, JMS, JDBC, etc.) the concepts behind the heuristics are generic and can be realized for other technologies, as well.

6. RELATED WORK

There is a large body of literature dealing with detection of performance problems and performance anti-patterns, comprising model-based and measurement-based approaches.

Model based approaches [4, 22, 25] analyze architecture and performance models in order to identify architecture-level performance anti-patterns. For instance, Trubiani et al. [22] formalize performance anti-patterns as a set of rules referring to elements of architectural meta-models. Structural information about architectural model instances as well as performance metrics gained from analyses of performance models are compared with the predefined rules in order to detect performance anti-patterns. While model-based approaches can already be applied in the design phase, their detection capabilities are limited by the lack of detailed information about the final system.

Measurement-based approaches analyze data from load tests or data gathered at operation time to find performance problems and anti-patterns. Jiang et al. [12] automatically compare performance metrics gathered during load tests against a predefined performance baseline. In this way they are able to identify performance anomalies. Grechnik et al. [7] apply feedback-directed learning during load tests to derive rules for meaningful selection of input data for further tests. Combining the selection of input data with an analysis of the resource consumption of single methods, performance bottlenecks are identified more effectively compared to random testing. Aguilera et al. [1] propose an approach for debugging performance characteristics in a distributed system of black-box components. The authors extract traces from messages transmitted between individual components. They introduce algorithms for inferring causal paths through the distributed system. An offline analysis of the traces is applied to identify bottlenecks in the system under test.

In [15] the authors apply non-intrusive monitoring of component interactions in J2EE systems. Based on [15], in another work Parsons et al. [16] reconstruct design models as well as run-time paths from gathered monitoring data. Using pattern matching and data mining techniques these artifacts are analyzed to identify performance anti-patterns. In [17] Parsons et al. describe how they use frequent sequence mining on run-time paths in order to reveal resource intensive call sequences. Finally, the authors match these sequences to performance design flaws in the system under test. Similar to the approach in [15], Crasso et al. extract communication traces between J2EE components. The authors use a tool called *Drools* to translate pre-defined anti-pattern rules to the records collected during system execution. Crasso et al. additionally suggest improvements to solve identified performance anti-patterns.

With their tool *Paradyn*, Miller et al. [14] introduce a goal-oriented approach to analyze root causes of performance problems at operation time. Therefore, Paradyn dynamically instruments the target system during the operation phase. Combining the dynamic instrumentation with a hierarchical model for performance problem analysis, the authors pinpoint the root cause of an occurring performance problem.

In our work, we extends the ideas from [16] and [14] with a systematic experimentation approach taking into consideration the sensitivity between performance metrics and the load. In this way we provide a novel, more effective approach for detection of communication related performance anti-patterns. While the approach in [16] is solely designed for J2EE systems, our approach is generally applicable on any Java system.

7. CONCLUSION

We presented an approach for automatic, measurement-based detection of communication performance anti-patterns in distributed systems. For a selected set of anti-patterns, we introduced five heuristics which describe detection strategies for individual anti-patterns. We evaluated the heuristics and Dynamic Spotter on four scenarios using an extended version of the TPC-W application. The results show that the communication performance anti-patterns can be accurately detected by our approach. Since some performance problems can be hidden by others, an iterative approach should be applied to detect and resolve the problems. For future work, we plan an evaluation of our heuristics on a large-scale enterprise system as well as development of heuristics for further performance anti-patterns, e.g. anti-patterns related to improper memory usage.

ACKNOWLEDGEMENTS

The research leading to these results has received funding from the DFG grant RE 1674/6-1 and the European Union Seventh Framework Programme (FP7/2007-2013) under grant no 317704 (CloudScale).

8. REFERENCES

[1] M. K. Aguilera, J. C. Mogul, J. L. Wiener, P. Reynolds, and A. Muthitacharoen. Performance debugging for distributed systems of black boxes. In *SIGOPS OSR*, volume 37, pages 74–89. ACM, 2003.

[2] B. W. Boehm. Software engineering economics. *IEEE TSE*, SE-10(1):4 –21, 1984.

[3] L. Bulej, T. Kalibera, and P. Tuma. Repeated results analysis for middleware regression benchmarking. *Performance Evaluation*, 60(1):345–358, 2005.

[4] V. Cortellessa, A. Di Marco, R. Eramo, A. Pierantonio, and C. Trubiani. Digging into uml models to remove performance antipatterns. In *Proc. ICSE*, pages 9–16. ACM, 2010.

[5] B. Dudney, S. Asbury, J. Krozak, and K. Wittkopf. *J2EE antipatterns*. Wiley, 2003.

[6] K. Foo, Z. Jiang, B. Adams, A. Hassan, Y. Zou, and P. Flora. Mining performance regression testing repositories for automated performance analysis. In *Proc. QSIC*, pages 32–41. IEEE, 2010.

[7] M. Grechanik, C. Fu, and Q. Xie. Automatically finding performance problems with feedback-directed learning software testing. In *Proc. ICSE*, 2012.

[8] G. Y. Guo, J. M. Atlee, and R. Kazman. *A software architecture reconstruction method*. Springer, 1999.

[9] M. Hsueh, T. Tsai, and R. Iyer. Fault injection techniques and tools. *Computer*, 30(4):75–82, 1997.

[10] J. Huang. Understanding gigabit ethernet performance on sun fire systems. *Sun BluePrints^{TM} OnLine*.

[11] R. Jain. *The art of computer systems performance analysis*. John Wiley & Sons Chichester, 1991.

[12] Z. Jiang, A. Hassan, G. Hamann, and P. Flora. Automated performance analysis of load tests. In *Proc. ICSM*, pages 125–134. IEEE, 2009.

[13] D. Menascé. Tpc-w: A benchmark for e-commerce. *Internet Computing, IEEE*, 6(3):83–87, 2002.

[14] B. Miller, M. Callaghan, J. Cargille, J. Hollingsworth, R. Irvin, K. Karavanic, K. Kunchithapadam, and T. Newhall. The paradyn parallel performance measurement tool. *Computer*, 28(11):37–46, 1995.

[15] T. Parsons, A. Mos, M. Trofin, T. Gschwind, and J. Murphy. Extracting interactions in component-based systems. *TSE*, 34(6):783–799, 2008.

[16] T. Parsons and J. Murphy. Detecting performance antipatterns in com-ponent based enterprise systems. *Journal of Object Technology*, 7(3):55–90, Mar. 2008.

[17] T. Parsons, J. Murphy, and P. O'Sullivan. Applying frequent sequence mining to identify design flaws in enterprise software systems. In *MLDM Posters*, pages 261–275, 2007.

[18] F. Pukelsheim. The three sigma rule. *The American Statistician*, 48(2):88–91, 1994.

[19] C. Smith and L. Williams. Software performance antipatterns. In *WOSP*, pages 127–136. ACM, 2000.

[20] C. Smith and L. Williams. Software performance antipatterns; common performance problems and their solutions. In *CMG-CONFERENCE-*, volume 2, pages 797–806, 2002.

[21] C. Smith and L. Williams. More new software performance antipatterns: Even more ways to shoot yourself in the foot. In *CMG-CONFERENCE-*, pages 717–725, 2003.

[22] C. Trubiani and A. Koziolek. Detection and solution of software performance antipatterns in palladio architectural models. In *Proc. ICPE*, pages 19–30. ACM, 2011.

[23] A. Wert. Performance problem diagnostics by systematic experimentation. In *Proc. WCOP*, pages 1–6. ACM, 2013.

[24] A. Wert, J. Happe, and L. Happe. Supporting swift reaction: automatically uncovering performance problems by systematic experiments. In *Proc. ICSE*, pages 552–561. IEEE Press, 2013.

[25] J. Xu. Rule-based automatic software performance diagnosis and improvement. In *Proc. WOSP*, pages 1–12. ACM, 2008.

Architectural Tactics Support in Cloud Computing Providers: The Jelastic Case

Jaime Chavarriaga
Universidad de los Andes,
Vrije Universiteit Brussel
jchavarr@vub.ac.be

Carlos Noguera
Vrije Universiteit Brussel
cnoguera@vub.ac.be

Rubby Casallas
Universidad de los Andes
rcasalla@uniandes.edu.co

Viviane Jonckers
Vrije Universiteit Brussel
vejoncke@vub.ac.be

ABSTRACT

When developing and deploying applications in the cloud, architects face the challenge of conciliating architectural decisions with the options and restrictions imposed by the chosen cloud provider. An architectural decision can be seen as a two-step process: selecting architectural tactics to promote quality attributes and choosing design alternatives to implement those tactics. Available design alternatives are limited by the offer of the cloud provider. When configuring the cloud platform and its services as directed by the chosen tactics, the architect must be mindful of conflicts among the available alternatives. These trade-offs amongst the desired quality attributes can be difficult to detect, understand and ultimately solve. In this paper, we consider the case of Jelastic, a particular cloud platform provider, to illustrate: 1) the modeling of architectural tactics and their corresponding design alternatives using cloud configuration options, and 2) a process that exploits these models to determine which options to use in order to implement a combination of tactics. Furthermore, we present an analysis for this cloud provider that explains which combinations of tactics and configurations lead to trade-offs.

Categories and Subject Descriptors

D.2.11 [**Software Architecture**]: Language, Patterns; D.2.13 [**Reusable Software**]: Domain engineering

Keywords

Cloud Computing; Quality Attributes; Architectural Tactics; Feature Model

1. INTRODUCTION

Software Architectural Tactics have been proposed [2] to promote quality attributes. Each architectural tactic de-

scribes which design alternatives help to achieve attributes such as performance, availability, maintainability or security. For a specific application, software architects must understand the architectural tactics that promote the quality attributes they strive for and select the proper design alternatives to implement them.

Several methods have been proposed to support architectural design based on architectural tactics. For instance, ADD [2, 18] and ACDM [12] support software architects to select architectural tactics based on the intended quality attributes for an application, select design alternatives that implement these tactics, and integrate these selections into an application design. In addition, methods such as ATAM [9] or CBAM [14] have been proposed to detect and solve conflicts on the chosen tactics and design alternatives. However, there is still little work discussing how to apply these tactics to support design in the context of cloud computing.

Cloud providers such as Amazon[1], Google[2] and Jelastic[3] offer platforms and services to implement and deploy software applications. Software Architects use and configure these services in different ways depending on the application requirements. As in other contexts, architectural tactics can be used as a foundation to decide which services and which configurations to use. For instance, to improve the performance of an application an architect might select the *maintain copies or computation* tactic, aiming to reduce the contention that would occur if all computation took place on a central place. This tactic can be implemented using diverse services offered by cloud platforms such as Amazon Elastic Bean *load-balanced web servers*, Jelastic's Glassfish *clustered application servers*, or Heroku's PostgreSQL *clustered database servers*.

Problems may arise when the selected design alternatives conflict with each other. A *trade-off* [2, 18] occurs when the chosen set of design alternatives helps to achieve some of the requirements but inhibits or reduces the satisfaction of others. As an example, consider an application striving for both performance and availability. To achieve performance, an architect selects the tactic *reduce computational overhead*, and implements it by configuring a Jelastic instance to use a *TCP/IP load balancer*. This design alternative distributes

Permission to make digital or hard copies of all or part of this work for personal or classroom use is granted without fee provided that copies are not made or distributed for profit or commercial advantage and that copies bear this notice and the full citation on the first page. Copyrights for components of this work owned by others than ACM must be honored. Abstracting with credit is permitted. To copy otherwise, or republish, to post on servers or to redistribute to lists, requires prior specific permission and/or a fee. Request permissions from permissions@acm.org.

QoSA'14, June 30–July 4, 2014, Marcq-en-Baroeul, France.
Copyright 2014 ACM 978-1-4503-2577-6/14/06 ...$15.00.
http://dx.doi.org/10.1145/2602576.2602580.

---

[1] http://aws.amazon.com
[2] http://cloud.google.com/products/
[3] http://www.jelastic.com

the traffic across several machines very quickly because it does not check or process header information of the data that is transmitted. In the other hand, the same architect aims to implement the *Active Redundancy* tactic to achieve high levels of *Availability* by configuring the *Clustering options* in a *Glassfish* application server. These clustering options require an *HTTP load balancer* to process headers of the web protocol. Without noticing it, the architect has decided to implement two tactics in a way that leads to a trade-off.

This paper presents our analysis on how to implement well-known architectural tactics on a particular cloud platform. It describes 1. how to implement the architectural tactics proposed by Bass et al. [2] on the Jelastic platform, and 2. which combinations of architectural tactics lead to trade-offs. To achieve this, we employ Feature Models [8, 6] to describe the catalog of architectural tactics, as well as the valid configuration options offered by Jelastic. These feature models are then related by a Feature-Solution Graph [4, 7]. Then, performing combinatorial analysis of all the possible configurations, we find out which decisions must be traded-off.

The remainder of this paper is structured as follows. Section 2 gives a motivation for our case study and research questions, Section 3 describes our approach to analyse how to implement architectural tactics using configuration options in a cloud platform, and which combinations of tactics lead to trade-offs. In addition, this section gives a background on the feature models and feature solution graphs used in our work; Section 4 describes how we model the architectural tactics, Section 5 how we model configuration options in Jelastic, and Section 6 how we model the implementation of tactics using these configuration options. Finally, Section 8 discusses the results of our analysis, Section 9 presents related work, and Section 10 concludes the paper.

2. MOTIVATION

Cloud computing has become prevalent. Software architects must now consider which design alternatives offered by cloud providers implement the architectural tactics of interest. Cloud computing providers offer different types of services. *Infrastructure as a service (IaaS)* providers offer virtual machines with predefined configurations, while *Platform as a service (PaaS)* providers offer predefined types of application servers and execution environments such as web and database servers. Every customer acquiring these services must use these services "as-is", i.e., using only the options and configurations already present.

Each type of cloud computing service targets specific stakeholders: While IaaS services allow IT administrators to configure, start and reorganize virtual machines based on their needs, PaaS services support software architects and developers during the design, development, testing and deployment of applications. In fact, many PaaS services based on the *OpenShift* and *Cloud Foundry* opensource projects run on IaaS services such as *Amazon EC2* or *OpenStack*.

Usually, PaaS offerings facilitate the deployment of applications in scalable settings. For example, *Google App Engine* offers proprietary platforms that dynamically scale applications in standard languages like Java, Python and PHP. These services automatically allocate new server resources as an application load grows, and reduce the resources when the load goes down. However, they impose limitations regarding operations (such as network and disk access) that

can be executed and libraries that can be invoked. Others services, such as *Jelastic* and *OpenShift*, offer available servers such as Tomcat, Glassfish, MySQL and PostgreSQL in auto-scalable settings with less limitations but restricting which settings and configurations can be used. In contrast, other platforms such as *Heroku* or *Cloud Foundry* allow the installation of almost any application or server but requires manual intervention or additional applications to scale.

Jelastic cloud platform.

Jelastic is one of the PaaS cloud platform supporting standard servers in auto-scalable settings. It includes a simple configuration system that allows software architects to choose which application servers and configurations to use and which options for replication to include. In addition, the configuration system allows the deployment of standard applications without using proprietary APIs and applying architectural designs used in private infrastructures. In theory, a simple application can scale easily in this platform without any modification.

In order to study how to implement tactics in cloud platforms, we chose Jelastic for two reasons: First, it is a cloud platform that is not as limited as platforms such as Google App Engine but still supports auto-scaling options not present in platforms such as Heroku or Cloud Foundry. And second, it is aimed to support standard applications without proprietary APIs or servers, allowing us to reuse existing knowledge about how to implement the architectural tactics.

Research Questions.

Considering that cloud providers offer diverse options for deploy application, but also limit which options can be used by software architects, we pose three research questions:

Q1 How to implement the architectural tactics using the servers and options offered by the Jelastic cloud platform?

Q2 Which architectural tactics can be implemented using only configuration options, and which require additional code in the application?

Q3 Which combinations of architectural tactics lead to trade-offs caused by conflicts in the configuration options?

3. FEATURE-SOLUTION GRAPHS TO ANALYZE ARCHITECTURAL TACTICS

In order to address the research questions, we use feature models to represent architectural tactics and design alternatives in the Jelastic cloud platform. In addition, we define feature-solution graphs to relate tactics and options in the cloud platform to reason about conflicts. This section gives an overview of our approach to analyze tactic implementations and interactions.

3.1 Analyzing tactic implementations and interactions

Our approach consists of four steps:

1. *Model the architectural tactics* using a feature model. This feature model represents the tactics defined in the literature and is reusable across several technical contexts.

2. *Model the design alternatives and configuration options of Jelastic* using another feature model. This model is specific to Jelastic and, therefore, can be only reused for applications to be deployed in that cloud platform.

3. *Relate tactics to the corresponding design alternatives* using Feature-Solution Graphs connecting the feature model of tactics with the feature model of Jelastic design alternatives. These relationships represent architectural knowledge about how to implement the tactics in the Jelastic cloud platform.

4. *Detect trade-offs caused by conflicts among design alternatives.* Selecting a set of tactics, we use the feature-solution graph to determine which design alternatives can be used to implement these tactics. Then, using combinatorial analysis we can find which tactics lead to conflicts in the corresponding design alternatives.

3.2 Feature Models

A *Feature Model* specifies the similarities and differences among the members of a family of products as well as the options that can be used to configure each product.

Feature models consist of mandatory features capturing commonalities, optional features capturing variations, and feature groups and relationships representing configuration constraints. Feature groups may be *Or (inclusive-or)*, where one or more features can be selected, or *Alternative (exclusive-or)* groups, where just one of the set can be selected. Features can constrain other through *requires* and *excludes* relationships that indicate that one feature must be selected when other is selected or that two features cannot be selected at the same time.

Figure 1 shows a feature model describing some of the design alternatives and configuration options in Jelastic. The feature model has a root feature *Jelastic* which has a mandatory subfeature: *Application Server* and three optional subfeatures: *Load Balancer*, *Session Server* and *Database*. In turn, the *Application Server* can be one of *Tomcat*, *Glassfish* or *Jetty* (i.e., an alternative group). In addition, the *Glassfish* application server has an optional *High Availability* option subfeature which requires the *Load Balancer* feature. In the other hand, the *Database* can be an *SQL* or a *NoSQL* database, or both (i.e., an or group). Alternative sub-features can be selected for both *SQL* and *NoSQL*.

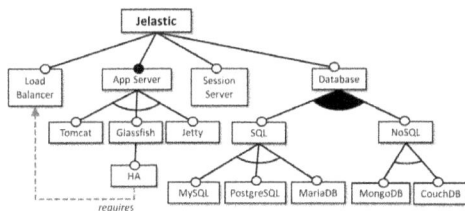

Figure 1: Example feature model representing Jelastic options

A feature model constrains which are the valid configurations by means of feature types (mandatory, optional), groups and relationships. For example, a configuration: App Server, Tomcat, Database, SQL, MySQL would be valid, whereas Load Balancer, Database, NoSQL, MongoDB would not since it does not include the mandatory feature App Server.

3.3 Feature-Solution Graphs

A *Feature-Solution Graph* relates two feature models where the left-side model represents requirements (or features) and the right-side model represents the components or the architecture elements that may be included in a product (or the solutions) [4]. In addition, it includes a set of "realized by" relationships that show for each feature on the left-side, the corresponding solutions on the right-side.

In order to represent architectural tactics, we extend feature-solution graphs to include additional relationships. As we will describe in Section 7, we introduce *forces* and *prohibits* relationships to denote that the implementation of a tactic forces or prohibits the selection of a configuration option.

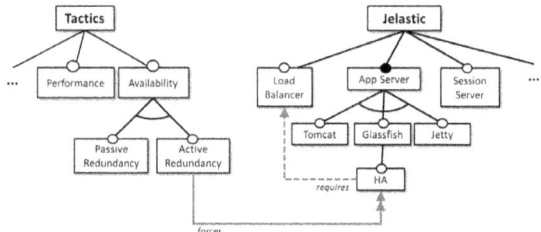

Figure 2: Example feature-solution graph

Figure 2 shows an excerpt of a feature-solution graph example relating two feature models. The left-side models quality attributes and architectural tactics and the right-side Jelastic configuration options mentioned above. Relationships relate tactics with the components that realize them. For instance, there is an *Active Redundancy* tactic for *Availability* in the left-side. In that tactic, servers in a group must be able to receive and process any request from any user. Represented as a graph to the right-side feature model, that tactic must be implemented in Jelastic by selecting the *High Availability* option of *Glassfish*.

4. MODELING THE ARCHITECTURAL TACTICS

An *Architectural Tactic* is a reusable architectural building block, a design decision that provides solutions to help achieve a quality attribute [2]. Bass et al. present 79 architectural tactics targeting six quality attributes: availability, performance, security, testability, interoperability and modifiability [2]. Software architects, concerned by these quality attributes, can review the corresponding tactics to select which design alternatives to use in an application.

The following is a brief description of these tactics and their organization.

Tactics for Availability there are 28 tactics organized in three groups:

Fault detection tactics, such interchanging *Ping/Echo* and *Heartbeat* messages, that recognize and identify faults in servers and components; *Fault recovery* tactics, such as *Rollback* and *Retry*, that continue any interrupted activity or processing after detecting a fault; and *Fault prevention* tactics, such as *Removal of service* and *Transactions*, that prevent faults or the propagation of these faults into other servers or components. Note that, When software architects choose a *Fault recovery* tactic, they must also select some *Fault detection* tactic. In addition note the *Rollback*

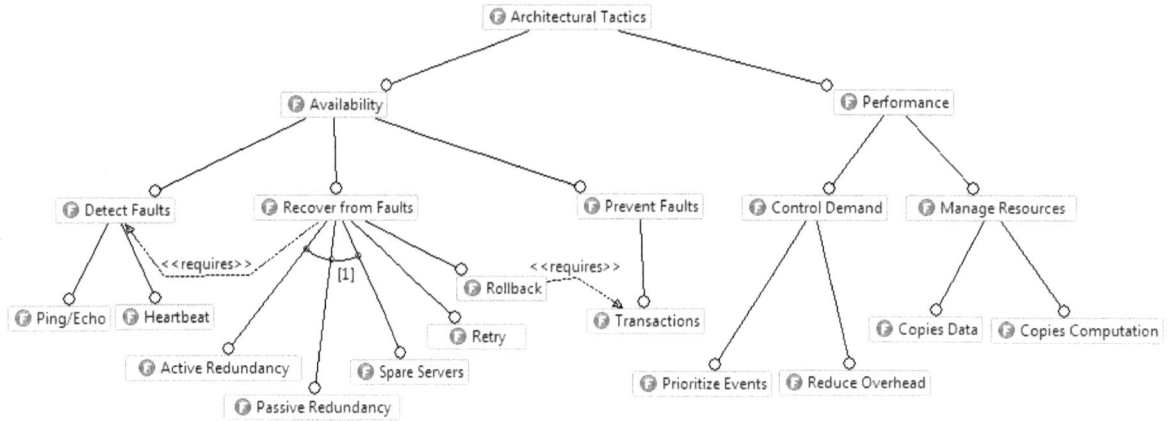

Figure 3: Excerpt of the Feature model of Architectural Tactics

fault recovery tactic requires the use of *Transactions* fault prevention tactic.

There are twelve **Tactics for Performance** divided into two groups[4]: *Control resource demand* tactics, such as *Prioritize Events* and *Reduce Overhead* aimed to reduce latency caused by the demand of computing resources; and *Manage resources* tactics, such as *Maintain Copies of computation* and *Maintain Copies of data*, aimed to reduce contention caused by simultaneous demands for the same resource and the inability to use a resource.

For **Security**, there are 17 tactics arranged into four groups: tactics to *Detect Attacks*, *Resist Attacks*, *React to Attacks* and *Recover from Attacks*. Note that the implementation of any tactic to *Recover from Attacks* requires the simultaneous implementation of a *Detect Attacks* Tactic. In addition, there is a *Recover from Attacks* tactic to *Recover* the system that requires the implementation of some *Recover from fault* tactic for *Availability*.

In addition, there are eight **Tactics for Testability** organized in two groups: tactics to *Control and Observe System State* such as using a *Sandbox* or *Record/Playback* mechanisms; and tactics to *Limit Complexity*.

Finally, for **Modifiability** there are eleven tactic in four groups: Tactics to *Reduce Size of Modules*, to *Increase Cohesion* of modules, to *Reduce coupling* and tactics to *Defer Binding*.

4.1 Feature Model for Architectural Tactics

As mentioned before, the first step of our analysis is modeling the set of architectural tactics. We created a feature model representing the architectural tactics where the top elements represent quality attributes and the elements at lower levels represent which tactics help to achieve each of these attributes. Figure 3 shows an excerpt of that feature model including tactics for availability and performance [5]. Note that relations between tactics are included in the model: *Recover From Faults* tactic requires a *Detect faults* tactic and *Rollback* tactic requires the *Transaction* tactic.

---

[4]This classification is consistent to Bass et al. [2]. Previous work from the same authors includes a different classification.

[5]The Feature Model for Architectural Tactics is available at `http://soft.vub.ac.be/~jchavarr/jelastic-fsg/`

5. MODELING DESIGN ALTERNATIVES IN JELASTIC

After modeling architectural tactics, we model the design alternatives and configuration options in Jelastic.

5.1 Configuration options in Jelastic

In *Jelastic*, software architects can customize the execution environment where their applications will be deployed. They can use a web-based application to select which servers include in that environment and configure the options of those servers. Based on the options provided by the configuration application and the platform documentation[6] we have extracted the available options and corresponding constraints.

For a Java application, a Jelastic environment must include an *Application Server* and can include other optional services: a *Load balancer*, an *SSL* certificate, a *Session server*, a *SQL database*, a *NoSQL database*, or a *Memcached* server.

For the **Load balancer** the only provided option is a *Nginx Load balancer*. It can be configured to act as a *TCP load balancer* without processing headers in the web protocol, an *HTTP load balancer* that analyzes the HTTP request before redirecting it, or as a *sticky-session load balancer* that redirects web requests from the same web browser to the same web server. In addition, Nginx has an additional option to support *Web caching*. This *Web caching* option cannot be selected along side the *TCP load balancer*.

Jelastic offers as **Application Servers** either an instance of *Tomcat*, *Glassfish* or *Jetty*. When the *Glassfish* is selected, a *High Availability* option may be selected to configure a cluster of application servers. This clustering option requires the selection of a *Load Balancer* other than *TCP Load Balancer*.

The optional **Session server** configures shared sessions on the application servers in order to allow any server respond to any web request. This session server can be configured using *Multi-cast Session Replication* that replicates session data across sets of servers and *Memcached Session Replication* that stores session data into an external caching server. The *High Availability* option for *Glassfish* requires the selection of the *Multicast session replication*. In addi-

---

[6]`http://docs.jelastic.com/`

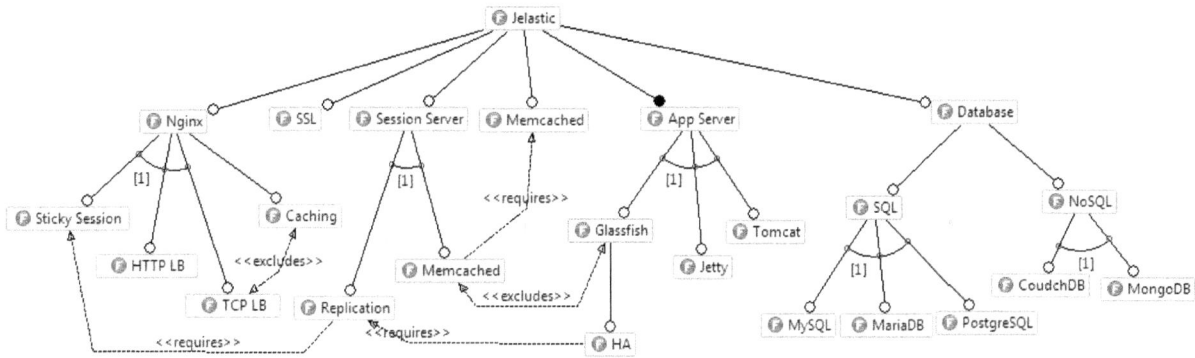

Figure 4: Feature model representing Jelastic configuration options

tion, this *Multicast session replication* requires the *Sticky-session load balancer* option.

The optional **Database Server** can be an *SQL database server* (either *MySQL*, *MariaDB* or *PostgreSQL*); and a *NoSQL database server* (either *CouchDB* or *MongoDB*).

Finally, a **Memcached server** provides a fast-access caching server. The above mentioned session server option *memcached session replication* requires a *Memcached* server.

5.2 Feature model of Jelastic

Figure 4 shows a Feature Model representing the mentioned configuration options. Note the *requires* and *excludes* relationships that represent the constraints about which combinations of options are allowed.

6. RELATING TACTICS AND DESIGN ALTERNATIVES

After modeling the architectural tactics and configuration options in Jelastic, we analyze how software architects can implement each tactic using features offered by the cloud platform.

Tactic implementation in Jelastic.

Jelastic can provide either direct, indirect or no support for architectural tactics:

Architectural tactics may be implemented in an application by special provisions in the design and code of the application or by the configuration of the platform. For instance, the above mentioned *Maintain copies of Data* tactic for Performance can be implemented using a caching library in the code. However, even an application without these libraries can benefit of implementing this tactic by configuring *Web Caching* in the *Load Balancer*.

Other tactics, such as the *Condition Monitoring* Availability tactic to detect faults, cannot be directly implemented using only configuration options in the platform. For instance, Jelastic does not offer a configurable service that monitors servers and perform actions when a fault is detected. However, the servers in the platform offer APIs and log files that can be used by a custom application or an IT administrator to perform that task.

We are interested in identifying tactics that can be implemented using only configuration options during deployment, i.e., those *directly supported* by Jelastic, and those that can be implemented using additional code and design that ex-

ploit platform supported APIs and libraries, i.e., those *indirectly supported* by the platform.

In the other hand, other tactics must be implemented completely by the application since *no support* for them exists in the provider. For instance, the *Ping/Echo* availability tactic to *Detect Faults* is not directly supported by the servers in Jelastic but can be implemented integrating design patterns and code in the application [10]. We consider that these tactics do not benefit from the use of a cloud platform, and the configuration options in the platform have no influence in their implementation.

Tables 1 and 2 show, for each architectural tactic (rows), which configuration options (columns) can or should be selected to implement it. In each row, the options are specified using the following conventions:

✓ if the option must be selected to implement the tactic. That means that the marked options can be used to directly implement the tactic without altering the design of the application. Here we assume that applications use standard JEE APIs and libraries and do not implement the tactic using special design patterns.

X if the option should be not selected. That means that the options marked with X impede the implementation of the tactic using only configuration options.

+ if the option can be used to indirectly implement the tactic, but is not supported automatically. This means that Jelastic offers APIs and applications that can be used by an external application or operator to implement the tactic.

(blank) if the option has no influence of the implementation of the tactic.

In these tables, some tactics are implemented by selecting a parent feature in the Jelastic feature model shown in Figure 4. For instance, some tactics are implemented by selecting *App Server* instead of a more specific server such as *Tomcat* or *Glassfish*. That means that any *App Server* can be included in the configuration.

Additionally, some rows in these tables include + marks for a parent and its children features. For instance, some tactics appear with a + mark for the *App Server* and some of its children (e.g. *Tomcat* and *Glassfish*). That means that the tactic can be implemented using provided APIs but the API is different for each server. If a tactic appears only

Table 1: Implementation of Architectural tactics on Jelastic

| | | | Nginx Load Balancer | | | | SSL | Session Server | | App Server | | | | SQL Database | | | NoSQL Database | | |
			TCP LB	HTTP LB	Sticky	Caching	SSL	Replication	Memcached	Jetty	Tomcat	Glassfish	HA (Clustering)	MySQL	MariaDB	PostgreSQL	MongoDB	CouchDB	Memcached
Availability	Detect Fault	Ping/Echo																	
		Monitor																	
		Heartbeat											✓						
		Timestamp																	
		Sanity Check																	
		Condition Monitoring	+					+		+	+	+	+	+	+	+	+	+	+
		Voting																	
		Exception Detection	✓					✓											
		Self Test																	
	Recover	Active Redundancy	✓										✓						
		Passive Redundancy	✓							✓									
		Spare	✓						✓	✓									
		Exception handling																	
		Rollback												✓			X		
		Software Upgrade								+	+	+	+	+	+	+	+	+	+
		Retry																	
		Ignore Faulty Behaviour																	
		Degradation	+				+		+	+	+	+	+	+	+	+	+	+	+
		Reconfiguration	+				+		+	+	+	+	+	+	+	+	+	+	+
		Shadow												✓					
		State Resynchronization											✓						
		Escalating restart																	
		Non-Stop Forwarding																	
	Prevent	Removal from Service								+	+	+	+	+	+	+	+	+	+
		Transactions												✓			X		
		Predictive Model																	
		Exception Prevention																	
		Increase Competence Set																	
Performance	Demand	Manage Event Rate										✓							
		Limit Event Response										✓							
		Prioritize Events										✓							
		Reduce Overhead		✓			X		X				X						
		Bound Execution Times	✓							✓				✓			✓		
		Increase Efficiency									✓						✓		
	Manage	Increase Resources								+				+			+		
		Introduce Concurrency	✓							✓							✓		
		Copies of Computation	✓					✓		✓									
		Copies of Data				✓													
		Bound Queue Sizes										✓							
		Schedule Resources								+				+					

with a + mark in the parent feature (e.g. *App Server*), that means that the tactic can be implemented with any of its children using the same API.

7. DETECTING TRADE-OFFS

Having modeled how to implement the architectural tactics using configuration options in Jelastic, we rely on the FAMA Framework[7] [3] to detect trade-offs.

FAMA includes several operations to analyze feature models, e.g., operations to determine if a feature model is valid and to find the set of valid configurations of a feature model. In a feature model, a **valid configuration** is a set of features that satisfy the constraints defined in the model i.e., mandatory features, group cardinality and feature relationships. Thus, in our feature model of tactics, a valid config-

uration is a combination of tactics that do not contradict each other. Similarly, in our feature model of Jelastic, a valid configuration is a set of configuration options that is accepted by that cloud platform.

FAMA also includes an operation to validate a partial configuration. A **valid partial configuration** for a feature model is a set of non-conflicting features that can be included in a valid configuration. This validation results helpful to determine, during a configuration process, after a stakeholder have selected some features, if the stakeholders can select other features and complete a valid configuration, or if they must remove some features before obtain a configuration without conflict.

We use both mentioned operations to analyze our feature-solution. To perform the analysis, we:

---
[7] http://www.isa.us.es/fama/?FaMa_Framework

Table 2: Implementation of Architectural tactics on Jelastic

			Nginx Load Balancer				SSL	Session Server		App Server				SQL Database			NoSQL Database		
			TCP LB	HTTP LB	Sticky	Caching	SSL	Replication	Memcached	Jetty	Tomcat	Glassfish	HA (Clustering)	MySQL	MariaDB	PostgreSQL	MongoDB	CouchDB	Memcached
Security	Detect	Detect Intrusion																	
		Detect Service Denial	✓																
		Verify Message Integrity																	
		Detect Message Delay																	
	Resist	Identify Actors								✓				✓			✓		
		Authenticate Actors								✓				✓			✓		
		Authorize Actors								✓				✓			✓		
		Limit Access	✓																
		Limit Exposure	✓																
		Encrypt Data					✓												
		Separate Entities								✓				✓			✓		
		Change Default Settings								✓				✓			✓		
	React	Revoke Access								+	+	+	+	+	+	+	+	+	
		Lock Computer								+	+	+	+	+	+	+	+	+	
		Inform Actors								+									
	Rcvr	Maintain Audit Trail	+					+		+	+	+	+	+	+	+	+	+	
		Restore	Use any **Recover from fault - Availability** tactic																
Testability	Limit & Control	Specialized Interface																	
		Record/Playback																	
		Localize State Storage								✓									
		Abstract data Sources								✓									
		Sandbox								+	+	+	+	+	+	+	+	+	+
		Executable Assertions																	
		Limit Complexity																	
		Limit nondeterminism																	

1. Transform the Feature-Solution Graph into a Feature Model using a technique based on the proposed by Classen et al. [5]: we integrate both feature models for tactics and Jelastic into a single feature model and where "forces" and "prohibits" relations in the FS-Graph are translated into "requires" and "excludes" relationships.

2. Find all the valid configurations of tactics (i.e. the valid combinations according to the feature model of tactics) using the FAMA framework, and

3. Determine which valid configurations of tactics are also a valid partial configuration for the feature model representing the feature-solution graph[8].

The valid configurations of tactics that are not valid partial configurations of the feature-solution graph represent combinations of tactics that lead to trade-offs caused by conflicts in the configuration.

8. RESULTS OF OUR ANALYSIS

Regarding the research questions presented in Section 2, answers to Q1 - How to implement the architectural tactics in Jelastic have been presented in Section 6.

To address Q2 and Q3, this section explains and summarizes the main findings for: 1. Which architectural tactics can be implemented using only the configuration options of the Jelastic platform, and which require additional design and code, and 2. Which combinations of tactics lead to trade-offs.

8.1 Architectural tactics supported by Jelastic

As mentioned before, Bass et al. [2] propose 79 architectural tactics for six quality attributes : availability, performance, security, testability, interoperability, and modifiability. While some of these tactics can be implemented using deployment options in a cloud platform, others require an special design and implementation.

According to our review, mainly the tactics for *Availability*, *Performance*, *Security* can be implemented using deployment options. In contrast, the tactics for *Testability*, *Interoperability* and *Modifiability* are usually implemented through design alternatives in the application code.

Among the tactics supported by a cloud platform, we can distinguish two types: those tactics that are supported by configuring options in the environment without using additional designs and code, and those that can be supported by using APIs and applications offered by the provider.

Availability.

For *Availability*, 9 of 28 tactics can be implemented by configuring options in the platform. These tactics can be implemented using the diverse alternatives that offer the application and database servers in the platform.

---

[8]Java programs used to automate the analysis are available at http://soft.vub.ac.be/~jchavarr/jelastic-fsg/

Table 3: Results after combining tactics for one and for a pair of Quality Attributes

	Availability				Performance				Security				Testability			
Combination with tactics of	Total	Valid	Conflict	%	Total	Valid	Conflict	%	Total	Valid	Conflict	%	Total	Valid	Conflict	%
Availability	289	25	264	91.3%	277,151	8	277,143	99.9%	54.527	4,487	50.040	91.7%	867	75	792	91.3%
Performance					959	31	928	96.7%	91,105	2,945	88,160	96.7%	2.877	93	2.784	96.7%
Security									95	95	0	0%	285	285	0	0%
Testability													3	3	0	0%

In addition, 5 tactics for *Availability* can be implemented using custom or third party applications integrated to Jelastic APIs and applications. Tactics such as *Condition monitoring* that monitors parameters on servers, *Software upgrade* that updates faulty applications, *Degradation* that deactivates non-critical systems, *Reconfiguration* that reconfigure the system and *Removal of service* that deactivates faulty servers, can be implemented using cloud provider APIs.

Performance.

For *Performance*, All the tactics are supported by Jelastic in some way. 10 of 12 tactics can be implemented by configuring different options in application and database servers. The other 2, *Increase Resources* and *Schedule resources* can be implemented using custom or third party applications integrated to the platform.

Many tactics for *Performance* are based on the use of queues for requests and responses. *Manage Event Rate*, *Limit Event Response*, *Prioritize Events* and *Bound Queue Sizes* must be implemented using the *Glassfish* application server that supports message queues. In contrast to other cloud providers such as Microsoft and Google, Jelastic does not offer other alternatives for queue management.

Security.

For *Security*, 10 of 17 tactics can be implemented by configuring the platform. Basically, these tactics refers to tactics such as *Detect service denial* and *Limit exposure* that can be configured in Firewalls and Security Filters, and tactics such as *Authenticate* and *Authorize Actors* that can be configured in application and database servers.

Also for *Security*, 5 of 17 tactics can be implemented integrating APIs and third party products. Tactics such as *Revoke Access*, *Lock Computer*, *Inform Actors*, *Maintain Audit Trail* can be implemented integrating custom or third-party applications to the logging system in Jelastic.

Testability.

For *Testability*, 2 of 8 tactics are aimed to facilitate the configuration of applications during testing. The tactics *Localize State Storage* and *Abstract data sources* can be easily implemented in Jelastic because the platform allow the definition of "environments" that share applications but differ on the configuration file.

In addition, the *Sandbox* tactic for *Testability* can be also implemented using the feature that allow software architects define alternative environments for the same applications.

Other tactics, such as *Specialized Interfaces* and *Executable Assertions* must be implemented by the application and cannot be implemented configuring the platform. The *Record/-Playback* tactic, aimed to reproduce test scripts and verify their results, is not supported by any service of Jelastic.

Other cloud providers such as SOASTA[9] and Skytap[10] offer Cloud-based testing services.

Others.

In contrast to the mentioned tactics, tactics for *Interoperability* and *Modifiability* are hardly supported by configuring the Jelastic platform (We omitted these tactics in Table 2 for that reason). For instance, regarding *Interoperability*, tactics refer to the discovery, orchestration and tailoring of services and interfaces. Although these tactics can be implemented using servers for integration and service buses such as the offered by CloudHub[11], these types of servers are not offered by Jelastic as configuration options.

About *Modifiability*, all tactics are oriented to take special considerations during application design or refactoring and cannot be implemented by configuring a platform for deployment.

8.2 Architectural tactic combinations that lead to trade-offs

We use the FAMA framework to perform a combinatorial analysis of the feature models and feature-solution graphs presented in figures 3 and 4.

From this analysis we find that there are 2,147,483,647 valid configurations for the tactics feature model (including all 79 tactics), and 1,536 possible configurations for Jelastic feature model. When restricting the architectural tactics model to only those tactics that are actually supported by Jelastic (see tables 1 and 2) we find 210,862,079 possible combinations of tactics.

Analyzing the feature-solution graph that maps tactics to their implementing configuration options in Jelastic, we find that the possible set of valid solutions is further reduced to 1,352.988. This reduction in the size of the valid configuration set is explained by the fact that some combinations of architectural tactics lead to conflicts in the configuration of the platform. That means that the elements and options in the configuration used to implement some tactic have conflicts with the elements and options used to implement other tactics.

Software architects striving for one or two quality attributes, may chose architectural tactics with conflicting implementations. Table 3 shows the number of valid combinations of tactics for each two quality attributes according to the feature model in Figure 3, and the number of these combinations that lead to conflicts in the Jelastic configuration according to our Feature-Solution graphs. For instance, the intersection of *Availability* and *Performance* shows the number of valid combinations of tactics for both quality attributes (277,551), the number of configurations that do not

---

[9] http://www.soasta.com/
[10] http://www.skytap.com/
[11] https://cloudhub.io/

lead to trade-offs (8) and the number of those that lead to trade-offs (277,143).

In Table 3, intersections in the diagonal show results for the combinations of tactics for a single quality attribute. For instance, the upper-left intersection shows information regarding the combinations of tactics for *Availability*. There are 289 valid combinations of tactics for Availability according to figure 3, however 264 of those lead to trade-offs (only 25 do not lead to trade-offs).

8.3 Discussion

Threats to validity.

The main threat to validity of our study is the configuration options selected to implement the architectural tactics. First, because other architects may decide for a different set of options to implement the tactics. And second, because future versions of the Jelastic cloud platform may include additional servers and options that allow software architects implement the tactics in a different way. Thus, results from the proposed analysis may vary too. However, we consider that we study a valid set of tactic implementations and the results of our analysis contributes to the understanding of architectural trade-offs in cloud computing platforms. In addition, our approach for analysis can be used by others to analyze a different set of tactic implementations.

Observations on architectural trade-offs.

When a software architect selects tactics for an application, based on our combinatorial analysis, we found that:

- Conflicts occur in tactics aimed to the same quality attribute. For instance, the *Reduce Overhead* and *Maintain copies of computation* tactics for *Performance* conflict one with the other. While *Reduce overhead* is aimed to improve response time by eliminating processing such as *HTTP load balancing* in *Nginx* and *Session Replication* in the *Session server*, the *Maintain copies of computation* for web application servers requires these mechanisms.

- Many tactics for traditionally considered conflicting quality attributes, can be implemented without a conflict. For instance, quality attributes such as *Performance* and *Security* are considered conflicting [13]. However, there are tactic combinations that can be implemented without configuration conflicts. According to our analysis, tactics for performance such as *Maintain copies of computation* and *Maintain copies of data* can be implemented concurrently with tactics for Security as *Detect Service Denial* and *Authenticate Actors*.

- Some tactics lead to trade-offs more frequently than others. Tactics such as *Reduce Overhead* and *Increase Efficiency* for performance aim to avoid additional processing in the system and usually conflict with Availability and Security tactics that introduce new processes to maintain redundant servers, encrypt data or detect attacks.

9. RELATED WORK

Architectural tactics on the cloud.

Recently, some work has focused on designing applications for cloud computing platforms. They propose reference architectures or design considerations to achieve high levels of availability or performance on platforms such as Amazon AWS or Microsoft Azure. However, few of them review how the existing architectural tactics can be applied on these platforms.

Alexandrov et al. [1] present some experiments about how to apply availability tactics in the Amazon cloud platform. They present many options to implement the tactics for detecting faulty servers and introducing servers into the cluster. These tactics can be used to achieve higher availability than the offered by default by the provider.

Kossman, Schad et al. [11, 15] discuss about the performance unpredictability in cloud providers and tactics to deal with it. Basically, all the different cloud providers provide different architectural options for their services, and software architects must understand these options and how to combine it to improve the performance of their applications.

Winkler et al. [17] propose a catalog of tactics and patterns that can be used to implement security tactics on different cloud platforms. They also propose some hints about how to design secure applications on these platforms. However, they do not consider how these options interact to tactics and patterns used to implement other tactics.

In contrast to these works, we are considering tactics for achieving several quality attributes. Additionally, we are also determining which combinations can be applied without conflicts in specific cloud platforms.

Architectural Trade-offs.

When software architects consider more than one quality attribute for the architectural design, they must consider potential conflicts in the corresponding design alternatives. ATAM [9] and CBAM [14] have been proposed as techniques to detect these trade-offs in an architectural design. They are based on peer-reviews to evaluate an architectural design, determine trade-off points and perform trade-off decisions. In contrast to our approach, they are focused on an specific application and require complete architectural specifications.

Other authors have been focused on providing information about architectural trade-offs using relationships among quality attributes [16, 13]. These studies try to determine if a quality attribute has *positive*, *negative* or *independent* relationships to other quality attributes, gathering that information from user surveys and controlled experiments. They produce a *dependency matrix* that explain that relationships. In contrast to our approach, these studies consider that quality attributes conflict one to the other independently of the technological context of the application or the chosen design alternatives. Thus, they do not consider interactions and trade-offs that are specific to a technology or platform.

10. CONCLUSIONS

We have presented our analysis of Q1 - how to implement architectural tactics in Jelastic, Q2 - which tactics can be implemented using only configuration options, and Q3 -

which combination of tactics lead to trade-offs. In addition, we presented a systematic approach to perform the analysis that is based on feature models and feature-solution graphs.

About Q1, We presented how to implement the architectural tactics proposed by Bass et al.[2] using configuration options in the Jelastic platform in Section 2.

Regarding Q2, We found that large number of tactics for availability, performance and security that can be implemented using configuration options in the cloud provider. In contrast, tactics for interoperability and modifiability cannot be implemented configuring the platform and requires an special design or refactoring of the applications.

And for Q3, In contrast to ideas from other authors [16, 13], we find that architectural trade-offs occur *not only by selecting specific combinations of quality attributes* but for selecting *conflicting design alternatives and configuration options* to achieve those attributes.

Current and Future Work.

We consider that the presented approach to analyze the implementation of architectural tactics can be applied on other cloud computing platforms. We are currently working on feature-solution graphs that combine more than two feature models and allow the integration of reusable feature models. In concrete, we are exploring how to reuse parts of our analysis such as the feature model of architectural tactics, that is not specific to Jelastic, and the set of options to configure servers such as Tomcat or MySQL that may be the same for any cloud provider.

We are also working on extending FAMA to analyze feature-solution graphs without transforming it first into a feature model. For instance, because this transformation, we can only consider relationships where a tactic "forces" or "prohibits" the selection of a configuration option. We are now interested on feature-solution graphs including soft-constraint relationships (e.g. a relationship denoting that a tactic "suggests" a configuration option).

11. ACKNOWLEDGMENTS

Jaime Chavarriaga is a recipient of a COLCIENCIAS fellowship. Carlos Noguera is funded by the FWO-AIRCO project of the Fonds Wetenschappelijk Onderzoek of the Flemish Region.

12. REFERENCES

[1] T. Alexandrov and A. Dimov. Software availability in the cloud. In *International Conference on Computer Systems and Technology (CompSysTech2013)*, pages 46–50, 2013.

[2] L. Bass, P. Clements, and R. Kazman. *Software Architecture in Practice*. Addison-Wesley Professional, 2012.

[3] D. Benavides, S. Segura, P. Trinidad, and A. Ruiz-Cortés. FAMA: Tooling a framework for the automated analysis of Feature Models. In *Proceeding of the First International Workshop on Variability Modelling of Software-intensive Systems (VAMOS 2007)*, 2007.

[4] H. Bruin and H. Vliet. Scenario-based generation and evaluation of software architectures. In *Proceedings of the Third Symposium on Generative and Component-Based Software Engineering (GCSE 2001)*, pages 128–139, 2001.

[5] A. Classen, A. Hubaux, and P. Heymans. A formal semantics for multi-level staged configuration. In *Proceedings of the Third International Workshop on Variability Modelling of Software-Intensive Systems (VaMoS 2009)*, pages 51–60, 2009.

[6] K. Czarnecki and U. W. Eisenecker. *Generative Programming*. Addison-Wesley, 2000.

[7] M. Janota and G. Botterweck. Formal approach to integrating feature and architecture models. In *Proceedings of the 11th International Conference Fundamental Approaches to Software Engineering (FASE 2008)*, pages 31–45, 2008.

[8] K. C. Kang, S. G. Cohen, J. A. Hess, W. E. Novak, and A. S. Peterson. Feature-Oriented Domain Analysis (FODA) feasibility study. Technical Report CMU/SEI-90-TR-021, Software Engineering Institute, Carnegie Mellon University, 1990.

[9] R. Kazman, M. Klein, M. Barbacci, T. Longstaff, H. Lipson, and J. Carriere. The Architecture Tradeoff Analysis Method. Technical Report CMU/SEI-98-TR-008, Software Engineering Institute, Carnegie Mellon University, 1998.

[10] S. Kim, D.-K. Kim, L. Lu, and S. Park. Quality-driven architecture development using architectural tactics. *Journal of Systems and Software*, 82(8):1211 – 1231, 2009.

[11] D. Kossmann, T. Kraska, and S. Loesing. An evaluation of alternative architectures for transaction processing in the Cloud. In *Proceedings of the SIGMOD'10*, 2010.

[12] A. Lattanze. *Architecting Software Intensive Systems: A Practitioners Guide*. CRC Press, 2008.

[13] D. Mairiza and D. Zowghi. Constructing a catalogue of conflicts among non-functional requirements. In *Proceedings of the Evaluation of Novel Approaches to Software Engineering (ENASE 2010)*, pages 31–44, 2010.

[14] R. Nord, M. Barbacci, P. Clements, R. Kazman, M. Klein, and J. Tomayko. Integrating the Architecture Tradeoff Analysis Method (ATAM) with the Cost Benefit Analysis Method (CBAM). Technical Report CMU/SEI-2003-TN-038, Software Engineering Institute, Carnegie Mellon University, 2003.

[15] J. Schad, J. Dittrich, and J.-A. Quiané-Ruiz. Runtime measurements in the cloud: Observing, analyzing, and reducing variance. In *Proceedings of the VLDB Endowment'10*, 2010.

[16] M. Svahnberg and K. Henningsson. Consolidating different views of quality attribute relationships. In *Proceedings of the ICSE Workshop on Software Quality (WOSQ '09)*, pages 46–50, 2009.

[17] J. R. V. Winkler. *Securing the Cloud: Cloud Computer Security Techniques and Tactics*. Syngress Publishing, 2011.

[18] R. Wojcik, F. Bachmann, L. Bass, P. Clements, P. Merson, R. Nord, and W. Wood. Attribute-Driven Design (ADD), version 2.0. Technical Report CMU/SEI-2006-TR-023, Software Engineering Institute, Carnegie Mellon University, 2006.

Performance-based Selection of Software and Hardware Features under Parameter Uncertainty

Leire Etxeberria
Mondragon Unibertsitatea
Mondragon, Spain
letxeberria@mondragon.edu

Catia Trubiani
Gran Sasso Science Institute
L'Aquila, Italy
catia.trubiani@gssi.infn.it

Vittorio Cortellessa
University of L'Aquila
L'Aquila, Italy
vittorio.cortellessa@univaq.it

Goiuria Sagardui*
Mondragon Unibertsitatea
Mondragon, Spain
gsagardui@mondragon.edu

ABSTRACT

Configurable software systems allow stakeholders to derive variants by selecting software and/or hardware features. Performance analysis of feature-based systems has been of large interest in the last few years, however a major research challenge is still to conduct such analysis before achieving full knowledge of the system, namely under a certain degree of uncertainty. In this paper we present an approach to analyze the correlation between selection of features embedding uncertain parameters and system performance. In particular, we provide best and worst case performance bounds on the basis of selected features and, in cases of wide gaps among these bounds, we carry on a sensitivity analysis process aimed at taming the uncertainty of parameters. The application of our approach to a case study in the e-health domain demonstrates how to support stakeholders in the identification of system variants that meet performance requirements.

Categories and Subject Descriptors

D.2.11 [**Software Architectures**]; C.4 [**Performance of Systems**]: Modeling techniques, Performance Attributes; D.2.8 [**Software Engineering**]: Metrics—*performance measures*

Keywords

Software Architectures; Performance Analysis; Feature Selection; Uncertainty.

1. INTRODUCTION

In Software Product-Line (SPL) engineering, many software systems include a set of configuration options, called *features* [15, 1], that allow stakeholders to build system products fulfilling their functional requirements. Software and

---

*Leire and Goiuria are members of the embedded system group supported by the Basque Government.

Permission to make digital or hard copies of all or part of this work for personal or classroom use is granted without fee provided that copies are not made or distributed for profit or commercial advantage and that copies bear this notice and the full citation on the first page. Copyrights for components of this work owned by others than ACM must be honored. Abstracting with credit is permitted. To copy otherwise, or republish, to post on servers or to redistribute to lists, requires prior specific permission and/or a fee. Request permissions from permissions@acm.org.
QoSA'14, June 30–July 4, 2014, Marcq-en-Baroeul, France.
Copyright 2014 ACM 978-1-4503-2576-9/14/06 ...$15.00.
http://dx.doi.org/10.1145/2602576.2602585.

hardware features are also used to specify multiple architectural choices early in the design of a system [17], and these features aim to develop, deliver, and evolve a portfolio of similar products. However, in both cases, a major challenge is left in the hands of system designers that have to find an optimal product, i.e., the one that also meets non-functional requirements.

Performance is considered today a very critical non-functional property, because it directly affects user perception. If performance targets are not met, a variety of negative consequences (such as damaged customer relations, business failures, lost income, etc.) can impact on the project success [10]. All these factors motivate the activities of software performance modeling and analysis at the earlier phases of the life cycle, when reasoning on predictive quantitative results can allow to avoid expensive rework. However, early in the life cycle, there is often lack of knowledge about the software system, thus the performance analysis unavoidably co-exists with a certain amount of uncertainty.

In our previous work [22] we demonstrated that uncertainty is particularly critical in the performance domain when it relates to values of parameters such as the resource demand of services, service time of hardware devices, etc. In this paper we broaden the scope of our research, since we focus on studying the influence of uncertain parameters on system performance while selecting software (e.g., services) and hardware (e.g., single-core or multi-core processors) variable features. We achieve our goal by providing the performance prediction of best and worst cases on the basis of the selected features embedding uncertain parameters; thereafter, in case of wide gaps between worst and best case performance results (i.e., large uncertainty propagates from parameters to indices) we devise two sensitivity analysis steps aimed at taming the uncertainty of parameters.

Figure 1 illustrates the process we envisage for this goal. Ovals in the figure represent operational steps whereas square boxes represent input/output data.

We assume that a set of *Performance Requirements*, among others, is defined. Some examples of performance requirements are as follows: the response time of a service has to be less than 3 seconds, the throughput of a service has to be greater than 10 requests/second, the utilisation of a hardware device shall not be higher than 80%, etc. Performance requirements will be used to interpret the results from the model-based performance analysis.

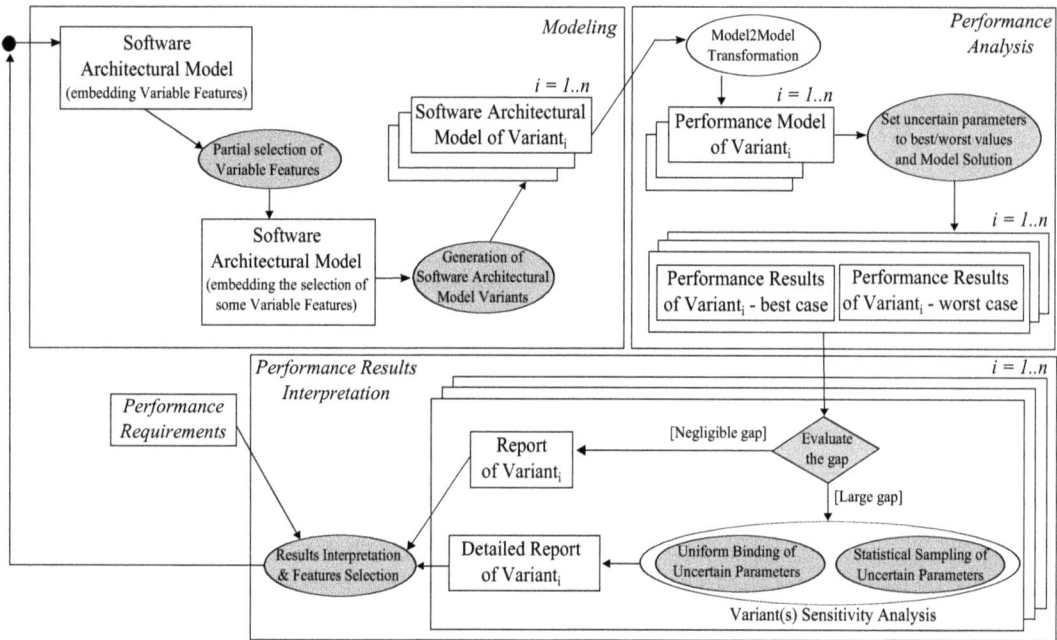

Figure 1: Model-based performance analysis process in presence of variable features embedding uncertain parameters.

Three macro phases have been identified in the process. In the *Modeling* phase, a software architectural model embedding variable features is built and, through the partial selection of variable features, a number of n software architectural model variants are generated. The modeling of variable features and the generation of variants are performed by using the SPL Conqueror tool [19]. In the *Performance Analysis* phase, we first transform software architectural models of the generated variants into performance models [3], then we set all uncertain parameters to their best and worst values, and at last we analyze the generated performance models. Note that we assume a property of monotonicity for the performance results with respect to uncertain parameters since the selected features of one variant (e.g., a system with four cores processors) only embed uncertain parameters (e.g., the service time of four cores processors may vary from 0.004 to 0.008 microseconds) that monotonically affect performance indices. Hence, the setting of uncertain parameters to best/worst values entails to solve the performance model of each variant twice and provides as output two different set of performance results for the best/worst case respectively. In the *Performance Results Interpretation* phase we evaluate, for each variant, the gap between performance results of best and worst cases. If the gap is negligible then a report of the variant is provided, otherwise we introduce two operational steps: (i) the uniform binding of uncertain parameters aims to reduce the uncertainty without further information, (ii) the statistical sampling of uncertain parameters aims to push ahead the uncertainty reduction given that parameter probability distributions are known. The comparison of results obtained by these two steps originates a detailed report of the variant under analysis. Finally, this report is provided to the system designers as support in the selection of software and hardware features that most likely fulfill the non-functional requirements. Integrating performance analysis into SPL in the early development phases allows to assess the impact of different choices on system performance. In case of unsatisfactory results, that is all variants do not fulfill performance requirements, a set of refactoring actions can be introduced to generate new software architectural models[1] that undergo the same process shown in Figure 1.

The novelty of our approach is that it is able to quantitatively compare multiple system variants generated from the specification of variable features, thus supporting the software designer in the process of selecting the software and hardware features that most likely tolerate the uncertainty of parameters.

The remainder of the paper is organized as follows. Section 2 presents related work; Section 3 describes our approach; Section 4 shows the approach at work on a case study from the e-health domain; Section 5 reports the open issues raised by the approach; and finally Section 6 concludes the paper and provides directions for future research.

2. RELATED WORK

In this section we discuss related work in the context of variability-aware performance prediction that relates to two main research areas: (i) model-based performance analysis; (ii) optimization of non-functional properties.

Model-based performance analysis. In [21] a model-driven approach to derive a performance model from an extended feature model has been presented. Such approach is intended to integrate the performance analysis in the development process of Software Product Lines (SPLs), and provides performance predictions on the basis of product and platform-specific annotations. Our approach goes beyond feature selection because it keeps into account the uncertainty of parameters that triggers performance sensitivity analysis for system variants. In [9] a model-based approach

---

[1]We do not detail the refactoring process here, as it is out of this paper focus. However, readers interested to this part can refer to [2].

to estimate the performance of multi-core systems has been illustrated. It proposes a performance model for general-purpose operating system schedulers that allows the performance analysis taking into account the influence of schedulers in Symmetric Multi Processing (SMP) environments. We used this work to model the variability of operating system schedulers. In our previous work [4] a model-based analysis process for embedded SPLs has been presented, however it takes into account only variability issues and do not consider uncertainty in the parameters. We relied on this work for the modelling of variable software and hardware features, and we extend it by focusing on the model-based performance analysis of each variant.

Optimization of non-functional properties. In [19] the SPL Conqueror tool has been presented to optimize non-functional properties in SPLs. It generates the system variants, execute and measure it. In order to reduce the effort of analyzing all variants, the SPL Conqueror tool allows to get the minimum set of variants that is needed to calculate the impact on performance of each feature. SPL Conqueror [18] also considers feature interactions that affect non-functional properties and provides heuristics for their detection. In our approach we use this tool for the generation of software model variants. Recently, in [8] a variability-aware approach to performance prediction via statistical learning has been proposed. Such approach works progressively with random samples of variants, without additional effort to detect feature interactions. In [6] a contract-based technique is proposed to characterise worst case execution times under uncertain parameters, and such technique is applied to code examples. All these approaches are oriented to code-based measurement, since variants are executed to measure performance properties. On the contrary, our approach works on model-based performance analysis of variants and additionally considers uncertainty on parameters.

3. APPROACH

In this section we describe our approach by providing details on the shaded boxes of Figure 1 that represent the focus of this paper.

3.1 Partial selection of variable features and generation of software variants

A Software Product Line (SPL) is a set of similar software systems built from a shared set of features satisfying a particular domain, where a feature is defined as a prominent or distinctive user-visible characteristic of a system [12] [14]. An important challenge in the context of SPL is to manage the variability between products, where the variability is defined as the ability to customize a system [23] and also occurs when multiple architectural choices are allowed early in the design of a system [17].

The spectrum of variability may be quite wide, in fact a software system may include variability in the selection of software (e.g., service characteristics) and hardware (e.g., platform characteristics) features. A key concept in many SPL approaches is the feature model that represents the variability between family members in a concise taxonomic form. Hence, a specific system variant is characterized by a valid feature combination derived by the feature model based on the system's requirements.

In this paper we use feature models to represent software and hardware features that inevitably affect the software ar-

chitecture as well as its performance. The selection of variable features is demanded to stakeholders, limitedly to the ones that are either optional or alternative. As a side effect, other features can be mandatorily required in the system configuration, once given the stakeholder's selection. This activity represent the first operational step in the *Modeling* phase (see Figure 1), and produces a software architectural model embedding the selection of some variable features.

Afterwards, the variability expressed in the feature model is analyzed and bound to specific system products that we name *variants* in the following. Stakeholders perform an initial selection of features, then the list of variants (the minimum to get the impact of each feature) is automatically generated by SPL Conqueror tool. Software architectural models corresponding to such list of variants are generated automatically [4]. This activity represent the second operational step in the *Modeling* phase (see Figure 1), and produces a set of n software architectural models representing all the relevant system variants.

Note that there are some software and hardware features including uncertain parameters. For example, if a certain service (i.e., a software feature) is selected, then such service may include an uncertain parameter related to its resource demand (e.g., the processor units of computation needed to accomplish a software operation may vary from 10 to 15 no. of visits). Consider as another example if a four cores processor (i.e., a hardware feature) is selected, then such processor may include an uncertain parameter related to its service time (e.g., the service time of four cores processors may vary from 0.004 to 0.008 microseconds). On the other hand, there are some features that do not include uncertainty in their parameters. For example, if a fix allocation for multi-core processors (i.e., a hardware feature) is selected, then such allocation affect the routing probability among cores, but no uncertain parameters are introduced.

3.2 Set uncertain parameters to best/worst values and model solution

In the *Performance Analysis* phase (see Figure 1) each software architectural model representing a system variant is firstly transformed into a Queueing Network (QN) [13] performance model [3]. Since software architectural models contain a certain number of parameters (e.g., resource demand of services and service times of hardware devices) whose values are subject to lack of knowledge in the early phases of the software life cycle, this uncertainty is propagated by the transformation into performance models.

Hence, QN models contain a set of variable parameters that cannot be deterministically assigned. However, such parameters are bound to concrete values by estimating their best and worst values that could be available in many cases [7]. Hence, the setting of uncertain parameters to best/worst values entails to solve the performance model of each variant twice and provides as output two different set of performance results for the best/worst case respectively. In our approach the solution of QN performance models is performed with the Java Modelling Tool (JMT) [5].

It is worth to remark that each variant only embed uncertain parameters that monotonically affect performance indices. Hence, this step of model solution uniformly takes best and worst values for all the uncertain parameters thus to provide evidence of best/worst values for the indices.

3.3 Variants sensitivity analysis and performance results interpretation

In the *Performance Results Interpretation* phase (see Figure 1), the gap between worst and best cases is evaluated for each variant. Designers pre-define a percentage threshold on such gaps, possibly by interacting with stakeholders to interpret their level of uncertainty acceptance. The threshold is then used to distinguish between negligible and large (but not overwhelming) gaps. Negligible gaps do not lead to further analysis because the ranges of performance results of those variants have been considered as acceptable, and a variant report is produced. On the contrary, large (but not overwhelming) gaps trigger two performance sensitivity analysis steps driven by different criteria for dealing with uncertain parameters, as detailed in the following.

Uniform binding. It is used when the parameter probability distributions are unknown. Consequently, we aim at taming the uncertainty of parameters without additional information by assigning uniformly distributed values to all uncertain parameters. For this goal, we analyze the performance of each variant by splitting the parameter ranges in a fixed number of intervals and binding the parameters to the extreme values of such intervals, as formalized here below. Let m be the number of uncertain parameters, and let p_k be a generic assignment of values to these parameters, i.e., p_k is a vector of m elements $\{p\_k^j, 1 <= j <= m\}$. We name $worst_j$ and $best_j$ the worst and best values of j-th parameter, respectively. If n represents the fixed number of uniform intervals set for uncertain parameters, then each interval range is given by $(worst_j - best_j)/n$. Hence, p_k^j values will be defined as follows([2]):

$$p\_k^j = best_j + k * \frac{(worst_j - best_j)}{n} \quad (\forall k = 1, ..., n-1) \ (1)$$

In other words, Equation 1 allows to calculate the value of j-th uncertain parameter related to the k-th assignment of values, where k varies in the interval $(1, ..., n\text{-}1)$ and n can be configured by the designer. As we show in Section 4, this step demonstrates that the propagation of parameter uncertainty on performance indices can be mitigated even in absence of further knowledge on the parameters.

Statistical sampling. It is used when the parameter probability distributions are known. Hence, we analyze the performance of each variant by sampling the values of uncertain parameters on the basis of their probability distributions. In our approach the sampling process is supported by ArcheOpteryx tool [16], where the number of samples can be configured by the designer.

As we show in Section 4, an increased knowledge on parameters (even if still non-deterministic) allows to decrease the level of uncertainty on performance indices, thus driving software designers to a better feature selection than the best achievable one without this knowledge. This could be considered as an obvious assertion by a qualitative viewpoint that does not need any experimentation to be proven. However, the benefit of our approach is that it is able to quantify the propagation of uncertainty from parameters to performance indices. Hence, designers have in their hands a quantitative approach that can be appropriately tuned to drive their choices in different cases.

---

[2]In the formula it is assumed that worst values are larger then best values (e.g., resource demands, service time, etc.). In cases where it holds the opposite (e.g., network bandwidth), $worst_j$ and $best_j$ must be swapped.

Both these two performance sensitivity analysis steps (i.e., uniform binding and statistical sampling) provide as output a detailed report for the system variant under analysis and it is used by the designers to select the software and hardware features that most likely fulfill the performance requirements.

4. CASE STUDY

The proposed approach has been applied on a case study in the e-health domain. Figure 2 depicts an excerpt of the E-Health System (EHS) software architectural model embedding variable features. The system supports the doctors' everyday activities, such as the retrieval of information of their patients. On the basis of such data doctors may send an alarm in case of warning conditions. Patients are allowed to retrieve information about the doctor expertise and update some vital parameters, e.g. heart rate, that are required to monitor their health status.

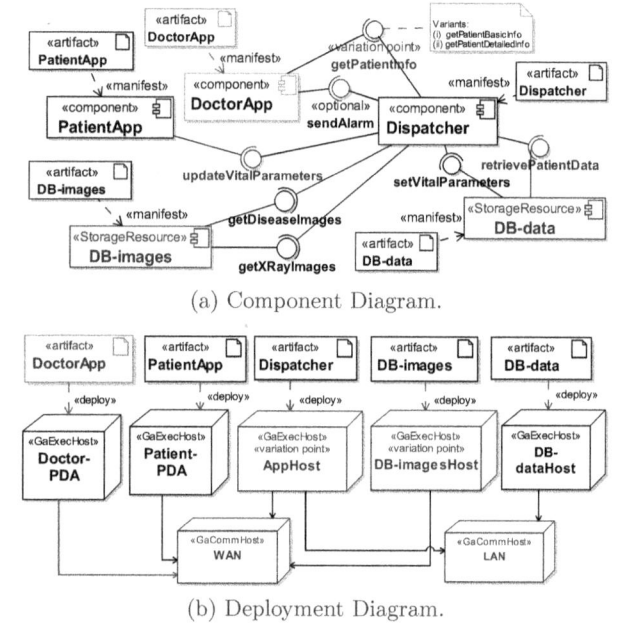

(a) Component Diagram.

(b) Deployment Diagram.

Figure 2: EHS- Software Architectural Model (embedding Variable Features).

The Component Diagram in Figure 2(a) describes the software components and their dependencies. *PatientApp* and *DoctorApp* components are connected to the *Dispatcher* component that forwards users' requests to the *DB-data* component and/or retrieves images from the *DB-images* component. The Deployment Diagram in Figure 2(b) shows that both the doctor's and the patient's applications are deployed on a Personal Digital Assistant (PDA), i.e. a mobile device in the hands of doctors and patients, respectively.

In the following we focus on *getPatientInfo* and *updateVitalParameters* services. When doctors require patient's information, their client application *DoctorApp* sends a request to the *Dispatcher* that manages the communication towards the database. Consequently, patient's medical history and disease data are retrieved by the *DB-data* storage resource, and if the battery of the doctor's PDA has a high charge level (regulated by a probability set to 0.75 in our case study) then the client application is notified by additionally sending x-rays and disease images retrieved by the

DB-images storage resource. When patients update their vital parameters, their client application *PatientApp* sends a request to the *Dispatcher* that manages the communication towards the database, and vital parameters are stored in the *DB-data* storage resource.

The system workload has been defined as follows: (i) a closed workload for the *getPatientInfo* service, with 50 users and an average thinking time of 5 minutes; (ii) a closed workload for the *updateVitalParameters* service, with 2500 users and an average thinking time of 1 hour. The performance requirements that we consider, under the stated workload of 50 doctors and 2500 patients, are:

RT: The average response time of the getPatientInfo service has to be less than 10 seconds.

RT: The average response time of the updateVitalParameters service has to be less than 5 seconds.

4.1 EHS Feature Modeling

Figure 3 reports the EHS feature model. *Hardware* features include the possibility to specify *multi-core* processors, with 2 or 4 cores for *AppHost* and *DB-imagesHost* (see Figure 2(b)). If a multi-core processor is selected, then *allocation* feature has to be defined. It can be fix or dynamic. In case of *fix* allocation it is possible to select the strategy to distribute classes of jobs: (i) Half and Half means that one half of the cores is dedicated to doctors' requests and the other half is dedicated to the patients' ones; (ii) One and Three can be selected in case of 4 cores only, and it means that one core is exclusively used by doctors' requests and three cores by patients' ones. In case of *dynamic* allocation we used the work in [9] to specify the variability in load-balancing policies of operating system schedulers. In our case, we devise two alternatives, that are: a more balanced one (i.e., 50%-50%) and a less balanced one (i.e., 80%-20%). In this latter case, doctors' and patients' requests are dynamically managed by an operating system balancing load among cores on the basis of the pre-defined probabilities. *Software* features include the possibility to specify different system functionalities (see Figure 2(a)). In EHS there are two alternative variants to get basic or detailed (i.e., doctors require the statistics of patients' vital parameters) patient information respectively. Furthermore, there is a service that can be optionally included in the system, i.e., doctors may send an alarm in case of warning conditions.

Table 1 schematically reports the output of SPL Conqueror tool on the EHS case study, given the feature model of Figure 3. After a partial selection where no multi-core is discarded, the tool provides a set of 7 system variants (over a set of 28 feasible variants) that need to be evaluated. As performance can only be measured per variant, SPL Conqueror automatically computes the minimum set of variants that include all the selected features (in this case 7), thus to get information about each feature. Note that $Variant_1$, $Variant_6$, and $Variant_7$ have the same hardware features, while they only differ for the set of provided functionalities. In fact, $Variant_1$ provides the *getPatientBasicInfo* service[3], $Variant_6$ provides the *getPatientDetailedInfo* service, and finally $Variant_7$ include the *sendAlarm* service. $Variant_2$ and $Variant_5$ are 4-cores configurations with a fix allocation: (i) half and half in case of $Variant_2$, (ii) one and three

---

[3]The *getPatientBasicInfo* service is shared by all the variants listed in Table 1, except for $Variant_6$ that provides the *getPatientDetailedInfo* service.

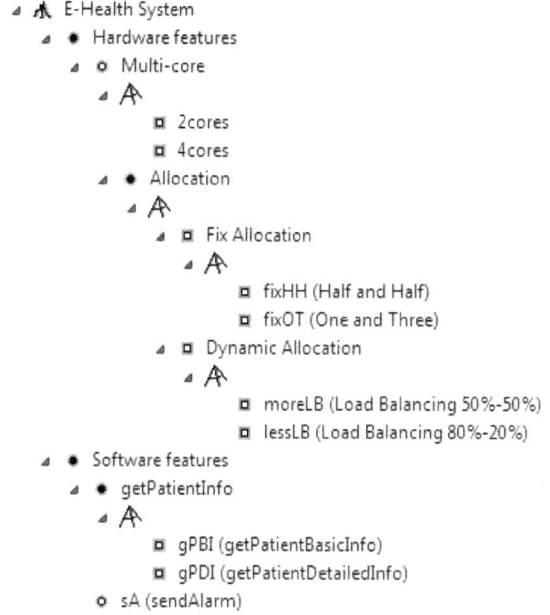

Figure 3: EHS- Feature model.

in case of $Variant_5$. Finally, $Variant_3$ and $Variant_4$ are 2-cores configurations with a dynamic allocation: (i) 50%-50% in case of $Variant_3$, (ii) 80%-20% in case of $Variant_4$.

4.2 EHS Performance Analysis

Table 2 reports the EHS uncertain parameters, in particular five parameters concern the resource demands of software services, and three parameters are related to the characteristics of hardware devices. Each parameter is detailed with best/worst bounds as well as *mean* (μ) and *variance* (σ^2) of parameter probability distributions.

Table 2(a) reports the resource demand of software services expressed in terms of cpu visits each service requires to the host it is deployed on. Each parameter is defined with the name of the service and the host to which the demand is required. For example, the *getPatientBasicInfo* service has a parameter named *gPBI-AppHost* representing the number of visits to the *AppHost* that varies between *20* and *30*.

Table 2(b) reports the characteristics of hardware devices. State-of-art values [11] have been used to set these bounds: the service time of 2-cores processors varies between *0.007* and *0.014* microseconds, whereas it varies between *0.004* and *0.008* microseconds in case of 4-cores processors. Wide Area Networks (WAN) bandwidths have been estimated to vary between *6* and *2* Mbps.

As said in Section 3.2, the setting of uncertain parameters to best/worst values entails to solve the performance model of each variant twice. Table 3 summarizes the performance results of the EHS variants for the best/worst case respectively. We report the response time (RT) of critical services, i.e, *getPatientInfo* (namely *gPI*), *updateVitalParameters* (namely *uVP*), and *sendAlarm* (namely *sA*). Note that the response time of *getPatientInfo* service refers to *getPatientBasicInfo* in all variants, except in $Variant_6$ where such service is replaced by *getPatientDetailedInfo* (see Table 1). Similarly, the response time of *sendAlarm* service is only reported for $Variant_7$, in fact it is the only variant including such service (see Table 1).

	HW features						SW features	
	2cores	4cores	fixHH	fixOT	moreLB	lessLB	gPDI	sA
$Variant_1$	X		X					
$Variant_2$		X	X					
$Variant_3$	X				X			
$Variant_4$	X					X		
$Variant_5$		X		X				
$Variant_6$	X		X				X	
$Variant_7$	X		X					X

Table 1: EHS- model variants.

(a) Resource demand of *software* services.

Parameter	Best value	Worst value	Mean (μ)	Variance (σ^2)	Unit of measure
gPBI-AppHost	20	30	25	0.308	no. of visits
uVP-AppHost	80	120	100	4.938	no. of visits
gPDI-AppHost	5	7.5	6.25	0.019	no. of visits
sA-AppHost	10	15	12.5	0.077	no. of visits
gPBI-DB-imagesHost	40	60	50	1.234	no. of visits

(b) Characteristics of *hardware* devices.

Parameter	Best value	Worst value	Mean (μ)	Variance (σ^2)	Unit of measure
2coresProcessor	0.007	0.014	0.0105	1.51E-07	microseconds
4coresProcessor	0.004	0.008	0.006	4.94E-08	microseconds
WAN	6	2	4	0.049	Mbps

Table 2: EHS- uncertain parameters.

4.3 EHS Performance Results Interpretation

Table 3 additionally reports the percentage GAP we get in performance results for the best vs worst case, as the following ratio: $((worst - best)/worst) * 100$. For example, the value in $Variant_1$, $gap(gPI)$ cell states that the gap between worst and best cases for response time of $getPatientInfo$ service in $Variant_1$ is 42.13%, and it has been obtained as $((3.94 - 2.28)/3.94) * 100$.

In our experimentation we focus on gaps from 60% to 90%, because the former value represents the acceptance threshold set by designers, whereas latter value guarantees to exclude unfeasible (i.e. too high) performance results that are usually originated by overstressing the system. For example, in $Variant_1$ the response time of $updateVitalParameters$ varies from 2.36 to 600 seconds, where latter value unambiguously indicates the presence of a software/hardware bottleneck that delays all requests. $Variant_6$ and $Variant_7$ also suffer of the same problem. Variants that show such a behavior are straightforwardly discarded.

On the contrary, $Variant_2$ and $Variant_5$ are the best ones since the gap between best/worst values is lower than 50%, which is very likely due to their common feature to embed 4-cores processors that provide enough computational power to handle the worst case. Variants that show such a behavior nicely tolerate the uncertainty on parameters, hence designers do not strictly need any further analysis to deal with them.

Shaded entries in Table 3 highlight the variants that evidently need to be further analyzed by our sensitivity analysis process, because they show gaps within the previously defined thresholds. In particular, in $Variant_3$ the response time of $updateVitalParameters$ varies from 2.15 to 6.15 seconds, whereas in $Variant_4$ the response time of $getPatientInfo$ varies from 2.33 to 13.85 seconds. Note that both these latter variants do not fulfill the stated performance requirements in their worst case, hence designers are induced to discard them in the process of selecting features.

Figure 4 reports the sensitivity analysis of the $updateVitalParameters$ response time in $Variant_3$.

In particular, Figure 4(a) shows the variation of RT(updateVitalParameters) on the basis of parameter values that have been set according to the Equation 1 with n=11. We conducted three different experiments: (i) *software* parameters have been varied only, and hardware parameters are set to mean values; (ii) *hardware* parameters have been varied only, and software parameters are set to mean values; (iii) both software/hardware parameters have been varied. Note that n=11 leads to get 10 different sets of values for software, hardware, and software/hardware parameters, i.e., $p\_1, \ldots, p\_10$ vectors reported on the x-axis of Figure 4(a). In particular, each p_i represents a set of values that have been calculated with Equation 1. This leads to a bench of 30 experiments. It is worth to notice that the increases of software uncertain parameters have little impact on the performance results since they lead the RT(updateVitalParameters) to vary from 2.80 to 3.72 seconds, whereas increases of hardware uncertain parameters lead the same index to vary from 2.51 to 4.3 seconds. Finally the variation of both software/hardware parameters has the highest impact on the performance results, as expected, since it leads the same index to vary from 2.28 to 5.30 seconds.

Figure 4(b) shows the response time histogram for these experiments, where the range of resulting RT(updateVitalParameters) values is reported on the x-axis and the number of occurrences on the y-axis. We remark that $(5 + 7 + 5 + 5 =)$ 22 times the RT(updateVitalParameters) falls between 2.58 and 3.79 seconds, thus providing a confidence value for this interval of 0.73 (equals to 22/30).

Figure 4(c) shows the variation of RT(updateVitalParameters) on the basis of parameter values that have been set by randomly sampling. We assumed that all parameters have a $NORMAL$ distribution and, they have variances between $\mu - 3 * \sigma$ and $\mu + 3 * \sigma$ (see Table 2). This means that in 99.73% of observed cases the parameter values fall in

	RT (sec) - Best case			RT(sec) - Worst case			GAP (%)		
	RT(gPI)	RT(uVP)	RT(sA)	RT(gPI)	RT(uVP)	RT(sA)	gap(gPI)	gap(uVP)	gap(sA)
$Variant_1$	2.28	2.36		3.94	600		42.13	99.61	
$Variant_2$	2.09	1.8		3.42	3.21		38.89	43.93	
$Variant_3$	2.31	2.15		4.68	6.15		50.64	65.04	
$Variant_4$	2.33	2.23		13.85	43.39		83.18	94.86	
$Variant_5$	2.09	1.79		3.42	3.01		38.89	40.53	
$Variant_6$	3.18	2.37		6.47	600		50.85	99.61	
$Variant_7$	2.28	2.36	0.52	3.94	600	0.93	42.13	99.61	44.09

Table 3: EHS- RT of services while varying system variants (best and worst cases).

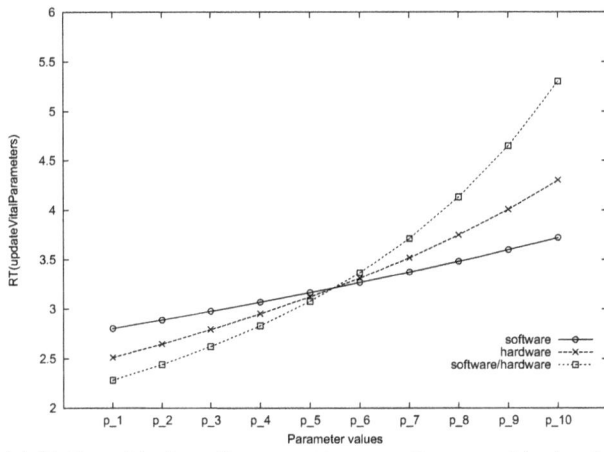

(a) Uniform binding: Response time vs software and/or hardware parameters.

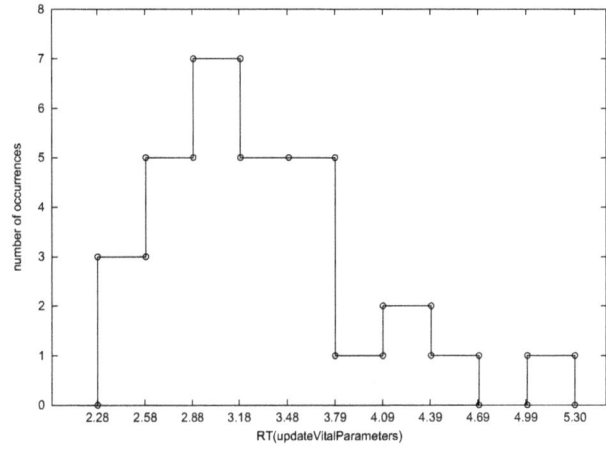

(b) Uniform binding: Response time histogram.

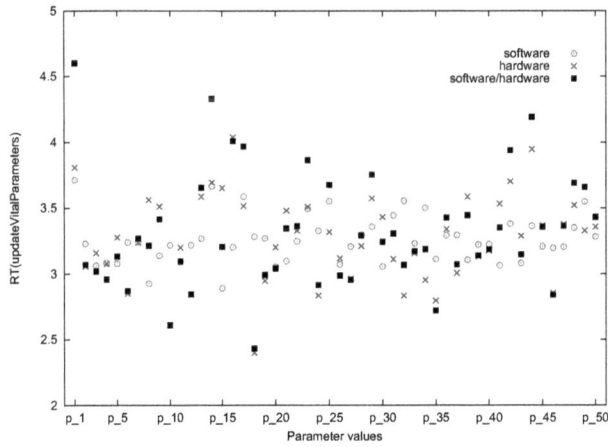

(c) Statistical sampling: Response time vs software and/or hardware parameters.

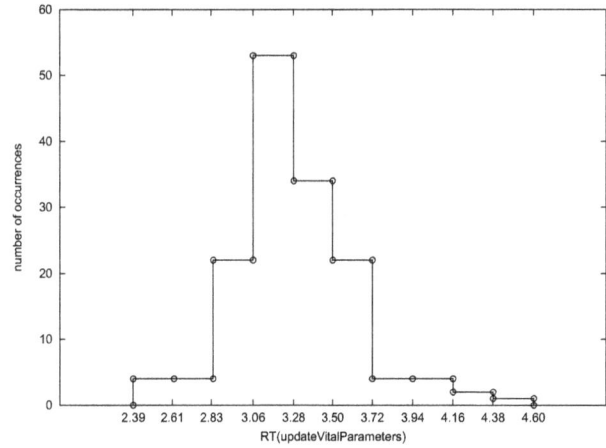

(d) Statistical sampling: Response time histogram.

Figure 4: EHS-$Variant_3$: RT(updateVitalParameters) sensitivity analysis.

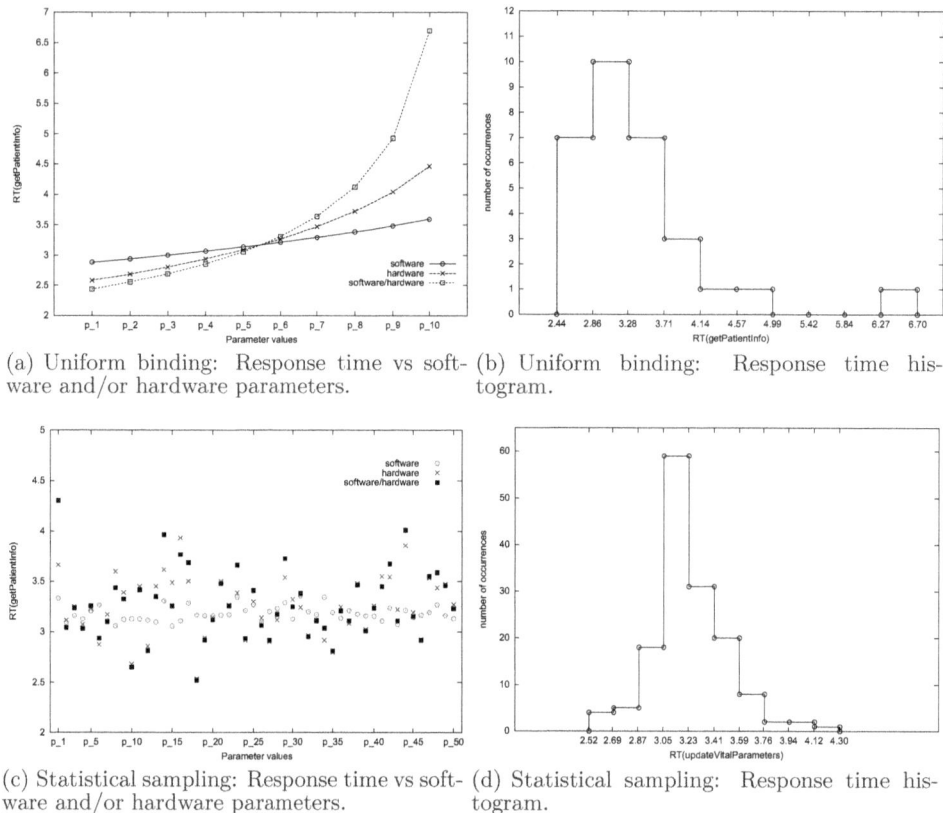

(a) Uniform binding: Response time vs software and/or hardware parameters.

(b) Uniform binding: Response time histogram.

(c) Statistical sampling: Response time vs software and/or hardware parameters.

(d) Statistical sampling: Response time histogram.

Figure 5: EHS-$Variant_4$: RT(getPatientInfo) sensitivity analysis.

the range of best and worst values. We conducted here the same three experiments shown in Figure 4(a). Note that 50 different values have been sampled for software, hardware, and software/hardware parameters, i.e., $p\_1, \ldots, p\_50$ vectors reported on the x-axis of Figure 4(c). In particular, each p_i has been randomly generated by ArcheOpteryx tool [16], and the sampling process does not guarantee any order among the p_i vectors. This leads to a bench of 150 experiments. Even though the performance results seem to be scattered over larger ranges, we notice that the result trends in Figure 4(c) are similar to the ones obtained in the case of uniform binding. In particular, software uncertain parameters have little impact on the performance results since they lead the RT(updateVitalParameters) to vary between 2.89 and 3.71 seconds, whereas hardware uncertain parameters lead the RT(updateVitalParameters) to vary between 2.39 and 4.04 seconds. Finally the binding of both software/hardware parameters has more impact on the performance results, as expected, since it leads the RT(updateVitalParameters) to vary between 2.42 and 4.60 seconds.

Figure 4(d) shows the response time histogram for these experiments. We remark that (22 + 53 + 34 + 22 =) 131 times the RT(updateVitalParameters) falls between 2.83 and 3.72 seconds, thus providing a confidence value for this interval of 0.87 (equals to 131/150).

Summarizing, for $Variant_3$ the RT(updateVitalParameters) falls in the interval (2.58, 3.79) with a confidence value of 0.73, whereas in the interval (2.83, 3.72) with a confidence value of 0.87.

Figure 5 reports the sensitivity analysis of the *getPatientInfo* response time in $Variant_4$.

Similarly to Figure 4, Figure 5(a) refers to the uniform binding step, and it again shows that software parameters have little impact on the performance results, and so on towards concurrent variations of software and hardware parameters. Figure 5(b) shows the corresponding response time histogram that provides a confidence value of 0.8 (equals to 24/30) from 2.44 to 3.71 seconds. Figure 5(c) refers to the statistical sampling step, and it once again shows that software parameters have little impact on the performance results, and so on towards concurrent variations of software and hardware parameters. Figure 5(d) shows the corresponding response time histogram that provides a confidence value of 0.85 (equals to 128/150) from 2.87 to 3.59 seconds.

Summarizing, for $Variant_4$ the RT(getPatientInfo) falls in the interval (2.44, 3.71) with a confidence value of 0.8, whereas in the interval (2.87, 3.59) with a confidence value of 0.85.

The above experimentation confirms that, while increasing the knowledge on uncertain parameters, it is possible to better tame uncertainty in the performance results, and this was an expected finding. An added value of our approach is that it allows to quantify such progressive decrease of uncertainty, as demonstrated above. For example, we have shown that in $Variant_3$ the response time of the *updateVitalParameters* service falls in the (2.58, 3.79) seconds interval with a confidence value of 0.73 with the uniform binding methodology, whereas with the statistical sampling we demonstrated that it falls in the narrower (2.83, 3.72) seconds interval with a higher confidence value of 0.87. Other approaches that do not utilize uniform binding and/or statistical sampling can only report about best and worst cases, i.e. a (2.15, 6.15) seconds interval for the service here considered. This would negatively affect the stakeholders' choices in that, with a response time requirement of 5 seconds on the *updateVitalParameters* service, they would be induced to discard $Variant_3$ because the requirement falls within the (2.15, 6.15) seconds interval. Instead our approach is able to find out that such variant fulfills the requirement with a high confidence value.

Beyond the generation of variants, SPL Conqueror allows to automatically detect feature interactions. An interaction among two features occurs when the performance of a variant embedding both features are heavily different from those of the variant where one feature does not appear.

We remark that this aspect is not the focus of this paper, although we retained worthwhile to start investigating it. Thus, we used SPL Conqueror to detect feature interactions in EHS. We intended to investigate possible interactions between software and hardware features. This kind of interactions pointed out by the tool on EHS are: (2cores, moreLB, gPDI), (2cores, lessLB, gPDI), (4cores, moreLB, gPDI), (4cores, lessLB, gPDI)([4]). Hence, the focus here is on the interactions between number of cores (i.e., hardware) and *getPatientInfo* service behavior (i.e., software).

For sake of space we only consider here the following interactions: (2cores, moreLB, gPDI) and (2cores, lessLB, gPDI). These two sets of features give rise to new system variants, namely $Variant_8$ and $Variant_9$ respectively. Through explicit performance analysis of these variants we meant to validate the SPL Conqueror output.

To this end, Table 4 reports the response time of the *getPatientInfo* service, where shaded rows represent the two additional system variants. In the table $Variant_3$ and $Variant_4$ are also reported, because they differ from the additional ones by the absence of the *gPDI* feature. For each variant the response time of the *getPatientInfo* service has been obtained by assigning a random set of values to uncertain parameters, because in this experiment our intent was to focus on interactions rather than uncertainty. We have repeated this assignment several times, but for sake of space Table 4 only reports 5 different assignments named as p_1, p_2, ..., p_5, one for each table column.

	RT(gPI)				
	p_1	p_2	p_3	p_4	p_5
$Variant_3$	3.24	2.73	2.83	3.29	3.00
$Variant_8$	6.18	4.56	5.20	6.24	4.94
$Variant_4$	3.69	2.85	3.06	3.88	3.23
$Variant_9$	12.30	5.57	7.71	13.62	6.46

Table 4: EHS- RT(getPatientInfo) service while considering two further system variants.

Numerical results provide good evidence to the correctness of SPL Conqueror output for these interactions. In fact, the system performance heavily vary, in both (2cores, moreLB) and (2cores, lessLB) cases, depending whether gPDI soft-

---

[4]Note that each detected interaction is represented by a 3-ple because the multi-core feature (i.e., 2cores and 4cores) implies a choice on the allocation feature (i.e., moreLB and lessLB).

ware feature is selected or not. For example, with the assignment p_1 for uncertain parameters we can notice that the RT(gPI) delta percentage between $Variant_8$ and $Variant_3$ is equal to $(6.18 - 3.24)/6.18 = 0.47$, and the same quantity for $Variant_9$ and $Variant_4$ is $(12.30 - 3.69)/12.30 = 0.7$. The order of magnitude of these deltas has been observed across all adopted parameter assignments.

We are aware that this is far from being a rigorous proof of SPL Conqueror output soundness, but first validation results seem promising to track a direction for this goal.

5. DISCUSSION

Our approach highlights the complexity of model-based performance analysis of software architectures while considering software and hardware variable features as well as their uncertain parameters. In the following we discuss some key points raised by this work.

Software Product Line (SPL) principles. A remarkable difference exists between a software architectural model (embedding variable features) and a performance model. An architectural model describes a set of software products containing a collection of configurable software and hardware features, which are building blocks for many products with different options and alternatives. A performance model is an instance-based representation of one product at runtime, as deployed on a given platform. Thus, SPL principles do not apply to performance models since, as stated in [20], it is impossible to build a performance model for the whole set of products or to predict the performance properties of a software architectural model (embedding variable features). Hence, it is not possible to exploit the commonalities across variants in this context, but we need to instantiate a product in order to predict its performance characteristics (i.e., response time, throughput, utilization) on a specific platform.

Detection of feature interactions under parameter uncertainty. The detection of feature interactions may be affected by uncertain parameters since features including uncertain parameters (e.g., the multi-core processors) may propagate this uncertainty on performance indices, whereas other features (e.g., hardware allocation) do not. This point opens an interesting direction of research that we aim to investigate in the future.

Scalability of the approach. In our experimentation we analyzed 7 different QN performance models (that basically represent the system variants generated by SPL Conqueror), and each performance model has been solved twice to get best/worst cases. Two system variants were subject to sensitivity analysis, where the performance models were solved 30 times for the uniform binding, and 150 times for the statistical sampling. The JMT queueing network solver has evaluated a number of $(7 * 2 + 2 * 30 + 2 * 150 =)$ *374* models in approximately 12 minutes, which can be considered more than acceptable at design time. In our future work we intend to investigate the scalability of our approach on larger QN models.

Limitations of the approach. Our approach to uncertainty taming only applies to parameters that monotonically affect performance indices. Consequently, there might be some parameters that cannot be considered by our approach because their influence on performance indices is non-monotonic. For example, the operational profile stochastically characterizes the way users interact with the system, hence it represents a good example of such a parameter.

6. CONCLUSION

In this paper we proposed an approach to quantify the correlation between selection of features embedding uncertain parameters and system performance. In particular, we provided best and worst case performance bounds on the basis of selected features and, in cases of wide gaps among these bounds, we performed a sensitivity analysis process aimed at taming the uncertainty of parameters.

We have shown, through a case study, how taming uncertainty in performance results while increasing the amount of information available on uncertain parameters. Our approach allows to quantify the level of confidence that stakeholders can achieve on performance results, hence they can enhance their capabilities of feature selection by identifying system variants that better meet performance requirements.

As future work, we first intend to apply our approach to other case studies, possibly coming from real world systems. This broader experimentation will allow us to study the scalability of the approach on larger systems and compare the analysis results achieved on the model level with measurements from the actual system implementation. Beside this, we intend to integrate more sophisticated techniques to consider the variance in performance indices and study the interactions among features, as well as the influence of features on other non-functional attributes.

7. ACKNOWLEDGMENTS

The authors would like to thank Norbert Siegmund and Sven Apel (University of Passau) for their valuable support while using the SPL Conqueror tool. This work has been partially supported by the CRAFTERS ARTEMIS Project Nr. 295371, and the National funding Ministerio de industria, energía y turismo.

8. REFERENCES

[1] S. Apel and C. Kästner. An overview of feature-oriented software development. *Journal of Object Technology*, 8(5):49–84, 2009.

[2] D. Arcelli, V. Cortellessa, and C. Trubiani. Antipattern-based model refactoring for software performance improvement. In *QoSA*, pages 33–42, 2012.

[3] S. Balsamo, A. Di Marco, P. Inverardi, and M. Simeoni. Model-based performance prediction in software development: A survey. *IEEE Trans. Software Eng.*, 30(5):295–310, 2004.

[4] L. Belategi, G. Sagardui, L. Etxeberria, and M. Azanza. Embedded software product lines: domain and application engineering model-based analysis processes. *Journal of Software: Evolution and Process*, 2012.

[5] G. Casale and G. Serazzi. Quantitative system evaluation with java modeling tools. In *ICPE*, pages 449–454, 2011.

[6] J. Fredriksson, T. Nolte, M. Nolin, and H. Schmidt. Contract-based reusable worst-case execution time estimate. In *RTCSA*, pages 39–46, 2007.

[7] H. Groenda. Improving performance predictions by accounting for the accuracy of composed performance models. In *QoSA*, pages 111–116, 2012.

[8] J. Guo, K. Czarnecki, S. Apel, N. Siegmund, and A. Wasowski. Variability-Aware Performance Prediction: A Statistical Learning Approach. In *International Conference on Automated Software Engineering (ASE)*, pages 301–311, 2013.

[9] J. Happe, H. Groenda, M. Hauck, and R. H. Reussner. A prediction model for software performance in symmetric multiprocessing environments. In *QEST*, pages 59–68, 2010.

[10] H. Harreld. NASA Delays Satellite Launch After Finding Bugs in Software Program, April, 1998.

[11] J. L. Hennessy and D. A. Patterson. *Computer Architecture, A Quantitative Approach*. Elsevier, fourth edition, 2007.

[12] K. C. Kang, S. G. Cohen, J. A. Hess, W. E. Novak, and A. S. Peterson. Feature-oriented domain analysis (foda) feasibility study. Technical report, Software Engineering Institute, November 1990.

[13] E. Lazowska, J. Kahorjan, G. S. Graham, and K. Sevcik. *Quantitative System Performance: Computer System Analysis Using Queueing Network Models*. Prentice-Hall, Inc., 1984.

[14] K. Lee, K. C. Kang, and J. Lee. Concepts and guidelines of feature modeling for product line software engineering. In *International Conference on Software Reuse: Methods, Techniques, and Tools*, pages 62–77, 2002.

[15] C. Lengauer and S. Apel. Feature-oriented system design and engineering. *Int. J. Software and Informatics*, 5(1-2):231–244, 2011.

[16] I. Meedeniya, A. Aleti, and L. Grunske. Architecture-driven reliability optimization with uncertain model parameters. *Journal of Systems and Software*, 85(10):2340–2355, 2012.

[17] R. Olaechea, S. Stewart, K. Czarnecki, and D. Rayside. Modelling and multi-objective optimization of quality attributes in variability-rich software. In *NFPinDSML*, 2012.

[18] N. Siegmund, S. S. Kolesnikov, C. Kästner, S. Apel, D. S. Batory, M. Rosenmüller, and G. Saake. Predicting performance via automated feature-interaction detection. In *International Conference on Software Engineering (ICSE)*, pages 167–177, 2012.

[19] N. Siegmund, M. Rosenmüller, M. Kuhlemann, C. Kästner, S. Apel, and G. Saake. SPL Conqueror: Toward optimization of non-functional properties in software product lines. *Software Quality Journal*, 20(3-4):487–517, 2012.

[20] R. Tawhid and D. C. Petriu. Automatic derivation of a product performance model from a software product line model. In *SPLC*, pages 80–89, 2011.

[21] R. Tawhid and D. C. Petriu. User-friendly approach for handling performance parameters during predictive software performance engineering. In *ICPE*, pages 109–120, 2012.

[22] C. Trubiani, I. Meedeniya, V. Cortellessa, A. Aleti, and L. Grunske. Model-based performance analysis of software architectures under uncertainty. In *QoSA*, pages 69–78, 2013.

[23] J. van Gurp, J. Bosch, and M. Svahnberg. On the notion of variability in software product lines. In *Working IEEE/IFIP Conference on Software Architecture*, pages 45–54, 2001.

Dealing with Uncertainties in the Performance Modelling of Software Systems

Diego Perez-Palacin
Politecnico di Milano
Dipartimento di Elettronica, Informazione
e Bioingegneria
Milano, Italy
diego.perez@polimi.it

Raffaela Mirandola
Politecnico di Milano
Dipartimento di Elettronica, Informazione
e Bioingegneria
Milano, Italy
raffaela.mirandola@polimi.it

ABSTRACT

Models play a central role in the assessment of software non-functional properties like performance and reliability. Models can be used both in the initial phases of development to support the designer decisions and at runtime to evaluate the impact of changes in the existing software. However, being abstraction, the models include *per-se* a certain degree of uncertainty. Nevertheless, often this aspect is neglected and models are used beyond their capabilities. Recognising the presence of uncertainties and managing them, would increase the level of trust in a given software model. In this paper we exploit a recently defined taxonomy that classifies the different types of uncertainties and we define a method that, starting from a given model, helps in recognising the existence of uncertainty, in classifying and managing it. We show the method at work on an example application considering the performance of the application as target non-functional property.

Categories and Subject Descriptors

D.2.4 [**Software Engineering**]: [Software/Program Verification]; I.6.4 [**Computing Methodologies**]: Simulation and Modeling

Keywords

Uncertainty; Models; Performance

1. INTRODUCTION

Software is increasingly permeating modern society, covering also critical areas of daily life. The ability to assess software non-functional properties like performance and reliability is therefore becoming of paramount importance to avoid possible unrecoverable damaging effects [4]. In this context, models (and abstraction) play a prominent role [23, 1, 14]. They are key in the initial development of an application, where they represent abstractions of the system-to-be. They may abstract both the real world in which the systems will be embedded and the systems themselves and they may be used to reason about requirements and possible architectural choices [1]. Models are now increasingly used also at run

Permission to make digital or hard copies of all or part of this work for personal or classroom use is granted without fee provided that copies are not made or distributed for profit or commercial advantage and that copies bear this notice and the full citation on the first page. Copyrights for components of this work owned by others than ACM must be honored. Abstracting with credit is permitted. To copy otherwise, or republish, to post on servers or to redistribute to lists, requires prior specific permission and/or a fee. Request permissions from permissions@acm.org.
QoSA'14, June 30–July 4, 2014, Marcq-en-Baroeul, France.
Copyright 2014 ACM 978-1-4503-2576-9/14/06 ...$15.00.
http://dx.doi.org/10.1145/2602576.2602582.

time to support continuous monitoring of compliance of the running system with respect to the desired model [27, 9, 5, 6]. A wide set of models has been proposed over time to support software engineers. They vary according to the level of formality and precision, the aspects they intend to describe, and the kind of reasoning they support [23, 4]. The emergence in the last years of the *model driven development* paradigm [14], has highlighted their importance and shown in practice their use and effectiveness for both functional and non-functional reasoning and verification.

However, being abstraction, the models include *per-se* a certain degree of uncertainty. The analyses carried out during the initial development phases cannot provide accurate results because the information of the environment where the application will be deployed may not be completely known when applications are initially architected. This is further exacerbated in software that is embedded in dynamic contexts, where requirements, environment assumptions, and usage profiles continuously change. Since these changes in the context happen in a way that is hard to predict when systems are initially built, the outcome of the model analysis are in these cases subject to higher uncertainty because assumptions upon which they rely on may not be true. Recognizing the presence of uncertainties and managing them, would minimize their influence and increase the level of trust in a given software model. The missing corrective potential of managing uncertainties could lead to exaggerate the claims of the models validity and to their uninhibited application to problems far beyond their capabilities [22].

New methods emerged to study these kind of uncertainties in the last decades. Natural science research areas, such as the weather forecasting or hydrological modeling of water basin fields, have been particularly prolific for the identification of model uncertainties [30, 2, 22]. Starting from [17], mathematical methods have been developed for the representation and management of uncertainties, such as probability theory or fuzzy methods [20]. The interest for the study of uncertainties in the computer science field is more recent. Discussions on uncertainties and proposals of methods to manage them can be found in [16, 36, 8, 19, 18, 24, 33, 35]. These approaches usually start from the knowledge of the existence of a given type of uncertainty and propose the most suitable method to deal with it. However, what often happens in reality is that the existence of uncertainty is not known in advance, and it can be suspected only when strange model results and/or behaviors are observed. But also in this case, the origin of such deviations is not known and should still be discovered.

In this paper we focus on this second and more challenging aspect. Specifically, we propose a methodology called MUSE (Managing Uncertainties in Software modEls) that, starting from a given model, guides the software engineers in recognizing the existence of uncertainty and in managing it. To this end, MUSE exploits a recently defined taxonomy that classifies the different types of uncertainties [28], together with their sources and existing approaches to handle them. The first step consists in building awareness about the existence of uncertainty in the model under exam. Once this fact is recognized, it is necessary to understand to which category of the taxonomy this uncertainty belongs to be able to manage it in the most suitable way. The step of identification of uncertainty is a challenging one and two different methods are analyzed. The last step of MUSE shows how the existing methods can be applied to mitigate the effect of uncertainties and to increase the accuracy and trustworthiness of model analysis results.

We then show MUSE at work through a concrete example concerning the model-based performance evaluation of a software system migration, which illustrates how the input data to create a system model may be incomplete and subject to uncertainties.

The paper is organized as follows. Section 2 presents the background and summarizes the related work. The proposed approach is described in Section 3 and some of the existing methods to manage model uncertainties are discussed in Section 4. The application of the proposed approach is then shown in Section 5 through an example considering the performance of the application as target non-functional property. Section 6 concludes the paper.

2. BACKGROUND AND RELATED WORKS

2.1 Background

Several definition of uncertainties can be found in different areas of the scientific literature ranging from the absence of knowledge, to the inadequacy of information or the deficiency of the modeling process [34, 15]. In the following we refer to a general definition of *uncertainty* in modeling given in [34] and used in [28] as: *"any deviation from the unachievable ideal of completely deterministic knowledge of the relevant system"*. Such deviations can lead to an overall "lack of confidence" in the obtained results based on a judgment that they might be "incomplete, blurred, inaccurate, unreliable, inconclusive, or potentially false" [30].

In the rest of the paper we make use of the taxonomy defined in [28], where uncertainties are classified regarding the following dimensions: *location*, *level* and *nature*.

In particular, as illustrated in Figure 1 and detailed in [28], considering the *location* dimension, i.e, the place where the uncertainty manifests itself within the model, we can specialise it in: *Input parameters*, model *Structure* and *Context*. The *level* describes where the uncertainty manifests itself along the spectrum between deterministic knowledge (0th level) and total ignorance (3rd level) passing through awareness of uncertainty (1st level) and unawareness of uncertainty (2nd level). The *nature* indicates whether the uncertainty is due to the lack of accurate information (*Epistemic*) or is due to the inherent variability of the phenomena being described (*Aleatory*).

In order to manage uncertainties in software systems, research works in the the literature [7, 16, 10] have investigated their possible sources. Examples of sources of uncertainty are: *Simplifying assumptions, Noise in sensing, Future parameters value, Human in the loop, etc*. The impact of these uncertainties on the trustworthiness of the information in the models and their relation with the taxonomy dimensions have been analysed in [28]. For example, *simplifying assumptions* is classified has being epistemic with location that can be both context or model structural. Due to space reasons, we do not provide here a complete description (interested readers are referred to works referenced above for further details). According to the identified type of uncertainties several methods can be applied to reduce their impact (see details in [28]). For

example, to deal with uncertainties located in *Input parameters*, reliability bound [36], confidence intervals [36], probability distributions [36], fuzzy methods, range of values, mean and variance, sensitivity analysis, sensitivity to information sources [7] have been applied so far. Some of these methods were proposed in computer science, while other are brought from other research areas. However, none of them at present is able to completely eliminate uncertainties. In the following subsection we provide a short overview of the most recent works dealing with the topic of uncertainty in the computer science field.

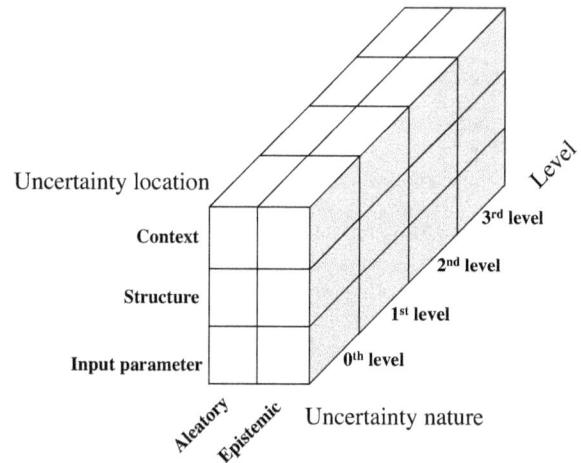

Figure 1: Model uncertainty dimensions

2.2 Related works

At present, in computing, the most used definitions of uncertainty simply distinguish between natural variability of physical processes (i.e., aleatory or stochastic uncertainty) and the uncertainties in knowledge of these processes (i.e., "epistemic" or state-of-knowledge uncertainty) [8, 19, 18, 24, 33, 12, 16].

We can devise two main kinds of works where uncertainty has been taken into account. The first one, includes works discussing the impact of uncertainty on requirements and on architectural decisions. Specifically, in [35] the authors deal with requirements specification of self-adaptive systems and present a requirement definition language that captures the existing uncertainties. Work in [31] proposes a methodology to manage uncertainties in the structure of system requirements models based on the utilization of partial models that allow to to capture, elaborate and change uncertainties. Techniques yielding to the choice of suitable architectures in the presence of uncertainty are presented in [12, 11]. To achieve this goal, they explain how to rank, compare and choose an architectural configuration that maximizes the likelihood of satisfying the system's quality preferences. In [10], authors provide a list of sources of uncertainties that may exist in self-adaptive software systems. They also extend their method to compare the utility of an architecture by including how this utility is expected to vary over time within given constraints.

The second set of works proposes specific techniques to deal with parameter uncertainties. Works in [13, 19, 8, 36] cope with prediction of reliability and availability of computer systems in presence of uncertainties. They share the usage of Markovian models as mathematical formalization for representing software systems and present formal methods that address the challenge of uncertainties in the parameters of these models. In [8] authors describe a Monte Carlo based approach and calculate the number of samples of uncertain parameter values necessary to produce availability results within a confidence interval. In [18, 19] authors use the method of moments for evaluating component-based software reliability under uncertainties. They deal with the presence of uncertainties in both the components estimated reliability and in the operational profile of software. Work in [13] estimates confidence levels of parameters of the software operational profile.

Model-based performance and reliability evaluation of software architectures in presence of uncertainties are tackled in [33, 25, 24]. Their methods are applied at software design time and aim at finding software designs or software component compositions that meet the non-functional requirements. They consider uncertainties in the values of the parameters of their models and propose to model this uncertainty through probability distribution functions. They extract samples of the parameter values and perform Monte-Carlo based simulations.

3. THE MUSE APPROACH

In this section we present the MUSE methodology for identifying the existence of uncertainties in the information represented in system models. Referring to the taxonomy described in Section 2, this means moving the level of an uncertainty from the second level, where the uncertainty in the model is not recognized, to a lower one, where not only the existence of an uncertainty but also its location (*context*, *structural* or *input parameter*) and nature (*aleatory* or *epistemic*) are discovered.

We first provide an overview of the overall concept, while in the following subsections we describe in detail its main steps. The rationale of MUSE is not to define a specific method to deal with a given uncertainty, but rather its focus is in helping the software engineering in the proper use of software (performance) models. To this end it includes a set of steps that can be followed to increase the grounds for credibility of a given model.

3.1 Overview

The proposed approach is illustrated in Figure 2. It starts considering as input the model, the analysis results and the definition of uncertainty. The first step consists in building awareness about the existence of uncertainty in the model we are considering (Section 3.2). Once this fact is recognized, it is necessary to understand to which category of the taxonomy this uncertainty belongs (Section 3.3), to be able to manage it in the most suitable way (Section 4). The step of identification of uncertainty is a challenging one. In the following we propose two different strategies that can be used to this end. The first one, called *bottom-up* is based on the knowledge of the possible sources of uncertainty in the given model while the other, called *top-down*, starts from the complete lack of knowledge about possible uncertainties.

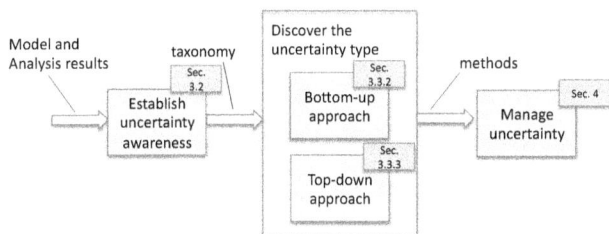

Figure 2: Overview of MUSE

3.2 Establish Uncertainty Awareness

This step aims at recognizing if there is some deviation of the model analysis results from the expected ones. This could be done in different ways, depending on the availability of data: (i) comparing data, (ii) using multiple models or (iii) through the intervention of a domain expert.

- **Data comparison.** Following the review of strategies given in [29], we should check whether there are available real observations to use as control data for model validation test. If the system is already deployed and running, the actual information of the system properties is available. In this case the deviation from the expected behavior can be easily checked comparing the actual data with the output of a model analysis. [1]

- **Multiple models.** If there is not available field data to check the model correctness, model imperfections cannot be assessed directly. This technique generates several plausible models using the available information, analyzes all of them to obtain the same kind of result, and compares their result values. More formally, being X the available information, n different analysis techniques, and f_i the analysis technique i that uses a subset X_i of data from X, we can derive that there is an uncertainty if

$$\neg(f_1(X_1) = ... = f_n(X_n)) \quad , \text{where } X_1, ..., X_n \subseteq X.$$

This technique raises the existence of uncertainty if the results of different model analysis are not the same. However, it does not provide guarantees in the opposite sense; i.e., if all the model analysis provide the same results, it cannot be ensured that there is not uncertainty in the model because it might happen that all the results are wrong.

- **Domain expert.** When the previous methods cannot be applied, expert elicitation of the uncertainty (technique described in [21]) may be used to proceed with the analysis.

3.3 Discover the Uncertainty Type

After the acknowledgment that some uncertainty is present in the given model, to be able to manage it, it is necessary to understand its *location* and its *nature*. We devise two different approaches that are summarised in Figure 3 and illustrated below.

3.3.1 Bottom-up

This is an empirical method that, in addition to the knowledge of the model and the domain, requires the awareness of both the potential sources of uncertainty of the system model and the way to check their presence in the model. Since each uncertainty is associated to an uncertainty class (or to several classes, depending on how the concrete uncertainty manifests itself in the model characteristics), when one of the uncertainties is identified in the model, its class can be discovered as represented in the lower part in Figure 3.

Consider for example that a part of a model represents the time to transfer a concrete file to a remote client, and that there is a running system where this time can be measured. It is known that *noise in sensing* is a possible source of uncertainty in this model, which affects the values of some its *input parameters*; concretely the parameter that represents the measure of the file transmission time. The

---

[1]The mismatch could be due to a problem in the model or to a wrong implementation of the mechanism to monitor the actual information of the system. In this work we will assume that the missed information is in the system model and we leave the differentiation of the source of the mismatch for a future work.

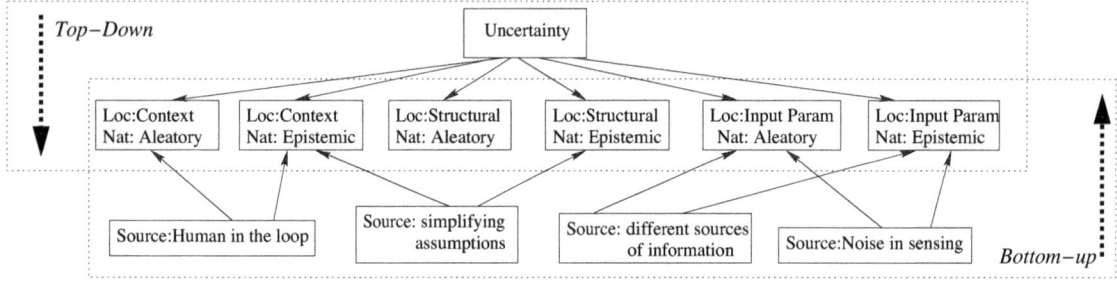

Figure 3: Two proposed methods to identify an uncertainty

nature of this uncertainty can also be classified as *aleatory* when, for example, it is known that the internet infrastructure may force the re-sending of some packets during some transmissions, then resulting in a higher measured transmission time, but not during others. The nature of this uncertainty can be classified as *epistemic* when the transmission time is measured considering only the moment in which the last packet of the file left the server, and not the moment in which it reached its destination and is usable by the remote client.

Under some circumstances this may be the only possible method to adopt for the classification of uncertainties in the model. However, this method may be tedious to use because: it requires a large amount of information and it needs to know all the possible sources of uncertainty that can affect the model together with the suitable methods to detect their presence. Moreover, the list of concrete sources of uncertainties is large and it is prone to be extended as new sources are found. Finally, since a concrete source of uncertainty can manifest itself in different parts according to the considered system, an implementation of this method is very tailored to a specific system model, so it is hardly reusable in other systems or generalizable to be applied in a broad type of models.

For these reasons, it is important to have a method that does not need to look into each possible source of uncertainty, but that can classify and manage uncertainties from a more broad perspective. Next subsection explains a possible method of such type.

3.3.2 Top-down

The aim of this method is to be able to identify the type of uncertainty only knowing that an uncertainty exists in the model as a result of the previous step. Therefore the ideal goal is defining the function:

$TypeOfUncert : model \rightarrow typeOfUncertainty$.

However, this is a difficult problem and we propose here an heuristic and iterative process that is able, given an uncertainty, to decide for its class. In other words, the process emulates the function $TypeOfUncert : model \rightarrow typeOfUncertainty$ through the execution of function:

$isTypeOfUncert : model, typeOfUncertainty \rightarrow boolean$.

The objective of the process is trying to explain the presence of the uncertainty by exploiting the existing taxonomy and starting from the easiest class to be managed and arriving to the hardest one, so changing the *typeOfUncertainty* value in a specific order. Figure 4 depicts the order in which types of uncertainties are checked, and the rationale for such an order is presented in the following paragraphs.

Motivation of iteration order: Let us consider at first the dimension *location* of the taxonomy. We consider reasonable assum-

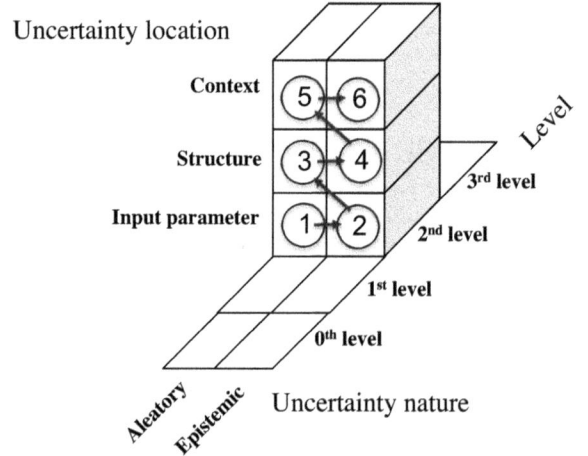

Figure 4: Proposed checking order to identify the type of an uncertainty

ing that an *input parameter* uncertainty is easier to manage than a *structural* one. In the same way, a *structural* uncertainty is easier to manage than a *context* one. The reason for this ranking is based on the fact that *input parameter* uncertainties are related to the values of the attributes in the model elements, *structural* uncertainties are related to the presence or not of some model elements, and *context* uncertainties are related to the type of elements that can be included in the model. Therefore, if some lack of knowledge can be explained as an uncertainty in attributes values, it will be easier to deal with than if it involves an uncertainty in the existence of model elements. Actually, the increment of parameter uncertainty was already proposed as a method to account for structural uncertainty [30]. In the same way, if some lack of knowledge can be explained as an uncertainty in concepts that can be included in the model (*structural*) it will be easier to deal with than if it involves an uncertainty in aspects that cannot be even represented in the model (*context*).

Regarding the *nature* dimension of an uncertainty, we consider that the *aleatory* is easier to be managed than the *epistemic* for the reasons presented in the following [2]: since an uncertainty due to the randomness in the values of some attributes or presence of some elements can be described up to some point using aleatory variables or statistical studies (e.g., probability distribution functions or co-

---

[2]This reasoning is based on the authors' current best of knowledge; nothing impedes that, in the future, other techniques that deal with *epistemic* uncertainty can be developed and this type of uncertainty may become the easiest to tame.

variances), uncertainties of *aleatory* nature can be managed with well-established techniques. On the other hand, uncertainties due to lack of enough data to build reliable knowledge (e.g., about the model attributes value or about whether some elements should be present in the model) are more difficult to manage. The cause of this higher difficulty is that in this case there are not even guarantees of the trustworthiness of the information to perform a reliable statistical study with it. As an example of this higher difficulty, consider the typical usage of the uniform distribution over a range when there are no clues of the possible values of a variable. This fact can be seen like relaxing of the lack of knowledge of a variable (i.e., an *epistemic* uncertainty) to treat it as a randomness in its value (i.e., as an *aleatory* uncertainty).

For these reasons, the iterative process modifies the $typeOfUncertainty$ parameter following the order illustrated in Figure 4.

Characteristics of the iterative process: One should be aware that this method does not ensure that the uncertainty is classified in its truly belonging class. For example, if a true *context* uncertainty can be easily explained as a *structural* uncertainty, it will be identified as *structural*. The same happens for the nature of the uncertainty: if some uncertainty that truly has an *epistemic* nature can be also easily explained as a random variability, it will be identified from the point of view of *aleatory* nature. What it shall not happen is that a simpler to tame uncertainty will be identified as a harder one.

Characteristics of *isTypeOfUncert* function: Function $isTypeOfUncert$ must be carefully implemented. This function should not force the explanation of an uncertainty under a certain type, but to check whether the uncertainty can be easily explained as such type. The reason is that it is easier to deal with a slight uncertainty of a harder type, than with a very large uncertainty of an easier type. For example, both an intricate variability of many parameters in the model and a light variation of model structure may provide an explanation of the uncertainty. Implementing an intricate $isTypeOfUncert$ function that is able to find the large set of unknown features in the *input parameters* that explain the uncertainty is less helpful to subsequently deal with the uncertainty than an $isTypeOfUncert$ function that returns `false` for the *input parameters* and tries with the next type. The idea is not to incur in the "law of the instrument": *I suppose it is tempting, if the only tool you have is a hammer, to treat everything as if it were a nail*; in this case, if it were absolutely better to deal with uncertainties due to the *aleatory* characteristics of *input parameter*, it could always be found a manner in which any uncertainty can be explained as belonging to such a type.

Since the behavior of the $isTypeOfUncert$ function is a critical part, a domain expert may orient its definition and implementation. For example, when looking for uncertainties in the *input parameters*, a sensitivity analysis [3] over model parameters can give information about the most influential parameters. Minor variations of these parameters have more impact in the output results than major variations on other parameters. Therefore, in order to provide a reason to explain a given deviation of the analysis output with respect to the expected output, a slight uncertainty in the most influential parameters is more plausible to happen than larger uncertainties in other parameters. If results improve in a significant quantity by assuming that most sensitive parameters are slightly uncertain (domain expert shall provide the amount of deviation until it can be considered "slight"), the existence of uncertainty in the input parameters will be acknowledged.

Following the same view, the $isTypeOfUncert$ function can decide that there is a structural uncertainty by assigning *variation points* in the model and applying heuristic genetic algorithms.

A structural uncertainty can be acknowledged if the analysis of a slight variation of the model ($\Delta model$) provides an output that is closer to the real values. The number of maximum allowed mutations of the original model should be bounded by a value given by the expert in order to avoid forcing the explanation of the uncertainty by a large amount of structural uncertainties. If a $\Delta model$ within the limit of mutations provides close enough results, the *structural* uncertainty will be acknowledged. It is worth noting that the outcome of this technique does not mean that the true model is the $\Delta model$ that provided the closest results to the expected ones. It just means that, more accurate results may be reached by acknowledging that there exists an uncertainty in the current model structure.

4. MANAGE UNCERTAINTY

The last step of the MUSE approach deals with the management of uncertainties of a concrete type. Goal of this step is to reduce and eventually to eliminate the impact of the discovered uncertainties on the model analysis results. Two paths can be followed: modify the model to improve the representation of information and eliminate the uncertainty or keep the current model and apply techniques to manage existing uncertainty.

Modify the model.

This path aims at including more information in the model in order to eliminate the type of uncertainty that has been found or at least reduce it to a negligible quantity; this is, move the uncertainty to the 0th level. Following this path, an appropriate model can be reached by refinements starting from a model where the location and the nature of its uncertainties have been identified .

This would require the availability of additional information useful for the uncertainty reduction. In this case, the available information can be included in the form of more accurate parameter values (then reducing *input parameter* uncertainty), or by refining the structure of the model to include this new information (then reducing *structural* uncertainty) or allowing to model new concepts that previously were out of the model context (reducing *context* uncertainty). This path is very simple, but unfortunately cannot be always followed because of lack of additional information to be included in the model or because the model size becomes huge.

Manage a model with uncertainty.

This path aims at working with the model being aware that it contains uncertainties, and taming it during the model analysis (i.e., manage the uncertainty in its 1st level).

Since at this point the type of the uncertainty to manage has been unveiled, we prefer to take advantage of existing techniques already proved as useful for managing uncertainties of a concrete type. We list and briefly explain some of them in the following.

If the uncertainty concerns a randomness in the values of the *input parameters* it can be applied the traditional solution of parameter description with probability distributions together with an analysis of the obtained results expressed with a confidence level. In case of *epistemic* uncertainty on the *input parameters*, it can be applied the solution that encloses the unknown parameter values within a range of values and associates the uniform probability distribution within the range. When considering the uncertainty in the model *structure*, probability distributions are hard to apply. However, we can exploit the same principles and create a discrete set of models with different structure (expecting that they represent a wide range of the characteristics of the potentially infinite models) and weight their analysis results. This approach represents the basics of the method called *model averaging* (e.g., as in [26]). For an *epistemic* uncertainty on the model *structure*, the *model discrepancy* technique can be applied (e.g., as in [32]). This technique requires supplying the estimation of some correct results during its initial calibration in order to be able to quantify the uncertainty in the model and use it in subsequent analysis.

5. MUSE AT WORK

In this section we apply MUSE to a concrete IT example illustrated in Figure 5. An organization is changing the working philosophy of its datacenter. In the past, each computerized service had dedicated hosts, which were managed by the IT department but selected and purchased by the responsible of the service. At a certain point, a change in the working philosophy has been introduced: instead of many and very heterogeneous servers, the IT department acquired powerful racked servers. Each of these servers, at present, are no longer dedicated to a single service but they run virtual machines (VM) that are the ones in charge of executing services. Each VM is in charge of at most one service, while a service can be deployed on a set of VM.

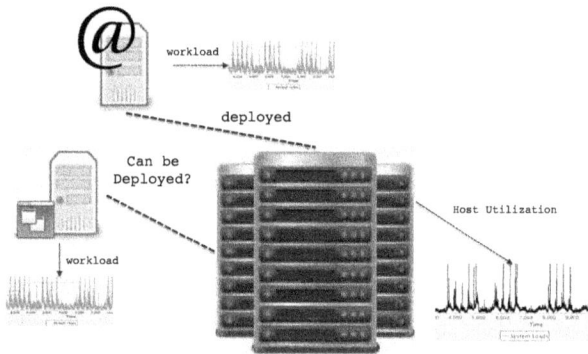

Figure 5: System example

The IT department is now organizing the migration of a service that works in batch. This service, the last day of each month, has to make some computations and generate a set of documents (e.g., payslip) for each of the organization's members and clients. Let us assume that there are 100,000 jobs completely parallelizable to be completed and each of them requires two seconds of computation in the new host (e.g., for the computation of worked hours and creation of the pdf document for members and users). The computation should finish during the day. The profit of virtualizing this service is obvious because in the past the dedicated servers were idle most days of the month.

The IT department is considering to deploy the VM of this service in the same host that manages one of the VM of the organization's email service, which consists of 16 processing cores. Currently, the VM of the email service has high priority in the host, and this should continue as the email service is considered as a low latency one. Thus, the VM of the batch service should use spare cores of the host. To avoid a tight solution that may become useless if the email usage varies slightly, the batch service will only be deployed in the host if it is still suitable for a variation in the email usage of +50%.

For assessing the suitability of deploying the new service VM in the same host, the IT department has been provided with some information of the email service and can also use some information of the server. Information regarding the email service concerns the variation in the arrival rate of email messages that the VM in this

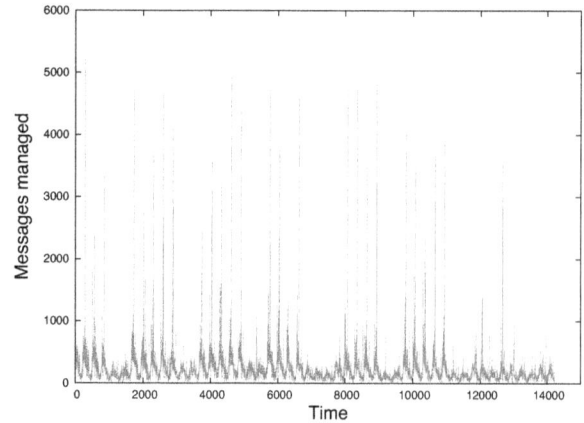

Figure 6: Arrival rate of requests received during 14225 consecutive periods of 5 minutes each

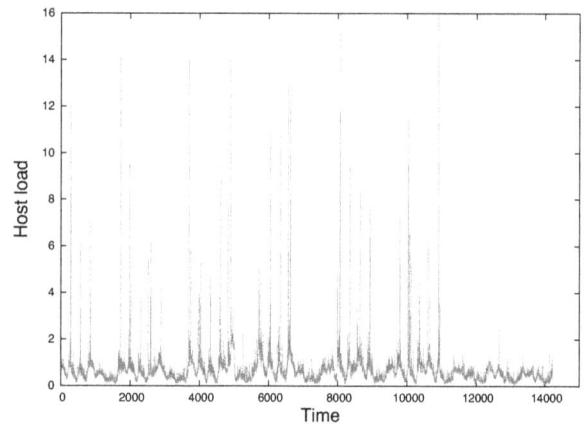

Figure 7: Server utilization during 14225 consecutive periods of 5 minutes each

host received as depicted in Figure 6 (called in the following λ_i), while information regarding the server concerns its load in terms of number of processor cores utilized over time as depicted in Figure 7 (called in the following N_i) [3]. In the rest of the section we impersonate the behavior of the IT department engineers.

5.1 System Model

We evaluate whether the server will be able to cope also with the new batch service. We decide to follow a model-based evaluation and propose a model as depicted in Figure 8. In such model, there is an object *server* with associated *services*, only the *email* service in this case, and performance information. Each service has associated information regarding: its workload in terms of number of jobs (i.e., managed messages) during concrete time intervals and computing requirements for each piece of work (execution time). The performance information associated with the server is the mean number of used processing cores during concrete time intervals.

Although the service time of email messages is an information required for performing the study, we have not been provided with

---

[3]This data usage corresponds to the messages managed by a University email system. Each value corresponds to the messages managed and mean system load during periods of 5 minutes. There are represented 14225 periods of 5 minutes, referring from 14:31 of 12 Nov. 2013 to 23:56 of 31 Dec. 2013

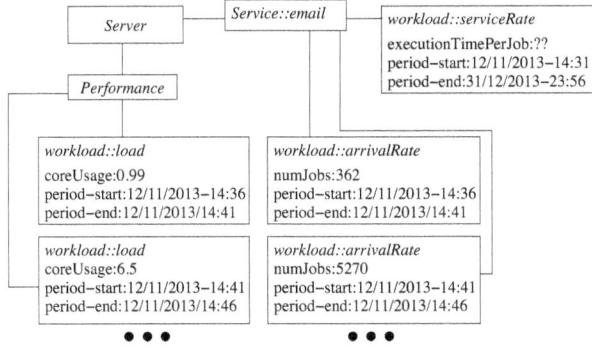

Figure 8: Model elicited by modelers

this information. This is due to the fact that the email performance was calculated for the first deployment of the service to assess whether the deployment fit the service requirements. However, since the email migration implied that the service was deployed into a more powerful host, the requirements were for sure satisfied and nobody cared about measuring the new computing requirements of email messages.

To complete the model to reason over it, we have to calculate a mean execution time of each message in the VM by using the mean arrival rate and the mean number of used cores in the system and assuming that the execution time of a message did not vary with time (i.e., messages did not increase its size, complexity, and the hardware was not upgraded).

Being $\overline{\lambda}$ the mean arrival rate and $\overline{N}$ the mean number of cores used in the server, we calculate the mean execution time $1/\overline{\mu}^*$ of each message using classical formulas from operational analysis [4] by $\overline{\mu}^* = \overline{\lambda}/\overline{N} = 224.04/0.678 = 330.4$. Note that the mean usage of host cores is only 0.678, then meaning that the host is always almost free but for some moments where the peak usage happen.

5.2 Establish uncertainty awareness

Following MUSE, the first step is to realize the presence of uncertainties in the model. This could be immediately acknowledged since the execution time of a message management is not known and the model was not completely defined. However, it may also happen that the previous $1/\overline{\mu}^*$ calculation gave the exact value for the execution time, case in which there would not be uncertainty in the system. We follow the *data comparison* method to check the presence of uncertainties through inconsistencies between the calculated and measured data. The measured data is the usage of cores in the host (N_i) and the calculated data is the core requirements of the email service (N_i^*) using (λ_i and $\overline{\mu}^*$).

Therefore, we calculate each N_i^* values as $N_i^* = \lambda_i/\overline{\mu}^*$, and we check whether N_i^* values match up with N_i ones. Since it is essentially unlikely that the calculated values of processing core requirements are exactly the same as the measured ones, we will accept that an N_i^* matches up with an N_i if its value is within a tolerance of $\pm10\%$; therefore $(N_i - 10\%N_i) \leq N_i^* \leq (N_i + 10\%N_i)$. To decide whether there are uncertainties or not, we grant one more tolerance level by allowing the 20% of time periods to be out of the interval. This additional tolerance level is reasonable because some messages need much more processing time than others: a plain-text message can be delivered much quicker than a message with com-

---
[4] As notation matter, we use the super-index "*" for calculated data (e.g., X^* for calculated value and X for the measured value

pressed attached file that has to be uncompressed and checked for virus. Therefore, depending on the proportion of messages with attachment during a time period, the service rate of messages may vary. We accept that the 20% of time periods have a completely dominant type of messages, then causing in the email service a requirement of much less or much more processing resources. Thus, following this *data comparison* method to check the presence of uncertainties, we will realize its existence if more than 20% of N_i^* values are not within their acceptable interval. We obtained that in only 1792 out of 14225 time periods the N_i^* data were within its allowed interval. This gives us a percentage of 87.4% of data out of the acceptable interval, which is higher than the allowed tolerance, and in consequence we acknowledge the presence of uncertainties.

5.3 Discover the uncertainty type

At this point the next step of MUSE guides the discovery of the uncertainty type. In the following the top-down approach is adopted and illustrated in the example. The first attempt is to check whether the uncertainty can be explained as an *input parameter* uncertainty due to the randomness on the parameters value.

Input-parameter aleatory.

Provided parameters of arrival rate and system usage are not prone to show randomness. Thus, in this case, the $isTypeOfUncert$ function looks for a possible randomness in the execution time parameter that lets the calculated and measured system load match up. Our belief about the system is that the mean service rate for serving emails over different time periods can show some variability, but not much, as discussed above. Examples given in the previous subsection to motivate the inclusion of tolerances during the checking of the existence of uncertainties apply also here.

For checking the variability in the service rate, we calculate as many μ_i^* values as arrival rate and system load elements are available, following the formula: $\mu_i^* = \lambda_i/N_i$. We see that the maximum and minimum values found for μ_i^* are $max_i(\mu_i^*) = 4194.04$ and $min_i(\mu_i^*) = 5.98$, which correspond to the period of 26 Dec. at 14:06 when there were received 3523 requests and the system load was 0.84 and the period of 29 Nov. at 15:11 when there were received 84 requests and the system load was 14.05, respectively. We calculate the standard deviation σ and the probability distribution of these μ_i^* values and we obtain $\sigma = 266.05$ and the graph depicted in Figure 9. From data in Figure 9 we calculate the minimum length range that includes the 95% of μ_i^* values and we obtain the interval [39.483, 885.47]. This range of variability of μ_i^* value can explain the uncertainty in terms of randomness in the input parameters. Now, it should be decided whether this obtained variability for the the μ^* parameter is within the accepted amount of variability for the service rate of emails. Since we are expecting a service rate almost constant and only allowing a slight variability, we assume that the obtained variability is too large to accept that the uncertainty is well explained by the randomness in μ^* value. Therefore, the $isTypeOfUncert$ function for this case will return false and we continue looking for the next type of uncertainty.

Input-parameter Epistemic.

After discarding the randomness in the input parameter as a reason to easily explain the uncertainty, the $isTypeOfUncert$ function with the *input parameter* location and *epistemic* nature of the uncertainty is evaluated. Parameters of the model are in *load*, *arrivalRate* and *serviceRate* objects. Assuming lack of knowledge of actual *numArrivals* or *numCores* parameters and modifying their values can of course make the formula that relates their values match, and therefore the uncertainty would be explained. How-

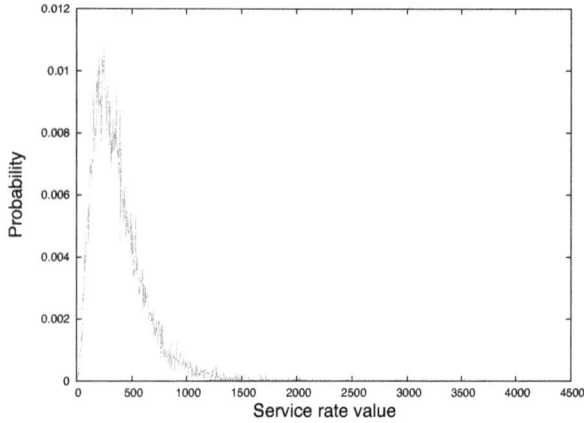

Figure 9: Probability distribution of μ_i^* values

ever, due to the simplicity of the measures, we prefer to assume that these pieces of information were collected correctly and the uncertainty should reside in other parameters. A possible uncertain parameter could be the *period-start* and *period-end* parameters, uncertainty that could come from the fact that the VM and the server do not share the same time (e.g., the email service is configured as working in the timezone of the organization headquarters, while the server has the timezone of the datacenter). We modified the values of *load* in periods of one hour up to a maximum shift of $\pm 12h$ (i.e., 25 studies), and we calculate the standard deviation of μ_i^* values in each study, called σ_h such that $h \in \{-12, ..., +12\}$. Figure 10 depicts these σ_h. The minimum standard deviation is found for $\sigma_0 = 266.0$ (i.e., the original phase of data), meaning that the best explanation is that there is not uncertainty in the parameter values of dates of the workload periods and system load periods.

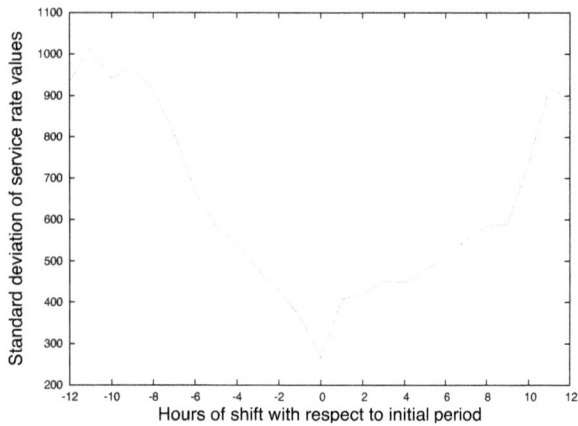

Figure 10: Mean service rate errors in function of the data shift

Next, to continue checking the epistemic uncertainty we try to find whether there could exist a value for the execution time required by email that could make the system model coherent, even if such value is different from the value we expected and we do not known its origin or what kind of behavior it shows. Therefore, the next considered parameters are in *serviceRate* objects. For doing this, we relax the previous assumptions and we only keep the very commonsense one: if $\lambda_i > \lambda_{i'}$ then $N_i \geq N_{i'}$ for any value considered for the execution time; that is, higher values of arrival rate should not show lower values of system active cores.

For checking it, we look in the input arrival rate and system load values whether the relaxed assumption hold, and we found a time period (the 4303-th time period) with an arrival rate $\lambda_{4303} = 1622$ and system load $N_{4303} = 0.53$, and another time period (the 10910-th one) with $\lambda_{10910} = 636$ and system load $N_{10910} = 16.8$. These values let us deduce that there does not exist any value for the *executionTime* parameter that could make the model coherent even only under the relaxed assumption. Since we are looking for the theoretical existence of the service rate value, we have not considered here any possible tolerance regarding the amount of cases we admit to observe where a $\lambda_i < \lambda_{i'}$ and $N_i \geq N_{i'}$; but it could have been considered too.

Using the last two studies, we can say that the observed uncertainty does not come from the fact that we do not know the real value of parameters and therefore the *epistemic* uncertainty in the *input parameters* is discarded. Following the process described in Section 3, it is now time to check whether there is a *structural aleatory* uncertainty.

Structural Aleatory.

Here we check the existence of some randomness in the model structure. In other words we investigate if there are elements of *workload*, *service*, or *server* that should be (or not be) present in the model. This may look like a huge uncertainty in the model that would prevent accurate analysis, but it could happen even in our simple example. For instance, this type of uncertainty could happen if, within the process of virtualization and migration of services to the processing host, service administrators were allowed, for some periods, to execute tests on the destination host. This fact would produce an uncertainty since it is not known when the services were proved, how much they were stressed by the test, how many services and how concurrently. The presence or absence of other services in the host is a decision taken by the responsible of such service, and therefore is a random event from the point of view of the host and host administrators. Therefore, the true structure of the model can be subject to randomness.

The function $isTypeOfUncert$ for the *structural aleatory* uncertainty check whether exists a possible alternative model with a slightly different structure that explains better the system. Note that this alternative model is not intended to be considered the "true" model, because under the assumption of randomness the true model may not even exist. Modifying the structure of the *arrival rate* elements of the email service or the *load* description of server is not appropriate since this is the piece of information that is assumed to be known out of random events. We investigate the *server* and *service* elements structure. The fact that there is only one host is pretty tight to the problem definition, so the study concentrates on possible modifications of the *services* that are attached to the server.

The checking process is separated into two parts: the first part calculates a service rate for the email service that is able to explain a fraction of the processing cores usage in the host over time in a coherent manner. The second part studies if the rest of loads that are not due to the email service could be explained by the temporal existence of other services, through the creation of alternative models ($\Delta model$) that include more services with their own workload associated with the server.

The first part calculates the service rate μ^* that coherently explains a part of the server usage. "Coherently" means that the load generated by the email VM working at a service rate of μ^* should not be higher than the load measured in the host. For achieving it, we should choose a high value of μ^*. Moreover, we also want to represent the fact that during the 10% of periods, the dominant type of messages required much less processing capacity than usual.

The value for μ^* that satisfies these two requirements is the 90th percentile in Figure 9; i.e., the μ_i^* value that is higher than 90% of the rest. This 90th percentile in Figure 9 corresponds to the value 697. An email VM that serves its emails at a a rate of $\mu^* = 697$ creates a usage of host cores as the graph depicted in Figure 11 that explains the 55.7% of host usage.

The second part tries to explain the remaining 44.3% of core usage through model modification. The sporadic deployment of other services can easily motivate this 44.3% remaining. The inclusion in the model of another *service* element that consumes such 44.3% of server load can then be done. Therefore, the study of the type of uncertainty finishes here because the $isTypeOfUncert$ function would return true for this type of *structural aleatory* uncertainty.

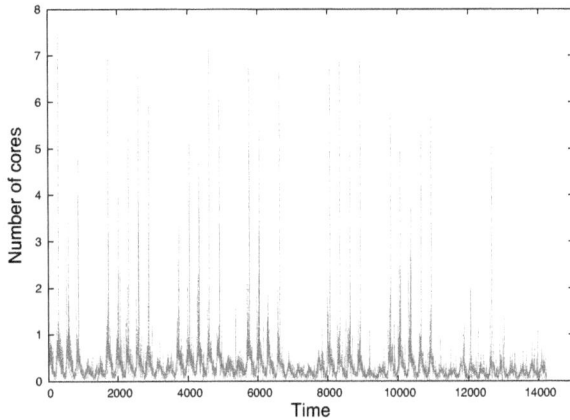

Figure 11: Usage of cores of the email service using the 90th percentile service rate $\mu = 697$

5.4 Dealing with uncertainty

We use in this example the *model discrepancy* technique for managing the identified *structural aleatory* uncertainty. This technique assumes that the model used is not the true model of the system. We use as model the elements and parameters that produced the information in Figure 11; i.e., the arrival rate of requests to the email service and the $\mu^* = 697$ for mail service rate values. The discrepancy term between the model and the expected results is represented by the subtraction of the total usage of host cores (i.e., data in Figure 7) and the calculated core usage of the email service (i.e., data in Figure 11).

We evaluate the time that the batch service requires to execute if the usage of host cores does not variate and we obtain a value of 3 hours and 37 minutes.

We analyze with two different manners the system usage under the situation that the email workload increases by 50%: with and without considering the *structural* uncertainties.

Considering uncertainties, we obtain the usage of cores in the server due to the new workload of the email service workload and we add the discrepancy term calculated previously. This gives us the expected usage of cores in the host. With this usage of cores, we calculate that the new batch service will require 3 hours and 40 minutes to execute.

Without considering uncertainties, all the usage of cores in the server is due to the workload of the email service. Therefore, and increment of 50% in the email service workload directly produces an increment of 50% in the server core usage. Using this usage of cores, we calculate that the new batch service will require a mean

time to execute of 3 hours and 42 minutes. From this experiment we obtain the following conclusions.

Since the email service only requires a minor use of the host capacity, results of the scenario where the email service receives a 50% more of workload are quite similar to the results of the scenario with the current workload. The batch service finishes within a day in any case. Depending on whether the analysis considers uncertainties or not, the expected execution time of the batch service varies in 3 or 5 minutes, respectively. The study that considers uncertainties predicts that the batch execution time increases only the 60% of the quantity predicted by the study that does not consider uncertainties. These fact illustrates the importance of considering uncertainties in the model analysis.

6. CONCLUSION AND FUTURE WORK

In this paper we have presented a methodology called MUSE that, starting from a given model, guides the software engineers in identifying the existence of uncertainty and in managing it.

MUSE is conceived around the use of a recently defined taxonomy that classifies the different types of uncertainties together with their sources and existing approaches to handle them. It starts establishing some awareness about the existence of uncertainties in a given model. It then proceeds trying to devise to which category of the taxonomy this uncertainty belongs to be able to manage it in the most suitable way. Finally, the last step of MUSE shows how the existing methods can be applied to mitigate the effect of uncertainties and to increase the accuracy and trustworthiness of model analysis results.

We have also shown MUSE at work through its application to a concrete example concerning the model-based performance evaluation of a software system migration. Specifically, using a set of realistic data logs, we have illustrated how the data used for the creation of a system model may be incomplete and subject to uncertainties, and how it is possible to manage them.

This research can be extended along several directions. We plan to investigate up to which degree the uncertainty identification process can be generalized and to implement it with the goal of being as general as possible; i.e., identify how much expertise on the domain problem is no longer required with respect to current approaches that work completely *ad-hoc* for a given problem. Besides, at present the identification step is focused on finding a single type of uncertainty. Allowing the discovery of a combination of types of uncertainties that are concurrently present in the model could increase the accuracy of results, probably at the cost of incrementing the complexity of uncertainty management step. Finally, we intend to analyze the different uncertainties in the context of real-world application scenarios, to assess possible correlation and identify best practice procedures.

Acknowledgments

This work has been partially supported by the FP7 European project Seaclouds.

7. REFERENCES

[1] D. Ardagna, C. Ghezzi, and R. Mirandola. Rethinking the use of models in software architecture. In *QoSA*, volume 5281 of *LNCS*, pages 1–27. Springer, 2008.

[2] B. Beck and G. van Straten. *Uncertainty and forecasting of water quality*. Springer-Verlag, 1983.

[3] J. T. Blake, A. L. Reibman, and K. S. Trivedi. Sensitivity analysis of reliability and performability measures for

multiprocessor systems. In *Proc. of the 1988 ACM SIGMETRICS*, pages 177–186, New York, NY, USA, 1988. ACM.

[4] R. Calinescu, C. Ghezzi, M. Z. Kwiatkowska, and R. Mirandola. Self-adaptive software needs quantitative verification at runtime. *Commun. ACM*, 55(9):69–77, 2012.

[5] R. Calinescu, L. Grunske, M. Z. Kwiatkowska, R. Mirandola, and G. Tamburrelli. Dynamic qos management and optimization in service-based systems. *IEEE Trans. Software Eng.*, 37(3):387–409, 2011.

[6] V. Cardellini, E. Casalicchio, V. Grassi, S. Iannucci, F. L. Presti, and R. Mirandola. Moses: A framework for qos driven runtime adaptation of service-oriented systems. *IEEE Trans. Software Eng.*, 38(5):1138–1159, 2012.

[7] L. Cheung, L. Golubchik, N. Medvidovic, and G. Sukhatme. Identifying and addressing uncertainty in architecture-level software reliability modeling. In *Int. Parallel and Distributed Processing Symposium. IPDPS 2007*, pages 1–6, 2007.

[8] A. Devaraj, K. Mishra, and K. S. Trivedi. Uncertainty propagation in analytic availability models. In *Proc. of the Symposium on Reliable Distributed Systems*, SRDS '10, pages 121–130, Washington, DC, USA, 2010. IEEE Computer Society.

[9] I. Epifani, C. Ghezzi, R. Mirandola, and G. Tamburrelli. Model evolution by run-time parameter adaptation. In *ICSE*, pages 111–121. IEEE, 2009.

[10] N. Esfahani and S. Malek. Uncertainty in self-adaptive software systems. In *Software Engineering for Self-Adaptive Systems II*, volume 7475 of *LNCS*, pages 214–238. Springer, 2013.

[11] N. Esfahani, S. Malek, and K. Razavi. Guidearch: guiding the exploration of architectural solution space under uncertainty. In *ICSE*, pages 43–52, Piscataway, NJ, USA, 2013. IEEE Press.

[12] N. Esfahani, K. Razavi, and S. Malek. Dealing with uncertainty in early software architecture. In *FSE*, pages 21:1–21:4, New York, NY, USA, 2012. ACM.

[13] L. Fiondella and S. Gokhale. Software reliability with architectural uncertainties. In *Int. Parallel and Distributed Processing Symposium, IPDPS 2008*, pages 1–5, 2008.

[14] R. B. France and B. Rumpe. Model-driven development of complex software: A research roadmap. In *FOSE*, pages 37–54, 2007.

[15] S. Funtowicz and J. Ravetz. *Uncertainty and Quality in Science for Policy*. Springer, 1990.

[16] D. Garlan. Software engineering in an uncertain world. In *Proc. of Future of Software Engineering Research workshop*, FoSER '10, pages 125–128, New York, NY, USA, 2010. ACM.

[17] C. F. Gauss and C. H. Davis. *Theory of the motion of the heavenly bodies moving about the sun in conic sections*. Boston,Little, Brown and company, 1809. http://www.biodiversitylibrary.org/bibliography/19023.

[18] K. Goseva-Popstojanova and S. Kamavaram. Assessing uncertainty in reliability of component-based software systems. In *ISSRE*, pages 307–, Washington, DC, USA, 2003. IEEE Computer Society.

[19] K. Goseva-Popstojanova and S. Kamavaram. Software reliability estimation under certainty: generalization of the method of moments. In *Proc. of International Symposium on High Assurance Systems Engineering*, pages 209–218, 2004.

[20] J. C. Helton, J. D. Johnson, W. Oberkampf, and C. J. Sallaberry. Representation of analysis results involving aleatory and epistemic uncertainty. *Int. J. General Systems*, (6):605–646, 2010.

[21] S. C. Hora. Acquisition of expert judgment: Examples from risk assessment. *Journal of Energy Engineering*, 118(2):136–148, 1992.

[22] V. Klemesă. Operational testing of hydrological simulation models. *Hydrological Sciences Journal*, 31(1):13–24, 1986.

[23] J. Kramer. Is abstraction the key to computing? *Commun. ACM*, 50(4):36–42, 2007.

[24] I. Meedeniya, A. Aleti, and L. Grunske. Architecture-driven reliability optimization with uncertain model parameters. *J. of Systems and Software*, 85(10):2340–2355, Oct. 2012.

[25] I. Meedeniya, I. Moser, A. Aleti, and L. Grunske. Architecture-based reliability evaluation under uncertainty. In *QoSA*, pages 85–94, New York, NY, USA, 2011. ACM.

[26] H. Moon, S. B. Kim, J. J. Chen, N. I. George, and R. L. Kodell. Model uncertainty and model averaging in the estimation of infectious doses for microbial pathogens. *Risk Analysis*, 33(2):220–231, 2013.

[27] B. Morin, O. Barais, J.-M. Jézéquel, F. Fleurey, and A. Solberg. Models@ run.time to support dynamic adaptation. *IEEE Computer*, 42(10):44–51, 2009.

[28] D. Perez-Palacin and R. Mirandola. Uncertainties in the modeling of self-adaptive systems: A taxonomy and an example of availability evaluation. In *Proc. of the 5th ACM/SPEC Int. Conf. on Performance Engineering*, ICPE '14, pages 3–14, New York, NY, USA, 2014. ACM.

[29] J. C. Refsgaard, J. P. van der Sluijs, J. Brown, and P. van der Keur. A framework for dealing with uncertainty due to model structure error. *Advances in Water Resources*, 29(11):1586 – 1597, 2006.

[30] J. C. Refsgaard, J. P. van der Sluijs, A. L. Højberg, and P. A. Vanrolleghem. Uncertainty in the environmental modelling process - a framework and guidance. *Environ. Model. Softw.*, 22(11):1543–1556, Nov. 2007.

[31] R. Salay, M. Chechik, J. Horkoff, and A. Sandro. Managing requirements uncertainty with partial models. *Requirements Engineering*, 18(2):107–128, 2013.

[32] M. Strong, J. E. Oakley, and J. Chilcott. Managing structural uncertainty in health economic decision models: a discrepancy approach. *Journal of the Royal Statistical Society: Series C (Applied Statistics)*, 61(1):25–45, 2012.

[33] C. Trubiani, I. Meedeniya, V. Cortellessa, A. Aleti, and L. Grunske. Model-based performance analysis of software architectures under uncertainty. In *QoSA*, pages 69–78, New York, NY, USA, 2013. ACM.

[34] W. Walker, P. HarremoŚs, J. Romans, J. van der Sluus, M. van Asselt, P. Janssen, and M. Krauss. Defining uncertainty. a conceptual basis for uncertainty management in model-based decision support. *Integrated Assessment*, 4(1):5–17, 2003.

[35] J. Whittle, P. Sawyer, N. Bencomo, B. H. C. Cheng, and J.-M. Bruel. Relax: A language to address uncertainty in self-adaptive systems requirement. *Requir. Eng.*, 15(2):177–196, June 2010.

[36] L. Yin, M. Smith, and K. Trivedi. Uncertainty analysis in reliability modeling. In *Proc. of Reliability and Maintainability Symposium, 2001*, pages 229–234, 2001.

Experiences with Modeling Memory Contention for Multi-core Industrial Real-time Systems

Thijmen de Gooijer
ABB Corporate Research
Västerås, Sweden
thijmen.de-gooijer@se.abb.com

K. Eric Harper
ABB Corporate Research
Raleigh, NC, USA
eric.e.harper@us.abb.com

ABSTRACT

Wide availability of multicore CPUs makes concurrency a critical design factor for the software architecture and execution models of industrial controllers, especially with messages passing between tasks running on different cores. To improve performance, we refactored a standardized shared memory IPC mechanism implemented with traditional kernel locks to use lock-free algorithms. Prototyping the changes made it possible to determine the speed-up when the locks were removed, but we could neither easily confirm whether the IPC performance would suffice for the communication patterns in our real-time system, nor could we tell how well the implementation would scale to CPUs with more cores than our test machine. In this paper we report on our experience with using a queuing petri net performance model to predict the impact of memory contention in a multi-core CPU on architecture level performance. We instantiated our model with benchmark data and prototype measurements. The results from our model simulation provide valuable feedback for design decisions and point at potential bottlenecks. Comparison of the prototype's performance with our model simulation results increases credibility of our work. This paper supports other practitioners who consider applying performance modeling to quantify the quality of their architectures.

Categories and Subject Descriptors

C.4 [**Performance of Systems**]: design studies; D.2.11 [**Software Engineering**]: Software Architectures; I.6.3 [**Simulation and Modeling**]: Applications

Keywords

performance modeling; queuing petri nets; multicore; real-time systems; industry; experience report

Permission to make digital or hard copies of all or part of this work for personal or classroom use is granted without fee provided that copies are not made or distributed for profit or commercial advantage and that copies bear this notice and the full citation on the first page. Copyrights for components of this work owned by others than ACM must be honored. Abstracting with credit is permitted. To copy otherwise, or republish, to post on servers or to redistribute to lists, requires prior specific permission and/or a fee. Request permissions from permissions@acm.org.
QoSA'14, June 30–July 4, 2014, Marcq-en-Baroeul, France.
Copyright 2014 ACM 978-1-4503-2576-9/14/06 ...$15.00.
http://dx.doi.org/10.1145/2602576.2602584.

1. INTRODUCTION

While it is difficult to find a modern desktop computer that does not have a multi-core CPU, many embedded real-time devices still contain single-core chips. These devices have been designed with the assumption that only one task is allowed to run at a time, typically in priority order. The IT and embedded software industries have shown it is non-trivial to remove this assumption from software designs [33] [35]. With multi-core steadily advancing in the embedded real-time domain, the software architecture and execution models of ABB's industrial real-time controllers now have to support task concurrency and scale to multi-core.

One of the mechanisms impacted is Inter-Process Communication (IPC), which has to scale while maintaining data integrity and consistency. Conservative IPC mechanisms often rely on kernel mode locking, which severely limits their concurrency. We prototyped a lock-free IPC mechanism to avoid this constraint, based on the Multi-core Association MRAPI and MCAPI specifications [4] [3]. The implementation uses atomic CPU instructions instead of global locks [29], achieving latency reductions up to 25x compared to those for lock-based implementations.

While our prototype demonstrates the scalability of the lock-free IPC mechanism, it does not help us understand its performance for the target workload in our control system. Furthermore, it is difficult to isolate and study performance parameters such as caching. Performance modeling promises to be a quicker way of predicting performance, scalability, and the impact of various parameters. Others have reported on application of performance models to real-time multicore systems (e.g. [26]) and contention in such systems (e.g. [12]), but often without a holistic software architecture view and rarely in industrial settings.

In earlier work we have shown how a performance model helped to find the theoretical maximum performance and thereby set goals for optimizing our prototype implementation [29]. In this paper we describe the performance model for our real-time system (RTS) case study in further detail. We discuss our requirements for a performance modeling tool and motivate the choice for QPME. We give a detailed description of our layered memory contention model and assumptions. We ran systematic simulation experiments to predict under what conditions we can meet our performance goals. One of the most interesting lessons is that with a relatively simple model we can provide valuable feedback to both the aforementioned prototyping activity and the architecture design process. Our findings suggest that comprehensive and accurate multicore performance models are difficult to construct, but that traditional modeling techniques are still relevant in the multicore era.

The rest of this paper is structured as follows. Section 2 introduces the problems that multicore poses to the embedded real-time domain, our prior work, and the Queuing Petri Net modeling technique. We explain our selection of QPME for our modeling problem in Section 3. Section 4 discusses the performance goal for our RTS case study and the shared memory IPC workload. Section 5 describes our memory contention performance model. We plan our simulation experiments in Section 6 and discuss the results in Section 7. Our lessons learned are listed in Section 8. Finally, Section 9 compares our work to the state of the art and Section 10 concludes this paper.

2. BACKGROUND

2.1 Embedded Real-time Multicore

Most classes of electronics are becoming embedded computer systems: internet-accessible with software defined features. These systems are computers with constraints, for example, size, cost and power. The predominant design constraint is TDP (Thermal Design Power) with expected battery life ranging from hours to days. This constraint [32] drives reduction in footprint both with regard to energy and physical size, because smaller form factors consume less power. Multicore technology is a tremendous enabler of footprint reduction providing more computing power per unit volume.

Unfortunately software that runs on a single processor core does not easily migrate to multicore in a way that leverages the additional computer resources. This is because many task synchronization and memory protection issues do not surface on single core where tasks cannot access resources concurrently. It may be beneficial to continue serializing a task on a single core, but implementing software on multicore exposes weaknesses in the software design that are difficult to detect and resolve.

Real-time system designs have deadlines by which execution of a task must be finished for the system to be useful. Tasks are typically executed periodically in a schedule. Deviations from the period, schedule and deadlines introduce jitter, which reduces the usefulness of the system. Latency variations in IPC are a potential source of jitter. This is one of the reasons that we seek to increase the predictability of IPC latency and increase the available capacity.

The control systems we work with in this paper have not been designed with concurrency in mind. The traditional design goals for control systems have been predictability and reliability of execution, because we need to be confident that industrial processes do the right thing in the right time to avoid disaster. Only recently the industry started its transition to multi-core processors, creating the challenge of evolving decades old designs to support concurrency, while avoiding impact on predictability and reliability.

2.2 Lock-free Algorithms

A recent paper by the authors [29] explores the benefit of using lock-free algorithms for data exchange between tasks running on separate cores. The experiments show that shared memory data exchange latency for embedded applications that are migrated from single core to multicore processor architectures can be improved up to twenty-five times

using a lock-free design. The paper also introduced a preliminary model of the lock-free exchange that predicts performance at the system architecture level and provides stop criteria for the lock removal refactoring.

The key assumptions in this previous work were that the data exchange was through shared memory on a single device for FIFO (First-In, First-Out) data exchange in a single address space. This paper expands on the details of the performance model and our on-going prototyping work extends these techniques to other types of data exchange and across more than one address space.

2.3 Queuing Petri Nets

Queuing Petri Nets (QPNs) combine queuing networks and colored Petri nets to construct rich performance models [30]. QPNs are made up of places and transitions that connect the places to form a graph. See Figure 2 for an example QPN. Places contain zero or more colored tokens. Places may be ordinary places and just hold tokens or queuing places. In queuing places, tokens enter a service station with a queue before they become available in the place. The same queue may be mapped to more than one place, i.e., places may share resources.

An initial assignment of tokens to places is given which is called a marking. Tokens flow through the QPN when a transition fires. Upon firing, the transition takes a defined mix of tokens from input places and puts tokens in output places, where input and output are relative to the transition. The conditions under which a transition fires are called modes and a transition may have several modes.

3. SELECTING A MODELING TOOL

Lacking previous experience with performance modeling of real-time systems, we first performed a short survey to identify tools that would be suitable for industrial use within this domain. The search process in this survey was guided by the requirements outlined below and our experience with applying the Palladio Workbench performance modeling tool in industry [22].

- It must be possible to represent multi-core processors in the model.

- The modeling concepts of the tool should map to real-time system components and concepts easily.

- The tool should be freely available or already licensed.

- The layered architecture of the RTS must easily map to the modeling formalism in a way that is understood by our technical stakeholders, who are software architects and engineers.

- A graphical representation of the model to use during stakeholder discussions must be easy to create.

- It must be possible to analyze the influence of design changes to the IPC mechanism on the performance of the overall architecture.

- The model analysis technique should have been shown to scale to complex systems by prior studies.

We consulted several sources ([15],[37],[31]) to find tools suitable for performance modeling of embedded real-time systems. Further, we reconsidered the tools reviewed from earlier work. The interesting tools were sorted into three categories: visual modeling tools, analytical/simulation tools, and tools that were relevant but quickly proved unsuitable.

3.1 Tools considered

Visual modeling tools and performance visualizations are simple and easy to grasp by non-technical audiences. We considered this class of tools, because in our experience constructing a model and reasoning about performance already helps identify performance issues, i.e., quantitative analysis may be skipped or performed later. We found two suitable tools: 1) Performance maps, which were developed in-house, similar to the value stream mapping [36] modeling technique developed by Toyota; and 2) the UML profile for Modeling and Analysis of Real-Time and Embedded systems (MARTE) [8].

Analytic and simulation models can be used to quantify the architectural differences between alternative designs. A quantitative study requires more complete models that are instantiated with measurements from the system or prototypes. Performance measurements take considerable time and effort to obtain, but afterwards enable quick analysis of use cases and performance scenarios in the architecture.

We considered two tools with support for analysis or simulation of performance models: 1) QPME supports Queuing Petri Nets (QPNs). QPNs combine the benefits of Petri Nets for state representation with the strength of Queuing Networks for expressing scheduling [30]; and 2) The Palladio Workbench tool, which implements the Palladio Component Model (PCM) [16]. The PCM is based on the component-based software engineering philosophy. PCM notation is similar to UML and therefore quite intuitive. A drawback of Palladio is that it was created with distributed web systems in mind, not real-time embedded systems.

3.2 Rejected tools

Besides the aforementioned tools, we found many others that we rejected for varying reasons. Mosquito is based on model transformations from UML system design models to queuing network performance models [1]. By default the tool uses a web service hosted by the university that created Mosquito, thus we cannot use it for confidentiality reasons.

The project "Components with Quantitative properties and Adaptivity" (COMQUAD) developed tools to check performance requirements on software components at runtime [28]. The approach is aimed at EJB and CORBA CCM systems and only prototypical implementations are available. While one of these is for real-time components, we could not find an industrial case study or download the tools.

Robocop is a component system model developed for component-based, embedded systems, and has been extended with a performance prediction framework [27]. Simulation can be used to detect missed deadlines based on response times and to detect overloaded resources by processor over-utilization. One industrial case study on a JPEG decoder has been published [17], but no mature toolkit could be downloaded.

Alcatel-Thomson's research laboratory developed UML extensions to specify latency constraints and resource usage for real-time systems. A transformation of the architectural models enables evaluation through simulation [23], but we did not discover further research publications.

3.3 Decision for QPME

We decided to use QPME for our study and against using a visual modeling tool, because this would limit how we could study the scaling behavior over the number of cores. While QPME doesn't have the option to automatically run simulations for model variants like Palladio does, it is more flexible for modeling different systems. Palladio was developed to model web applications and service systems. Resource models in Palladio also do not have a model element to represent memory resources, but have specific elements for CPU, disk and network resources. While QPNs are powerful and flexible, the models are more difficult to understand, and larger models may suffer from state space explosion that inhibits analysis of large models. QPME is one of few tools that supports nesting of QPNs. The possibility of layering combined with the flexibility of the modeling concept means that we can express our high-level architecture on the top layers and detail the lock-free IPC on lower layers. Furthermore, we wanted to gain experience in applying QPN models.

4. PERFORMANCE GOAL AND WORKLOAD DEFINITION

Our primary relevant design goal for the overhaul of the real-time system architecture is efficient use of multicore hardware. Several requirements or sub-goals have been derived from this design goal. We list those that are relevant to our work on the IPC mechanism.

1. Execute control tasks with cycle times from 1 to 100 milliseconds.

2. Process all I/O and system messages in time.

3. Keep memory bus utilization by IPC below 20%.

4. Have an IPC mechanism that scales from 1 to 16 cores.

4.1 Workload Definition

Based on experience and market requirements we were given two workload scenarios. The first scenario is for a system running a small number of large applications with 100 millisecond execution cycle times. The second scenario is for a control application system that executes in 1 millisecond cycles. The latter scenario is more time critical as there is only one millisecond to complete all communication and tasks. Furthermore, the tasks generate more I/O signals being read and written on average per millisecond, which puts a higher load on the IPC mechanism. Therefore, we opted to explore this second scenario.

The system architecture suggested that there would be three main components using the IPC mechanism: application tasks, I/O and peer-to-peer (P2P) communication modules. Their workloads interact with shared memory as shown in Figure 1. The first workload is execution of cyclic real-time application tasks that read inputs and perform a computation to generate output. Application tasks interact with the communication modules and thus shared memory when reading input and writing output. During computation the application tasks mostly load the CPU and block it from being used by the communication modules. The tasks are executed once every millisecond in the chosen scenario. The computation resources available in this millisecond are divided over some dozen tasks. The second workload

Table 1: Benchmark references and their values for memory access latency in nanoseconds (ns).

Latencies (all in ns)	L1 cache	L2 cache	L3 cache	Main Memory
Google Rules of Thumb [24]	0.5	7		100
Intel Core i5 (full random) [6]	1.33	3.33	16.66	108.4
Intel Core i5 (sequential) [6]	1.33	3.33	4.33	8.5
Multi-socket SMP AMD [2]	1	7	25	135
PowerPC 440 (random-read) [5]				100-300
X86 cache disabled (random-read) [9]				1100-2000
Ptrchase (random pointer read) [7]	1	10		300-700

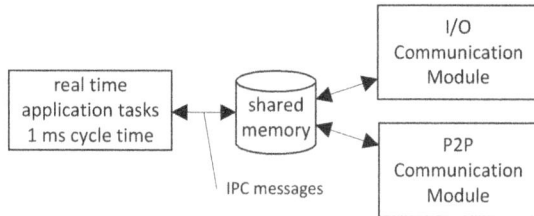

Figure 1: Modeled workloads on the system memory.

is created by the I/O communication module, which reads values from sensors and writes outputs to actuators that are connected to the real-time system via various protocols. The third and final workload is generated by the P2P communication module responsible for interactions with other nodes. The communication modules keep the values that have not been consumed by a task or waiting for transmission in shared memory.

We make several assumptions and simplifications in the described workload:

1. The model only considers IPC workload. Other demands on the memory system, for example reading program code from memory, are not modeled. This leads to an optimistic view of the system performance. We took this assumption into account by introducing a pre-fetch workload in part of our model simulations (see Section 6.1).

2. The real-time applications that execute every millisecond are relatively small and therefore all their program code fits in cache. Traditionally storage on similar systems is measured in megabytes, rather than gigabytes. This assumption should hold as newer processors have relatively large caches to accommodate applications such as multimedia.

3. Communication with supervision systems and the resulting workloads are not modeled. These workloads can be ignored as the cycle time for I/O copies to a supervision system is on the order of 500 milliseconds.

4. Security, safety and redundancy mechanisms that may put additional demand on resources are not modeled. We could not include these as their design was not yet finished. This assumption leads to an optimistic view of the system performance.

5. The various communication modules and real-time applications have equal execution priority. All tasks are dynamically allocated to CPU cores and not constrained to run on a dedicated core. The impact of both assumptions has been studied using the performance model, but are not reported upon in this paper to maintain confidentiality.

5. MEMORY CONTENTION MODEL

The speed of computer memory is declining relative to the speed of CPUs. Increasingly many cores share the same memory in SMP and multi-core systems. Using atomic CPU instructions in user mode for task synchronization eliminates the operating system computation overhead associated with traditional shared memory transactions, including possible context switches from user to kernel mode. Therefore, we assume that shared memory access will be the bottleneck for lock-free IPC message exchange rather than computing capacity in the individual cores. In this Section we discuss the assumptions we make about the RTS memory system (Section 5.1), describe our memory contention performance model (Section 5.2) and how we calibrated the model (Section 5.3).

5.1 Memory System Assumptions

We obtained data about memory access times from various public benchmarks in Table 1. References to the benchmarks are listed in the table. The benchmark data shows that modern consumer systems have a memory latency of about 100ns (nanoseconds) and older systems are slower with 300-700ns. Based on this information we made the pessimistic assumption that the latency to main memory would be 200ns in our embedded system. We made this assumption because the hardware platform design was not finalized and no prototypes or development boards were available yet.

We disregard transfer time in the model. We motivate this decision with the following example calculation. Typical DDR memory has a peak transfer rate of at least 1600MB/s. Based on existing applications we assume the size of an IPC message averages 40 bytes. Transferring these bytes, without regard for access latency, takes 40bytes / 1600MB/s = 23.8 ns. The transfer time is an order of magnitude lower than the assumed latency, thus we ignore transfer time for all memory operations.

We made a number of additional assumptions to simplify our model:

1. One memory transaction (read or write) takes on average 200ns and the transaction times follow an exponential distribution. The latency value can be seen as a pessimistic estimate based upon the benchmarks presented earlier.

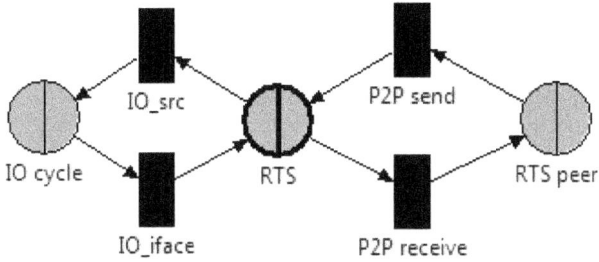

Figure 2: QPN model layer for the system environment

2. There can be only one request on the memory bus at a time and no other request is served until that request completed. This disregards some optimizations that are available in modern systems, but in the past those optimizations have often been disabled in real-time systems to increase predictability.

3. Writers and readers in IPC calls are not blocked by lock contention, only by contention for CPU and memory access. This assumption follows from the use of our lock-free algorithms [29].

4. The lock-free IPC mechanism uses a minimal number of CPU execution cycles. In reality of course IPC message passing will busy the CPU, but we expect the number of cycles needed for task execution to be at least an order of magnitude higher.

5. No pre-emption of tasks takes place: we assume run to completion for all tasks. Thus, while a CPU core is waiting for a memory transaction or application task execution to complete, no other task is allowed to run on that core. Not only does this assumption simplify our model significantly, but it fulfills the desire for more predictable execution time.

6. Look-up of a cached value does not incur a memory transaction, nor does it trigger a cache coherency protocol. The validity of this assumption is heavily dependent on what CPU features are disabled and how processes are allocated to improve real-time predictability.

5.2 QPN Model of the RTS

The QPN model of the RTS has a single queue representing the memory shared by a limited, configurable number of cores. The model's layers, Petri-net places, and transitions represent the architecture of our system. Colored Petri-net tokens flow through the system and represent the expected communication workload between the components of the system. An overview of the token colors used in the model is given in Table 2.

Figure 2 shows the environment layer of the model, which has two queuing places, *IO cycle* and *RTS peer*, that regulate the flow of requests to and from the system subnet place *RTS*. The queuing places delay the flow of IO and P2P tokens in the Petri net in such a way that the latencies obtained approximate those of our workload scenario.

The *RTS* subnet is shown in Figure 3 and contains most of the model logic. Requests from the environment model enter the subnet through the *input-place* and leave through

Table 2: Overview of the token colors used in our QPN model

Token color	Description
IO	I/O message exchange
P2P	P2P message exchange
CPU core	CPU core for execution
Task	Application task
Memory op	Creates pre-fetch load

Table 3: Translation of workload scenario to QPN resource demands

Workload	Original Quantity	QPN Representation
Reading and writing of I/O signals	I/O signals with X signals per I/O message	For each I/O message, one IPC is issued to the shared memory
P2P module messages	X values send via P2P messages	X IPC messages per ms
Application task execution	X values used from Y communication modules	Y IPC messages

the *output-place*. The *actual population* place keeps track of the number of tokens in the subnet.

When an IO or P2P token enters the subnet, it is immediately forwarded to the *CPU* place, where it has to wait for a CPU core token to become available in the *CPU* place. If a CPU core token is available, the *CPU scheduler* transition fires and the token is sent to the *IO comm mod* or *P2P comm mod* place. The communication module places are queuing places that map to the memory bus queue, thereby modeling the contention for the single memory bus. The *Application Task Execution* design is slightly more complex and therefore modeled in a subnet, which contains ABB intellectual property and is therefore not included in this paper. However, the subnet contains a queuing place that maps to the same memory bus queue to model the third contending workload. The *application task scheduler* has a function similar to the *IO cycle* and *RTS peer* queuing places; it regulates the number of Task tokens that show up at the CPU every millisecond.

We can vary the number of cores available in the model by changing the number of CPU core tokens in the network. Every token represents one core and an increase in tokens leads to an increase in concurrency. This describes how all three workloads from our workload model map to the same queue representing the system's memory bus, thereby exposing the concurrent memory access bottleneck.

5.3 Resource Demands and Calibration

The workload scenario we selected in Section 4.1 contains estimates of the number of I/O signals and P2P messages exchanged. We refined these estimates and converted them to the number of IPC messages sent/received for the QPN model according to Table 3. None of the actual estimates are included in this paper to maintain confidentiality.

Initially we assumed that each IPC message would incur two memory transactions for send and receive respectively.

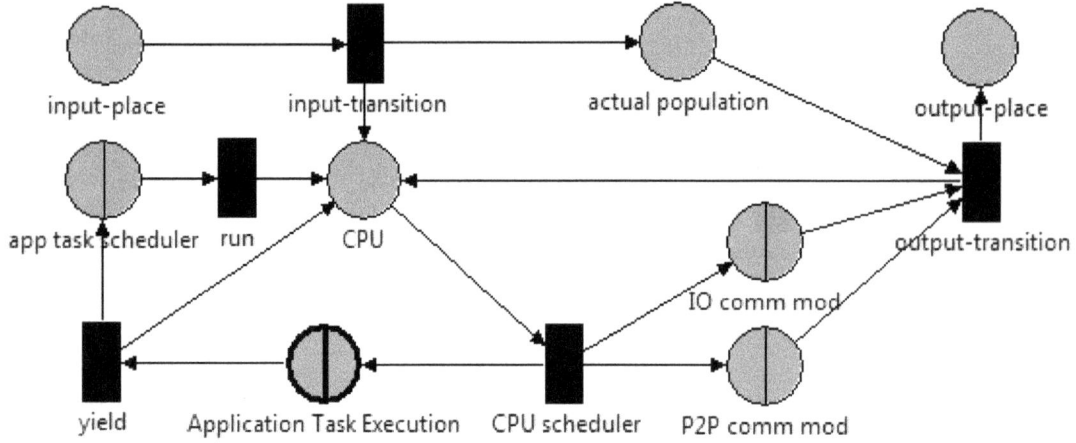

Figure 3: RTS core system QPN model layer

Simulating the model with varying numbers of CPU cores under these assumptions gives throughputs at least an order of magnitude above what our prototype suggests is possible. We reverse engineered the prototype source code to capture the procedures and created UML sequence diagrams of the lock-free message exchange implementation. From these diagrams we extracted the number of memory transactions needed for sending and receiving a message. To simplify the model we did not distinguish between read and write operations, nor did we consider any special execution path that might require less or more memory operations.

6. EXPERIMENT DESIGN

We simulated the QPN model to predict whether our performance goals can be met given the defined workload (see Section 4). The simulation experiments of our QPN model are organized based on model variations (Section 6.1) and key metrics (Section 6.2). Both are discussed in this Section and lead to the selection of experiments (Section 6.3).

6.1 Variation Points

We studied several design parameters with the QPN model. Below we specify the variation points used in this paper.

Number of cores and big applications. We considered both single and multi-core designs and evaluated multi-core configurations from two to 16 cores. Exploratory simulation runs showed that the modeled workload is not demanding enough to keep a large number of cores busy, thus we created a new version of the workload. In the 'big apps' variant of our workload, we increased the CPU time consumed by each application task by an order of magnitude.

Cache hit rate. It is difficult to determine what the cache hit rate of the IPC in our RTS might be. It depends on the locality of the applications, the chosen schedule, and CPU hardware. Furthermore, the hit rate differs for various operations. Therefore, we simulated different cache hit rates from 0% up to 90% with 10% intervals. We assumed that a memory look-up that hits the cache takes no time from the memory bus and that all tasks benefit equally from increased caching. The increased performance is modeled by reducing the amount of memory operations needed by the

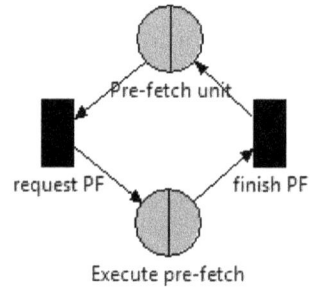

Figure 4: Pre-fetch workload model

hit rate for an IPC send or receive transaction. For example, if an IPC receive transaction takes x memory operations we then model a 50% cache hit rate by demanding only $0, 5 \times x$ memory operations.

Pre-fetching memory load. Fetching program and OS instructions, and pre-fetching memory contents put a base workload on the memory bus that we did not model explicitly in Section 5. We assume that this workload may be utilizing the memory bus for 30%. We created a model variant that captures this load by generating extra memory operations and putting them in the memory queue. The model for this workload is shown in Figure 4 and is part of the same QPN model as the parts shown in Figures 2 and 3. The *Execute pre-fetch* place shares its memory queue with those mentioned in Section 5.2, e.g. the *IO comm mod* place. The pre-fetch workload does not consume CPU core tokens because a pre-fetching unit is often part of the memory management unit that operates independently from the CPU's execution units. All pre-fetch memory operations are modeled to take 200ns just like normal memory operations.

6.2 Metrics

The following metrics are used in our experiments. For each metric we set a specific performance goal derived from the general goals and workload definition in Section 4. In addition to these metrics, we tracked memory bus contention as the time that tokens wait to get access to the resource,

Table 4: Model configurations simulated in the first set to explore the variation points

cache hit rate	normal workload	normal workload + pre-fetch
0% - 90%	1,2	2

Table 5: Model configurations for the scalability simulations

cache hit rate	normal workload + pre-fetch	big apps workload + pre-fetch
60%	1,2,4,6,8,16	1,2,4,6,8,16

and contention for CPU cores as the average waiting time from when a task is ready until it starts executing. These additional metrics are informative and useful but do not strictly relate to our performance goal.

Timeliness of task execution. All application and communication module tasks must be executed within the 1 ms cycle. The measured throughput of tasks in the system should match or exceed the throughputs specified in the workloads. In this paper we show the timeliness as a percentage of tasks that completed on within their cycle.

Message throughput. The measured number of IPC messages in each execution cycle compared to the goal defined in our workload definition shows the performance as the percentage of messages exchanged relative to the goal.

Memory bus utilization. The IPC workload may not block the memory bus for more than 20% of the cycle time. We verify this by recording the utilization of the queue that represents the memory bus in our model.

6.3 Simulation Experiments

Running and analyzing all possible combinations of our variation points would be too large of an effort. Instead, we conducted two sets of QPN model simulations. The first set determined the feasibility of the set workload and evaluated the impact of cache hit rates and the pre-fetch workload. The second set explored the scalability of the modeled IPC mechanism in more detail. The second set was constructed after completing experiments in the first set.

The configurations for the first set of simulations are listed in Table 4, comparing single versus dual core performance at various cache hit rates for the normal workload. We quickly learned that the workload could not be handled by a single core. Therefore, the comparative experiments for the addition of the pre-fetch load were only done for the dual core configuration of the model.

The configurations for the second set of simulations are shown in Table 5. The first experiments show that the throughput requirements are met at 60% and higher cache hit rates for dual core configurations. Therefore, in the second set we evaluated the effect of scaling the number of cores at a 60% cache hit rate. We ran experiments with the normal application tasks and the big applications variant where the pre-fetch workload was active. The pre-fetch workload is unaffected by scaling the number of CPU cores, but makes for a more realistic contention scenario.

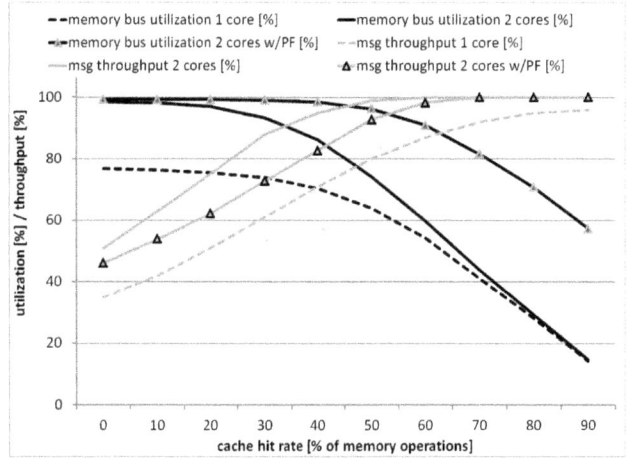

Figure 5: Results of the experiments in the first set. The results for the runs with the pre-fetch workload are marked w/PF.

7. RESULTS

In this Section we first discuss the results of our simulations (Section 7.1). Then, we summarize some of the recommendations we gave to the RTS architecture team (Section 7.2). Finally, we identify threats to the validity of our results and the benefits of our recommendations (Section 7.3).

7.1 Simulation Results

A summary of the results for the first simulation set is shown in Figure 5. It shows the memory bus utilization and message throughput (in percent) as a function of cache hit rate. Timeliness is not shown, but it follows the same pattern as message throughput.

Looking at Figure 5, the gray dotted line shows that we cannot achieve the target message throughput with a single core. The solid gray lines show that in the dual core scenario we only achieve the target message throughput at cache hit rates of 60% and higher. The effect of the pre-fetch workload is clearly visible from the solid black lines. Only at a ninety percent cache hit rate is the memory bus utilization lower than the targeted 20% (black solid line) due to the message exchange.

The results of the second set are shown in Figures 6 and 7. The normal application workload results in Figure 6 show that our memory bound workload does not benefit from more than two cores. These results confirm the need for more computationally intensive tasks if we want to observe CPU contention. In Figure 7, the impact of the big applications workload variant is clearly visible. Only with ten or more cores is full execution timeliness achieved. Note in Figure 7 that we ran additional experiments to increase the resolution compared to Figure 6. We conclude that both workload variations can be executed on two and ten cores respectively, if a 60% cache hit rate for the IPC mechanism can be expected. Unsurprisingly though, the memory bus utilization does not decrease as the number of cores increases and the utilization does not go below the 20% target.

The results presented in our previous paper [29] show that the prototype results are close to the theoretical maximum. The fastest measured latency is twice that of the calculated maximum, which assumes most message pass-

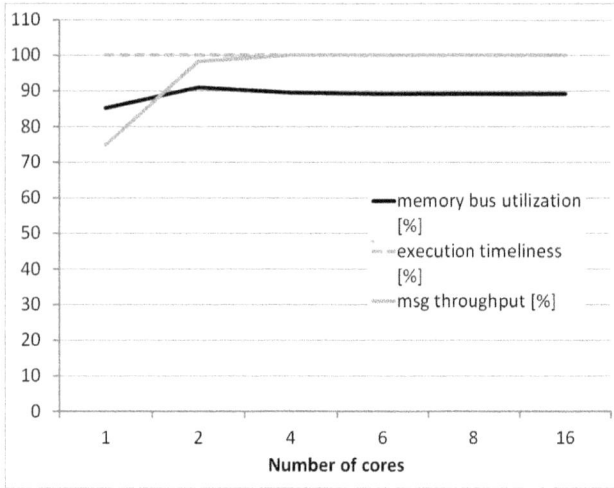

Figure 6: Results of the experiments in the second set with the *normal* applications.

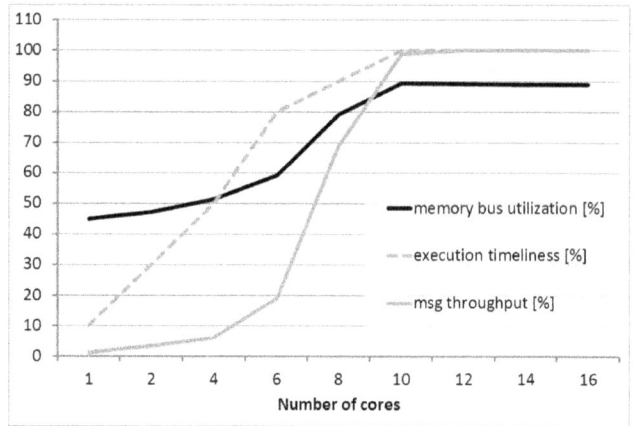

Figure 7: Results of the experiments in the second set with the *big* applications.

ing happens in cache (i.e., no delay is caused by trips to memory). Our model makes the more pessimistic assumption that most transactions are served by memory. Yet, the measured throughput for FIFO messages in our prototype ranges from just 35% lower to 37% higher than that obtained in our model simulations. It is encouraging that the model simulation and prototype measurements results are so close. This increases trust in the simulation results and our architectural recommendations.

7.2 Recommendations

Central to all recommendations is the observation that the simulations suggest the expected workloads can only be supported at high cache hit rates or with faster memory. Based on the simulation results we can make various recommendations to the architecture design team.

- Measure cache hit rates for the IPC messaging prototype to find out what cache hit rate might be expected in the IPC mechanism. Note that the overall cache hit rate may be different. The simulation results suggest that the workload scenario is only feasible if the cache hit rates are high.

- Limit the amount of supported I/O sources and/or optimize the packing of I/O signals in I/O messages to limit the amount of IPC messages created by the communication modules. The simulation results suggest that the current I/O message packing results in too high load on the memory subsystem due to the I/O messages being relatively small. A higher number of sources will lead to less flexibility in optimizing the packing of I/O messages, as messages from different sources cannot easily be packed together.

- Trade capacity and/or bandwidth for low latency when selecting memory for the RTS hardware. The simulation results and our calculations on bandwidth suggest that latency is a key parameter due to the small size of the IPC messages.

- Look at how data locality may be increased to limit the need for IPC. First, because we have seen that

the memory demands of IPC are rather high. Second, we are concerned with the possible penalty of cache coherency protocols between cores slowing down real-time communication.

7.3 Threats to validity of the results

The presented results and recommendations are subject to the assumptions that we made explicit in Sections 4.1 and 5.1. We have made an attempt to indicate the impact of each assumption. However, unforeseen impacts may exist and the validity of each assumption is subject to changes in the RTS architecture or IPC mechanism.

The model has been calibrated against our prototype. However, as the hardware architecture for the RTS was not finalized yet, the prototype measurements were done on x86 hardware. The behavior of the real-time platform is likely to vary because it will be equipped with a different processor.

The communication modules interact with various types of I/O devices and protocols, for example, Ethernet-based for the P2P communication. Neither the overhead of nor the interaction with the network stack is modeled. Yet, the system bottleneck may turn-out to be related to I/O rather than memory contention.

8. LESSONS LEARNED

During our work on the performance modeling we recorded several lessons and observations that reflect our experience with using QPME in an industrial setting. Our earlier experience is mostly with Palladio, which therefore is our point of reference.

Concurrent prototyping and modeling gives synergies. It would have been very difficult to accurately estimate the IPC memory access pattern without the prototype implementation. Our initial guess of just two operations for each message exchange was off by an order of magnitude. At the same time the model directed our prototyping activity because it showed what performance would be possible even with a high memory latency. Performing the activities simultaneously we could continuously compare results to improve the accuracy of the model and the performance of the prototype.

Imperfect multicore model may suffice. Multicore processors pose many new challenges to accurately create performance models. Our effort shows that building upon strong assumptions and combining modeling with prototyping can work. Just like back of the envelope calculations have their place, imperfect models can still provide valuable feedback to the architecture and design process.

Stakeholders find QPN models are not intuitive. Even though some of our stakeholders have basic knowledge of Petri nets and queuing models, they did not easily understand the QPN model. The QPN concepts are not natural to computer scientists and software performance modeling was new to our real-time and control systems experts. We conclude that QPNs are more flexible in expressing different system types than Palladio at the cost of hidden complexity. Palladio's four view modeling slightly increases the modeling effort, but is easier to understand for stakeholders.

QPME is close to a production quality tool. The QPN Model Editor (QPME) is among the most advanced and best QPN tools known to us. However, it is still an academic tool with minor shortcomings. A couple of bugs required us to manually edit the underlying XML to clean-up the model and several defects were reported to the developers through SourceForge. Some were fixed in the QPME 2.0.1 release. We would like to automatically run simulations for various values of a variable (i.e., initial marking) to make analysis of alternatives easier. Despite these minor issues QPME is a very usable tool that enabled us to get the expected results with reasonable effort.

Simulation results analysis tooling are limited. We consider the QPME simulation results analysis features less user-friendly than those of Palladio. For example, the user interface does not show individual measurements, while the simulation time needed for accurate results does not seem to differ for practical purposes. We suggest that improved usability or new tools for analysis of performance model simulation results could increase industry adoption of such tools for architectural decision making.

9. RELATED WORK

Most existing work applies state-of-the-art performance modeling techniques to either real-time systems or shared-memory problems. Quiñones et al. use simulation to study cache replacement policies in real-time systems touching both topics, but they used an in-house tool [34]. Frieben and Heutger have applied the Palladio Workbench to simulate the performance of real-time PLCs [26]. Their work however focuses on CPU utilization in multicore processors. Several other papers discuss contention caused by multicore chips in real-time systems, but do not model the performance of an application at the software architecture level. For example, Dasari and Nelis study the impact of contention on multi-core real-time systems [21]. Cho et al. study cache sharing in manycore real-time systems and increase predictability of performance by extending OS memory management [19].

There is an interesting line of work on the modeling of cache and resource sharing by Babka. He shows how to separate the functional and resource sharing model [12] and uses QPNs to shorten analysis times and increase accuracy

[10]. Later he applies his findings to QImPrESS performance models [11]. Babka further investigates how to accurately model cache sharing [14], [13]. We have tried to apply some of the lessons from this work, but were limited by not knowing what CPU might be used in the RTS and thus not being able to take some of the measurements needed for the accuracy Babka achieved.

Chandra et al. have created a detailed model to predict multicore cache contention between threads [18]. However, their work requires a detailed model of the CPU, which is not feasible in our case. Mandke Dani et al. created a thread contention prediction tool to create a profile of multi-threaded application data accesses [20]. They use the tool to predict what last level on-chip cache access policy is more profitable in multicore processors. Their tool could be of use for tuning our system, but is too fine-grained for the architecture level predictions that we needed. Eklov created profiling tools for performance analysis of software on modern processors with hierarchical caching [25]. Using such tools to study contention with a running prototype implementation of our software architecture may be an alternative approach to our problem.

10. CONCLUSIONS

We set performance goals for our lock-free IPC mechanism on a multi-core real-time system and created a QPN model to analyze the performance of our workload. The resource demands in the model are based on publicly available benchmark data and static analysis of a prototype. The model contains some strong assumptions, because many aspects of the design were still open when it was created. Yet, the model enabled us to give useful recommendations to the architecture design of the real-time system. We documented valuable lessons learned that help practitioners decide when the application of QPN models and the QPME tool may be useful. Finally, the success of our effort suggests that more opportunities exist to apply existing performance modeling techniques to new multicore problems.

11. REFERENCES

[1] Mosquito CASE tool. http://sealabtools.di.univaq.it /tools.php. (last accessed on 2014-04-15)
[2] Multi-socket SMP latencies. http://blogs.utexas.edu /jdm4372/tag/memory-latency/. (last accessed on 2014-04-15)
[3] Multicore Communications API Working Group (MCAPI). http://www.multicore-association.org /workgroup/mcapi.php. (last accessed on 2014-04-15)
[4] Multicore Resource Management API Working Group (MRAPI). http://www.multicore-association.org /workgroup/mrapi.php. (last accessed on 2014-04-15)
[5] PowerPC 440 TLB regular memory versus static TLB latency comparison. http://www.mcs.anl.gov/~kazuto mo/hugepage/bglion.html. (last accessed on 2014-04-15)
[6] SiSoft Intel Core i5 measurements for the Westmere architecture. http://www.sisoftware.net/?d=qa &f=ben_mem_latency. (last accessed on 2014-04-15)
[7] The ptrchase memory-latency benchmark. http://tom.womack.net/computing/ptrchase.html. (last accessed on 2014-04-15)

[8] UML profile for MARTE. http://www.omgmarte.org/. (last accessed on 2014-04-15)

[9] X86 cache disabled memory latency benchmark. http://www.mcs.anl.gov/~kazutomo/hugepage/x86 laptop-cachedisabled.html. (last accessed on 2014-04-15)

[10] V. Babka. Resource Sharing in QPN-based Performance Models. *Proc. of WDS*, 1:202–207, 2008.

[11] V. Babka. Cache Sharing in QImPrESS Performance Models. In *Proc. of WDS*, pages 28–33, 2009.

[12] V. Babka, M. Děcký, and P. Tuma. Resource Sharing in Performance Models. In K. Wolter, editor, *Formal Methods and Stochastic Models for Performance Evaluation (LNCS 4748)*, pages 245–259. Springer Berlin / Heidelberg, 2007.

[13] V. Babka, P. Libic, and P. Tuma. Timing Penalties Associated With Cache Sharing. In *MASCOTS*, pages 583–586, 2009.

[14] V. Babka, L. Marek, and P. Tuma. When Misses Differ: Investigating Impact of Cache Misses on Observed Performance. *15th Int. Conference on Parallel and Distributed Systems*, pages 112–119, 2009.

[15] S. Balsamo, a. Di Marco, P. Inverardi, and M. Simeoni. Model-based performance prediction in software development: a survey. *IEEE Transactions on Software Engineering*, 30(5):295–310, May 2004.

[16] S. Becker, H. Koziolek, and R. Reussner. The Palladio component model for model-driven performance prediction. *Journal of Systems and Software*, 82(1):3–22, Jan. 2009.

[17] E. Bondarev, M. R. V. Chaudron, and E. A. de Kock. Exploring Performance Trade-offs of a JPEG Decoder Using the Deepcompass Framework. In *Proc. of the 6th Int. Workshop on Software and Performance*, WOSP '07, pages 153–163, 2007. ACM.

[18] D. Chandra. Predicting Inter-Thread Cache Contention on a Chip Multi-Processor Architecture. In *11th Int. Symposium on High-Performance Computer Architecture*, pages 340–351. IEEE, 2005.

[19] S. Cho, L. Jin, and K. Lee. Achieving Predictable Performance with On-Chip Shared L2 Caches for Manycore-Based Real-Time Systems. *13th IEEE Int. Conference on Embedded and Real-Time Computing Systems and Applications*, 1(c):3–11, Aug. 2007.

[20] A. M. Dani, B. Amrutur, Y. Srikant, and C. Bhattacharyya. TCP: Thread Contention Predictor for Parallel Programs. In *20th Euromicro Int. Conference on Parallel, Distributed and Network-based Processing*, pages 19–26. IEEE, Feb. 2012.

[21] D. Dasari and V. Nelis. An Analysis of the Impact of Bus Contention on the WCET in Multicores. In *High Performance Computing and Communication & 2012 IEEE 9th Int. Conference on Embedded Software and Systems (HPCC-ICESS), 2012 IEEE 14th Int. Conference on*, pages 1450–1457, Liverpool, 2012.

[22] T. de Gooijer, A. Jansen, H. Koziolek, and A. Koziolek. An Industrial Case Study of Performance and Cost Design Space Exploration. In *ICPE '12 Proc. of the third joint WOSP/SIPEW Int. Conference on Performance Engineering*, pages 205–216, Boston, MA, USA, 2012.

[23] M. de Miguel, T. Lambolais, M. Hannouz, S. Betgé-Brezetz, and S. Piekarec. UML extensions for the specification and evaluation of latency constraints in architectural models. In *Proc. of the 2nd Int. Workshop on Software and Performance*, WOSP '00, pages 83–88, 2000.

[24] J. Dean. Software Engineering Advice from Building Large-Scale Distributed Systems, 2009. http://static.googleusercontent.com/external_content/untrusted_dlcp/research.google.com/en//people/jeff/stanford-295-talk.pdf

[25] D. Eklöv. *Profiling Methods for Memory Centric Software Performance Analysis*. Phd thesis, Uppsala University, 2012.

[26] J. Frieben and H. Heutger. Case Study: Palladio-based Modular System for Simulating PLC Performance. In *Palladio Days 2012*, Paderborn, Germany, 2012.

[27] J. Gelissen. Robocop: Robust open component based software architecture., 2004. http://www.hitech-projects.com/euprojects/robocop/deliverables.htm.

[28] S. Göbel, C. Pohl, S. Röttger, and S. Zschaler. The COMQUAD Component Model: Enabling Dynamic Selection of Implementations by Weaving Non-functional Aspects. In *Proc. of the 3rd Int. Conference on Aspect-oriented Software Development*, AOSD '04, pages 74–82, 2004.

[29] K. E. Harper and T. de Gooijer. Performance Impact of Lock-Free Algorithms on Multicore Communication APIs. In *Embedded World Conference*, 2013.

[30] S. Kounev, S. Spinner, and P. Meier. QPME 2.0 - A Tool for Stochastic Modeling and Analysis Using Queueing Petri Nets. In K. Sachs, I. Petrov, and P. Guerrero, editors, *From Active Data Management to Event-Based Systems and More*, pages 293 – 311. Springer, Berlin / Heidelberg, 2010.

[31] H. Koziolek. Performance evaluation of component-based software systems: A survey. *Performance Evaluation*, 67(8):634–658, Aug. 2010.

[32] T. Mudge. Power: a first-class architectural design constraint. *IEEE Computer*, pages 52–58, 2001.

[33] V. Pankratius, C. Schaefer, A. Jannesari, and W. F. Tichy. Software engineering for multicore systems: an experience report. *Proc. of the 1st Int. workshop on Multicore software engineering*, pages 53–60, 2008.

[34] E. Quinones and E. Berger. Using randomized caches in probabilistic real-time systems. In *Real-Time Systems, 2009. ECRTS '09. 21st Euromicro Conference on*, pages 129–138, 2009.

[35] R. Vincke, S. Van Landschoot, E. Steegmans, and J. Boydens. Refactoring sequential embedded software for concurrent execution using design patterns. *Twenty-first Int. Scientific and Applied Science conference*, pages 157–160, 2012.

[36] J. Womack and D. Jones. *Lean Thinking: Banish Waste and Create Wealth in Your Corporation*. Simon and Schuster, Inc., 2003.

[37] M. Woodside, G. Franks, and D. C. Petriu. The Future of Software Performance Engineering. *Future of Software Engineering (FOSE '07)*, pages 171–187, May 2007.

Using Architecture-Level Performance Models as Resource Profiles for Enterprise Applications

Andreas Brunnert
fortiss GmbH
Guerickestr. 25
80805 München, Germany
brunnert@fortiss.org

Kilian Wischer, Helmut Krcmar
Technische Universität München
Boltzmannstr. 3
85748 Garching, Germany
{wischer, krcmar}@in.tum.de

ABSTRACT

The rising energy and hardware demand is a growing concern in enterprise data centers. It is therefore desirable to limit the hardware resources that need to be added for new enterprise applications (EA). Detailed capacity planning is required to achieve this goal. Otherwise, performance requirements (i.e. response time, throughput, resource utilization) might not be met. This paper introduces resource profiles to support capacity planning. These profiles can be created by EA vendors and allow evaluating energy consumption and performance of EAs for different workloads and hardware environments. Resource profiles are based on architecture-level performance models. These models allow to represent performance-relevant aspects of an EA architecture separately from the hardware environment and workload. The target hardware environment and the expected workload can only be specified by EA hosts and users respectively. To account for these distinct responsibilities, an approach is introduced to adapt resource profiles created by EA vendors to different hardware environments. A case study validates this concept by creating a resource profile for the SPECjEnterprise2010 benchmark application. Predictions using this profile for two hardware environments match energy consumption and performance measurements with an error of mostly below 15 %.

Categories and Subject Descriptors

C.4 [**Performance of Systems**]: measurement techniques, modeling techniques; D.2.8 [**Software Engineering**]: Metrics—*performance measures*

General Terms

Measurement; Performance

Keywords

Performance Modeling; Palladio Component Model; Resource Profile; Energy Consumption; Capacity Planning

Permission to make digital or hard copies of all or part of this work for personal or classroom use is granted without fee provided that copies are not made or distributed for profit or commercial advantage and that copies bear this notice and the full citation on the first page. Copyrights for components of this work owned by others than the author(s) must be honored. Abstracting with credit is permitted. To copy otherwise, or republish, to post on servers or to redistribute to lists, requires prior specific permission and/or a fee. Request permissions from permissions@acm.org.
QoSA'14, June 30–July 4, 2014, Marcq-en-Baroeul, France.
Copyright is held by the owner/author(s). Publication rights licensed to ACM.
ACM 978-1-4503-2576-9/14/06 ...$15.00.
http://dx.doi.org/10.1145/2602576.2602587.

1. INTRODUCTION

Enterprise applications are the backbone of many business processes. These applications need to meet performance requirements (i.e. response time, throughput, resource utilization) to avoid problems during the process execution. Detailed capacity planning effort [17] is therefore required before new enterprise applications are deployed in a data center. This effort is driven by a basic question: How much hardware resources are required to fulfill performance requirements for the expected workload? This question leads to a more specific inquiry about the applications demand for hardware resources such as central processing units (CPU), hard disk drives (HDD) and memory. The capacity planning finally requires an assessment of the workload impact on the resource demand.

At the same time, the rising energy consumption is a major cost driver in data centers nowadays [8, 22]. The energy consumption is defined as the power consumption integrated over time. It would thus be beneficial to know how much power will be consumed by the resources utilized by an application in beforehand [6].

Estimating hardware requirements and energy consumption of new enterprise application deployments is only possible if different parties work together [4]. First of all, enterprise application vendors (EAV, i.e. software or consulting companies) need to quantify the resource demand of their software products. Enterprise application users (EAU, i.e. companies who source software from EAVs) need to specify the expected workload for their use cases. Finally, enterprise application hosts (EAH, i.e. data center providers) need to specify the characteristics of the hardware environment on which the applications can be deployed. Nowadays, the communication between these parties lacks a medium in which all these aspects are captured. The resource profile concept introduced in this work serves as such a communication medium and helps to answer the questions raised above.

This work proposes the use of architecture-level performance models to represent resource profiles. The contribution of this work therefore includes the resource profile concept as a use case for these models in between their traditional application domains: software performance engineering [24] and application performance management [18]. Additionally, an approach is presented to adapt these models to different hardware environments. Furthermore, a performance modeling approach is extended to allow predictions of the energy consumption. A case study finally evaluates the feasibility of the resource profile concept.

53

(a) Resource profile

(b) Use cases for a resource profile

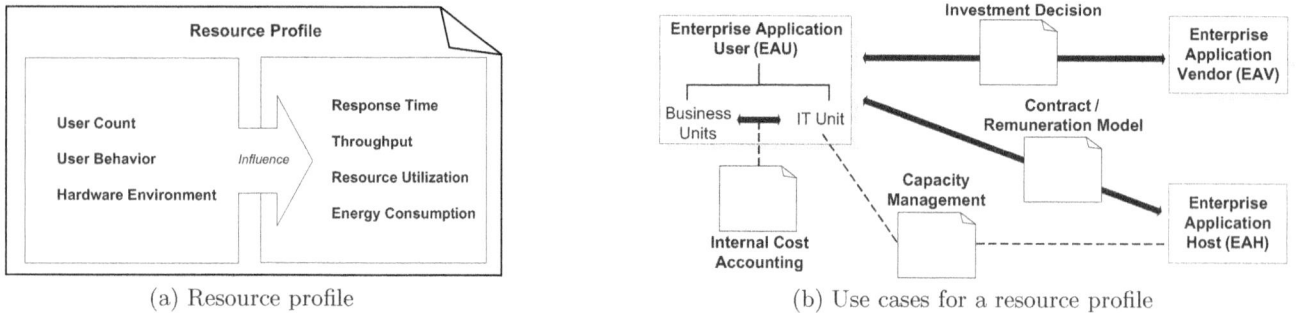

Figure 1: Resource profiles for enterprise applications

2. RESOURCE PROFILES

Resource profiles are models that allow evaluating energy consumption and performance of enterprise applications (see figure 1(a)). In an ideal case, a resource profile is constructed once by an EAV and can then be used by EAUs and EAHs for several use cases as shown in figure 1(b). The intended use cases are similar to the ones of system requirements for end user desktop software (such as games or office tools). System requirements show whether a user is able to run a software on his current environment. If an end user needs to modify his soft- or hardware environment, this often has a huge impact on his purchasing decision. If EAUs would have similar information at hand during a software purchasing scenario, it would also influence their investment decisions.

2.1 Content and Structure

The energy consumption and performance of an enterprise application is influenced by several factors as depicted in figure 1(a). One of the key factors is the hardware environment on which an enterprise application is deployed. As hardware resources (e.g. the CPU) have different performance and power consumption characteristics, the resource demand (e.g. required CPU time) and energy consumption of single transactions is directly dependent on the components used within a server. Different hardware environments thus have a big impact on the performance and energy consumption of an application. Resource profiles therefore provide a means to represent different hardware environments.

Besides the hardware environment, the workload on a system directly influences the performance and energy consumption of an application. The workload of an enterprise application is typically specified by the amount of users accessing the system and their behavior [16]. Depending on the workload, the hardware environment is utilized on different levels, which lead to varying performance and energy characteristics. Consequently, the user count and their behavior can be represented in a resource profile.

To evaluate the impact of different hardware environments and workloads on energy consumption and performance, a model is required that describes the performance-relevant aspects of an enterprise application architecture independently from these influencing factors. These aspects include the components of an enterprise application, their interfaces, relationships, control flow, parametric dependencies and resource demands [12]. Resource profiles describe these aspects independently from the workload and hardware environment. To simplify their use, the aforementioned as-

pects are hidden for resource profile users (i.e. EAU, EAH). Resource profiles abstract these aspects on the level of detail of single deployment units of an enterprise application. These deployment units represent a collection of application components and thus reduce the complexity for the users. Instead of dealing with individual application components, they can use these deployment units for specifying allocations on different hardware environments.

To represent the workload, resource profiles describe external interfaces provided by an enterprise application (e.g. functionalities provided by user interfaces). These external interfaces can be used for specifying the workload. Based on these specifications, the influence of different workloads and hardware environments on performance and energy consumption can be evaluated as shown in figure 1(a).

The knowledge required for constructing a resource profile and for specifying the input variables for the evaluation is often distributed between different parties (i.e. EAV, EAU and EAH, see figure 1(b)). Resource profiles are therefore meant to be used differently depending on the available information. An EAV should create resource profiles for all enterprise applications sold (off-the-shelf and custom developments), which then can be adapted by EAUs and EAHs for their specific needs. They can modify the workload and the hardware environment but reuse the specifications provided by an EAV.

2.2 Use Case Examples

The primary use case of a resource profile is to estimate the required hardware resources for an enterprise application. As this task is required in different contexts, the following paragraphs explain some use cases in which the transferable nature of resource profiles helps to simplify the relationships of EAUs, EAVs and EAHs.

If an EAU is interested in a new enterprise application, he could use the corresponding resource profile as one component in an overall investment decision. The EAU can specify the expected amount of users, their behavior and his existing hardware environment to evaluate if this hardware would be sufficient to run the application for his needs. At the same time, the EAU could evaluate the impact of this particular application on his energy bill. If new hardware is needed for the application, the resource profile helps to compare different hardware configurations in terms of their impact on performance and energy consumption. Resource profiles can also be used to choose between different off-the-shelf software products with similar functionality with regard to the above mentioned criteria.

When software is purchased and hosted by an EAU internally, a resource profile supports the internal cost accounting between different business units and the IT unit [3]. Using resource profiles, the resource demand and power consumption of an enterprise application can be broken down to user profile levels or transaction classes. Brandl et al. [3] showed how such a breakdown of the resource consumption on the level of transaction classes can be used to allocate costs to different business units according to their workload.

If an EAU does not want to host an application himself, resource profiles can be used to negotiate a contract between an EAU and an EAH (e.g. cloud providers). As cloud computing is gaining more popularity, the demand for usage-based costing will increase [3]. Similar to the internal cost accounting approach explained above, EAUs and EAHs could agree on a remuneration model which is directly dependent on the resource and energy consumption of the hosted application [13]. Resource profiles help both parties to better estimate their costs in such a scenario.

If an enterprise application is already running in a production environment, resource profiles help in the capacity management process. For example, the impact of an increased user load on performance and energy consumption of an application can be examined in beforehand and appropriate conclusions can be drawn.

The next section explains the construction of resource profiles based on architecture-level performance models.

2.3 Performance Models as Resource Profiles

Evaluating the performance of an application is a common problem in the software engineering domain. Numerous performance modeling approaches have been proposed to address this challenge [1, 12]. A performance model of an enterprise application typically contains performance-relevant aspects of an application architecture, the hardware environment and the workload. Using these models as input for analytical solvers or simulation engines allows predicting response time, throughput and resource utilization for the modeled software system. Several case studies (see section 4) showed the applicability of performance models for predicting these performance metrics.

Performance models thus seem to be generally suitable to represent resource profiles. As resource profiles must be adapted to different target environments, a key requirement for their representation is that performance-relevant aspects of an application architecture, the hardware environment and the workload can be modeled independently from each other. In an ideal case, an EAV can model the performance-relevant aspects of an application architecture and distribute this incomplete model to an EAU who complements the model with the expected workload. Afterwards, an EAH can add the hardware environment to the resource profile.

Conventional performance modeling approaches [1] such as Queuing Networks, Layered Queuing Networks (LQN) or Queuing Petri Nets depict all these aspects nested in one single monolithic performance model. It is therefore hard to change a single aspect like the hardware environment or the workload without needing to substantially change the whole performance model. Architecture-level performance models [12] try to separate these aspects to simplify the modeling process. A popular architecture-level performance model is the Palladio Component Model (PCM) [20]. PCM separates all the aspects mentioned above and is thus used as meta-model to represent resource profiles.

PCM is described by Reussner et al. [20] as a software component model for business information systems to enable model-driven quality of service (QoS, i.e. performance) predictions. A software system is represented in PCM by several model layers which can reference each other [20]. The most important model within PCM is called repository model. This model contains the components of a software system and their relationships. The control flow of a component operation, its resource demand and parametric dependencies are specified in so called Resource Demanding Service Effect Specifications (RDSEFF). Components are assembled in a system model to represent an application. User interactions with the system are described in a usage model. The other two model types in PCM are the resource environment and allocation model. A resource environment model allows to specify available resource containers (i.e. servers) with their associated hardware resources (CPU or HDD). An allocation model specifies the mapping of system model elements on resource containers.

A resource profile can thus be represented using this meta-model by creating a system model. Such a system model describes the external interfaces of an enterprise application and references repository model components (including RDSEFFs) to describe the performance-relevant aspects of an application architecture. Several approaches to construct these models, either based on design model transformations [2] or dynamic analysis [5], already exist and are therefore not described in detail in this work. The workload for a PCM-based resource profile can be specified in a usage model. The hardware environment can be specified by the resource environment model whereas the deployment on this environment is specified in the allocation model.

Even though PCM provides a good foundation for building resource profiles, just creating a performance model is not sufficient for supporting the structure and use cases of a resource profile outlined earlier. The remainder of this section therefore focuses on questions that cannot be answered by the PCM modeling capabilities:

- How can resource profiles based on the PCM meta-model be adapted to different hardware environments?

- How can the PCM meta-model be extended to support energy consumption predictions?

2.4 Adapting Resource Profiles to Different Hardware Environments

Hardware environments are specified in PCM resource environment models. An example of a resource environment model is shown in figure 2(a). In this example, the resource environment consists of two hardware servers which are connected via a network connection. The model depicts the CPU and HDD of both servers. The CPU of *Server1* consists of 16 cores (number of replicas) and the CPU of *Server2* consists of 8 cores. Each core has a processing rate of 1000. The HDDs of both servers also specify a processing rate of 1000. A processing rate of 1000 means that one CPU core respectively the HDD can process 1000 units of work within a simulated time frame. In this example, one simulated time frame is interpreted as one second. Thus, each CPU core and HDD can process 1000 milliseconds (ms) of work per simulated time frame.

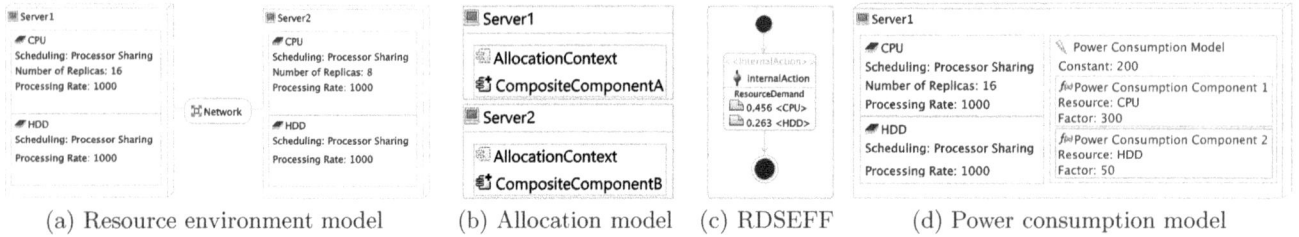

| (a) Resource environment model | (b) Allocation model | (c) RDSEFF | (d) Power consumption model |

Figure 2: PCM models

An allocation model defines how system model elements are mapped on servers in the resource environment model. To simplify the use of a resource profile for evaluating different deployment options, an EAV should represent indivisible deployment units using composite components [20]. Composite components allow to combine several repository model components so that they can only be allocated as a whole and not individually. This representation ensures that EAUs or EAHs cannot evaluate deployment options which are not supported by an EAV. The allocation model in figure 2(b) shows the allocation of two composite components on the two servers modeled in the resource environment model. *CompositeComponentA* is mapped on *Server1* and *CompositeComponentB* on *Server2*.

A component implements several operations which can be invoked by users or other components. The resource demand of an operation is defined in internal actions of an RDSEFF. It is specified as the amount of units of work needed on a particular hardware resource to be processed. This resource demand is thus modeled relative to the processing rate of a hardware resource in the resource environment model. Figure 2(c) shows a simplified RDSEFF. The internal action consumes 0.456 units of work on the corresponding CPU resource and 0.263 units of work on the HDD. If this component is mapped on a resource container with a CPU core that can process 1000 units of work within one second, the 0.456 units of work can also be interpreted as 0.456 ms CPU time required by the component operation. The same interpretation is valid for the HDD demand.

This dependency between resource demands in RDSEFFs and processing rates of hardware resources in resource environment models avoids the need to adapt resource demands of every internal action in every RDSEFF if hardware resources are changed. It is only necessary to adapt the processing rate of modeled hardware resources if they are replaced by other types of the same resource. If more attributes of a hardware environment are changed (e.g. the number of servers), the allocation model must also be changed to map the (composite) components on the new resources. What needs to be done to model these structural changes is described by Reussner et al. [20].

If a resource profile is used to predict performance and energy consumption for a hardware environment that is not the one the resource profile was initially created with, the profile must be adapted to the target environment. To adapt the resource profile from one environment to another, the processing rate of resources must be scaled according to the performance of the hardware resources.

Following Menascé [16], the processing rate of a resource is scaled according to the hardware benchmark results of the initial and target hardware resource. After performing a suitable benchmark on the initial and the target server, we assume to get two benchmark scores of the investigated hardware resource. The benchmark score of the initial ($b_{initial}$) and target (b_{target}) server and the initial processing rate ($r_{initial}$) allow to calculate the new processing rate (r_{target}) for the target server's resource as follows:

$$r_{target} = \frac{b_{target}}{b_{initial}} * r_{initial} \qquad (1)$$

For example, when benchmarking a specific hardware resource, an initial server gets a benchmark score of 40 whereas a score of 50 is achieved on the target server. By using formula 1 with an initial processing rate of 1000 a target processing rate of 1250 can be calculated. This calculation is possible for different hardware resources. For CPU benchmarks it is important that the benchmark can evaluate the performance of a single core, otherwise it is much harder to adapt the resource environment model from one server to another. If standardized benchmarks are used for this purpose, the benchmarks must not necessarily be performed by the user of a resource profile, as results for common hardware systems are often available on the web sites of the benchmark providers. Nevertheless, processing rates and benchmark scores of hardware resources used to derive resource demands need to be distributed along with a resource profile.

This approach assumes that all resource demands in the RDSEFFs of a repository model are initially derived from measurements on the same hardware types. Otherwise, it would be necessary to adapt the resource demands in an RDSEFF individually if a component is moved from one server to another in the allocation model. Similarly, the network traffic between all components needs to be represented in a resource profile even if the profile is created on a single machine. Without this information, it would not be possible to distribute components in a resource profile to different machines connected by a network.

2.5 Predicting Energy Consumption

To the best of our knowledge, there is no performance modeling approach available which is able to predict the energy consumption of an application. Hence, it can also not be predicted using PCM. As energy consumption is defined as the power consumption integrated over time, the PCM meta-model is extended by a *power consumption model* element. The PCM simulation engines SimuCom [2] and EventSim [19] are also extended to use the new *power consumption model* element. Simulation results now allow to evaluate the power consumption of servers in a resource environment over time. The integral of the resulting function can be used to predict the energy consumption of an application. The construction of a *power consumption model* is explained in the following.

PCM is already capable of predicting the utilization rate of modeled hardware resources such as CPU or HDD. The full server power consumption can thus be modeled based on the utilization of the server's hardware resources as shown in several existing works on this topic [8, 21]. Full server power consumption refers to the power consumed by the power adapters of the server. As shown in section 2.2, this is the key figure from an economic point of view.

Rivoire et al. [21] and Fan et al. [8] showed that simple linear power models based on resource utilization metrics produce very accurate results. Even very simple models, which only capture the CPU utilization to predict the power consumption, are very accurate. A linear model with the predicted power consumption of a server as the dependent variable P_{pred} and multiple resource utilization metrics as the independent variables u_i can therefore be specified by the following equation [8, 21]:

$$P_{pred} = C_0 + \sum_1^i C_i * u_i \qquad (2)$$

In PCM resource environment models a hardware server is represented by a resource container. The new *power consumption model* element is thus attached to the existing resource container meta-model element. It represents a linear model in the form of equation 2. Figure 2(d) shows an example of such a *power consumption model* for one server with 16 CPU cores and a HDD resource. A *power consumption model* contains a constant (C_0) which represents an approximation of the idle power consumption of a server. The independent variables of equation 2 are represented by multiple *power consumption components*. A *power consumption component* contains a multiplication factor (C_i) and a reference to the utilization of a hardware resource of the resource container (u_i). In the example of figure 2(d), the *power consumption model* represents the equation: $P_{pred} = 200 + 300 * u_{CPU} + 50 * u_{HDD}$. A CPU utilization of 50 % and a utilization of the HDD of 20 % would thus lead to a predicted power consumption of 360 watts (W).

The best way to construct such a linear *power consumption model* is a calibration run on the target hardware similar to the approach presented by Economou et al. [7]. In a calibration run, hardware resources are stressed independently from each other with changing intensity. Meanwhile the corresponding resource utilization metrics reported by the operating system and the resulting power consumption of the full server system are measured. Modern enterprise servers implement power measurement sensors for single hardware resources and the whole system. A common way to offer their measurements is to use the Intelligent Platform Management Interface (IPMI)[1]. Thus, there is often no need to use an external power meter device. After finishing the calibration run, a linear regression on the measured metrics is done to generate a linear *power consumption model*.

3. EVALUATION

In this section, a case study using the SPECjEnterprise-2010 industry standard benchmark demonstrates the feasibility of the resource profile concept. A resource profile

based on the extended PCM meta-model is generated for the SPECjEnterprise2010[2] benchmark application on an initial hardware environment and is adapted to a target hardware environment by using the SPEC CPU2006[3] benchmark. Afterwards, workloads using varying amounts of users are executed both as a simulation using the resource profile and on deployments on the initial and target hardware environment. The simulated and measured response time, throughput, power consumption and resource utilization values are afterwards compared with each other. The evaluation steps and the quantitative validation ensure that the extended PCM meta-model provides a solid base for representing resources profiles with the properties explained in section 2.1.

3.1 SPECjEnterprise2010

The SPECjEnterprise2010 benchmark application represents business processes of an automobile manufacturer and is divided into three different domains: the Supplier domain, the Manufacturing domain and the Orders domain. The Orders domain is used by automobile dealers to sell and order cars. By doing so, they drive the demand for the Manufacturing domain. This domain simulates car manufacturing sites. It interacts with the Supplier domain to order parts required during the manufacturing process.

The evaluation in this paper focuses on the Orders domain as it is intended to be used by end users, whereas the other two domains are used by other applications as (web-) services. The communication between the domains is disabled in order to avoid the need to model and evaluate all domains.

The Orders domain is a Java Enterprise Edition (EE) web application that is composed of Servlet, JavaServer Pages (JSP) and Enterprise JavaBean (EJB) components. The automobile dealers access this application using a web interface over the hypertext transfer protocol (HTTP). The automobile dealers can perform three different business transactions: Browse (B), Manage (M) and Purchase (P). These three business transactions are composed of several HTTP requests to the system.

The dealer interactions with the system are implemented as benchmark driver in the Faban harness[4]. Faban is a load generation framework which is used to execute load on a SPECjEnterprise2010 deployment. For each benchmark run one can specify the number of dealer clients that interact with the Orders domain (benchmark scale). The official driver is implemented in a way that the benchmark scale not only influences the total number of clients but also the behavior of a single simulated client. As this is not typical for an enterprise application, the benchmark driver is patched so that the behavior of a dealer client is now independent of the total number of clients.

---

[1]http://www.intel.com/design/servers/ipmi/

[2]SPECjEnterprise is a trademark of the Standard Performance Evaluation Corp. (SPEC). The official web site for SPECjEnterprise2010 is located at http://www.spec.org/jEnterprise2010.

[3]The SPECjEnterprise2010 and SPEC CPU2006 results or findings in this publication have not been reviewed or accepted by SPEC, therefore no comparison nor performance inference can be made against any published SPEC result. The results in this publication should thus be seen as estimates as the benchmark execution might deviate from official run rules. The official web site for SPEC CPU2006 is located at http://www.spec.org/cpu2006.

[4]http://java.net/projects/faban/

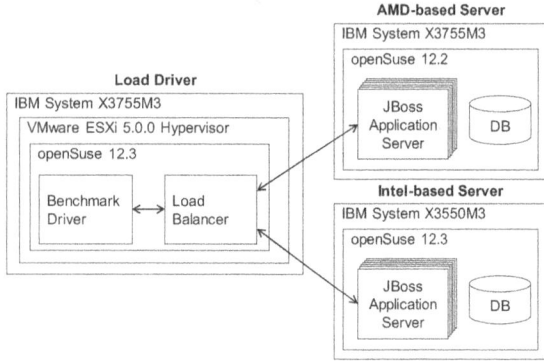

Figure 3: SPECjEnterprise2010 system topology

3.2 System Topology

An overview of the system topology is given in figure 3. The initial server, on which a resource profile represented as a system model is created, is an IBM System X3755M3 server. This machine, hereafter referred to as AMD-based server, contains 256 gigabytes (GB) random-access memory (RAM) and four AMD Opteron 6172 processors with four cores and a 2.1 GHz frequency each. The target server, which is represented by adapting the model as explained in section 2.4, is an IBM System X3550M3 server. This machine, hereafter referred to as Intel-based server, contains 96 GB RAM and two Intel Xeon E5645 processors with 6 cores and a 2.4 GHz frequency each. The hyper-threading capability of the Intel processors is disabled for this evaluation. The operating system on the AMD-based server is open-Suse 12.2 whereas openSuse 12.3 is used on the Intel-based server. Six JBoss Application Server (AS) 7.1.1 instances are deployed on both servers, all running the SPECjEnterprise2010 benchmark application. Every AS instance uses its own Apache Derby DB in version 10.9.1.0 as persistence layer. The JBoss AS instances and the Apache Derby DBs are executed within a 64 bit Java OpenJDK Server virtual machine (VM) in version 1.7.0. The mod_cluster[5] web server module is used as load balancer for the JBoss AS clusters on a separate VM. The benchmark driver which generates the load on the systems under test (SUT) is also deployed on the same VM. The VM is mapped on the same type of hardware server as the AMD-based server explained above using the VMware ESXi 5.0.0 (build 469512) hypervisor. The VM runs openSuse 12.3 as operating system and is configured to have eight virtual CPU cores and 80 GB RAM. All servers are connected using a one gigabit per second (Gbit/s) network connection.

3.3 Creating & Adapting the Resource Profile

To construct a system model of the SPECjEnterprise2010 benchmark application on the AMD-based server, we use an automatic performance model generation approach presented in our previous work [5]. The PCM model generator is configured to represent the CPU resource demand in ms in the generated repository model components used within the system. A moderate load (~50 % CPU utilization) is generated using the benchmark driver for a period of 20 minutes. During this time, data is collected and afterwards used to generate a system model for the SPECjEn-

terprise2010 benchmark application. Details of this process can be found in [5]. Afterwards, the system model is complemented with a usage model, which represents the workload generated by the benchmark driver, and a resource environment model that represents the hardware environment of the AMD-based server.

As outlined in section 2.4, the RDSEFFs of repository model components used within the system model contain CPU demand values specific for the AMD-based server. To adapt this information for the Intel-based server, the processing rate of CPU cores represented in the resource environment model needs to be changed. Additionally, the number of CPU cores needs to be reduced. SPEC CPU2006 is used to benchmark the CPU cores of both servers. The benchmark consists of an integer (SPECint) and a floating point (SPECfp) benchmark which again consist of several sub-benchmarks [9]. To calculate the adapted processing rate, the SPEC CPU2006 integer benchmark is executed on the AMD- and Intel-based servers. The AMD-based server achieved a benchmark score of 12.91 for the SPECint_base2006 metric. The Intel-based server achieved a benchmark score of 18.92. By using equation 1, a processing rate of 1464 is calculated for CPU cores in the adapted resource environment model of the Intel-based server.

In a next step, *power consumption models* are added to the resource environment models of the AMD- and Intel-based servers, as explained in section 2.5. As these models only depict the CPUs of both servers, their *power consumption models* can only model the dependency between the CPU utilization rate and the power consumption. This constraint is acceptable as Capra et al. [6] state that the CPU consumes the majority of the overall power of a server and the power consumption is significantly dependent on the CPU's utilization rate. All other hardware resources consume roughly the same amount of power independent of their utilization rate [6].

To calibrate the *power consumption models*, the command line tool lookbusy[6] is used to stress the CPU. Using lookbusy the hardware resources CPU, HDD and memory can be utilized with a fixed utilization rate. To stress the CPU, lookbusy generates a consecutive CPU utilization in steps of 10 % starting from 0 % to 100 %. Each utilization step lasts for five minutes. After each step the server is kept idle for two minutes. A self written Java tool meanwhile captures the CPU utilization rate and the full server power consumption using IPMI interfaces provided by the servers every second. The IPMI power sensors used in this evaluation showed some ramp-up and ramp-down effects in every utilization step. To avoid these effects, only measurements taken between a ramp-up phase of two minutes and a ramp-down phase of another two minutes are used. This dataset is used to perform a linear regression to construct a *power consumption model* in the form of equation 2. The measurements and the thereof derived *power consumption models* for the AMD- and Intel-based servers are shown in figure 4(a) and figure 4(b).

The system model of the SPECjEnterprise benchmark application, complemented with a usage model describing the benchmark driver workload and a resource environment model representing one of the two hardware environments, is hereafter called AMD- or Intel-based model respectively.

---

[5]http://www.jboss.org/mod_cluster

[6]http://www.devin.com/lookbusy/

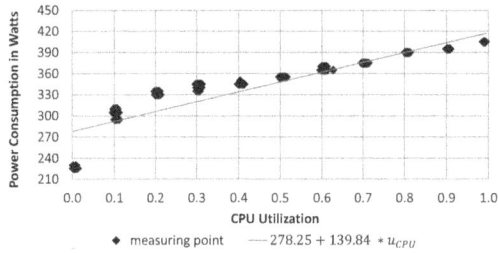

(a) AMD-based server

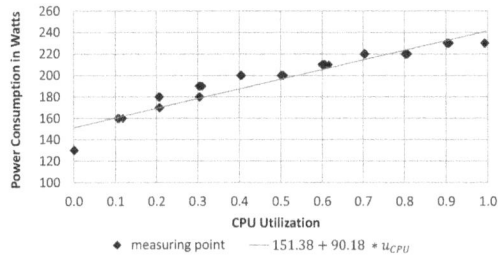

(b) Intel-based server

Figure 4: Power consumption models

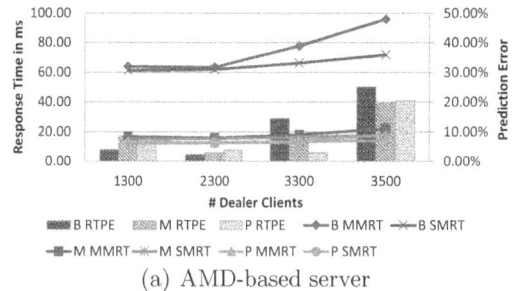

(a) AMD-based server

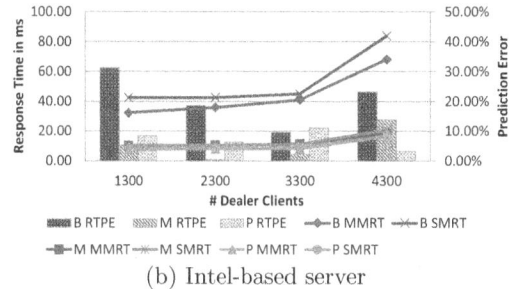

(b) Intel-based server

Figure 5: Measured and simulated response times

3.4 Comparing Measurements & Simulations

In this section, the simulation results of the AMD- and Intel-based models are compared with measurements on the corresponding servers. The comparison is conducted for different load conditions. Four benchmark runs are executed on both SPECjEnterprise2010 server deployments with varying amounts of dealer clients. The number of clients is increased in steps of 1000 from 1300 to 4300. Benchmark runs on the AMD-based server showed that the system cannot handle 4300 concurrent dealer clients. In a benchmark run with 3500 clients the AMD-based server shows a CPU utilization of approximately 86 % which is equal to the utilization of the Intel-based server in a run with 4300 clients. Therefore, the highest load level is reduced from 4300 to 3500 dealer clients for the AMD-based server.

For each load level the AMD- and Intel-based models are used to predict performance and energy consumption for the respective amount of dealer clients. To simulate such high amounts of dealer clients, the event-oriented simulation engine EventSim [19] is used instead of the default process-oriented simulation engine SimuCom [2]. EventSim performs better under such load conditions.

For every load level a benchmark and simulation run of 30 minutes is executed. To avoid side effects during the benchmark and simulation runs, only results during a steady state between a five minute ramp-up and a five minute ramp-down phase are considered in the following.

To evaluate the accuracy of the simulation results, the measured and simulated results for each of the following metrics are compared: CPU utilization, power consumption as well as response time and throughput of the three business transactions. To measure the CPU utilization and the power consumption, the same Java tool is used as for the construction of the *power consumption models* in section 3.3.

The benchmark driver reports measurements for throughput and response time of the three business transactions performed by the dealer clients. However, the reported response times cannot be used for this evaluation since they contain the network overhead between the driver and the SUT whereas the generated model does not include this information. The simulated and measured response times can thus not be compared with each other. To measure comparable response times, a Servlet filter is used to log the response time of each HTTP request executed during a benchmark run. The mean response times of these HTTP requests are used to calculate the mean response times of the three business transactions. The measurement has an influence on the CPU utilization. To reduce this distortion, the Servlet filter is only deployed on one of the six application server instances. The throughput is taken directly from the benchmark driver. It is included in this comparison as using different thread pool configurations could lead to good response time measurements while the throughput is very low. Therefore, the throughput comparison is important to ensure the validity of the evaluation results.

Table 1 and figure 5(a) show the comparison of the measured and simulated results for the AMD-based server and model. Table 1 shows for every load level specified by the number of dealer clients (C) and for every business transaction (T) the Measured Throughput (MT), the Simulated Throughput (ST), the Throughput Prediction Error (TPE), the Measured Mean CPU Utilization (MMCPU), the Simulated Mean CPU Utilization (SMCPU), the CPU Prediction Error (CPUPE), the Measured Mean Power Consumption (MMPC), the Simulated Mean Power Consumption (SMPC) and the Power Consumption Prediction Error (PCPE). Figure 5(a) shows the Measured Mean Response Time (MMRT), the Simulated Mean Response Time (SMRT) and the Response Time Prediction Error (RTPE). Table 2 and figure 5(b) show the same measurement and simulation results for the Intel-based server and model.

The AMD-based model predicts the response times of the business transactions for low (1300 clients) and medium (2300 clients) load conditions with an error below 10 %. Under high load conditions (3300/3500 clients) the error

Table 1: Measured and simulated results for the AMD-based server

C	T	MT	ST	TPE	MMCPU	SMCPU	CPUPE	MMPC	SMPC	PCPE
1300	B	78623	78557	0.08 %						
	M	39378	39245	0.34 %	33.37 %	30.04 %	9.97 %	367.55 W	320.26 W	12.87 %
	P	39259	39135	0.32 %						
2300	B	139328	138383	0.68 %						
	M	69685	70186	0.72 %	57.38 %	52.89 %	7.82 %	403.87 W	352.22 W	12.79 %
	P	69932	69514	0.60 %						
3300	B	200174	199166	0.50 %						
	M	99643	99930	0.29 %	82.53 %	76.00 %	7.92 %	433.76 W	384.52 W	11.35 %
	P	99673	99315	0.36 %						
3500	B	211585	211314	0.13 %						
	M	105454	105506	0.05 %	86.10 %	80.59 %	6.40 %	436.47 W	390.95 W	10.43 %
	P	105708	105557	0.14 %						

Table 2: Measured and simulated results for the Intel-based server

C	T	MT	ST	TPE	MMCPU	SMCPU	CPUPE	MMPC	SMPC	PCPE
1300	B	78502	78333	0.22 %						
	M	39464	39376	0.22 %	24.05 %	27.24 %	13.26 %	197.05 W	175.94 W	10.71 %
	P	39367	39297	0.18 %						
2300	B	139603	138961	0.46 %						
	M	69314	69490	0.25 %	45.08 %	48.29 %	7.12 %	220.47 W	194.93 W	11.58 %
	P	69266	69576	0.45 %						
3300	B	199517	199646	0.06 %						
	M	99254	99936	0.69 %	64.86 %	69.34 %	6.92 %	241.67 W	213.91 W	11.49 %
	P	99890	99355	0.54 %						
4300	B	259548	259591	0.02 %						
	M	130239	129641	0.46 %	86.03 %	90.16 %	4.80 %	264.29 W	232.69 W	11.96 %
	P	129909	129293	0.47 %						

stays below 26 %. The response time prediction of the Intel-based model is slightly less accurate. The response times are mostly predicted with an error below 20 %. Only the prediction of the browse transaction in the case of 1300 clients and at the highest load level with 4300 clients show deviations of 31.23 % and 23.19 % respectively compared to the measurement results.

Both models predict the throughput with an error below 1 %. This low error is caused by the fact that the average think time of a dealer client between two transactions with approximately 9.9 seconds is much higher than the response time of a single transaction. Thus, the prediction errors of the response times only have a low impact on the prediction accuracy of the throughput. The CPU utilization is mostly predicted with an error below 10 % by both PCM models. Only the CPU utilization prediction for the Intel-based server in a setting with 1300 clients has a higher error of 13.26 %. The power consumption of both servers is predicted with an error below 13 %. As the power consumption values are relatively stable during the steady state of all load levels, the energy consumption can be predicted by multiplying the mean power consumption values by time.

This evaluation shows that energy consumption and performance of two deployments of the same enterprise application can be predicted with an accuracy that is acceptable for capacity planning purposes [17]. The approaches to adapt resource profiles to different hardware environments and to predict energy consumption using an extended PCM metamodel could thus be validated. It is therefore technically feasible to realize the resource profile concept.

4. RELATED WORK

The resource profile concept relates to several existing research directions. This section is therefore structured according to different directions that contribute to our work. First, we review existing approaches to support capacity planning for enterprise applications using performance models. Afterwards, research in the area of energy consumption of enterprise applications is presented. Finally, approaches that predict energy consumption and performance of enterprise applications are outlined. The review of related work concludes with approaches to improve the relationships of EAVs, EAUs and EAHs using resource demand data.

Capacity planning using performance models

A model-driven capacity planning tool suite for component- and web service-based applications is proposed by Zhu et al. [25]. The tool suite can be used in early software design phases to support the performance evaluation. It consists of tools to transform existing design models into performance models and benchmark drivers to derive resource demands for the performance models. These performance models and benchmarks can then be used to support capacity planning tasks. Their tooling is intended to be used early in the development process and not as a final capacity planning tooling, as the implementation might have different characteristics as the generated benchmark code.

Liu et al. [14] show how LQN models can be used to support the capacity sizing for EJB applications. In a later work, Liu et al. [15] use LQN models to realize a capacity sizing tool for a business process integration middleware by taking different CPU configurations into account. The authors introduce a way to deal with different hardware environments in the context of LQN models. They implemented a model transformation tool which dynamically constructs LQN models from XML documents representing the application model on the one hand and the hardware configuration on the other hand. However, in their current implementation one is limited to only change the processing speed of the CPU of a server and one is not able to change the hardware environment more radically, for example from a one server deployment to multiple servers.

Tiwari and Nair [23] are using LQNs to predict the performance of two deployments of the same Java EE sample application. Similar to the approach in this work, they show how the SPEC CPU benchmark can be used to adapt a LQN model to a different hardware environment. However, as already discussed in section 2.3, LQN models do not allow to change the workload or the hardware environment without reconstructing the whole model. Their approach is thus less flexible than the one proposed in this work.

Energy consumption of enterprise applications

Capra et al. [6] developed energy benchmarks for enterprise resource planning (ERP), customer relationship management (CRM) and database management system (DBMS) applications. They showed that under the same workload different applications with similar functionality have a significant divergent energy consumption. They concluded that energy efficiency is a quality metric that should be considered when buying or developing new software.

An overview of existing power models and metrics to describe the energy consumption of computer systems can be found in the work of Rivoire et al. [22]. The authors show several metrics that can be used to model the energy consumption of computer systems. This work is thus not focused on the energy consumption of a specific enterprise application but rather on the system level.

Johann et al. [10] propose methods to measure the energy efficiency of software. The authors define energy efficiency as the ratio of useful work done relative to the energy required for performing the work. The authors suggest to calculate the energy efficiency of single methods or components throughout the software development process to create energy efficient applications. However, even though this is a very promising research direction it is challenging to really measure the efficiency if the system on which an application will be deployed has a different power profile than the one on which the application is developed.

Jwo et al. [11] propose an energy consumption model for enterprise applications. The authors calculate the overall energy consumption by multiplying the time a transaction spends on a machine with the machine's mean power consumption. As the time spend on a machine and its power consumption is workload dependent, the resource profile approach is more flexible as it allows to include this perspective.

Combination of performance and energy prediction

One of the few examples that combines energy consumption and performance prediction approaches with a business perspective can be found in the work of Li et al. [13]. The authors propose a sizing methodology for ERP systems which is based on closed queuing networks. Their methodology allows to optimize sizing decisions using multiple dimensions. They allow to perform Total Cost of Ownership

(TCO) decisions that include hardware purchasing as well as energy consumption costs for new ERP systems. Unfortunately, their approach is limited to ERP systems with a predefined set of deployment options and is thus not transferable to other types of applications. However, their multi objective optimization (MOO) approach might be an interesting enhancement for the resource profile concept introduced in this work as resource profiles could be used as the input for such a MOO solver.

Relationships between EAV, EAU and EAH

The term resource profile was already used by Brandl et al. [3] in their work on cost accounting for shared IT infrastructures. The authors introduce an approach to associate resource demands to specific IT services (e.g. email) and to store these resource demands for different user types in service-specific vectors (called resource profiles). Using these resource demand vectors they propose an approach to exactly bill the service consumers by the number of users and types of services they are using. Compared to the approach presented in this work, their resource profile concept is mainly intended to be used to allocate costs for existing applications and services more precisely. The approach presented in this work is intended for new applications and services that should be integrated into a data center. However, the data in our resource profile can also be used for the cost accounting approach presented by Brandl et al. [3].

5. CONCLUSION & FUTURE WORK

This work introduced the concept of resource profiles for enterprise applications. Their main purpose is to simplify the integration of new enterprise applications into data centers with given performance requirements. To achieve this goal, resource profiles support the capacity planning process by allowing to evaluate energy consumption and performance for different workloads and hardware environments before an enterprise application is deployed.

The required information to specify a resource profile and the input parameters for the evaluation can be provided by different parties such as EAVs, EAUs and EAHs. This is achieved by leveraging PCM as meta-model to represent resource profiles. This meta-model is enhanced to allow predictions of the energy consumption. Additionally, an approach is presented to adapt these enhanced PCM models to different hardware environments. The evaluation showed that a resource profile for the SPECjEnterprise2010 benchmark application predicts energy consumption and performance for two hardware environments with high accuracy.

Additional case studies are required to validate further use cases outlined in section 2.2. To make resource profiles better applicable in different scenarios, several extensions are required. First of all, the representation of external systems (e.g. CRM or ERP systems) reused by an enterprise application needs to be investigated. As resource profiles are intended to describe a specific enterprise application, approaches to represent external systems as black-box components which can be replaced by EAUs or EAHs need to be introduced.

Enterprise applications are often executed in runtime environments (e.g. Java EE servers) that are available by different vendors. It would be helpful for the capacity planning if these platforms were represented explicitly in a resource profile and could also be changed by EAUs or EAHs.

Further extensions are required in the underlying PCM meta-model to support the representation of varying workloads and to represent memory demands. The meta-model should also be enhanced to allow representations of the power consumption using nonlinear models. Additionally, the simulation engine EventSim needs to be enhanced to support more elements of the PCM meta-model.

Another area of future research is better automation to create resource profiles. Our evaluation shows how a resource profile can be created and adapted for Java EE applications. Other enterprise application frameworks need similar automation. Even though the underlying performance models could be created using different means such as static or dynamic analysis, our future research will focus on better dynamic analysis as these approaches tend to generate more accurate models from a resource demand perspective.

6. REFERENCES

[1] S. Balsamo, A. Di Marco, P. Inverardi, and M. Simeoni. Model-based performance prediction in software development: A survey. *IEEE Transactions on Software Engineering*, 30(5):295–310, 2004.

[2] S. Becker. *Coupled Model Transformations for QoS Enabled Component-Based Software Design*. Karlsruhe Series on Software Quality. Universitätsverlag Karlsruhe, 2008.

[3] R. Brandl, M. Bichler, and M. Ströbel. Cost accounting for shared it infrastructures. *Wirtschaftsinformatik*, 49(2):83–94, 2007.

[4] A. Brunnert, C. Vögele, A. Danciu, M. Pfaff, M. Mayer, and H. Krcmar. Performance management work. *Business & Information Systems Engineering*, http://dx.doi.org/10.1007/s12599-014-0323-7, 2014.

[5] A. Brunnert, C. Vögele, and H. Krcmar. Automatic performance model generation for java enterprise edition (ee) applications. In *Computer Performance Engineering*, pages 74–88. Springer, 2013.

[6] E. Capra, G. Formenti, C. Francalanci, and S. Gallazzi. The impact of mis software on it energy consumption. In P. M. Alexander, M. Turpin, and J. P. van Deventer, editors, *ECIS*, 2010.

[7] D. Economou, S. Rivoire, C. Kozyrakis, and P. Ranganathan. Full-system power analysis and modeling for server environments. In *Workshop on Modeling, Benchmarking, and Simulation*, Boston, Massachusetts, USA, 2006.

[8] X. Fan, W.-D. Weber, and L. A. Barroso. Power provisioning for a warehouse-sized computer. *Computer Architecture News*, 35(2):13–23, 2007.

[9] J. L. Henning. Spec cpu2006 benchmark descriptions. *Computer Architecture News*, 34(4):1–17, 2006.

[10] T. Johann, M. Dick, S. Naumann, and E. Kern. How to measure energy-efficiency of software: Metrics and measurement results. In *Proceedings of the International Workshop on Green and Sustainable Software*, pages 51–54, Zurich, Switzerland, 2012.

[11] J.-S. Jwo, J.-Y. Wang, C.-H. Huang, S.-J. Two, and H.-C. Hsu. An energy consumption model for enterprise applications. In *Proceedings of the IEEE/ACM International Conference on Green Computing and Communications*, pages 216–219, Washington, DC, USA, 2011. IEEE.

[12] H. Koziolek. Performance evaluation of component-based software systems: A survey. *Performance Evaluation*, 67(8):634–658, 2010.

[13] H. Li, G. Casale, and T. Ellahi. Sla-driven planning and optimization of enterprise applications. In *Proceedings of the First Joint WOSP/SIPEW International Conference on Performance Engineering*, pages 117–128, New York, NY, USA, 2010. ACM.

[14] T.-K. Liu, S. Kumaran, and Z. Luo. Layered queueing models for enterprise javabean applications. In *Proceedings of the IEEE International Conference on Enterprise Distributed Object Computing*, pages 174–178, Washington, DC, USA, 2001. IEEE.

[15] T.-K. Liu, H. Shen, and S. Kumaran. A capacity sizing tool for a business process integration middleware. In *Proceedings of the IEEE International Conference on E-Commerce Technology*, pages 195–202, Washington, DC, USA, 2004. IEEE.

[16] D. A. Menascé and V. A. F. Almeida. *Capacity Planning for Web Services: Metrics, Models, and Methods*. Prentice Hall, Upper Saddle River, New Jersey, 2002.

[17] D. A. Menascé, V. A. F. Almeida, F. Lawrence, W. Dowdy, and L. Dowdy. *Performance by Design: Computer Capacity Planning by Example*. Prentice Hall, Upper Saddle River, New Jersey, 2004.

[18] D. A. Menascé. Load testing, benchmarking, and application performance management for the web. In *Proceedings of the Computer Measurement Group (CMG) Conference*, pages 271–282, Reno, Nevada, USA, 2002. CMG.

[19] P. Merkle and J. Henss. EventSim – an event-driven Palladio software architecture simulator. In *Palladio Days 2011 Proceedings (appeared as technical report)*, Karlsruhe Reports in Informatics ; 2011,32, pages 15–22, Karlsruhe, 2011. KIT, Fakultät für Informatik.

[20] R. Reussner, S. Becker, E. Burger, J. Happe, M. Hauck, A. Koziolek, H. Koziolek, K. Krogmann, and M. Kuperberg. The Palladio Component Model. Technical report, KIT, Fakultät für Informatik, Karlsruhe, 2011.

[21] S. Rivoire, P. Ranganathan, and C. Kozyrakis. A comparison of high-level full-system power models. In *Proceedings of the Conference on Power Aware Computing and Systems*, Berkeley, CA, USA, 2008. USENIX Association.

[22] S. Rivoire, M. Shah, P. Ranganathan, C. Kozyrakis, and J. Meza. Models and metrics to enable energy-efficiency optimizations. *Computer*, 40(12):39–48, 2007.

[23] N. Tiwari and K. Nair. Performance extrapolation that uses industry benchmarks with performance models. In *International Symposium on Peformance Evaluation of Computer and Telecommunication Systems*, pages 301–305, Ottawa, ON, USA, 2010.

[24] M. Woodside, G. Franks, and D. C. Petriu. The future of software performance engineering. In *Future of Software Engineering (FOSE)*, pages 171–187, Washington, DC, USA, 2007. IEEE.

[25] L. Zhu, Y. Liu, N. B. Bui, and I. Gorton. Revel8or: Model driven capacity planning tool suite. In *ICSE*, pages 797–800. IEEE, 2007.

Empirical Resilience Evaluation of an Architecture-based Self-Adaptive Software System

Javier Cámara
Institute for Software Research
Carnegie Mellon University
jcmoreno@cs.cmu.edu

Pedro Correia
Department of Informatics Engineering
University of Coimbra
pcorreia@dei.uc.pt

Rogério de Lemos
School of Computing
University of Kent
r.delemos@kent.ac.uk

Marco Vieira
Department of Informatics Engineering
University of Coimbra
mvieira@dei.uc.pt

ABSTRACT

Architecture-based self-adaptation is considered as a promising approach to drive down the development and operation costs of complex software systems operating in ever changing environments. However, there is still a lack of evidence supporting the arguments for the beneficial impact of architecture-based self-adaptation on resilience with respect to other customary approaches, such as embedded code-based adaptation. In this paper, we report on an empirical study about the impact on resilience of incorporating architecture-based self-adaptation in an industrial middleware used to collect data in highly populated networks of devices. To this end, we compare the results of resilience evaluation between the original version of the middleware, in which adaptation mechanisms are embedded at the code-level, and a modified version of that middleware in which the adaptation mechanisms are implemented using Rainbow, a framework for architecture-based self-adaptation. Our results show improved levels of resilience in architecture-based compared to embedded code-based self-adaptation.

Categories and Subject Descriptors

D.2.11 [**Software**]: SOFTWARE ENGINEERING—*Software Architectures*; D.2.4 [**Software**]: SOFTWARE ENGINEERING—*Software/Program Verification*

General Terms

Experimentation, Measurement, Reliability

Keywords

Resilience evaluation, Architecture-based self-adaptation, Probabilistic model checking, Rainbow

Permission to make digital or hard copies of all or part of this work for personal or classroom use is granted without fee provided that copies are not made or distributed for profit or commercial advantage and that copies bear this notice and the full citation on the first page. Copyrights for components of this work owned by others than ACM must be honored. Abstracting with credit is permitted. To copy otherwise, or republish, to post on servers or to redistribute to lists, requires prior specific permission and/or a fee. Request permissions from permissions@acm.org.
QoSA'14, June 30–July 4, 2014, Marcq-en-Baroeul, France.
Copyright 2014 ACM 978-1-4503-2577-6/14/06 ...$15.00.
http://dx.doi.org/10.1145/2602576.2602577.

1. INTRODUCTION

During the last decade, the software industry has seen a continuous increase in the complexity of software systems, as well as in the uncertainty of the environments in which they have to operate. This trend has led to an increasing growth in the cost of both developing and operating such systems, but more importantly, has put their *resilience* (*i.e.*, their ability to provide service that can justifiably be trusted when facing changes [24]) in the spotlight as a central concern [13].

Initial approaches to tackle the development and run-time management of complex systems that must operate in ever-changing environments consisted either in making use of human oversight (which is expensive and unreliable), or in embedding low-level error-handling mechanisms in application code that trigger specific responses to anomalies observed in the system at run-time (*e.g.*, exceptions, timeouts). However, although the latter approach can be effective in specific situations, it lacks flexibility and is not well suited to dealing with more subtle, but important kinds of anomaly (*e.g.*, progressive performance degradation).

Autonomic computing, or self-adaptive systems [10, 13, 22], have emerged more recently as an alternative to overcome the shortcomings presented by the aforementioned approaches. In particular, architecture-based self-adaptation [17, 23, 25] leverages architecture models to enable high-level reasoning about the best way of adapting a system, and is regarded as a promising approach to building *resilient* software systems in a cost-effective manner. However, although architecture-based self-adaptation has been applied in practice and recent results indicate its potential benefits in terms of cost compared to embedded code-based adaptation mechanisms [8], there is still a lack of evidence supporting the arguments for its beneficial impact on system resilience [31].

This paper aims at providing empirical evidence that architecture-based self-adaptation has the potential to endow systems with improved levels of resilience, compared to the use of embedded code-based adaptation mechanisms. Our main contribution is an empirical study about the impact of architecture-based self-adaptation on resilience, which employs a framework for evaluating resilience in self-adaptive systems [7] incorporating the notion of *changeload* [1], which includes changes in the system and its environment.

In this study, our framework for resilience evaluation is applied to an adaptive industrial middleware system developed by Critical Software - called Data Acquisition and Control Service (DCAS), which is used to monitor and manage highly populated networks of devices in renewable energy production plants. Specifically, we compare the results of resilience evaluation between the original version of DCAS in which adaptation is implemented using embedded code-based mechanisms, and a modified version in which adaptation is implemented using the Rainbow framework for architecture-based self-adaptation [17]. Rainbow has been chosen for performing the experiments since its software has been widely available, its structure facilitates access to its internal components, its design is amenable to the injection of faults, and controllers built using it are fairly robust [9].

As a result of our analysis, we demonstrate that incorporating architecture-based self-adaptation in DCAS has a beneficial impact on resilience, mainly due to the: (i) higher level of abstraction of the information used by architecture-based self-adaptation, which enables better informed decision-making and flexibility, and (ii) reduced vulnerability of the external control layer to changes (e.g., failures) occurring at the system level (in contrast with embedded code-based adaptation mechanisms, which are prone to be affected by system failures, thereby interfering with adaptation).

The rest of this paper is structured as follows. Section 2 presents the general structure and objective of DCAS middleware, as well as, its two different versions, i.e., Original DCAS and Rainbow-DCAS, that are implemented using, respectively, embedded code-based and architecture-based adaptation mechanisms. Section 3 introduces resilience properties and their formalization, the notion of changeload, and provides an overview of the process followed for resilience evaluation. Next, Section 4 details the design of our experimental study, whereas Section 5 discusses experimental results. Section 6 discusses threats to validity. Section 7 describes related work. Finally, Section 8 presents some conclusions and indicates directions for future work.

2. DATA ACQUISITION AND CONTROL SERVICE

This section presents the general structure and objective of Data Acquisition and Control Service (DCAS) middleware, as well as, the adaptation mechanisms used in the two versions of the system employed for our study: (i) embedded code-based, and (ii) architecture-based.

2.1 Structure and objective

The Data Acquisition and Control Service (DCAS) [8] is a middleware from Critical Software that provides a reusable infrastructure to manage the monitoring of highly populated networks of devices. In particular, the middleware is designed to be seamlessly integrated with Critical's Energy Management System (csEMS)[1], which is a platform that provides asset management support for power producing companies based on renewable energy sources. The overall csEMS architecture aims at high scalability, flexibility and customization with management capabilities that enable the operation of control centers independently of the underlying application (e.g., wind, solar, etc.). The basic building blocks in a DCAS-based system (Figure 1) are: [2]

[1]http://solutions.criticalsoftware.com/products_services/csems/
[2]We herein consider a simplified version of the DCAS architecture. Further details about DCAS can be found in [8].

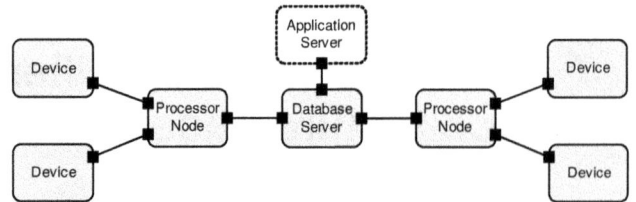

Figure 1: Architecture of a DCAS-based system

- **Devices** are equipped with one or more sensors to obtain data from the application domain (e.g., from wind towers, solar panels, etc.). Each sensor has an associated *data stream* from which data can be read. Each type of device has its particular characteristics (e.g., data polling rate, or expected value ranges) specified in a *device profile*.

- **Processor nodes** pull data from the devices at a rate configured in the device profile, and dispatch this data to the database server. Each processor node includes a set of processes called *Data Requester Processor Pollers* (DRPPs or *pollers*, for short) responsible for retrieving data from the devices. Communication between DRPPs and devices is synchronous, so DRPPs remain blocked until devices respond to data requests or a timeout expires. This is the main performance bottleneck of DCAS.

- **Database server** stores the data collected from devices by processor nodes.

- **Application server** is connected to the database server to obtain data, which can be presented to the operators of the system or processed automatically by application software. However, DCAS is application-agnostic, so the application server will not be discussed in the remainder of this paper.

The main objective of DCAS is collecting data from the connected devices at a rate as close as possible to the one configured in their device profiles, while making an efficient use of the computational resources in the processor nodes. Specifically, the primary concern in DCAS is providing service while maintaining acceptable levels of performance, measured in terms of processed data requests per second (rps) inserted in the database, while the secondary concern is optimizing the computational cost of operating the system, measured in number of active DRPPs in the processor nodes.

2.2 Adaptation Mechanisms

DCAS implements two adaptation mechanisms to keep an acceptable level of performance while making an efficient use of computational resources: (i) *Rescheduling* aims at avoiding performance degradation caused by devices which fail to respond in a timely manner when polled. It consists in decreasing the priority of the data streams associated with the failing devices, so that they are polled less often (thus reducing the average time that DRPPs remain blocked waiting for device data).(ii) *Scale up* aims at improving performance by exploiting as much as possible CPU and memory in processor nodes by (de)activating DRPPs as required.

Original DCAS. Scale up and rescheduling run in two separate control loops embedded in different sub-components of the processor node. Moreover, the C# adaptation logic that corresponds to these control loops is scattered across different parts of the code, and based on low-level information that indirectly indicates which aspect of the system needs to be improved. In the case of scale up, if the size of a data request queue associated with a particular processor node remains close to zero consistently, the adaptation mechanism considers this as an indicator of good performance, implying that there are active DRPPs which probably are not necessary and have to be deactivated. On the contrary, if the queue size increases consistently, scale up tries to increase performance by activating new DRPPs.

Rainbow-DCAS. Scale up and rescheduling are implemented as adaptation strategies inside of a single control loop running in a controller external to the DCAS system. The adaptation logic is implemented in Stitch [12], a language specifically tailored for representing adaptation strategies in Rainbow. Stitch adaptation strategies make use of system information reified into an architecture model of the underlying DCAS system. Scale up and rescheduling adaptation strategies replicate functionality of the adaptation logic in Original DCAS. However, in the case of scale up, the strategy is also informed by a direct performance measure obtained by a probe that measures the rps in the database, in contrast to the embedded code-based mechanisms, which make use of an indirect performance indicator.

3. RESILIENCE EVALUATION

This section: (i) introduces some general concepts related to resilience evaluation, as well as, the kind of resilience properties that we deal with in our study and their formalization, (ii) describes the notion of changeload, which is central to the framework used for resilience evaluation, and (iii) describes the process followed for resilience evaluation.

3.1 Resilience Properties

A *resilient* system is one that delivers a service that *can justifiably be trusted when facing changes* [24]. In the context of self-adaptive systems, changes (which can occur in the system itself, its environment, or even in its goals) can induce anomalies in the system at run-time, changing its current *operational profile*. Specifically, within a self-adaptive system, we may distinguish between a *conventional operational profile* (COP) that corresponds to the region of the state-space in which the system is operating without experiencing any anomalies, and *non-conventional operational profiles* (NCOPs), associated with anomalies induced by changes in the system or its environment. NCOPs correspond to regions of the state-space in which the system is experiencing a particular anomaly [6]. When the self-adaptive system enters a NCOP, this typically triggers adaptation mechanisms whose purpose is driving the system back into its COP by performing some actions on the system to correct the experienced anomaly. Once the system has entered into a NCOP, resilience can be assessed by quantifying the probability of returning to the system's COP by a given time deadline.

To express resilience properties about the system, we use PCTL [3], a logic language inspired by CTL [15]. With the aid of PCTL, a designer can express properties about the system that are typically domain-dependent. Furthermore, to ease the formulation of probabilistic properties, we make use of property specification patterns [14] that describe generalized recurring properties in probabilistic temporal logics. In our case, we are interested in how the system responds to changes, so we restrict ourselves to properties that can be instanced by using probabilistic response patterns [19],

PCTL Formulation	Description
$\mathcal{P}_{\geq 1}[G(\Phi_1 \Rightarrow \mathcal{P}_{\bowtie p}(F^{\leq t}\Phi_2))]$	**Probabilistic Response.** After state formula Φ_1 holds, state formula Φ_2 must become *true* within time bound t, with a probability bound $\bowtie p$.
$\mathcal{P}_{\geq 1}[G(\Phi_1 \Rightarrow \mathcal{P}_{\bowtie p}(\neg\Phi_2 U^{\leq t}\Phi_3))]$	**Probabilistic Constrained Response.** After state formula Φ_1 holds, state formula Φ_3 must become *true*, without Φ_2 ever holding, within time bound t, with a probability bound $\bowtie p$.

Table 1: Probabilistic response patterns

adapted to PCTL syntax (see Table 1). These patterns include a premise Φ_1 representing the initial conditions after a change in the system or its environment occurs, and a subformula enclosed by the probabilistic operator $\mathcal{P}_{\bowtie p}(.)$, representing the response to that change expected from the system (with a probability bound p and a time bound t).

EXAMPLE 1. *In DCAS, we are interested in assessing how the system reacts to low responsiveness in part of the devices connected to the system. Let* rps *be the variable associated with performance (defined as the number of requested data items inserted in the database per second), and* drpps *be the cost variable (defined as the number of active DRPPs in the system). We can then define the following predicates:*

$$\text{rpsViolation} \triangleq \text{rps} < \text{MIN\_RPS}$$
$$\text{hiCost} \triangleq \text{drpps} \geq \text{MAX\_POLLERS}$$

where MIN_RPS *is a threshold that establishes the minimum acceptable level of performance of the system, and* MAX_POLLERS *determines a maximum acceptable number of active pollers. Let us also express a predicate associated with the COP in DCAS as* dcasCOP $\triangleq \neg$rpsViolation $\wedge \neg$hiCost *. Based on these predicates, we may instantiate the following PCTL property, using the probabilistic response pattern included in Table 1:*

$$\mathcal{P}_{\geq 1}[G(\text{rpsViolation} \Rightarrow \mathcal{P}_{\geq 0.9}(F^{\leq 100}\ \text{dcasCOP}\ ))]$$

This property reads as: "When performance falls below threshold MIN_RPS *, the probability of raising performance again above* MIN_RPS *with a cost below the* MAX_POLLERS *threshold within 100 seconds is greater or equal to 0.9". It is worth observing that the instantiation of the probabilistic response patterns, as well as, the predicates used for the specification of the properties can be more general or specific, depending on the particular aspect of the system resilience that we want to study (e.g., we can employ* ¬rpsViolation *instead of* dcasCOP *in the property above if we are interested in evaluating resilience exclusively w.r.t. the performance of the system).*

3.2 Changeload

Evaluating the resilience of a self-adaptive system requires identifying the most relevant (sequences of) system or environmental changes that might affect system resilience. Such changes always occur under some system and environment conditions that provide a context for them. A *scenario* is a postulated sequence of events that captures the state of the system, its environment, and its goals during a given time frame, as well as changes affecting all the aforementioned elements. It is defined in terms of state (system and environment), changes applied to that state, and system goals.

Scenarios fall into two categories: *base scenarios* and *change scenarios*. A base scenario is defined in terms of typical

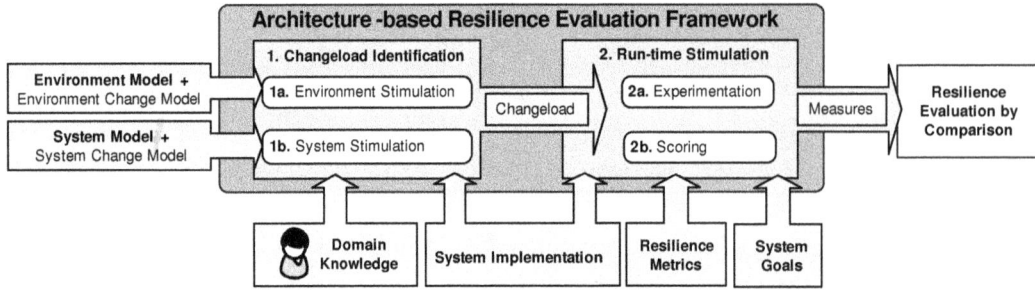

Figure 2: Overview of the resilience evaluation framework

conditions during the execution of the system, which includes: a typical (stable) state of the system and its environment, and a set of goals. [3]

The workload of a base scenario should be representative of the typical amount and type of work assigned to (or expected from) the system during a specified time period. Typical operation conditions comprise the typical setup of systems in the domain, as well as representative characterization of the system's environment, including the hardware and software resources typically used. Hence, a base scenario reflects the operational characteristics of systems in the domain while running a typical workload and operating in the absence of changes, setting the baseline for comparison with situations in which the system faces with changes that may drive it into an adaptation process. It should be noted that "typical" does only imply a stable state of the system with no abnormal conditions, not that the workload or operation conditions cannot be dynamic.

Change scenarios are derived from a base scenario, but include a representative sequence of changes that may affect the system and its ability to achieve and maintain its goals.

A changeload, is a set of representative change scenarios, comprising changes both in the system and its environment.

3.3 Evaluation Process Overview

Our framework for evaluating the resilience of self-adaptive systems consists of two main stages (Figure 2):

1. **Changeload identification** consists in identifying the sequence of changes (*i.e.*, the changeload) relevant for the run-time stimulation of the system and its environment. This stage requires human intervention and is divided in:

   (a) **Environment Stimulation**, identifies the environmental changes required to drive the environment towards conditions that trigger system adaptations.

   (b) **System Stimulation**, identifies system changes that can affect the ability of the system to return to its COP when experiencing an anomaly.

2. **Run-time stimulation** of the system and its environment, according to the changeload identified. This stage is fully automatic and divided into:

   (a) **Experimentation**, during which the system and its environment are stimulated according to the changeload,

[3]Our approach to resilience evaluation assumes fixed goals.

and information regarding the system's execution is collected, according to the metrics, as sets of execution traces for each scenario in the changeload. The exper-

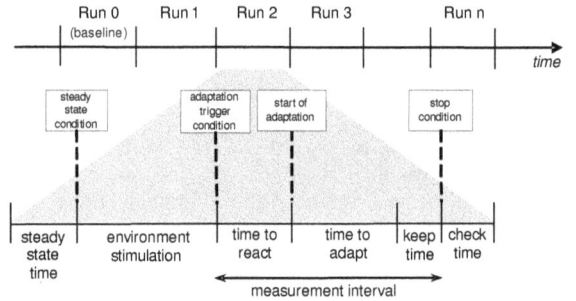

Figure 3: Experimental profile

imental profile, depicted in Figure 3, includes a set of runs, in which run 0 consists only of performing environmental stimulation to trigger adaptation to collect baseline information about adaptation behavior in the absence of system changes. This baseline will be used later as reference to understand the impact of system changes in the execution of the adaptation strategies. During Runs 1...N the system is run in such a way that: (i) it executes without stimulation for a *steady state period* to reach a *steady state condition*, (ii) *environment stimulation* is applied to induce the *adaptation trigger condition* required for adaptation (iii) the system detects the adaptation trigger condition and starts the execution of adaptation after a period of *time to react*, (iv) system changes are injected on top of the environmental stimulation during the *time to adapt*, and (v) continues running without further disturbance after adaptation has finished execution during a *keep period* used to collect further data about the effects of adaptation until some *stop condition* is met (*e.g.*, time deadline, etc.). The *measurement interval* in every run starts when the adaptation trigger condition is met, and ends with the stop condition.

(b) **Scoring**, where each set of collected traces for a particular scenario is transformed into a probabilistic response model of the system, and used as input to a probabilistic model-checker in addition to the resilience properties obtained from system goals to quantify resilience.

Our framework enables the evaluation of adaptation by comparison, which makes use of relative resilience metrics to compare how different adaptive solutions respond to a particular set of (system or environmental) conditions. This approach for evaluating resilience is intended to be used by the developer of the system just before its deployment, since the process often involves putting the system through adverse conditions inadequate for production environments.

4. EXPERIMENTAL DESIGN

Resilience is related to the system's ability of maintaining service provision without deviating from the fulfillment of system goals, despite changes that might affect the system or its environment. The primary goal in DCAS is maintaining an acceptable level of performance, therefore we designed our study with a focus on evaluating resilience *w.r.t.* performance. Hence, our experiments are designed to enable us to assess the system's ability to return to its COP, once it has been driven to the NCOP associated with the low performance anomaly rpsViolation (as defined in Example 1).

In this context, we formalize the following PCTL properties [4] in accordance with the objective of our study:

- *N1*. To address the primary performance related goal in DCAS, we formalize a property that enables us to quantify the probability of eliminating the rpsViolation anomaly (*i.e.*, raising performance again above threshold MIN_RPS) within t time units as: $\mathcal{P}(F^{\leq t} \neg\text{rpsViolation})$.
- *N2*. Moreover, we also want to evaluate resilience in the context of the associated cost of improving performance, so we also quantify the ability of the system to free the resources used for adaptation once they are not required anymore (*i.e.*, deactivation of DRPPs below a threshold α that can be instanced with different values) by a given deadline t as: $\mathcal{P}(F^{\leq t} \text{drpps} \leq \alpha)$.

In our study, we analyze and compare the levels of resilience quantified on the properties described above for both Original DCAS and Rainbow-DCAS, in order to determine whether the incorporation of architecture-based self-adaptation in the system improves its resilience.

Moreover, we provide some context for our evaluation of resilience. We have complemented our study with additional evidence collected according to some of the run-time evaluation criteria proposed in [20] that indicate the ability of the system to return to its COP after a disturbance:

- *WAT*. Working *vs.* adaptivity time of the system, where the working time is the time needed to perform the usual function of the system, and the adaptivity time concerns the time needed to adapt to changes in the system or its environment. In our specific case, we consider as *working time* all the measurement interval in our experiments (time to react + time to adapt + keep time, Figure 3), whereas adaptivity time corresponds to "time to adapt" (working and adaptivity times overlap in DCAS, since the system continues to work while it is adapting).

$$WAT = \frac{WorkingTime}{AdaptivityTime}$$

- *TA*. Time for adaptation, or time required to return to a nominal behavior after a perturbation. In DCAS, this is the time required to return to the COP since the time instant in which the system enters the NCOP associated to anomaly rpsViolation .

Finally, we also provide further context for resilience evaluation by including a measure of *experimental availability* taken from dependability benchmarking [28] [5]. In this context, a system is considered to be available when it is able to provide service as specified (*e.g.*, in DCAS, when performance levels are above threshold MIN_RPS). We refer to the sum of the duration of all time periods in which the system is available during the working time of the experiments as *uptime*. Experimental availability is defined as:

$$EA = \frac{Uptime}{WorkingTime}$$

The rest of this section details the: (i) identification of the changeload, (ii) procedure followed for run-time stimulation, and (iii) experimental setup used for our study.

4.1 Changeload Identification

This section details first the environmental part of the changeload identified to drive DCAS towards adaptation conditions, followed by system stimulation, in which representative system changes that might affect the resilience of DCAS are identified.

4.1.1 Environment Stimulation

The first step to identify a representative changeload to compare alternative adaptation mechanisms in terms of resilience is determining which environmental changes can trigger adaptations. To this purpose, we need to identify the anomalies associated to NCOPs. In DCAS, the primary focus of adaptation mechanisms is recovering from situations in which the system is running under the acceptable levels of performance. Therefore, in this case we identified potential sources of system states in which anomaly rpsViolation holds.

The only representative source of low performance that can be attributed to the environment in DCAS corresponds to the case in which connected devices fail to respond data requests in a timely manner (*e.g.*, due to high network latency, failures in devices, etc.). Specifically, we identified two representative scenarios to stimulate the environment:

- *Device delay*, in which devices fail to respond in a timely manner (inducing a delay of 2 seconds in the response of 25% of connected devices when they are requested for data). The number of devices and the amount of delay applied have been chosen to recreate representative situations in which high network latency is given in DCAS-based systems deployed in the field.
- *Device failure*, where we replicate more extreme situations in which 25% of de devices fail to respond by inducing a 30-second delay in the devices. This causes a timeout in data requests performed by the DRPPs in processor nodes, simulating effectively device failure.

4.1.2 System Stimulation

To identify relevant stimulation of the system, we follow a risk-based approach based on the Software Risk Evaluation

---

[4]Specifically, we evaluate the results obtained from applying the probabilistic quantifier $\mathcal{P}(.)$ to system response according to the probabilistic response pattern displayed in Table 1. The implicit premise in the properties specified is rpsViolation .

[5]Assessing availability in global terms is difficult since it depends on many factors that influence the system Mean Time Between Failures (MTBF).

(SRE) method [32] that considers both the probability and impact of system changes. This is a manual process that uses field data (if available) and expert knowledge, and consists in identifying relevant system changes that might impact system goals during adaptation. Field data was unavailable for DCAS, so the probability and impact of system changes was analyzed with the help of field experts.

The candidate system changes for system stimulation were classified in a risk exposure matrix for the case of the NCOP associated to the anomaly rpsViolation (Table 2). Grayed-out cells in the exposure matrix area contain changes which are left out of the changeload due to their low representativeness when considering the combination of their impact and probability of occurring.

We can observe in the matrix that, when facing performance issues, failures in the components involved in adaptation have a high probability of occurring. Moreover, these failures might have a critical impact if they fail to respond properly since they are used intensively during adaptation. Such is the case of the effectors used to activate DRPPs or the probes to check the status of data request queues, which are intensively used during scale up adaptation. Other effectors and probes, such as, the ones used for rescheduling (device delay probe and change rate delay effector) have also a high probability of occurring, but a marginal or negligible impact on performance, since the effects of rescheduling are limited compared to those of scale up. The rest of system changes, included in the white area of the exposure matrix, involves failures in different system coarse-grained components (e.g., processor node, database server), and finer-grained sub-components of the processor node (e.g., service engine, data requester, data persister, polling scheduler) all with potentially either critical or even catastrophic impact on service provision[6] (e.g., a crash in the database server would reduce rps to 0 by impeding insertions the database).

4.2 Run-time Stimulation

To evaluate the resilience of the two different versions of DCAS, we carried out run-time stimulation using a changeload in which all scenarios include a workload and operating conditions characteristic of a typical deployment of a DCAS-based system in production. Scenarios have a duration of 40 minutes (2400s), which is enough to collect sufficient data to characterize system behavior and synthesize the probabilistic models required to quantify resilience. All experiments incorporate a workload that includes 100 data streams (devices) with a data polling rate of 1 second.

In our experiments, the system is driven towards the triggering of adaptation to improve performance, and in which scenarios conform to the following pattern: (i) 600s of normal activity to let the system achieve a steady state; (ii) 600s of disturbance, during which we induce low responsiveness in data streams; and (iii) 1200s of normal activity. Scenarios in our experiments are divided in two groups:

1. Environment stimulation. Contains 2 scenarios including only environment stimulation, according to the cases described in Section 4.1.1 (device delay and device failure).
2. Environment+System stimulation. Contains 11 scenarios. Each scenario combines environmental stimulation (device delay) with one of the system changes identified

as relevant in the exposure matrix shown in Table 2. Environment stimulation is used in these scenarios as a way to trigger system adaptation without interfering with the system. This avoids potential interactions between system changes triggering adaptation conditions, and those applied during the execution of adaptation. Specifically, we have favored the use of device delay over device failure as environmental stimulation because it is enough to trigger adaptation, but at the same time has a more moderate impact, enabling us to better assess the contribution of system changes to variation in resilience levels.

For every scenario, we built a probabilistic model of system behavior during a period of 900s, which corresponds to system traces collected during the time frame $[600, 1500]$ of every system run, out of which the first 600s correspond to the disturbance period. Each probabilistic model has a time discretization parameter of $\tau = 1s$, and quantization parameters for the performance and cost variables of $\eta_{rps} = 10$ and $\eta_{drpps} = 1$, respectively[7]. Each model is synthesized from data obtained from 30 different runs of the same scenario (i.e., our experiments required (11+2)*30*2=780 runs).

4.3 Experimental Setup

For our experimental setup, we deployed both versions of DCAS across three different machines. In the case of Original DCAS (Figure 4, left), dcas-db acts as the back-end database running on Oracle 10.2.0, dcas-main acts as a processor node, running DCAS, and (dcas-devs) is used to simulate the response of network devices from which DCAS retrieves information (device response simulation is implemented as a simple Web service whose response time can be set in a configuration file). In the case of Rainbow-DCAS (Figure 4, right), Rainbow's master is deployed in an additional machine (dcas-master). All machines run on Windows XP Pro SP3 (DCAS is deployed as a Windows service), and an Intel core i3 processor, with 1GB of RAM.

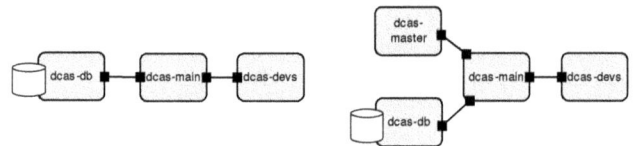

Figure 4: Experimental setup: Original DCAS (left) and Rainbow-DCAS (right)

5. EXPERIMENTAL RESULTS

In line with the system's goals of keeping an acceptable performance level while keeping down the cost of running the system, we study the resilience of Original DCAS and Rainbow-DCAS in the different scenarios identified in our changeload. Specifically, in this section we report on: (i) results regarding general run-time evaluation criteria related to the system's ability to return to its COP, and (ii) results regarding the evaluation of the resilience properties defined according to DCAS goals, described in Section 4.

5.1 General Run-time Evaluation Criteria

Table 3 displays the experimental results for WAT, TA, and EA both for Original DCAS and Rainbow-DCAS.

---

[6]A detailed discussion of the functionality of the different sub-components of the processor node can be found in [8].

[7]Details about time sampling, quantization, and the type of probabilistic models used for our study can be found in [7].

Impact		Probability			
		Very High	High	Low	Very Low
	Catastrophic			DB Crash Service Engine Crash	Processor Node Crash
	Critical		Add Poller Effector Crash DB-DCAS Conn. Shutdown Queue Status Probe Crash	Polling Scheduler Crash Data Persister Crash Data Requester Crash	
	Marginal		ChangeRateDelay Effector Crash Remove Poller Effector Crash	System Monitor Crash	Alarmer Crash Alarmer Publisher Crash
	Negligible		Device Delay Probe Crash	Device Monitor Crash	Alarmer Monitor Crash

Table 2: Exposure matrix for system changes in DCAS non-conventional operational profile rpsViolation

	WAT. Working *vs.* Adaptivity Time		TA. Time for Adaptation (s)		EA. Exp. Availability (%)	
	Orig.DCAS	Rainbow-DCAS	Orig.DCAS	Rainbow-DCAS	Orig.DCAS	Rainbow-DCAS
Device Delay	1.247	6.185	243	80	19	84
Device Failure	$\to 1$	$\to 1$	∞	∞	0	0
AddPoller Eff. Crash	$\to 1$	$\to 1$	∞	∞	0	0
Remove Poller Eff. Crash	1.200	7.058	362	88	15	45
ChangeRateDelay Eff. Crash	1.242	6.741	336	60	19	85
QueueStatus Probe Crash	1.226	8.695	291	62	18	88
DB-DCAS Conn. Shutdown	1.115	6.818	348	51	10	85
DB Crash	$\to 1$	$\to 1$	∞	∞	0	0
Service Engine Crash	$\to 1$	$\to 1$	∞	∞	0	0
Polling Scheduler Crash	$\to 1$	$\to 1$	∞	∞	0	0
Data Persister Crash	1.176	7.407	357	54	11	86
Data Requester Crash	1.123	6.060	315	72	15	83
Processor Node Crash	$\to 1$	$\to 1$	∞	∞	0	0

Table 3: Experimental results for general run-time evaluation criteria and availability

Regarding WAT, it can be observed that Rainbow-DCAS spends in most cases from 6 to 8 times more time working than adapting, whereas the original version of DCAS is prone to spend most of the time adapting to changes, with WAT values always close to 1. It is worth observing that some specific cases in which disturbances cannot be dealt with by adaptation mechanisms in both versions of DCAS (*e.g.*, device failure, service engine crash) make the system spend most of the working time also trying to (unsuccessfully) adapt to changes, resulting in WAT values that closely approach 1 (indicated by $\to 1$ in Table 3).

Concerning TA, Rainbow-DCAS also takes considerably less time to eliminate the anomaly, with times that range between 50 and 90 seconds *vs.* the 240-350 seconds required by Original DCAS, depending on the case. Cases in which adaptation mechanisms were unable to eliminate the performance anomaly are indicated with an infinite TA in the table. An interesting phenomenon that can be initially perceived as somewhat strange in the case of Rainbow-DCAS is that there are cases that yield a shorter TA in the presence of system and environment changes (*e.g.* data persister crash) *w.r.t.* cases in which there is only environment stimulation (device delay). This happens because adverse system conditions can influence the decision-making process in Rainbow (*e.g.*, the controller can try to further compensate the adverse situation by increasing the rate at which DRPPs are activated), resulting in a more aggressive adaptation *w.r.t.* cases in which decision-making is not influenced by such unfavorable changes. This phenomenon is in line with previous experience using Rainbow in other case studies [7].

Finally, it can also be observed that availability is much higher in Rainbow-DCAS, with values ranging between 80-90% in most cases in which the system is able to adapt, compared to the 10-20% in Original DCAS.

5.2 Resilience Evaluation

Table 4 shows the experimental results for resilience evaluation in the NCOP associated with the rpsViolation anomaly for Original DCAS (top), and Rainbow-DCAS (bottom).

Performance-related property $N1$ is instanced with different time bounds (t), in intervals of 50s, and up to time 600s, coinciding with the end of environmental stimulation. Each instance of the property describes the probability of recovering an acceptable performance by the given time bound.

Results for property $N1$ show that in general, resilience values obtained in Rainbow-DCAS tend to be higher than in Original DCAS in many of the scenarios.

Regarding scenarios that only include environment stimulation, we can observe that in the case of the device delay scenario, Rainbow-DCAS reacts much faster to the anomaly with values for $N1$ already of 90% by $t = 100$, whereas Original DCAS only reaches values above 90% by $t = 400$. This is motivated by the fact that in Rainbow-DCAS, the controller can exploit an explicit model of the system's expected behavior (in this case expected performance), as well as high-level information about the current performance of the system (updated at run-time in the system's architecture model). Having this explicit information readily available to the controller enables early detection of anomalies in the case of architecture-based self-adaptation. In contrast, embedded code-based adaptation mechanisms in Original DCAS do not have a global picture of the system's state, and for that, they have to rely on low-level local information that implicitly indicates potential performance problems (*e.g.*, data request queue size growth rate). In this case, there is a time gap between the occurrence of the anomaly causing the performance problem, and the time by which queue growth rate increases enough to trigger adaptation mechanisms. This results in late detection of the anomaly and increased reaction time of adaptation, hindering the ability of the system to recover its intended performance levels in a timely manner.

In the case of device failure, the results obtained are similar for both versions of the system since the changeload cannot be accommodated with the computational resources available, independently of the adaptation mechanism used.

In the case of scenarios that combine system and environment stimulation (device delay), we can observe that in some of the scenarios that involve component crashes in the system (*e.g.*, Data Persister and Data Requester), Rainbow-DCAS does not show any noticeable degradation of performance with respect to the device delay scenario. However, performance in Original DCAS is further degraded, showing values of 50% and 68% by $t = 400$ in the scenarios for the Data Persister and Data Requester crashes respectively,

		N1.$\mathcal{P}(F^{\leq t} \neg \text{rpsViolation})$												N2.$\mathcal{P}(F^{\leq 600} \text{drpps} \leq \alpha)$			
		$t=50$	$t=100$	$t=150$	$t=200$	$t=250$	$t=300$	$t=350$	$t=400$	$t=450$	$t=500$	$t=550$	$t=600$	$\alpha=10$	$\alpha=20$	$\alpha=30$	$\alpha=40$
Orig. DCAS	Device Delay	0	7	20	37	58	70	85	93	97	97	97	100	0	93	100	100
	Device Failure	0	0	0	0	0	0	0	0	0	0	0	0	53	93	100	100
	AddPoller Eff. Crash	0	0	0	0	0	0	0	0	0	0	0	0	100	100	100	100
	Remove Poller Eff. Crash	0	0	3	7	26	30	37	50	53	53	56	93	20	33	71	100
	ChangeRateDelay Eff. Crash	0	0	0	0	13	26	45	47	53	76	78	98	27	100	100	100
	QueueStatus Probe Crash	0	0	7	17	35	40	50	59	88	94	96	100	20	97	100	100
	DB-DCAS Conn. Shutdown	0	0	0	3	7	17	23	25	33	49	60	95	100	100	100	100
	DB Crash	0	0	0	0	0	0	0	0	0	0	0	0	43	93	100	100
	Service Engine Crash	0	0	0	0	0	0	0	0	0	0	0	0	-	-	-	-
	Polling Scheduler Crash	0	0	0	0	0	0	0	0	0	0	0	0	-	-	-	-
	Data Persister Crash	0	0	0	0	17	28	40	50	60	64	78	100	28	100	100	100
	Data Requester Crash	0	7	13	26	40	53	59	68	74	85	90	99	16	95	100	100
	Processor Node Crash	0	0	0	0	0	0	0	0	0	0	0	0	-	-	-	-
Rainbow-DCAS	Device Delay	0	90	100	100	100	100	100	100	100	100	100	100	100	100	100	100
	Device Failure	0	0	0	0	0	0	0	0	0	0	0	0	100	100	100	100
	AddPoller Eff. Crash	0	0	0	0	0	0	0	0	0	0	0	0	100	100	100	100
	Remove Poller Eff. Crash	0	92	100	100	100	100	100	100	100	100	100	100	0	0	10	100
	ChangeRateDelay Eff. Crash	0	96	97	100	100	100	100	100	100	100	100	100	100	100	100	100
	QueueStatus Probe Crash	13	100	100	100	100	100	100	100	100	100	100	100	100	100	100	100
	DB-DCAS Conn. Shutdown	0	91	100	100	100	100	100	100	100	100	100	100	100	100	100	100
	DB Crash	0	0	0	0	0	0	0	0	0	0	0	0	0	0	0	0
	Service Engine Crash	0	0	0	0	0	0	0	0	0	0	0	0	-	-	-	-
	Polling Scheduler Crash	0	0	0	0	0	0	0	0	0	0	0	0	-	-	-	-
	Data Persister Crash	0	93	100	100	100	100	100	100	100	100	100	100	100	100	100	100
	Data Requester Crash	0	77	100	100	100	100	100	100	100	100	100	100	100	100	100	100
	Processor Node Crash	0	0	0	0	0	0	0	0	0	0	0	0	-	-	-	-

Table 4: Experimental results for resilience evaluation

v.s. the 93% shown for that same time bound in the device delay case. Considering that the Data Persister and Data Requester components are in charge of requesting data to devices and dispatching the processed data to the database, respectively, one might expect a radical drop of the values in $N1$ to 0% throughout these scenarios. However, both versions of DCAS include a redundancy mechanism that detects the absence of a Data Persister or a Data Requester working properly, and automatically instances a new one, facilitating the progressive recovery of performance. In Original DCAS, performance recovery is slower because the implementation of the scale up adaptation mechanism is embedded within the failing component, and therefore needs to be restarted and run for some time until it stabilizes again. In contrast, scale up in Rainbow-DCAS is implemented in the Rainbow controller external to the target system, which is not directly affected by the failure in the component.

Regarding the cost-related property $N2$, we can observe that the probabilities of deactivating DRPPs that are not required is 100% even below the minimum threshold of pollers ($\alpha = 10$) almost in all cases of Rainbow-DCAS. There are two cases which are an exception. First, as expected, in the case in which the remove poller effector crashes no pollers can be removed and the system remains at the maximum level of active pollers that were required while scaling up (always above 20, as indicated by the probability 0% of $N2$ when $\alpha = 20$). Second, in the case in which the database crashes, the lack of data item insertions in the database is perceived by the controller as a lack of performance that has to be corrected, impeding the deactivation of pollers. Cases in which the number of pollers cannot be monitored due to the malfunction of the failing processor node (sub)component (cases service engine crash, polling scheduler crash, and processor node crash) are indicated by "-" in the table.

In Original DCAS, the probability of reducing the number of pollers below all values of threshold α tends to be smaller than in Rainbow-DCAS, mainly because detecting when pollers are not needed anymore by looking exclusively at queue growth rates is not as efficient as factoring in explicit performance information. However, the cases for the database crash and the remove poller effector crash are exceptions. In the database crash, the fact that Original DCAS

does not use performance information probed in the database to (de)activate pollers avoids the activation of additional pollers by the scale-up mechanism. For the crash in the remove poller effector, these higher probabilities are a consequence of the scale-up mechanism not activating initially as many pollers as in Rainbow-DCAS for the same situation.

6. THREATS TO VALIDITY

Regarding the internal validity of our study, the main concern is related to determining whether the improvement observed in resilience values in the case of Rainbow-DCAS *w.r.t.* Original DCAS is indeed caused by incorporating architecture based self-adaptation *vs.* other factors, such as, the lack of equivalence between the adaptation logic implemented in Original DCAS and the Stitch strategies implemented in Rainbow-DCAS. In this regard, rescheduling and scale-up adaptation logic in Rainbow-DCAS replicates as closely as possible the original adaptation logic in their respective embedded code-based counterparts. However, it is important to identify two main differences between the alternative implementations of adaptation mechanisms:

1. In Original DCAS, each adaptation mechanism resides in its own independent control loop in different sub-components of the processor node. This is an imposition of the OOP paradigm used to develop DCAS, which enforces encapsulation and information hiding, favoring good modularization, but also constrains the access of embedded adaptation mechanisms to information (e.g., for anomaly detection) and restricts actuation to their local scope (hampering coordinated adaptation). In contrast, the two adaptation mechanisms in Rainbow-DCAS reside within the same control loop in the external control layer that decides which one should be used, in a coordinated manner.

2. As a consequence of the limited scope of embedded adaptation mechanisms, Original DCAS can only use low-level information that indirectly indicates the system's performance (e.g., queue sizes). However, Rainbow-DCAS has access to high level information about whether performance goals are being met.

In our opinion, the abovementioned differences in the implementation of adaptation mechanisms in Rainbow-DCAS *w.r.t.* Original DCAS do not undermine the internal validity of the study. Regarding (1), it could be argued that since Rainbow is a centralized controller, its resilience compared to a decentralized control alternative might be worse, because it represents a single point of failure. However, in our study we consider resilience in the presence of changes only at the target system level and its environment (leaving controller failures out of the scope of this paper). Moreover, it is worth emphasizing that in Original DCAS, adaptive mechanisms are embedded in different target system components and are therefore prone to be affected by target system failures. Concerning (2), the ability to factor high level information, like performance, into the decision-making process is possible because of architectural descriptions. These descriptions allow systematical reasoning in terms of the actual goals of the system, rather than ad-hoc about low-level, indirect indicators.

Regarding external validity, the main concern might be the limited scope of our study, since it is restricted to:

1. A particular class of systems. Our results are set in the context of DCAS and Rainbow. Generalization requires experimenting with further types of controllers and systems. However, despite the recent appearance of other frameworks for developing self-adaptive systems [27, 2], Rainbow is the only one that has been widely available and evaluated in real-world scenarios [11, 8].

2. A set of (representative) change scenarios. This restriction stems from the large number of potential changes (especially in complex systems). This is an issue pervasive to many testing techniques in which not all inputs to or paths through a program can be tested. In practice, many of the changes identified by DCAS engineers present a low probability of occurrence or have a low impact in the system. Hence, the adequate use of a risk-based approach analogous to the Software Risk Evaluation (SRE) method, proposed by SEI, enables the selection of the most representative change scenarios.

7. RELATED WORK

There are some recent contributions that deal with the evaluation of self-adaptive systems.

The criteria for evaluation of adaptive properties presented in [20] and [30] aim at assessing the impact of self-* properties on different aspects of the system, such as, performance, in addition to comparing the adaptive features of different systems. Concretely, the criteria in [20] are grouped in different categories, among which "run-time evaluation" is the one that has a stronger relation with resilience. The definition of the different criteria relies on concepts such as *self-* situations* and *nominal situation*, comparable to NCOPs and COP, respectively (even if they are not formally defined).

The set of metrics presented in [26] aims at evaluating the adaptability of software at the architectural level, defining a relationship between the values of the proposed metrics and QoS levels that the system must guarantee. Although this approach is intended to help architects in the generation of adaptable architectures at development-time, the authors propose as future work its integration at run-time, extending it with the metrics presented in [20].

Other contributions, based either on probabilistic modeling or direct measurement of an existing system rely on the analysis of non-functional properties. Modeling approaches are useful during development, but heavily rely on parameter estimations obtained from domain experts or existing similar systems. For instance, Calinescu and Kwiatkowska [5] introduce an autonomic architecture that uses Markov-chain quantitative analysis to dynamically adjust the parameters of an IT system according to its environment and goals. However, this approach requires the specification of Markov-chains for describing the probabilistic behavior of components of the system. Concerning direct measurement, Epifani *et al.* [16] present a framework to keep models alive updating their internal parameters with run-time data. The framework uses Discrete-Time Markov Chains (DTMCs) and Queuing Networks to reason about reliability and performance. The approach by Calinescu *et al.* [4] combines [5] and [16] for defining a framework for developing adaptive service-based systems in which QoS requirements are translated into probabilistic temporal logic formulae used for identifying optimal system configurations.

Our resilience evaluation framework focuses on quantitative analysis using measurements, and does not assume the existence of Markov-chains describing the behavior of system components. Moreover, while other proposals deal with estimates of the future system behavior for optimizing its operation, our approach focuses on evaluating levels of confidence *w.r.t.* the self-adaptive capabilities of the system.

Another area related to resilience evaluation is resilience benchmarking, which encompasses techniques from prior efforts in performance [18], dependability [21], and security benchmarking [29]. Compared to established benchmarks, a resilience benchmark is specified following the same basic approach, but comprising a wide-ranging changeload (including, but not limited to, faults) and resilience metrics [1].

In our study, we use an architecture-based framework that evaluates by comparison the resilience of adaptation mechanisms of a self-adaptive software system [7].

8. CONCLUSIONS

In this paper, we have reported on our experience evaluating the resilience of a self-adaptive industrial middleware (DCAS) employed for collecting and processing data in highly populated networks of devices. Concretely, we have compared the resilience of the original version of DCAS (Original DCAS) in which adaptation mechanisms are implemented as embedded code-based logic, against a version in which adaptation is performed by an external controller implemented using the Rainbow framework (Rainbow-DCAS), which relies on architecture-based self-adaptation.

The empirical evidence of this evaluation indicates a positive impact of architecture-based self-adaptation on resilience, showing a substantial increment in the resilience values obtained in Rainbow-DCAS *w.r.t.* Original DCAS. In particular, resilience evaluation results regarding performance reveal a much faster recovery of acceptable performance levels in half of the scenarios used for our experiments. These results are consistent with the measures obtained for general run-time evaluation criteria and availability, which also show a remarkable improvement in Rainbow-DCAS, thus reinforcing the results of resilience evaluation.

We identified two main factors that influence improvement in resilience evaluation results in the case of Rainbow-DCAS. First, the controller has access to a global picture of the state of the system and its environment, reflected in the architecture model of the system updated at run-time. This enables faster anomaly detection and better-informed decision making based on an explicit model of the expected behavior of the system *vs.* the use of low-level, local information that is only an indirect indicator of whether the system goals are being met. Second, the fact that the adaptation logic resides within a control layer external to the target system reduces its vulnerability to failures at the target system. This can be observed if we consider for instance the crash of a component in Original DCAS that includes embedded adaptation logic. In such cases, not only the capability of proper repair cannot be relied upon (since part of the adaptation logic is compromised), but even if the system can recover, the affected part of the adaptation logic has to be restarted, requiring a ramp-up period until it achieves stable operation.

Regarding future work, we plan on: (i) investigating how further run-time evaluation criteria for adaptive properties presented in [20] and [30] can be instanced in the context of our resilience evaluation framework, and (ii) evaluate these additional properties in DCAS. Studying such properties in the context of DCAS will not only enable us to explore any potential correlations between resilience and adaptive properties, but will also provide further evidence about the potential improvement on other adaptive properties resulting from incorporating architecture-based self-adaptation. Finally, we also plan to include other controller types and systems to confirm the generality of our results.

9. ACKNOWLEDGMENTS

Co-financed by the Foundation for Science and Technology via project CMU-PT/ELE/0030/2009 and by FEDER via the "Programa Operacional Factores de Competitividade" of QREN with COMPETE reference: FCOMP-01-0124-FEDER-012983.

10. REFERENCES

[1] R. Almeida and M. Vieira. Changeloads for resilience benchmarking of self-adaptive systems: A risk-based approach. In *EDCC*. IEEE, 2012.

[2] R. Asadollahi, M. Salehie, and L. Tahvildari. Starmx: A framework for developing self-managing java-based systems. In *SEAMS*. IEEE, 2009.

[3] C. Baier and J.-P. Katoen. *Principles of Model Checking*. MIT Press, 2008.

[4] R. Calinescu et al. Dynamic QoS Management and Optimization in Service-Based Systems. *IEEE Trans. Software Eng.*, 37(3), 2011.

[5] R. Calinescu and M. Z. Kwiatkowska. Using Quantitative Analysis to Implement Autonomic IT Systems. In *ICSE*. IEEE, 2009.

[6] J. Cámara and R. de Lemos. Evaluation of Resilience in Self-Adaptive Systems Using Probabilistic Model-Checking. In *SEAMS*. IEEE, 2012.

[7] J. Cámara et al. Architecture-based resilience evaluation for self-adaptive systems. *Computing*, 95(8), 2013.

[8] J. Cámara et al. Evolving an Adaptive Industrial Software System to Use Architecture-based Self-Adaptation. In *SEAMS*. IEEE, 2013.

[9] J. Cámara et al. Robustness evaluation of controllers in self-adaptive software systems. In *LADC*. IEEE, 2013.

[10] B. H. Cheng et al. SEfSAS. volume 5525 of *LNCS*, chapter Software Engineering for Self-Adaptive Systems: A Research Roadmap. Springer, 2009.

[11] S.-W. Cheng et al. Evaluating the Effectiveness of the Rainbow Self-Adaptive System. In *SEAMS*. IEEE, 2009.

[12] S.-W. Cheng and D. Garlan. Stitch: A language for architecture-based self-adaptation. *J. Syst. Software*, 85(12), 2012.

[13] R. de Lemos et al. Software Engineering for Self-Adaptive Systems: A Second Research Roadmap. In *SEfSAS 2*, number 7475 in LNCS. Springer, 2012.

[14] M. B. Dwyer et al. Patterns in Property Specifications for Finite-State Verification. In *ICSE*, 1999.

[15] E. A. Emerson and E. M. Clarke. Using branching time temporal logic to synthesize synchronization skeletons. *Sci. Comput. Program.*, 2(3), 1982.

[16] I. Epifani et al. Model Evolution by Run-Time Parameter Adaptation. In *ICSE*. IEEE CS, 2009.

[17] D. Garlan et al. Rainbow: Architecture-Based Self-Adaptation with Reusable Infrastructure. *IEEE Computer*, 37(10), 2004.

[18] J. Gray. *Benchmark Handbook: For Database and Transaction Processing Systems*. Morgan Kaufmann, 1992.

[19] L. Grunske. Specification Patterns for Probabilistic Quality Properties. In *ICSE*. ACM, 2008.

[20] E. Kaddoum et al. Criteria for the evaluation of self-* systems. In *SEAMS*. ACM, 2010.

[21] K. Kanoun and L. Spainhower. *Dependability Benchmarking for Computer Systems*. Wiley-IEEE Computer Society Pr, 2008.

[22] J. O. Kephart and D. M. Chess. The vision of autonomic computing. *Computer*, 36, 2003.

[23] J. Kramer and J. Magee. Self-managed systems: an architectural challenge. In *FOSE*, 2007.

[24] J.-C. Laprie. From Dependability to Resilience. In *DSN Fast Abstracts*. IEEE CS, 2008.

[25] P. Oreizy et al. An architecture-based approach to self-adaptive software. *IEEE Intell. Syst.*, 14, 1999.

[26] D. Perez-Palacin et al. Software architecture adaptability metrics for qos-based self-adaptation. In *QoSA/ISARCS*. ACM, 2011.

[27] G. Tamura et al. Improving context-awareness in self-adaptation using the dynamico reference model. In *SEAMS*, 2013.

[28] M. Vieira and H. Madeira. A dependability benchmark for oltp application environments. In *VLDB*. VLDB Endowment, 2003.

[29] M. Vieira and H. Madeira. Towards a security benchmark for database management systems. In *DSN*. IEEE CS, 2005.

[30] N. M. Villegas et al. A framework for evaluating quality-driven self-adaptive software systems. In *SEAMS*. ACM, 2011.

[31] D. Weyns and T. Ahmad. Claims and evidence for architecture-based self-adaptation: A systematic literature review. In *ECSA*, volume 7957 of *LNCS*. Springer, 2013.

[32] R. Williams et al. *Software Risk Evaluation (SRE) Method Description: Version 2.0*. CMU-SEI, 1999.

Architecture Management and Evaluation in Mature Products: Experiences from a Lightweight Approach

Mikko Raatikainen
Department of Computer
Science and Engineering
Aalto University
Finland
mikko.raatikainen@aalto.fi

Juha Savolainen
Danfoss
Denmark
juhaerik.savolainen
@danfoss.com

Tomi Männistö
University of Helsinki
Finland
tomi.mannisto@cs.helsinki.fi

ABSTRACT

Software architecture evaluation is an essential part of architecture management and a means to uncover problems and increase confidence in the capability of the software architecture in fulfilling the most critical requirements. Architecture evaluation is typically carried out at an early stage of a software development. However, development efforts are often related to further development of existing software. We present a case study of the software architecture board (SWAB) initiative carried out at in a company called NSN. SWAB employed a lightweight architecture evaluation and management approach to exchange architectural experiences with related products and assess ability to fulfill future requirements. SWAB operated for two years but ultimately came to an end because the desired objectives were not achieved. The case study provides lessons for the evaluation of architecture in mature products and for using a lightweight evaluation approach: Evaluation in mature products seems not to be about finding problems and risk or making trade-offs, but about architecture management such as better communication, raising awareness about the architecture, and increased confidence to the architecture throughout the organization; and a lightweight architecture evaluation seems to be a good approach especially for mature products. However, the motivation and justification for architectural evaluation of mature products remains challenging, as their architecture is already in place and evolved over years towards good candidates, although the need for inter-product communication and alignment of architectural issues can be argued for.

Categories and Subject Descriptors

D.2.9 [**Software Engineering**]: Management

Keywords

architecture evaluation; architecture management; case study; software architecture

Permission to make digital or hard copies of all or part of this work for personal or classroom use is granted without fee provided that copies are not made or distributed for profit or commercial advantage and that copies bear this notice and the full citation on the first page. Copyrights for components of this work owned by others than ACM must be honored. Abstracting with credit is permitted. To copy otherwise, or republish, to post on servers or to redistribute to lists, requires prior specific permission and/or a fee. Request permissions from permissions@acm.org.
QoSA'14, June 30–July 4, 2014, Marcq-en-Baroeul, France.
Copyright 2014 ACM 978-1-4503-2576-9/14/06 ...$15.00.
http://dx.doi.org/10.1145/2602576.2602583.

1. INTRODUCTION

Software architecture can be understood as the fundamental structures of a system, and in addition, to capture the fundamental understanding of the system in its domain [16]. Furthermore, a software architect is responsible for all the important issues that need to be dealt with during the design of a system [12], and makes and provides rationale for the architectural design decisions that lead to the structures [17].

In the management of software architecture, architecture evaluation is an approach to examine, rather than design, existing or planned architecture in terms of how well the architecture accommodates current and future requirements [10, 2]. The main purposes of architecture evaluation include to uncover problems, or if no problems are discovered, to increase the level of confidence in the architecture [4]. In particular, architecture evaluation aims to assess non-functional characteristics, such as reliability, maintainability and performance, of a system [25][8][18]. Architecture evaluation has been identified as one of the three essential activities of software architecture design in addition to architectural analysis and architectural synthesis [15]. From the reports about specific architecture evaluation methods, SAAM [20] being the earliest one and ATAM [21] being most likely the best known one, the field has matured to the categorization of different approaches for architecture evaluation [6], comparison of specific evaluation methods [12][9][13][3], combining methods for architecture evaluation [6][19], and reports about empirical evidence about architecture evaluation in industrial application [1][23][30].

The existing architecture evaluation methods, which are often accompanied with reports about experiences, often carry out the evaluation in the early stages of a development project, even before implementation, on the basis of documentation or models since implementation has not been yet started and, thus, does not exist yet [7][5][32]. However, although the effort involved in architecture evaluation is not necessarily large compared with the size of an entire project [4], an evaluation often seems to be considered time-consuming or heavyweight and, therefore, is rarely done in practice at least following specific methodologies [1][3][30][30]. This may be because, even if the evaluation itself is not especially laborious, the preparations can also require significant effort. In fact, there seems to be a call for more lightweight approaches [30]: For example, although the recent agile and lean architecture practices are increasingly lightweight [8], focus is mostly on new product development rather than on architecture evaluation and management.

Moreover, the software development effort in industry is often targeted to maintenance or further development for existing software, but the basic functionality of the existing software, which is stabilized over the years, remains relatively unchanged. Such products that already implement the basic functionality are not under pressure for drastic changes and requirements do not constantly change, are referred here as *mature products*. The development efforts typically focus on implementing new requirements on top of the basic functionality. Nevertheless, these products are also under time and cost pressures so that development practices need to be efficient and effective.

In such mature products, architecture evaluation starts from different premises than in new product development: even if for the existing software the required information for evaluation, such as models or documentation, does not exist in appropriate forms, the software, as implemented, can be evaluated. Moreover, the existing models and documents can be used and their validity can be assessed against the implementation. Thus, for the existing software, the role and nature of architecture evaluation can be different than for newly-designed software: the evaluation of planned software on the basis of specifications versus the evaluation of the design of an existing implementation. However, little has been reported on architecture evaluation of mature products especially in a lightweight manner.

We provide a case study about the operationalization and experiences of the software architecture board (SWAB) as a lightweight approach to architecture evaluation and management for existing mature products that the company called NSN had been developing for several years. SWAB was developed and applied internally at NSN while this study is about SWAB by a means of a case study research approach [31, 26]. Architecture evaluation was a central activity and key in the original objectives in SWAB. Yet, compared with typical architecture evaluation approaches, architecture evaluation in SWAB was relatively lightweight especially in terms of time spent but also in terms of total effort including preparations as well as required and specified practices. The primary aim set for SWAB was to yield significant architectural advice regarding the alignment with architecture objectives. This aim of SWAB was not met as such, and in hindsight, can be considered overly ambitious or unrealistic for such mature products in question. SWAB was, nevertheless, operated for two years. However after that, the other benefits and contributions, such as communication and explicating architecture, realized with SWAB were not valued enough or deemed exhausted to justify the continuation. Thus, we give an in-depth account of the SWAB approach including appropriateness of having such a board, as well as its limitations. Moreover, on the basis of the findings about experiences and lessons learned we discuss the lightweight architecture evaluation as well as the architecture evaluation of mature products.

The paper is organized as follows. In Section 2, we describe NSN and its product lines as the subject of the study. Section 3 describes the applied case study method. An account of practices in SWAB is given in Section 4 and the experiences from SWAB are highlighted in Section 5. The lessons learned from SWAB in terms of light-weight evaluation approach for mature products are described in Section 6. Section 7 discusses the results and provides comparison with related work while Section 8 discusses construct, internal and external validity, and reliability. Section 9 draws the conclusions.

2. CASE COMPANY: NSN

NSN (Nokia Solutions and Networks) is a part of Nokia: Earlier NSN was Nokia Networks and then after a joint corporation with Siemens (Nokia Siemens Networks) but now again owned by Nokia. NSN is made up of several business units and employs thousands people having operations globally.

The business units are responsible for product lines consisting of several products. Each product line delivers different elements of a mobile phone or other kind of radio network. Thus, the products typically contain hardware and software parts but the focus of this study is only the software part of the products. The product lines together provide all the necessary elements for a telecommunication operator to construct an operational network although elements from other vendors can also be used. In fact, many telecommunication operators use various elements from several vendors in their network infrastructure. Interoperability between different vendors is in practice achieved by standardization. The products and the product lines are long-lived: For example, the operation time of an installed product can be over ten years.

Development in NSN is conducted in the so-called programs that create iterations to product line development. Typically, programs implement new requirements on top of unchanged basic functionality. The product lines of NSN had become relatively independent of each other being developed by separate organizations although cooperation, such as reuse, had been encouraged.

3. RESEARCH METHOD

We conducted a case study [31, 26] to capture the objectives, realization, and experiences of SWAB. The case study was carried out post-mortem meaning that SWAB was already discontinued. The objectives were to form an account about the entire SWAB life-cycle.

The research data is based on interviews, archival material and first-hand experiences. We carried out a two-hour interview with one of the key facilitators and participants of SWAB. The interview was transcribed for the analysis. The interview was open-ended rather than structured in a sense that predefined questions were not prepared but the interview was planned to thematically follow practices that took place in SWAB. The focus was on unclear issues but also confirmations that both emerged especially from the analysis of archival data about SWAB. The archival data included the minutes for the meeting covering seventeen SWAB workshops and supporting slide presentations describing SWAB principles. In practice, the latter covered all instructions that were prescribed about operations in SWAB. Finally, one of the authors had participated in SWAB actively such as in defining the principles for the above mentioned presentation. Therefore, he hold first-hand experience of the practices.

The data analysis was carried out following the principles adopted from Grounded Theory [28, 29] with an aim to generate an account about SWAB identifying commonalities by saturating data around common patterns as well as identify exceptions as specialties. The analysis was carried to the research data that all was produced into textual form. The analysis was validated by providing NSN a possibility to review the analysis results. We also compared our findings with the existing accounts about architecture evaluation reported in the literature.

4. DESCRIPTION OF SWAB

In the following, we give an account about setting up and objectives of SWAB followed by an account of operationalization and practices over the operational period of two years.

4.1 Objectives of SWAB

The SWAB charter stated the objectives of SWAB that was agreed upon and supported by management as follows:

> *Under the supervision of [management], SWAB gives advice on whether technical decisions in a starting program are aligned with architecture objectives.*

The practical and main means to meet these objectives were architecture evaluation of the products.

This generic objective was further refined. First, SWAB was to define NSN's general software architecture objectives based on strategic business drivers. SWAB was also mandated to maintain information about architectural issues. Second, SWAB was to advise selected programs. The responsibilities included close cooperation with the programs throughout the program's life-cycle; early involvement in the plans and requirements of the programs; validation that architectural requirements, drivers, and risks had been handled properly; and the provision of the advice and recommendations of the course of the actions based on NSN's general architecture objectives. Third, SWAB was to improve general architectural awareness and practices internally within NSN: For example SWAB was a means to facilitate cooperation, share good practices and lessons learned, and advise competence development efforts. Furthermore, because programs were from practically all different product units of NSN and needed to collaborate with SWAB, the architectural practices were expected to gradually become unified and compliant with SWAB practices across all programs and product lines.

We also uncovered unofficial objectives in which the focus was slightly different. For example, there were actually no real concerns or lack of trust about the capabilities of the architects to design good architecture or notice risks, or problems. Thus, it was unclear if an oversight board was needed, and it remained questionable whether or not anything critical was expected to be found. In fact, an unofficial objective, or hidden agenda, was to actually develop, test, and establish practices for lightweight architecture evaluation in order to keep track of the progress and plans of different programs. However, the existing evaluation methods such as ATAM were not considered feasible for mature products because they were too heavyweight and documentation-oriented. In general, more lightweight and transparent practices were needed. A final objective — one that was even more ambitious than the unified practices found in the SWAB charter — was to work toward a uniform architecture for NSN and even facilitate reuse between programs. In the end, these unofficial objectives largely shaped the actual practices of SWAB.

The role of SWAB was to be a technical advisory body rather than to make decisions. The aim was to be in close contact with the business units and to provide recommendations from a technological perspective, but decisions were left to the responsible business unit. The technical perspective meant focusing on architecture, and the technologies and practices related to architecture, rather than on organizational, business, or project management issues, such as milestones or resources. Nevertheless, SWAB was to be valued and all programs would request an audit, especially if they wanted guidance or anticipated problems. The management supported SWAB and was active in intiating SWAB.

4.2 Practices of SWAB

SWAB operated using half- to full-day workshops consisting of roughly an opening session, a special session, and an architecture evaluation session. During the opening session, recent news, rumors, and general problems were discussed openly without a predefined agenda. Special sessions, which were not always included, presented a specific topic of interest for SWAB members such as advances in specific technology or new methods for development.

Each architecture evaluation was based on the presentation, questions, and discussion about the architecture of a specific product that a program was developing. The questions that were raised led to the clarifications, further explanations or confirmations, and identification of potential issues. The presentations and questions were interwoven, but each took roughly an hour so that each architecture evaluation took in total roughly two hours.

The architecture presentation was advised to be light-weight, with short preparations as summarized by the slide in Figure 1a. In practice, the preparation effort was typically estimated to be less than a day. In fact, existing material could be used if such material existed in an appropriate form resulting minimal preparations. The presentation adhered to state-of-the-practice architecture presentation guidelines rather than requiring specific expertise, such as notations. There were also example templates (Figure 1b) to ensure the coverage of relevant characteristics and usage of appropriate conventions for architecture presentation. For example, a presentation was expected to include a diagram that showed the main runtime elements of the architecture and the context in which the product operated. In total, each presentation contained five to ten diagram slides.

The core team members of SWAB, meaning the people who were present several times, seemed to consist of thirteen members. However, SWAB was a secondary responsibility for all members who worked primarily in other organizational units and, therefore, were not able to always participate. Two key people established SWAB and later also acted as facilitators. On the one hand, the core team included architects who were working with and experts on a specific product line. A few of the members used to be architects but were, at the time, in managerial positions. All business units were relatively well-represented. On the other hand, the core team also included experts from supporting organizational units, such as the corporate research unit. Those invited to be on the core team were technically knowledgeable, had extensive experience with products, and were able and willing to express their opinions and share knowledge. Most of the core team members were familiar with each other from past working relationships.

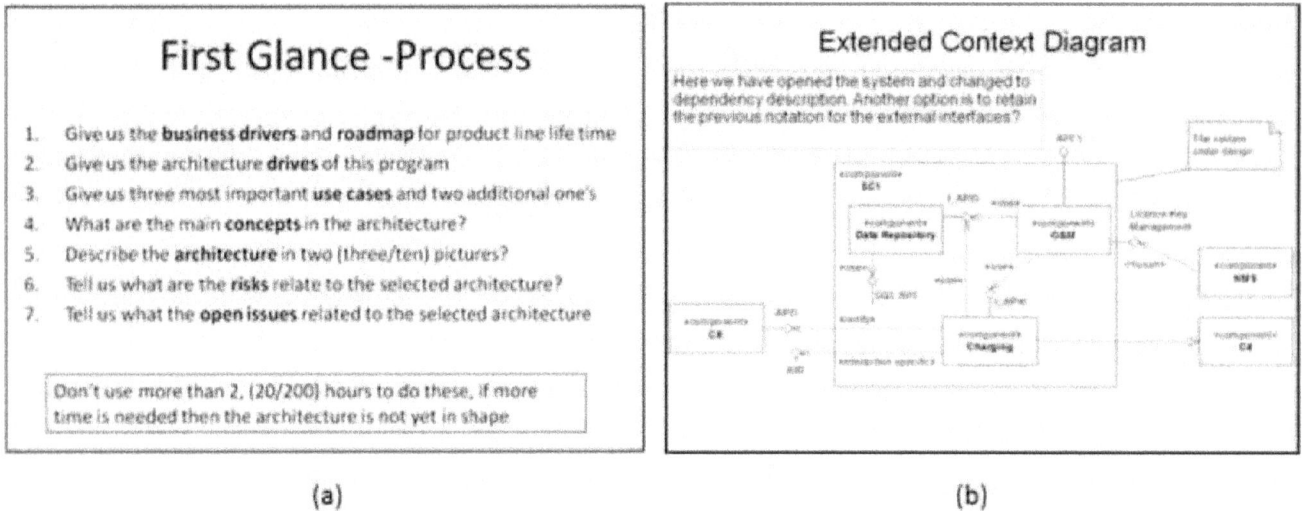

Figure 1: Example slides from the SWAB guidelines representing (a) guidelines for presentation and (b) an example diagram.

Several other people attended some of the workshops. Typically, an architect of a program presented a specific product sometimes accompanied by a few coworkers. Sometimes, independent experts gave presentations in the special sessions.

Each workshop resulted in documentation in the form of an architecture presentation given in the SWAB workshop and the minutes for the meeting. The minutes for the meeting included a concluding statement, possible recommendations resulting from the architecture evaluation, and a summary of the discussion. The minutes for the meeting were available for a wider audience but were not actively distributed. In fact, material from SWAB seemed to be read rarely people not actively participating in SWAB. Finally, some unofficial discussions took place and separate notes were created for confidential content.

The selection criteria of programs defined for SWAB evaluation were that the programs were developing a new product or a significant architectural change, a source of large expected revenues, a large resource investment, or a spearhead program. However, only one new product was eventually included in the evaluation workshops. Thus, practically all products were mature. Moreover, the domain stable was so few of the programs actually were even undergoing a drastic change. In the end, management also affected to the selection of the products.

To sum up, SWAB workshops were lightweight. There were few enforced or defined practices except the loose guidelines for the architecture presentation. Even the presentation guidelines just required the state-of-the-practice view-based documentation of a software architecture (cf. Figure 1b) rather than specifying a special notation. The SWAB workshops relied largely on peer-level expert discussion rather than defined or strict practices. The preparation effort was small: the architect needed to prepare the architecture presentation while for the others there were no preparations so that time spent at the individual level was just the workshop day that typically covered two product lines. Even for the architecture presentation, existing diagrams or material could be used because guidelines did not enforce a specific

kind of presentation in detail. However, cumulative expert time can be considered moderate due to the number of experts involved. That is, even if less than a day was used in preparations, the workshop involving more than ten participants accumulated the required expert-time.

5. EXPERIENCES OF SWAB

SWAB lasted roughly two years; during those two years, seventeen SWAB workshops was held, each with roughly ten participants. In total, eighteen products were evaluated including one new product and seventeen existing and mature products.

The first three workshops were more about setting up SWAB and agreeing on the mode of operation. It became soon evident that the presentations needed more detailed guidelines such example diagrams (cf. Figure 1b). The guidelines were introduced relatively early and adjusted over time. However, SWAB was not able to develop guidelines that, alone, would have ensured successful architecture presentations. Instead, the experience was that the architects needed to be coached in order to have the right focus in their presentations. A proper coach was identified to be a member of core SWAB team that worked in the same program or product line as the presenting architect. However, this was not tried in practice.

Small adjustments were made occasionally also afterward to the practices of SWAB. For example, in the seventh workshop, it was decided to add more time for the architecture evaluations, request the material beforehand, and assign special roles for SWAB members so that each could focus on a specific characteristic such as security or performance issues.

Nevertheless, the pre-defined practices that the presenters needed to adhere to remained relatively informal similarly as did the entire format. For example, the sixth workshop contained only several special sessions and there was no architecture evaluation.

After the first year and thirteen workshops, workshops were not organized for six months. The reason for the break was a decision that was made after the completed evaluations of initially-identified programs and certain frustrations regarding the results. The first workshops after the break were still successful, but later, fewer participants attended and evaluations were no longer prepared. Workshops were no longer organized, although SWAB was not yet officially terminated. At the same time, major organization changes took place, adding to employee workload and it seems that the reorganization caused changes and uncertainties that contributed to the final breakdown of SWAB.

The first SWAB workshops ended with high expectations for significant contributions, as expressed in a conclusion of the minutes for the meeting:

> "Feedback from [the management], SWAB is in the right track."

The first SWAB workshops discussed how to communicate with the business units and ensure management support for findings and conclusions. For the new product, major changes were actually recommended because the plans and requirements were considered unrealistically laborious and expectations for use too ambitious. However, in later evaluations, SWAB failed to uncover any significant issues with products, often offering general conclusions such as the following:

> "Architecture seems well thought out and suited for the purpose."

Because recommendations were not given, the initial main working mode of SWAB to evaluate architecture resulting in significant contributions, and advices or recommendations was gradually considered insignificant and even unsuccessful. This was in fact inline with one of the hidden assumption. On the one hand, the presenting architects were familiar with the products, unlike the listeners who often needed to ask simple questions. Simply gaining general understanding about the architecture required a major part of the presentation, reducing the amount of time that would have been spent on discussing architectural issues relevant and interesting for the presenting architect. On the other hand, even when potential issues were identified by SWAB members, they were not unknown to the presenting architect and solutions had already been considered. That is, despite the fact that SWAB consisted of highly experienced engineers, SWAB could not provide much direct guidance to the architects who had been tackling with problems and potential solutions for years. The added confidence to and verification of the architecture were not immediate, tangible, or large enough contributions. Typically, minor issues were brought up, but the perceived direct benefits were not as expected. For a product, working under high cost pressure, easy actions to changes were not found. Although SWAB participants tried to adjust the mode of operation by focusing on specific issues such as specific quality attributes and adjusting the template, the outcomes remained relatively similar.

Although SWAB did not find new issues, the discussions explicated relevant issues identified by a group of experienced architects, which were even recorded in the minutes for the meeting. Despite the fact that these issues were typically known by the architect or even trivial, the knowledge was mostly tacit and was being shared only among the members of a small team within the program. Sometimes, initial plans for corrective actions already existed, but such plans were similarly tacit and not being explicated anywhere before SWAB.

In fact, discussions about the architecture per se became more relevant than trying to discover new findings. Typically, discussions concerned rationales and design decisions that were previously only known by the architect and few others but were now summarized in the minutes for the meeting and architecture presentation. For instance, the following exchange took place in one of these discussions explicating rationales behind strategy to upgrade software:

> "Q: Upgrades without down-time?
> A: No, too expensive: OK to be down."

In these kinds of discussions, a special focus was paid on the quality attributes:

> "Q: Is this a performance problem?
> A: No the bottleneck seems to be the [database] server side."

Although the general format of SWAB remained relatively similar, there were in practice difference in the architecture evaluations because of the differences in the presentations. Some architects gave only a general overview, whereas others were well-prepared. Some architects presented the architecture in a good light, whereas others focused on problematic issues in the architecture. The differences in focus seemed to be due to lack of preparation time rather than, e.g., being afraid of judgmental discussion.

Paradoxically, those architects who came best prepared gained the least. Careful preparations did not result in better outcomes. The focus did not seem that relevant to evaluation outcomes, although focusing on issues resulted in somewhat greater benefit. It was reported that well-prepared presentations did not provoke as much discussion and, therefore, the benefits were minor. Well-prepared presentations pointed out not only issues in the architecture but also the solutions the architects had already considered. The presentation of thoroughly analyzed design decisions did not leave much room for discussion, even with experienced architects being the evaluators.

Beyond architecture evaluation, SWAB workshops provided value by facilitating the sharing of experience and technologies between different product lines. Because the SWAB members represented different organizational units, they were able to point out products with similar problems or solutions in other product lines as well as share their knowledge of specific technologies. SWAB also brought together architects who had struggled with similar problems in order to facilitate the sharing of knowledge and experience with problems as well as group problem solving. Thus, cooperation between product lines was initiated, which had diminished to a large extent. However, the cooperation did not reach the level of software reuse or common architecture across groups as originally was in the objectives. Similarly, SWAB did not operate long enough to achieve the objectives of common practices or the envisioned common architecture. In the end, the general software architecture objectives received little attention in SWAB.

Nevertheless, the general format of one-day workshops that occurred less than dozen times a year seemed to work well as such. The format was not considered to hinder the findings; the mature architectures were thoroughly considered and evolved towards a good candidate.

Similarly, the overall format of including an opening session, a special session, and an evaluation was regarded successful. In particular, the special sessions were interesting and members were motivated to participate because these sessions efficiently covered relatively advanced topics among other experts.

Otherwise, the participants were busy with their primary responsibilities in their respective programs, which meant they had limited time and scheduling problems, although in general, the effort to make time was not deemed inconveniently high.

On the one hand, the lack of a decision-making role and being secondary responsibility was challenging; at the best, SWAB could persuade management or provide support in communication with management. On the other hand, the lack of decision-making power was considered successful and good characteristics of SWAB because they allowed SWAB to focus on the technology. Despite the focus on technology, discussions remained relevant because the architects were cost-aware, rejecting excessively costly or laborious hypothetical solutions.

6. FINDINGS ABOUT LESSONS LEARNED

We elaborate in the following the findings in terms of lessons learned about the SWAB experiences and discuss about these findings more in the next section. This means lightweight architectural evaluation in mature products primarily focusing on technical issues.

6.1 Unknown Findings of Evaluation Are Rare or Irrelevant

When evaluating the architecture of a mature product, the findings, such as risks or problems that the evaluators make are rarely unknown or surprising for the responsible architect. Most of the novel findings seem even to be irrelevant; that is, they suggest small improvements or changes that do not have any significant effects on the entire system. Alternatively, the previously unknown risks are so improbable that preparation for the realization of risks may require unfeasible large effort.

In the case of a mature product, the architects have gained thorough understanding of the architecture in question over the years and the architecture has been shaped and improved over many years towards a good candidate. Mature architecture can have issues, but often, these issues are already widely known — for example, when the architecture has become obsolete and requires refactoring.

6.2 Evaluation Explicates Architectural Knowledge for Wider Audience

Even though they are rarely unknown, the findings, such as issues or risks, are not necessarily widely known and are explicated during the discussions in the evaluation for a wider audience. Over time, knowledge seems easily become tacit or is considered self-evident by the architects. This tacit knowledge includes design rationales, the key points of architecture, technical evolution and roadmaps, and technical problems or shortcomings of the architecture. The developers who are unfamiliar with the technical details of the product, such as those from other organizational units, new

recruits, or even management, cannot be aware of such tacit knowledge. Inherently, such tacit knowledge is not documented or documented scarcely, at best.

The documentation produced during the evaluations seems to provide a relatively efficient overview of the architecture. That is, even a short presentation of architecture in lightweight evaluation summarizes the key points, while the discussions with the other architects highlight what has been considered self-evident and omitted from the presentation. Thus, documentation of these discussions provided beneficial explications of previously tacit or little-known information.

6.3 Benefits Are Mutual

In contrast to new product development in which few or no solutions actually exist, mature products have existing and tested designs. The evaluated architecture can adopt solutions from other products, but the evaluation itself also facilitates the sharing of solutions and experiences across product lines, making the benefits mutual. The areas of shared knowledge include architectural practices, good and bad principles of design, and even reuse of software between product lines.

However, a key challenge then includes to communicate and disseminate the results of architecture evaluation. Otherwise the benefits remain among the evaluators: For example, architectural knowledge was primarily shared just a handful of people participating in the SWAB evaluation workshops.

6.4 Contributions Are Rarely Immediate

The nature of the previously explicated contributions means that, in practice, direct and immediate contributions or actions take place rarely. A typical contribution of an evaluation over time is growing awareness and confidence about software architecture and the implementation of planned requirements. The architect is then also supported by a larger audience in making decisions. Similarly, architectural practice and principles of design make their way to other products with a delay.

6.5 Lightweight Approach Is Sufficient

A lightweight evaluation approach seems to be in mature products often sufficient compared to more heavyweight approaches because, although the expected results do not seem to differ, the required effort is significantly smaller. The observation that less thorough presentations were more fruitful than well-prepared presentations also suggests that adding effort does not directly result in significant additional benefits. Rather, additional effort in preparations seems to increase expectations. Moreover, well prepared presentations seemed to come with well thought out solutions in mind. This leaves less room for the desired open dialogue. Thus, a more thorough evaluation seems to result in different kinds of contributions that are not necessarily more valuable, because the existing implementation limits alternative solutions. The focus of preparations seem to be more significant than the effort spent for the preparations: the preparations should focus on relevant aspects and concerns that can result in fruitful discussion. In a similar manner, more time spent in evaluation does not seem to directly result in more significant findings.

In the end, the number of findings could increase with more thorough evaluations and preparations, but considering that novel significant findings are rare, increased thoroughness may result in an increase in the number of insignificant findings rather than significant ones. In fact, one of the evaluated products was new and the contributions of the evaluation resembled results similar to what is expected of a more thorough evaluation.

6.6 Only Simple Guidelines Are Required

SWAB operated as a lightweight workshop with practically no special or enforced guidelines. There was basically only very general guidelines for architecture presentation that should adhere to the state-of-practice architecture documentation. Because the SWAB as an method was not considered sufficient and the results are more tied with the maturity of products and software architecture, it seems that additional guideline would not have resulted in significant improvements. Rather, it seems to be enough to be advised to use the state-of-practice methods when it can be expected that existing material can be taken advantages of, thus saving effort in preparations. The discontinuation of SWAB seemed not be due to methods and practices applied but rather on the expectations and role of SWAB.

6.7 Organizational Issues Become a Key Challenge

A major challenge in architecture evaluation is motivating people to commit themselves and to contribute. This can be especially true when the evaluation and evaluated product is not the primary responsibility of the architects involved because they primarily work with other products. The challenge for motivating is emphasized by the nature of evaluation results being indirect and intangible. However, experienced technical staff members seem to be even harder to motivate for more heavyweight approaches.

A challenge is also to find the right people. In order to carry out evaluations, the evaluators need to be familiar with the requirements and the existing implementations of products. On the one hand, in order to make an objective assessment, the evaluators should not be too tightly tied with the existing implementation. On the other hand, SWAB wasted efforts in trivial familiarization with products. In order to streamline the evaluation, the evaluators should familiarize themselves with the product before the evaluation. One approach that was proposed, but not applied in practice, is that preliminary introduction to the product would be made by someone other than the architect, possibly even in a separate session. A benefit of this approach would be that the technical details are not discussed during this introductory section.

The organizational culture also needs to be open, rather than judgmental or competitive, because the benefits largely depend on peer-level discussion. The architects must dare to describe even the deficiencies in the architecture or past mistakes to be avoided. In fact, many architectural issues often concern wicked problems for which there is not only one solution. Openness should not limit criticism. For example, some SWAB members were sometimes reluctant to be critical of each other because of their existing personal relationships. Such reluctance can seriously limit productive discussion.

7. DISCUSSION AND RELATED WORK

SWAB lasted a while at NSN but gradually discontinued. SWAB essentially in the end failed to achieve the expected primary objectives of, e.g., finding new problems and risks, but at the same time provided other kinds of value to NSN. This, however, was not appreciated or understood at that time. In the light of SWAB, we discuss in the following about lightweight architecture evaluation in mature products. Maturity means here that development is carried out within existing architecture in which the basic functionality has been stabilized over years and the basic features are well known. For example, in the case of SWAB, telecommunications domain is relatively stable and standardized application domain where major changes do not often take place.

In contrast to SWAB, the reported experiences in the literature about evaluating a software architecture are that key issues contributed include assessing the trade-offs especially resulting from different quality attributes, and problems and risks in architecture [5][1]. However, these kinds of experiences are mainly from the evaluation of new products or products facing challenges such as refactoring. In mature products as in the case of SWAB, the design decisions, which are expensive to change, have already been made and design has become stable and known over years. Trade-offs can be just described in terms of design decision taken rather than assessing alternatives. Discussion about making trade-offs and other design alternatives can only be hypothetical or speculative in nature because changes cannot be realistically made due to time and costs constraints.

However, when comparing the experiences of SWAB with applying ATAM to mature products, we observe several similarities: The findings were unsurprising, and minor than expected for the experienced architects, but evaluation resulted in other benefits, such as explicating risks, better communication and raising awareness about the architecture [11]. These kinds of other benefits are observed in addition to above discussed trade-offs, problems and risks also in general [1] and in the evaluation of new projects [23]. Consequently, the evaluation of a mature software architecture seems to result in especially these kinds of benefits.

A similar method to SWAB is the Tiny Architectural Review Approach (TARA) [30] that addresses lightweight evaluation primarily for existing software. The motivation is similar i.e. the organization is reluctant for more thorough architecture evaluation. The accumulated effort seems roughly similar in TARA and SWAB although the former presumes effort from one evaluator while the latter requires effort from a group of evaluators. A notable difference is in the purpose so that SWAB was a more general architecture management and evaluation approach whereas the assessment in TARA is done for a sponsor to answer a specific need: For example, in the TARA case study [30], the ownership and responsibility of the software had changed and the sponsor wanted to know how good the software was. This specific focus might have resulted in that the results of TARA are more concrete. Because one person is responsible for the assessment in TARA, the exchange of architectural knowledge does not seem to take place similarly as in SWAB. Therefore, the assessment is also done more reporting-oriented manner than as a presentation and workshop but both approaches result in roughly the same kind of information having similar guidelines adhering to similar state-of-the-practice methods (cf. Fig 2) although

TARA encourages additionally the analysis of code. The resulting information, and used effort is appreciated in both approaches.

Consequently, it seems that the method of evaluation does not make a large difference in mature products; even a very lightweight and loosely defined method seems to suffice to contribute these kinds of benefits as exemplified by SWAB and TARA: For example, effort was quite small, guidelines really simple, and practices informal. Thus, there is no need for special knowledge or learning new methods. In fact, accumulated experience about architecture review [23] indicates similar benefits taking into account what is expected of mature products but using a significantly higher effort. The experiences of SWAB also highlight that challenges are not in the practices of architecture evaluation per se but, e.g., in communication about results within the organization and finding and motivating the required experts as well as explicating the purpose.

The term lightweight architecture evaluation is used to refer to architecture evaluation practices that take relatively little time and effort, including all preparations. In particular, architecture evaluation is done quickly in a matter of hours. However, lightweight does not mean that total effort, for example, in terms of man-hours of experts, is necessarily very small but merely moderate because several experts are involved in accumulating the total effort. Naturally, the accumulated effort would be smaller if less experts are involved but the effort can be anyway considered significantly smaller than is typical in architecture evaluation methods.

Architecture evaluation in a lightweight manner relies heavily on the knowledge of existing architecture as was in the case of SWAB. Furthermore, SWAB seemed to largely benefit from expert evaluators who were able to cost-conscious manner focus on relevant discussions. In fact, in order to successfully apply a lightweight evaluation approach, the material, such as documents, models, and scenarios, for evaluation would need to be readily available; however, in practice, such documentation rarely exists appropriately. Producing relevant material from the scratch can be quite laborious resulting in a significantly less lightweight approach. Alternatively, architecture evaluation can be based on presentation where the presenter needs to be familiar with the product, have extensive knowledge of the architecture, be able to easily construct relevant material, and be able to answer questions and provide details from the experience. In fact, this was the case of SWAB where presentations were used rather than documents, and the presenting architect was able to provide necessary additional details when needed.

It seems that the failure to, e.g., find unknown problems was not due to the deficiencies of SWAB as an architecture evaluation method or that lightweight approach in general is not adequate. We argued that such problems are unlikely unknown and even if such problems existed, it seems possible that SWAB workshop would have identified those kinds of issues: For example, SWAB quite successfully evaluated the one new product identifying several relevant but unknown problems.

In a case when new problems are discovered and actions are considered a necessity as the result of a lightweight evaluation, then after a more thorough and rigorous analysis could take place using established and well defined evaluation methods or even more formal analyses. These kinds of

methods, however, require more effort, and if there are no issues, the benefits would be similar if applied to all products. Therefore, in the first place, more thorough evaluation does not seem practically feasible for mature products under constant time and money pressure. Lightweight evaluation methods seem more feasible and beneficial to start with compared with heavyweight approaches, at least for mature products in terms of required effort and commitment.

For new product development, the above conditions about knowledge about architecture is unlikely met: Material unlikely fully covers the planned architecture realistically and the architect cannot have yet gained deep experience. The presented architecture can be a candidate, partial, or draft architecture, for example. Therefore, in the case of new product development, the nature of lightweight architecture evaluation and feasibility of generalizing the lessons learned remain open for further studies. Similarly, thorough refactoring, or rewriting software, can be considered a special case that is not included in the scope of mature software development covered in this paper.

In the end, a lightweight architecture evaluation seems to be an approach that is sufficient to apply especially in the case of mature products producing specific kinds of results. However, another point is whether architecture evaluation is profitable or the effort spent is larger than the benefits gained. It seems that evaluation is easier to justify in new product development facing large development investment whereas in mature products uncertainties do not pertain as much to technological risks so that that need for architecture evaluation is more questionable. The profitability of architecture evaluation, in general, remains open and is ambiguous [1][23] due to indirect and unquantifiable benefits such as peer-level discussion and knowledge sharing.

8. VALIDITY AND RELIABILITY

Validity refers to correct relationship between a phenomena and an account as well as more general concepts covering the phenomena [14, 24]. In the following, we discuss validity in terms of the commonly used taxonomy differentiating construct, internal, and external validity [27, 31].

Construct validity refers to valid measures about the phenomena. Threats to construct validity are that the study was carried out after termination of SWAB rather than as a longitudinal and observational study, the limited number of informants, and the limited amount of data. These threats were mitigated by trying triangulate between the two key informants and archival data. For example, the minutes for the meetings provided a chronologically documented archival about phenomena that was possible to asses against the participant's recollections. Finally, the study results indicate similarities with earlier research as discussed in Section 7 thus alleviating some threats to construct validity.

Internal validity refers to the relationships of proposed constructs in terms of causality. The study indicates this kind of relationship merely about discontinuation of SWAB. A threat in uncovering correct relationships remains especially due to the limited sources of information and timing the study after the termination of SWAB. There is not either other similar case or case account available for comparison. On the other hand, the timing provides also insights for past events and to the experience as a whole. These threats were tried to mitigate similarly as in the case of construct validity.

Nevertheless, there can be other underlying hidden causes or confounding variable that were not uncovered in the study. Therefore, the proposed causes remain a proposition that can be an insufficient account about the phenomena.

External validity refers to generalizations about the results [22]. Because the research was carried out as a case study we made theoretical generalization [31] by conceptualizing rather than generalizing to population. The generalizations concern architecture evaluation in mature products and lightweight architecture evaluation. However, the contextual factors where the study was made was software intensive systems containing both software and hardware, mature products that are being maintained and developed long time and in use even over a decade, stable application domain, and very large organization. Thus, applicability of the results beyond these contextual factors remains a hypothesis to be tested.

Reliability refers to the repeatability of a measure [14, 31]. To address reliability, we stored as much original data and measures in order to maintain the chain-of-evidence. For example, we defined and stored the themes of the interview as well as notes, audio recordings, and transcripts.

9. CONCLUSIONS

We gave an account of software architecture board (SWAB) as a lightweight architecture evaluation and management approach at NSN for mature products where the evaluation was the essential and major activity. SWAB operated as expert workshops in a lightweight manner in terms of required guidance and practices. The required preparation effort was minor although accumulated expert time used during the evaluation was moderate due to the number of experts involved.

In the end, SWAB did not realize its original objectives of architecture and requirements management, such as the alignment of product lines with NSN's overall software architecture strategy. As an architecture evaluation approach, SWAB did not meet its expectations and objectives, which seemed to have been misplaced and quite ambitious in the first place: For example, new risks or problems were not found.

SWAB cannot be considered a complete failure but the experiences and lessons learned shed light on the nature of architecture evaluation in mature products that are similar that are found also in the case of new product evaluation. These, however, seemed not to be appreciated or understood at the time. The main contributions typical in new product evaluation such as unknown risks were not found.

Although new risks or problems might not be found and relevant discussion about making trade-offs does not necessarily take place as in the evaluation of new architecture, it also seems highly questionable or improbable whether the evaluation of mature products even can result in such findings. That is, trade-offs have been made in design and it is merely about communicating the rationales for design decisions as well as the risks and problems that are known by the experienced architect. Discussion beyond these seems largely hypothetical or irrelevant especially when taking into account costs and time pressures on product development.

Consequently, there were findings and benefits that SWAB contributed although different than expected: For example, better communication and collaboration, raising awareness about the architecture, and increased confidence to the architecture throughout the organization. In fact, these findings resemble additional or side benefits observed also in other evaluation methods in general and even emphasized in a more thorough evaluation of mature products. It seems that architecture evaluation in a mature product often delivers these kinds of contributions that seem to be inherent to the maturity of products where the architecture has evolved towards a good candidate. Nevertheless, accumulated experience from several different kinds of organizations would strengthen this finding.

Moreover, SWAB evidenced that architecture evaluation can be carried out in a lightweight manner especially for mature products. It also seems that the guidelines of the evaluation per se had no major influence on the outcome of the evaluation but loosely defined guidelines adhering to state-of-the-practice architecture design methods seem to be sufficient. The results of a lightweight approach seemed to be equaling other more laborious approaches but with significantly minor effort and preparations. A lightweight architecture evaluation seems to require, or at least highly benefit from expert knowledge about the evaluated architecture and general expertise of the evaluators.

A more detailed assessment about the feasibility of a lightweight architecture evaluation to new product development remains an open question for future work. Similarly, when considering refactoring, the evaluation concerns mature features but the architecture can be only a candidate so that thorough experience does not exist paralleling architecture evaluation with new product development.

In the end, the overall benefits and profitability of architecture evaluation in mature products are difficult to quantify and estimates should also carefully take into account the indirect and intangible benefits.

10. ACKNOWLEDGMENTS

We acknowledge the participants of the study. This work was financially supported by TEKES – the Finnish Funding Agency for Innovation.

11. REFERENCES

[1] M. Babar and I. Gorton. Software architecture review: The state of practice. *Computer*, 42(7):26–32, 2009.

[2] M. Babar, L. Zhu, and R. Jeffery. A framework for classifying and comparing software architecture evaluation methods. In *Australian Software Engineering Conference*, pages 309 – 318, 2004.

[3] L. Bass and R. L. Nord. Understanding the context of architecture evaluation methods. In *Joint Working IEEE/IFIP Conference on Software Architecture (WICSA) and European Conference on Software Architecture (ECSA)*, WICSA-ECSA '12, pages 277–281. IEEE Computer Society, 2012.

[4] J. Bosch. *Design and Use of Software Architectures: Adapting and Evolving a Product-Line Approach.* Addison-Wesley, 2000.

[5] N. Boucké, D. Weyns, K. Schelfthout, and T. Holvoet. Applying the atam to an architecture for decentralized contol of a agv transportation system. In *In 2nd International Conference on Quality of Software Architecture, (QoSA), LNCS 4214*, pages 180–198, 2006.

[6] G. Buchgeher and R. Weinreich. An approach for combining model-based and scenario-based software architecture analysis. In *International Conference on Software Engineering Advances (ICSEA)*, pages 141–148, 2010.

[7] P. Clements, R. Kazman, and M. Klein. *Evaluating Software Architectures—Methods and Case Studies.* Addison-Wesley, 2002.

[8] J. O. Coplien and G. Bjørnvig. *Lean Architecture: for Agile Software Development.* Wiley, 2010.

[9] L. Dobrica and E. Niemelä. A survey on software architecture analysis methods. *IEEE Transactions on Software Engineering*, 28(7):638–653, 2002.

[10] L. Dominick, R. Hilliard, E. Kahane, R. Kazman, K. P., W. Kozaczynski, H. Obbink, H. Postema, A. Ran, and W. Tracz. Software architecture review and assessment (SARA) report, version 1.0. Technical report, 2002.

[11] S. Ferber, P. Heidl, and P. Lutz. Reviewing product line architectures: Experience report of ATAM in an automotive context. In *Revised Papers from the 4th International Workshop on Software Product-Family Engineering (PFE), LNCS 2290*, pages 364–382, 2002.

[12] M. Fowler. Who needs an architect? *IEEE Software*, Jul/Aug, pages 11–13, 2003.

[13] A. Grimán, M. Pérez, L. Mendoza, and F. Losavio. Feature analysis for architectural evaluation methods. *Journal of Systems and Software*, 79(6):871–888, 2006.

[14] M. Hammersley. Some notes on the terms 'validity' and 'reliability'. *British Educational Research Journal*, 13(1):73–81, 1987.

[15] C. Hofmeister, P. Kruchten, R. L. Nord, J. H. Obbink, A. Ran, and P. America. A general model of software architecture design derived from five industrial approaches. *Journal of Systems and Software*, 80(1):106–126, 2007.

[16] ISO/IEC/(IEEE). ISO/IEC 42010 (IEEE Std) 1471-2000 : Systems and Software engineering - Recomended practice for architectural description of software-intensive systems, 07 2007.

[17] A. Jansen and J. Bosch. Software architecture as a set of architectural design decisions. In *Working IEEE / IFIP Conference on Software Architecture (WICSA)*, pages 109–120. IEEE Computer Society, 2005.

[18] R. Kazman, M. Barbacci, M. Klein, S. Jeromy Carriere, and S. Woods. Experience with performing architecture tradeoff analysis. In *International Conference on Software Engineering (ICSE)*, pages 54–63. ACM, 1999.

[19] R. Kazman, L. Bass, and M. Klein. The essential components of software architecture design and analysis. *Journal of Systems and Software*, 79(8):1207 – 1216, 2006.

[20] R. Kazman, L. Bass, M. Webb, and G. Abowd. SAAM: a method for analyzing the properties of software architectures. In *International Conference on Software Engineering (ICSE)*, pages 81–90. IEEE Computer Society Press, 1994.

[21] R. Kazman, M. Klein, and P. Clements. ATAM: Method for architecture evaluation. Technical Report CMU/SEI-2000-TR-004, Carnegie Mellon University, Software Engineering Institute, 2000.

[22] A. S. Lee and R. L. Baskerville. Generalizing generalizability in information systems research. *Information Systems Research*, 14(3):221–243, 2003.

[23] J. F. Maranzano, S. A. Rozsypal, G. H. Zimmerman, G. W. Warnken, P. E. Wirth, and D. M. Weiss. Architecture reviews: Practice and experience. *IEEE Software*, 22(2):34–43, Mar. 2005.

[24] J. A. Maxwell. Understanding and validity in qualitative research. *Harvard Educational Review*, 62(3):279–300, 1992.

[25] N. Rozanski and E. Woods. *Software Systems Architecture: Working With Stakeholders Using Viewpoints and Perspectives.* Addison-Wesley Professional, 2005.

[26] P. Runeson and M. Höst. Guidelines for conducting and reporting case study research in software engineering. *Empirical Software Engineering*, 14(2):131–164, 2009.

[27] W. Shadish, T. Cook, and D. Campbell. *Experimental and Quasi-Experimental Designs for Generalized Causal Inference.* Houghton, Mifflin, Boston, 2002.

[28] A. Strauss and J. Corbin. *Basics of Qualitative Research.* Sage, 2 edition, 1998.

[29] C. Urquhart, H. Lehmann, and M. D. Myers. Putting the 'theory' back into grounded theory: guidelines for grounded theory studies in information systems. *Information Systems Journal*, 20(4):357–381, 2010.

[30] E. Woods. Industrial architectural assessment using TARA. In *Working IEEE/IFIP Conference on Software Architecture (WICSA)*, pages 56–65, 2011.

[31] R. K. Yin. *Case Study Research.* Sage: Thousand Oaks, London, 3 edition, 2003.

[32] A. Zalewski and S. Kijas. Beyond ATAM: Early architecture evaluation method for large-scale distributed systems. *Journal of Systems and Software*, 86(3):683–697, 2013.

Failure Data Collection for Reliability Prediction Models: A Survey

Barbora Buhnova
Masaryk University
Brno, Czech Republic
buhnova@mail.muni.cz

Stanislav Chren
Masaryk University
Brno, Czech Republic
chren@mail.muni.cz

Lucie Fabriková
Masaryk University
Brno, Czech Republic
fabrikova@mail.muni.cz

ABSTRACT

Design decisions made early in software development have great impact on the software product quality. Design-time reliability prediction is one of the techniques that support software engineers in early design decisions, based on the evaluation of reliability impact of the individual design alternatives. The accuracy of reliability prediction is critically dependent on the accuracy of reliability prediction models, which relies on uncertain failure parameters (such as the failure probability of component-internal actions). Although the effectiveness of the failure-parameter estimation critically influences the usability of the prediction techniques, the parameter estimation often relies on expert knowledge and is not receiving systematic attention. This paper aims to survey existing techniques for estimation and collection of failure parameters in architecture-based reliability prediction models, and presents the findings that can be learned from their detailed analysis.

Categories and Subject Descriptors

D.2.11.d [**Software Engineering**]: Software Architectures—*Languages*; G.3.k [**Mathematics of Computing**]: Probability and Statistics—*Reliability and life testing*

Keywords

Reliability prediction models; Failure parameters; Value estimation; Data collection; Survey

1. INTRODUCTION

The central goal of reliability prediction is to estimate the expected reliability of a software product. During software architecture design, reliability prediction can be successfully employed to identify critical software components, quantify their influence on the overall system reliability, and optimise future testing activities [32]. Early quantification of expected system reliability allows software engineers to assess the reliability impact of their design decisions (e.g. the

Permission to make digital or hard copies of all or part of this work for personal or classroom use is granted without fee provided that copies are not made or distributed for profit or commercial advantage and that copies bear this notice and the full citation on the first page. Copyrights for components of this work owned by others than ACM must be honored. Abstracting with credit is permitted. To copy otherwise, or republish, to post on servers or to redistribute to lists, requires prior specific permission and/or a fee. Request permissions from permissions@acm.org.
QoSA'14, June 30–July 4, 2014, Marcq-en-Baroeul, France.
Copyright 2014 ACM 978-1-4503-2576-9/14/06 ...$15.00.
http://dx.doi.org/10.1145/2602576.2602586.

effect of different fault-tolerance mechanisms) and increases the maturity of the software engineering process.

Design-time reliability prediction depends on detailed system models, whose accuracy is often questioned, since they rely on the knowledge of failure rates of system components and their internal actions, which is hard to estimate before system implementation. Various techniques can be employed to estimate failure model parameters or collect failure data from related systems and port it to the design-time reliability models. The information about the techniques is however scarce, which makes it difficult to identify the best fitting parameter estimation technique for a new project.

The aim of this paper is to gather and classify existing data collection and parameter estimation techniques applicable in the context of architecture-based reliability prediction, and hence support mature reliability engineering.

The paper is structured as follows. Section 2 introduces our research method together with the discussion of related surveys. Section 3 details technique classification, Section 4 surveys the identified techniques, and Section 5 systematically discusses the techniques based on the introduced classification. Finally, Section 6 concludes the paper.

2. RESEARCH METHOD

For the purpose of this survey, we have examined a number of research areas, collected relevant approaches with respect to the defined goal, identified three dimensions of approach classification, and for each dimension studied existing approaches from the dimension point of view. This section overviews the examined research areas and information sources, explains the dimensions of technique classification, and discusses related surveys.

2.1 Examined research areas

The issue of parameter estimation for architecture-based reliability prediction models is rarely discussed in isolation. The richest source of information on reliability parameter estimation and collection are the evaluation sections of reliability prediction papers where the prediction techniques are applied to case study examples and reliability model construction is therefore detailed in (close to) real settings. The papers introducing design-time reliability prediction techniques, such as [29, 6, 3] hence became the primary source of information for this survey.

Unfortunately, most of the existing reliability-prediction techniques are only accompanied with demonstrating examples, whose value for our purpose is limited because of low complexity of the examples and high reliance on simplifying assumptions about model parameters. The most popular parameter estimation techniques in this context are expert knowledge and failure parameters being set to constant values, which may be sufficient for demonstration purposes but does not offer much guidance for real-world projects [3].

The most realistic parameter collection and estimation techniques can be identified in case-study papers discussing the experience from reliability analysis applied to a real-world system [32, 25]. Case study papers provide detailed description of the reliability-prediction process including the model parameter estimation or collection. On the other hand, the number of realistic studies is very limited and the papers often target reliability analysis in late development stages only (when the source code is already available).

2.2 Classifications of the techniques

The analysis of essential characteristics of existing parameter estimation/collection techniques resulted in the following three dimensions reflecting the viewpoints of technique classification, which is elaborated in Section 3.

- **WHAT** – **Reliability model parameters**. This dimension describes what kind of data the techniques collect or estimate based on the parameters of architecture-based reliability prediction models that shall be constructed.

- **WHERE** – **Sources of data collection**. This dimension characterizes the information sources exploited by the data collection techniques, i.e. where the analysed data comes from.

- **HOW** – **Collection process**. This dimension represents the activities contributing to the data collection/estimation process, i.e. how the data collection techniques obtain and process the data.

2.3 Related surveys

One of the first overviews of failure data collection techniques in reliability engineering dates back to 1996, when it became part of the *Handbook of Software Reliability Engineering* [33]. The book describe the whole process of failure data collection, including the steps that should be performed to setup the data collection process, and the mathematical background. However, the primary focus is on the overview of black-box reliability growth models and related testing and analytical procedures. Our survey complements this work with a detailed overview of reliability prediction model parameters, sources of data collection and concrete techniques applicable in architecture-based reliability analysis, which have mostly been introduced after 1996.

Dimov et al. [14] give a short survey on testing methods that generate data for reliability analysis. The study relates the testing methods to either white-box or black-box reliability approaches, but without much detail on transferring the test results to reliability model parameters. Moreover, since it concentrates on testing of existing systems, it overlooks failure data collection techniques for earlier development artefacts.

Murphy et al. [39] provide brief overview of traditional reliability-related data collection methods based on customer-related data, such as questionnaires, customer service calls or bug reports. However, it does not discuss if and how the methods could be used to derive reliability model parameters. Furthermore, it focuses on the collection techniques applicable only to already deployed systems.

Mannhart et al. [36] compare available methods for modelling expert judgement, and discuss their limits when applied to software reliability prediction. Besides arguing that most methods are unsuitable for software reliability analysis as they require excessive effort, the survey does not related the techniques to reliability prediction model parameters, which is one of the contributions of our survey.

Koziolek et al. [32] present a case study of a large industrial control system, which includes brief overview of several useful data collection techniques applicable in this specific case. The overview focuses on the component failure rate, outlining five failure-rate collection techniques. Although this study contains very useful information, is not aimed as a survey. Therefore, it lacks more detailed discussion and misses techniques inapplicable in the analysed case.

3. CLASSIFICATION ATTRIBUTES

This section presents the details of the technique classification structured according to the three views outlined in Section 2.2.

3.1 Reliability model parameters

Reliability prediction models vary in the types of parameters they utilize. The parameters depend on the analytical purpose of the reliability model (e.g. whether we want to predict the probability of system failure on demand, frequency of failure occurrences or only identify the least reliable system component) and the scope of the reliability model, which may incorporate failure data on different levels of abstraction (e.g. failure rate of the whole component vs. failure rate of each component-internal action) and span across different layers of the system.

In architecture-based reliability prediction [30], we distinguish prediction models that consider only the software layer of the analysed system and those that examine also the execution environment (hardware, network, operating system, etc.). This implies two classes of reliability model parameters: software parameters and execution environment parameters. To keep the survey focused, we discuss only failure parameters falling into the two classes, although one could argue that other system parameters, such as the behavioural parameters (e.g. transition probabilities among components, system operational profile), are also an important constituent of reliability prediction models.

Software parameters.
Software parameters of reliability models are dependent on the architectural abstraction of the reliability prediction models, which are often classified as black-box and white-box models [30]. The *black-box* reliability prediction ignores the internal structure of the system and requires the failure data of the system as a whole. *White-box* models on the other hand exploit the architecture of the system and the internal behaviour of system components in order to predict the overall system reliability based on the low level reliability of component-internal actions. Some reliability prediction models combine the black-box and white-box approach into *grey-box* models, where the white-box view of software architecture uncovers only the hierarchical structure of composite components and views the low-level components as black boxes [32, 51].

The failure behaviour of the system as a whole (in black-box models), system components (in grey-box models), or component-internal actions (in white-box models) is usually defined as a failure rate, time-dependent failure intensity, or probability of failure on demand [21]. Failure rate is the frequency in which the failures occur. Time-dependent failure intensity is defined as the rate of change of the expected number of failures with respect to time [33]. The probability of failure on demand is understood as $1 - r$ where r is the probability of failure-free operation of a software system for a specified period of time in a specified environment [30]. Additionally, we may also need the data that can help us to localise the faults that caused the failures in order to estimate the reliability of a component accurately [25].

In general, the failure behaviour can be specified in greater detail by additional parameters, such as the failure dependencies, their durations or latency [4]. However, these parameters are rarely utilised in existing reliability models.

Execution environment parameters.

Several reliability prediction approaches consider the execution environment, in which the system is deployed, in order to improve the plausibility of the reliability analysis [15, 6]. Execution environment comprises of hardware resources and network infrastructure.

The reliability of hardware resources is most commonly expressed via the *Mean Time To Failure (MTTF)* and *Mean Time To Repair (MTTR)* attributes that are later translated into availability values inside the reliability model [6].

Reliability in networks may be defined either as a probability of successful communication between a specified pair of nodes within the network, or as the ratio of correctly delivered data. The reliability is often modelled either with a random variable or with a fixed constant [53].

Unlike in software components, the execution environment parameters are often supplied by hardware vendors and infrastructure providers, and are easier to benchmark (e.g. as in [46]). For this reason, we further concentrate on the software parameter estimation techniques only.

3.2 Sources of data collection

The values of reliability model parameters can be collected from various sources, such as the implementation of previous system versions or user documents. This subsection overviews the possible sources in more detail.

Predecessor or similar system.

Previous versions of a system together with its historical artefacts provide a significant source for failure data [11, 24]. In case no previous versions of the software are available, similar systems may be leveraged [29, 6]. However, the data obtained from similar systems may not be straightforwardly portable to the newly designed system [57]. Moreover, information about sensitive data (e.g. security problems) may not be accessible.

This category also includes the *Commercial Off The Shelf (COTS)* components [29], which embody reusable system elements. However, the concept of accompanying COTS components with quality characteristics, such as software failure parameters, is still in its infancy.

Design-time artefacts.

In the early lifecycle stages, the system implementation is often not available. However, other artefacts can be em-

ployed, including requirements document [24, 11], UML diagrams [54, 12, 26], or project schedules [56]. Such artefacts describe the functionality of the system on various levels of abstraction. The requirements document may for example indicate the dependencies between system components (through common functionality). The project schedule may be leveraged in time-dependent system consideration. The UML diagrams may indicate the complexity of system architecture and, if accompanied with proper annotation, they can be used for derivation of the formal reliability model [4].

Late-stages artefacts.

In late stages of system development, the system is being implemented and may be exposed to various kinds of techniques. In particular, the source code can be subjected to fault injection [42], code coverage measurements [22] or metrics collection [13]. Additionally, the change logs from the version control system may be examined [25], for instance to reveal error propagation or linking of system faults (code discrepancies) to failures observable by system users.

Runtime artefacts.

An executed system or its parts (if executable) may produce large amount of artefacts. Primarily, the application logs may contain information about failures, their extent and severity. Next, the system can be exposed to various kinds of tests. Test results, for example, passing or failing tests under certain circumstances (e.g. various usage profiles, execution environment, workloads) serve as an input to many data collection techniques [43, 13, 52].

If the system or its parts are not yet available, a prototype may be created to simulate the demanded functionality. The prototype creation may however be a time-consuming task with an ineffective result. As an alternative, there are ways to simulate executable design models and design artefacts of the system [55].

User information.

User feedback may become valuable information source, communicated for instance via failure and bug reports, or modification requests [9]. The reports may serve as a basis for failure rate estimates. The modification requests may indicate the fault proneness of various system parts (caused by the modifications). Additionally, expected system usage, defined in terms of an operational profile, is an essential information source for a number of reliability estimation techniques called input domain techniques [7].

Expert knowledge.

Under the term expert knowledge we understand any available source of information that supplies us with the value of demanded data directly, without additional effort. E.g. knowledge and experience of domain expert, practices broadly accepted in the community, industry standards [11]. Although the sources mentioned above enable us to obtain data straightforwardly with very little effort, the data obtained this way use to be associated with high uncertainty. Instead of a constant number, an interval reflecting confidence of the estimate should be considered.

3.3 Collection process

Each failure-data collection or estimation technique describes a process of transforming input data into failure parameters. The process may be composed of several successive activities, which are discussed in this subsection.

Measurement.

Measurement activities aim at either measuring a specific aspect of a system behaviour (e.g. time between failures) or parsing system's artefacts to extract required data (e.g. the number of failure occurrences from application logs). Another measurement activity related to the processing of system artefacts is data filtering, such as the selection of those bug reports that satisfy certain conditions. Furthermore, this group includes system simulation [11], execution of test cases and processing of test results. We also consider code instrumentation methods (driven by code coverage) and fault injection methods to fall in this category.

The measurement activities may leverage predecessor or similar systems, design time, late-stage or runtime artefacts.

Metrics.

This category encompasses activities of software metrics collection. We understand software metric as a measure that quantifies some property of a software system or its artefacts. For instance, the property could be system complexity and the corresponding metric would be the length of code. Apart from the metrics characterizing the system itself, metrics can also describe system context (like the skills of programmers, the programming language or risk factors associated with system's complexity) [19]. Moreover, the classification of information, such as the assignment of severity classes to bug reports also belongs to metrics activities.

Analytical.

Analytical activities involve mathematical functions or model-based computations that transform a given set of input parameters into reliability-relevant information that can be utilized in reliability-prediction models. The activities usually input values obtained from measurement and metrics activities and result in failure parameters. Analytical methods usually consist of one or more mathematical formulae. They range from simple ones such as a fraction of failed test cases to the total number of test cases [43], to complex ones, such as software reliability growth models [52]. In order to provide credible results, they often impose restrictions on input data format, quality or origin [52, 33].

4. SURVEY OF THE TECHNIQUES

This section discusses the details of the identified data collection and estimation techniques for reliability prediction models. The techniques are structured into nine classes, each discussed together with its characteristics and limitations. A detailed analysis, classification and comparison of the techniques then follows in Section 5.

Application log parsing.

The parsing of application logs is one of the most popular approaches for failure data reconstruction, which may be also employed for reliability-model parameter estimation. The logs are often voluminous, containing much information irrelevant from the reliability point of view. Hence the log files must be filtered first. Afterwards, the remaining entries are scanned to produce traces of system and user failure-related behaviour.

One of the approaches that employ log parsing to estimate failure probability is the work of Banerjee et al. [2], who tar-

get reliability prediction of web applications. Once the logs are filtered, the traces of user activity in the approach are represented through a series of http requests that can be mapped to particular services of the application. Additionally, each request is assigned a status code that was included in web server response to the request. From this data, the failure per request and probability of failure per session are derived through the *Nelson's model* (described later in this section).

Besides the evidence of failures, detailed context of application failures may be obtained (e.g. debug information for error analysis from Java logging library Apache `log4j`, C library `nglogc`, and others).

Limitations: The usability of the discussed techniques in early development stages may be problematic, since they rely on an already implemented and running system. However, this problem may be bypassed by simulations, prototypes or execution of the techniques on former system versions. Moreover, logging mechanisms are often application-specific which makes it difficult to provide general instructions or tools for the processing of application logs.

Bug report analysis.

One of the most significant measures of system quality are the feedback reports submitted by system users and developers, or automatically collected during system usage (e.g. failure reporting in OS Windows). Bug reports in particular include failure profile information (e.g. hardware failures, illogical inputs, problems with drivers or third-party components), which may be stored in a bug reporting database (e.g. *Bugzilla*) [25] and similarly to application logs serve as the basis for reliability-model parameter estimation.

In a number of works, bug tracking databases have become an essential source for failure data collection [32, 52]. The reliability-model parameter estimation process in these approaches typically consists of two phases, where the first filters and analyses bug reports to collect raw failure data, which is then injected into an analytical model to compute the expected parameter values. The latter phase is most commonly based on *Software Reliability Growth Models (SRGMs)*, which are discussed later in this section.

Koziolek et al. [32] filter bug reports according to multiple criteria, including the status of the failures (if fixed or not), their severity (if high or low), and phase of the project (if released already). Furthermore, it is assumed that every failure was caused by a fault located in the same component that caused the failure. This assumption allows simpler assignment of reports to the individual components so that the reliability can be estimated on a component level, although it may cause deviations in the estimation accuracy.

Another approach involving error analysis was proposed by Nakagawa et al. [41], who divide the error records into several classes based on the error's complexity. Although the authors propose one specific classification scheme, they argue that different classifications are possible. The approach involves calculation of the error ratios of each class to the total error count. The computation is performed for the analysed application and one more reference application that is already mature and reliable. Afterwards, the data is used in a set of formulae that results in a probability of failure for the whole application.

In [5], the authors use bug tracker data only to determine the relative weight w of particular failures. The probability of occurrence of specific failure types is computed with the formula 10^{-b+w}, where b denotes the baseline parameter and is supplied by the developers based on their experience.

Limitations: Although bug tracker databases are common source of failure relevant information, processing their content into a failure rate might be problematic [5]. Bug reports describe circumstances of a failure, not frequency of its occurrence. Additionally, the data inside the reports is filled manually by a user or developer, which makes it prone to errors, duplicates or other inconsistencies. Furthermore, unlike the application logs which are usually well structured and thus can be parsed automatically, bug reports contain entries with sentences in natural language, such as description of failure circumstances or developer comments that have to be examined manually.

Failure-fault linking.

Failures within software architecture may be observed on various levels (e.g. crash of the whole application or failure of a single service), which together with the complexity of system control flow makes it nontrivial to identify which faults in the system caused the failures. The models often use simplifying assumptions such as that each failure was caused by a specific fault located in the same component, which causes estimation deviation [29, 28].

A combination of four methods to identify the faults corresponding to failures is presented in [25]. Two of the methods are automated, which is the scanning of change logs and test results. The remaining two, which are based on the search through the bug tracker database and CVS logs to trace the source-code modifications, require manual assistance due to the information inconsistencies.

Another helpful sources for failure-fault linkings are bug reports from previous system versions, similar systems dealing with the same problem or developer experience [28].

Limitations: Although these techniques can together identify most of the faults that lead to failures, as demonstrated on a case study, they can account only for the faults that have been already detected and fixed.

Moreover, they do not take into account more complex phenomena, such as failure propagation or dependencies between failures.

Input domain techniques.

The input domain techniques are based on random testing driven by the knowledge of system operational profile. First, the test cases are developed or generated according to an expected distribution of the input elements (i.e. operational profile). Next, the sampled test cases are executed and the number of failed tests is recorded. Last, the test data is evaluated with analytical methods discussed below.

The most basic technique in this category is the *Nelson's model* [43], which calculates the probability of failure as a $\frac{n_f}{n}$ where n_f is the number of failed test cases and n is the total number of executed tests. It implicitly assumes that the selection of test cases corresponds to the application's operational profile.

Further improvements of this model were made by Brown and Lipow [7] who explicitly consider the operational profile by weighting the above fraction with the probability of selecting the given inputs in the operational usage.

A similar technique was proposed by Ramamoorthy and Bastani [45] who include a metric for the confidence of reliability measure. Unlike the previous techniques, it provides an estimate of the conditional probability that the program is correct for all possible inputs given that it is correct for a specified set of inputs. Moreover, it does not require the random testing strategy to be used.

The above mentioned techniques face the problem that if no test cases fail (i.e. the failures are very unlikely to occur under the expected operational profile), the estimated probability of failure is estimated to be 0. However, that might not reflect the real reliability. Miller et al. [37] introduce a technique that is able to estimate non-zero (albeit small) probability of failure even when testing does not reveal any failures, and is therefore useful for ultra-reliable applications. Their approach is based on Bayesian estimation and regards the probability of failure as a random variable that follows the $Beta(a, b)$ distribution. The parameters a and b represent the prior belief about program's reliability. For example, if there is no prior assumption about the reliability, they should be both set to 1. Otherwise, their determination is either a subject of expert knowledge or the authors provide formulae that use mean and variance statistics of the reliability previously measured by other approaches, such as *Software Reliability Growth Models (SRGMs)* discussed below. Moreover, this technique is able to adjust the estimates when testing input distribution differs from the operational input distribution.

Limitations: Input domain techniques assume that input distribution (operational profile) is known. Often, this is not true, especially for green-field application development. Next, most of the techniques require large number of executed test cases in order to attain reasonable confidence in estimated probabilities. Some authors [16] even argue about the effectiveness of random testing versus non-random testing. Furthermore, the presence of an oracle that unambiguously classifies any input/output pair as either correct or incorrect is assumed [37].

Software Reliability Growth Models (SRGMs).

Software Reliability Growth Models (SRGMs) are one of the oldest and widely applied black-box analytical techniques to predict failure behaviour of a software. SRGMs are used to estimate the future failure data based on the system historical data. In particular the past data such as the number of faults or unique failures in a given time period is fit to an analytical function specific for the particular SRGM so that the parameters of the function together with the mean value function representing cumulative number of faults or failures for a given unit of time can be derived. The input failure data for the model is usually gathered during the testing phase. If test data is not available, the filtered reports from bug tracking database can be used as a substitute for failure counts [52]. Alternatively, source code metrics can be used to determine parameters of some SRGMs [34].

Limitations: The SRGMs are dependent on several underlying assumptions, such as that the faults are repaired immediately after their discovery or that testing follows the system's operational profile [52]. Satisfaction of these assumptions in real-world projects is the biggest challenge of the SRGMs. Case studies [52, 32, 1] reported credible results even if some assumptions were violated. On the other hand, application of SRGMs in [44] was unsuccessful due to their violation.

Furthermore, there is no single perfect SRGM suitable for every project. Multiple models should be verified and the one best fitting the data shall be chosen [50]. There are software tools such as *CASRE* [8] or *SMERFS* [48] that support multiple models and comparison of their results.

Test code coverage techniques.

During the attempts to alleviate the drawbacks of SRGMs, namely the assumed knowledge of the operational profile, several authors discovered that the *growth of test code coverage* is also directly related to the reliability growth and could be integrated with SRGMs to increase their usability [31, 35]. The test code coverage is a measure that describes the degree to which certain elements of the source code have been tested.

Gokhale et al. [22] propose a technique for test code coverage that adopts *Enhanced Non-Homogeneous Poisson Process* that is used in SRGMs. However, unlike the previous authors, they rely solely on the coverage growth data and do not require the data about failure growth. Their model utilizes two parameters. The first is the expected number of faults a residing in the software and can be estimated from functional testing data or from metrics. The second is the coverage function $c(t)$, which can have either continuous or discrete form. For the former, the formulae of the SRGMs are fitted to coverage data instead of the failure data. The latter form can be defined from the measured coverage obtained from code coverage tools such as *ATAC* [23].

Limitations: The assumptions of SRGMs are valid also for code coverage models. However, the necessity of known operational profile is diminished. Furthermore, some techniques require additional validation [22].

Fault injection.

Fault injection is a multi-purpose technique that is used for simulating events or conditions that are difficult to observe otherwise. It can be performed both on the code-level or at runtime. The program with injected faults is usually examined to evaluate the fault propagation, latency, fault-recovery mechanisms or test effectiveness in connection with mutation testing [42].

Several authors [25, 20] determine various failure parameters (time-dependent failure intensity, constant failure rate and probability of failure) of a system or its components by re-inserting previously detected and removed faults into the program. Afterwards, the program can be subjected to SRGMs, such as in [10] where it results in the value of time-dependent failure intensity, or to *Nelson's model*, such as in [25] where the failure probabilities of individual components are estimated.

While in small scale applications the faults can be re-injected manually, in large scale applications it is more practical to take advantage of old system versions (where the faults have been naturally present) as the basis for executing test cases from newer system versions [25].

Another parameter that can be estimated with the help of fault-injection is the total number faults in a program or its components, which can be obtained using the capture-recapture models such as Mill's hypergeometric model [38]. It is based on the assumption that the ratio of detected injected faults to the number of total injected faults is approximately equal to the ratio of detected real faults to the total number of real faults. The resulting total number of faults may serve as an input for SRGMs.

Limitations: The obtained values of the failure parameters represent the state of the program with injected faults and not the present version of the program. Therefore, they are more suitable for demonstration purposes rather than for real-world reliability analysis.

In the approach of Popstojanova et al. [25], it is also necessary to maintain the change logs for test cases and to track whether the failure of a test case was caused by the inserted fault or by testing a new feature not yet implemented in the older version of the program. Moreover, it is assumed that after the fault is detected and repaired, the new test cases are added as well.

The Mill's model further assumes that injected faults are randomly distributed in the program and that both injected and real faults have equal probability to be detected.

Multiple-factor metrics analysis.

Metrics are a well established technique to deduce quality parameters, which include the number of defects or fault density in a system or its parts.

There have been several attempts to derive the probability of failure or failure rate based on defect density [49, 33]. However, the transition is not straightforward due to the nature of failure-fault relationship, which is known to be complex [25]. Additionally, the existing approaches fail in empirical validations [18].

Since the derivation of failure parameters from a single characteristic proved to be inaccurate [18], several authors attempt to derive failure parameters from a combination of multiple different characteristics of an application.

Davidsson et al. [13] introduce a technique to estimate the probability of failure based on the JUnit testing framework and a set of metrics. Their Eclipse based tool called *GERT* incorporates testing, size and complexity metrics from the *Software and Reliability Early Warning (STREW)* metric suite [40] in a regression model with reliability as a dependent variable. The parameters of the regression equation are determined from the set of historical values from STREW metrics that are continuously collected during software development. The reference reliability values are obtained with the help of unit tests and *Nelson's model*. The tool allows selective analysis of application parts. Thus, it can be used for estimating failure probability of the whole application, its components or packages and individual files or classes.

Another technique for modelling complex relationships between different metrics and failure parameters is the *Bayesian Belief Network (BBN)*. A BBN is a graph that comprises nodes and arcs, where nodes represent uncertain variables and arcs casual relationships between variables [18]. With BBNs, it is possible to express expert beliefs about dependencies between different variables and their impact on uncertain outcomes, such as the probability of failure. At the beginning, expert knowledge can be used as an initial input that can be later continuously refined when more realistic data is available. The BBNs can incorporate many different kinds of metrics including metrics examining the application's development process or development team. There are several authors that make use of BBNs in software reliability analysis, for a detailed overview see [47].

Limitations: GERT needs to be used throughout the whole implementation so that more accurate analytical function for probability of failure can be constructed. Although the BBNs can capture complex relationship between multiple factors, the influences between the variables are specified by domain experts and therefore require further validation.

Results from techniques dependant on metrics or expert knowledge suffer from high uncertainty. In general, they are not suitable for point estimates of failure parameters. However, they can be still used for tasks such as identification of critical components or relative comparison of components from reliability standpoint.

Object-oriented metrics analysis.

Object-oriented (OO) design metrics were developed for the purpose of an early assessment of software quality. Originally, the connection to software reliability was studied through general fault-proneness of an application [17]. Presently, there exists several approaches that use OO metrics to estimate different failure parameters.

Goseva-Popstojanova et al. in [26] employ OO design metrics to compute the reliability-based risk factor of each component per execution scenario and the risk factor of the whole system, based on the failure probability and failure severity. The necessary data is collected from UML statechart and sequence diagrams. The numerical values for severity classes are mined from existing hazard statistics, and assigned to individual components by a domain expert. The background formal model employs *Discrete Time Markov Chains (DTMC)* similar to those commonly used by white-box reliability prediction approaches.

Another technique that gathers metrics from UML diagrams was proposed by Hong et al. [29], who compute failure rate of a component in a given scenario. The component failure rate is expressed as a probability that within a given scenario a fail of some component method in any of its busy periods will occur. Busy period is an OO metric obtainable from UML sequence diagram. Alternatively, this technique can be used in reversed direction. Provided we already have the failure probability of components(e.g. it was established by one of the methods in this section, or we use reliability certified COTS), we are able to calculate the failure probabilities of methods.

Limitations: Technique by Popstojanova et al. [26] actually outputs risked-based parameters instead of failure parameters. Despite their similarities, the assumption of using the risk-based parameter as a substitute for probability of failure needs to be validated.

Although the approach by Hong et al. [29] uses the OO metrics, it also requires further data about component or method failures which have to be collected from executable application or from certified COTS or provided by an expert. That makes it difficult to apply in early stages of development.

5. DISCUSSION OF THE FINDINGS

This section discusses our observations about the techniques surveyed in Section 4. The aggregated data structured according to the classification devised in Section 3 is shown in Table 1. The following subsections discuss the information in greater detail.

5.1 Parameter type

The most common parameter in present architecture-based reliability models is the probability of failure, although it is argued to be the least accurate of the studied parameter types [20]. Failure probability is usually a result of input domain techniques [43, 7, 37] (especially the *Nelson's model*), or of techniques that in some way incorporate input domain

techniques in their collection process, such as the application log analysis [2] and fault-injection [25].

Other techniques estimating the probability of failure are those that rely on uncertain data, e.g. metrics and expert knowledge. Such techniques can be found in several classes, most notably in multiple-factor and object-oriented metrics analyses [13, 47], but also in bug report analysis [41, 5].

The time-dependent failure intensity parameter has been only identified as a result of SRGMs or techniques integrating SRGMs [32] or inspired by SRGMs, such as test code coverage techniques [23].

The same holds true for the constant failure rate. There are either SRGMs that output the failure rate directly [35, 34], or specify it through a fixed time value for the failure intensity function. The time can be chosen, for example, according to the project schedule, e.g. by selecting the time of the product's release [22].

Overall, it can be observed that the more rigorous the data collection technique is (e.g. SRGMs compared to metrics analysis), the more detailed parameters it produces (time-dependent failure intensity compared to failure probability).

5.2 Level of detail

We distinguish three main levels of detail within a software architecture for which all failure parameters can be estimated. On the system level, the systems is assessed as a whole. On the component level, failure parameters of components or packages are evaluated. On the method level, the reliability of individual services, methods or actions is estimated, typically in connection to a usage profile.

Since the components are usually regarded as autonomous units (especially in component-based architectures), they can be considered as "mini-systems" on their own. Therefore, when a technique is intended for the whole system, it can be also applied to individual components. However, this also means that additional data, such as the origin of failures or faults, must be available [25].

Some categories of studied techniques are applicable to all the three levels of detail. The input domain techniques do not distinguish different elements being tested as long as the expected operational profile is respected [43, 7]. Therefore, they can employ functional tests for the system and its components or unit tests for individual methods. Additionally, Banerjee et al. [2] utilize data from web server logs with the *Nelson's model* to estimate the probability of failure per request and session.

The achieved level of detail is also proportional to the effort required to process the data. In bug report analysis category, Nakagawa et al. [41] compute the probability of failure for the whole system and require only simple classification of reports into groups of complexity. Koziolek et al. [32] are able to calculate time-dependent failure intensities for the components of the system. Since they are using SRGMs to do so, the parsing and filtering of the reports is more demanding, because they need to adhere to the assumptions of SRGMs. Brosch [5] can estimate the probability of failure for the individual actions of application's usage scenario. To achieve that, after the initial filtration, the bug reports have to be examined manually including the natural language description and the discussion threads between developers associated with the given report.

On the other hand, the technique by Hong et al. [29] from the OO metrics analysis category can be used for the esti-

Technique	Parameters		Data sources	Process	References
	Parameter type	Level of detail			
Application log parsing	probability of failure	system, component, method	run-time artefacts	measurement, analytical	[2]
Bug report analysis	time-dep. failure intensity, probability of failure	system, component, method	user information, similar system, expert knowledge	measurement, metrics, analytical	[32, 41, 5]
Failure-fault linking	failure-fault relationship	system, component	late-stage artefacts, run-time artefacts, user information, expert knowledge	measurement, analytical	[25]
Input domain techniques	probability of failure	system, component, method	late stage artefacts, run-time artefacts, expert knowledge	measurement, analytical	[43, 7, 45, 37]
Software reliability growth models	time-dep. failure intensity, constant failure rate	system, component	late stage artefacts run-time artefacts user information	analytical, measurement, metrics	[52, 34, 32]
Test code coverage	time-dep failure intensity, constant failure rate	system, component	late stage artefacts, run-time artefacts	measurement, analytical,	[22, 23]
Fault injection	time-dep. failure intensity, constant failure rate, probability of failure	system, component, method	late stage artefacts, predecessor system	measurement, analytical	[10, 25, 38]
Multiple-factor metric analysis	probability of failure	system, component	late stage artefacts, run-time artefacts, expert knowledge	metrics, measurement, analytical	[13, 47]
Object-oriented metrics analysis	probability of failure	system, component,	design-time artefacts, expert knowledge, COTS	metrics, analytical	[26, 29]

mation on either component level or method level but not on both at the same time, since the knowledge of component reliability is needed for the computation of method's reliability and vice versa.

5.3 Data sources

Majority of the techniques require multiple data sources. The most frequent combination are different late-stage artefacts, namely the source code with the run-time artefacts, such as test cases and testing reports. The source code can be subjected to fault injection [42, 10], instrumentation with probes measuring the code coverage [27] and for the collection of metrics [13, 34]. Test cases and testing reports are necessary for input domain techniques and can be useful for SRGMs [52] and test code coverage techniques [27]. Moreover, unit tests and test results are used for calibration of the Davidsson et al. metric-centred technique [13].

The most self-contained data source appears to be the application logs. After initial parsing and filtering, application logs can provide all necessary data needed for the input domain techniques [2].

The user information is dominant in bug report analysis, which may produce inputs for SRGMs. Although the input data for SRMGs can also be gathered from run-time artefacts (test reports) [52] and late-stage artefacts (source code metrics) [34], the case studies by Koziolek et al. [32] and Wood [52] show that bug reports could be sufficient.

Design-time artefacts are not extensively leveraged and in general, they have to be accompanied with additional data, such as the reliability of methods or components [29]. The technique by Popstojanova et al. [26] comes close as it is almost entirely based on OO metrics from UML diagrams. However, it still requires expert knowledge to some extent.

The expert knowledge is a data source recurring in most of the techniques. It is less significant among the techniques with strong measurement background such as SRGMs or test code coverage techniques. On one hand, expert knowledge brings uncertainty into the parameter estimation process so further result validation is required. On the other hand, it might bring benefits of higher flexibility of the model, for example as in the techniques by Miller et al. [37] or in BBNs.

Several authors suggest that relevant failure data can also be obtained from previous system versions or from systems of similar functionality [27, 40]. However, only few techniques actually use these sources. The technique of Nakagawa et al. [41] employs error reports from a similar system to determine all parameters of their analytical formula. Popstojanova et al. [25] requires multiple versions of the same system to simplify the fault injection process.

5.4 Process

By observing the collection processes, we can see that all types of techniques follow a similar pattern. In order to estimate failure parameters, the measurement and/or metric activities precede the application of analytical functions.

The parsing and filtering of application logs or bug reports are one of the most versatile and heterogeneous activities. They are used by several techniques [2, 32, 41, 5], each of them using these artefacts in different manner.

Execution and evaluation of test cases forms the core of input domain techniques [43, 7, 37]. Additionally, they can be leveraged by SRGMs, for instance, when the data from bug tracking database is not available. However, the SRGMs utilise also the information about the testing process (e.g. duration of tests or testing methodology) in contrast to input domain techniques that are primarily interested only in the final outcome of individual test cases. Furthermore, unit testing is an important part of the technique by Davidsson et al. [13], which is purely metrics-centred otherwise. Testing accompanied with modification of source code is used by code coverage [23] and fault injection approaches [38, 20].

Collection of metrics plays mostly a support role, especially in bug report analysis techniques [41] or SRGMs [34]. Although they are important in multiple-factor and object oriented metrics analyses and in the approaches by Popstojanova et al. [26] and Davidsson et al. [13] in particular, even there they are accompanied by either additional measurement activities or by inputs from domain experts.

Among analytical techniques, some use custom formulae [41, 5, 22, 38, 2, 26, 29], others make use of formuale provided by either SRGMs or input domain models.

One of the obstacles preventing application of the techniques is the extent of automation of the whole process. Test case generation, execution and evaluations or analytical computations can be well supported with automated tools [32]. The same is true for code instrumentation with coverage probes or collection of metrics from design-time or late-stage artefacts [26, 13, 23]. On the other hand, when unstructured data is being analysed or the insight of domain expert is necessary, specialized tools might aid the data collection but the manual processing is still unavoidable [5, 25].

6. CONCLUSION

The goal of this paper was to create a survey of failure-data collection and estimation techniques for reliability prediction models. To accomplish this goal, we studied possible reliability-model parameters, failure data sources, methods and analytical capabilities of existing techniques. The techniques have then been analysed and classified according to devised classification attributes, and the findings from technique classification discussed in a separate section.

In summary, it appeared that most of the techniques for failure data collection and estimation exploit the artefacts of late stages of software development while the early stages are rather neglected. The future research could attempt to bridge this gap by introducing new techniques making greater use of design-time artefacts, or by examining failure parameter portability among different system artefacts or reliability models.

7. REFERENCES

[1] V. Almering, M. van Genuchten, G. Cloudt, and P. J. Sonnemans. Using software reliability growth models in practice. *IEEE Software*, 24(6):82–88, 2007.

[2] S. Banerjee, H. Srikanth, and B. Cukic. Log-based reliability analysis of software as a service (saas). In *Proc. of ISSRE'10*, pages 239–248. IEEE, 2010.

[3] N. Benes, B. Buhnova, I. Cerna, and R. Oslejsek. Reliability analysis in component-based development via probabilistic model checking. In *Proc. of CBSE'12*, pages 83–92. ACM, 2012.

[4] S. Bernardi, J. Merseguer, and D. C. Petriu. A dependability profile within marte. *Software & Systems Modeling*, 10(3):313–336, 2011.

[5] F. Brosch. *Integrated Software Architecture-Based Reliability Prediction for IT Systems*. PhD thesis, Karlsruher Institut für Technologie, Karlsruhe, Germany, 2012.

[6] F. Brosch, H. Koziolek, B. Buhnova, and R. Reussner. Architecture-based reliability prediction with the palladio component model. *IEEE Trans. on Software Engineering*, 38(6):1319–1339, 2012.

[7] J. Brown and M. Lipow. Testing for software reliability. *ACM SIGPLAN Notices*, 10(6):518–527, 1975.

[8] CASRE. http://www.openchannelfoundation.org/projects/CASRE_3.0/.

[9] S. Chandran, A. Dimov, and S. Punnekkat. Modeling uncertainties in the estimation of software reliability–a pragmatic approach. In *Proc. of SSIRI'10)*, pages 227–236. IEEE, 2010.

[10] M.-H. Chen, A. P. Mathur, and V. J. Rego. Effect of testing techniques on software reliability estimates obtained using a time-domain model. *IEEE Trans. on Reliability*, 44(1):97–103, 1995.

[11] L. Cheung, R. Roshandel, N. Medvidovic, and L. Golubchik. Early prediction of software component reliability. In *Proc. of ICSE'08*, pages 111–120. ACM, 2008.

[12] V. Cortellessa, H. Singh, and B. Cukic. Early reliability assessment of uml based software models. In *Proc. of WOSP'02*, pages 302–309. ACM, 2002.

[13] M. Davidsson, J. Zheng, N. Nagappan, L. Williams, and M. Vouk. Gert: An empirical reliability estimation and testing feedback tool. In *Proc. of ISSRE'04*, pages 269–280. IEEE, 2004.

[14] A. Dimov, S. K. Chandran, and S. Punnekkat. How do we collect data for software reliability estimation? In *Proc. of CompSysTech'10*, pages 155–160. ACM, 2010.

[15] S. Distefano and A. Puliafito. Dependability evaluation with dynamic reliability block diagrams and dynamic fault trees. *IEEE Trans. on Dependable and Secure Computing*, 6(1):4–17, 2009.

[16] J. W. Duran and S. C. Ntafos. An evaluation of random testing. *IEEE Trans. on Software Engineering,*, SE-10(4):438–444, 1984.

[17] K. El Emam, W. Melo, and J. C. Machado. The prediction of faulty classes using object-oriented design metrics. *Journal of systems and software*, 56(1):63–75, 2001.

[18] N. E. Fenton and M. Neil. A critique of software defect prediction models. *IEEE Trans. on Software Engineering*, 25(5):675–689, 1999.

[19] J. Gaffney and C. F. Davis. An approach to estimating software errors and availability. In *Proc. of Minnowbrook workshop on software reliability'88*, 1988.

[20] S. Gokhale and K. Trivedi. Analytical models for architecture-based software reliability prediction: A unification framework. *IEEE Trans. on Reliability*, 55(4):578–590, 2006.

[21] S. S. Gokhale. Architecture-based software reliability analysis: Overview and limitations. *IEEE Trans. on Dependable and Secure Computing*, 4(1):32–40, 2007.

[22] S. S. Gokhale and K. S. Trivedi. A time/structure based software reliability model. *Annals of Software Engineering*, 8(1):85–121, 1999.

[23] S. S. Gokhale, W. E. Wong, K. S. Trivedi, and J. Horgan. An analytical approach to

architecture-based software reliability prediction. In *Proc. of IPDS'98*, pages 13–22. IEEE, 1998.

[24] K. Goseva-Popstojanova and M. Hamill. Architecture-based software reliability: Why only a few parameters matter? In *Proc. of COMPSAC'07*, pages 423–430. IEEE, 2007.

[25] K. Goseva-Popstojanova, M. Hamill, and R. Perugupalli. Large empirical case study of architecture-based software reliability. In *Proc. of ISSRE'05*, pages 43–52. IEEE, 2005.

[26] K. Goseva-Popstojanova, A. Hassan, A. Guedem, W. Abdelmoez, D. E. M. Nassar, H. Ammar, and A. Mili. Architectural-level risk analysis using uml. *IEEE Trans. on Software Engineering*, 29(10):946–960, 2003.

[27] K. Goseva-Popstojanova and K. S. Trivedi. Architecture-based approach to reliability assessment of software systems. *Performance Evaluation*, 45(2):179–204, 2001.

[28] M. Hamill and K. Goseva-Popstojanova. Common trends in software fault and failure data. *IEEE Trans. on Software Engineering*, 35(4):484–496, 2009.

[29] D. Hong, T. Gu, and J. Baik. A uml model based white box reliability prediction to identify unreliable components. In *Proc. of SSIRI-C'11*, pages 152–159. IEEE, 2011.

[30] A. Immonen and E. Niemelä. Survey of reliability and availability prediction methods from the viewpoint of software architecture. *Software and Systems Modeling*, 7(1):49–65, 2008.

[31] R. Jacoby and K. Masuzawa. Test coverage dependent software reliability estimation by the hgd model. In *Proc. of ISSRE'92*, pages 193–204. IEEE, 1992.

[32] H. Koziolek, B. Schlich, and C. Bilich. A large-scale industrial case study on architecture-based software reliability analysis. In *Proc. of ISSRE'10*, pages 279–288. IEEE, 2010.

[33] M. R. Lyu et al. *Handbook of software reliability engineering*, volume 3. IEEE Computer Society Press CA, 1996.

[34] Y. K. Malaiya and J. Denton. What do the software reliability growth model parameters represent? In *Proc. of ISSRE'97*, pages 124–135. IEEE, 1997.

[35] Y. K. Malaiya, M. N. Li, J. M. Bieman, and R. Karcich. Software reliability growth with test coverage. *IEEE Trans. on Reliability*, 51(4):420–426, 2002.

[36] A. Mannhart, A. Bilgic, and B. Bertsche. Modeling expert judgment for reliability prediction - comparison of methods. In *Proc. of RAMS'07.*, pages 1–6. IEEE, 2007.

[37] K. W. Miller, L. J. Morell, R. E. Noonan, S. K. Park, D. M. Nicol, B. W. Murrill, and J. M. Voas. Estimating the probability of failure when testing reveals no failures. *IEEE Trans. on Software Engineering*, 18(1):33–43, 1992.

[38] H. Mills. On the statistical validation of computer programs. *IBM Federal Syst. Div., Tech. Rep*, pages 72–6015, 1972.

[39] B. Murphy and T. Gent. Measuring system and software reliability using an automated data collection process. *Quality and reliability engineering international*, 11(5):341–353, 1995.

[40] N. Nagappan. *A Software Testing and Reliability Early Warning (STREW) Metric Suite*. PhD thesis, North Caroline State University, US, 2005.

[41] Y. Nakagawa and S. Hanata. An error complexity model for software reliability measurement. In *Proc. of ICSE'89*, pages 230–236. ACM, 1989.

[42] R. Natella, D. Cotroneo, J. A. Duraes, and H. S. Madeira. On fault representativeness of software fault injection. *IEEE Trans. on Software Eng.*, 39(1):80–96, 2013.

[43] E. Nelson. Estimating software reliability from test data. *Microelectronics Reliability*, 17(1):67–73, 1978.

[44] E. A. Nguyen, C. F. Rexach, D. P. Thorpe, and A. E. Walther. The importance of data quality in software reliability modeling. In *Proc. of ISSRE'10*, pages 220–228. IEEE, 2010.

[45] C. Ramamoorthy and F. B. Bastani. Software reliability - status and perspectives. *IEEE Trans. on Software Engineering*, 8(4):354–371, 1982.

[46] B. Schroeder and G. A. Gibson. Disk failures in the real world: What does an MTTF of 1,000,000 hours mean to you. In *Proc. of FAST'07*, pages 1–16. Citeseer, 2007.

[47] J. Sigurdsson, L. Walls, and J. Quigley. Bayesian belief nets for managing expert judgement and modelling reliability. *Quality and Reliability Eng. International*, 17(3):181–190, 2001.

[48] SMERFS. http://www.slingcode.com/smerfs/.

[49] T. Stalhane. Practical experiences with safety assessment of a system for automatic train control. *Proc. of SAFECOMP'92*, 1992.

[50] C. Stringfellow and A. A. Andrews. An empirical method for selecting software reliability growth models. *Empirical Software Engineering*, 7(4):319–343, 2002.

[51] R. Tripathi and R. Mall. Early stage software reliability and design assessment. In *Proc. of APSEC'05*, pages 619–628. IEEE, 2005.

[52] A. Wood. Software reliability growth models. *Tandem Technical Report*, 96, 1996.

[53] L. Xing. Fault-tolerant network reliability and importance analysis using binary decision diagrams. In *Proc. of RAMS'04*, pages 122–128. IEEE, 2004.

[54] S. Yacoub, B. Cukic, and H. Ammar. A scenario-based reliability analysis approach for component-based software. *IEEE Trans. on Reliability*, 53(4):465–480, 2004.

[55] S. M. Yacoub, H. H. Ammar, and T. Robinson. Dynamic metrics for object oriented designs. In *Proc. of METRICS'99*, pages 50–61. IEEE, 1999.

[56] M.-L. Yin, C. Hyde, and L. James. A petri-net approach for early-stage system-level software reliability estimation. In *Proc. of RAMS'00*, pages 100–105. IEEE, 2000.

[57] T. Zimmermann, N. Nagappan, H. Gall, E. Giger, and B. Murphy. Cross-project defect prediction: a large scale experiment on data vs. domain vs. process. In *Proc. of ESEC/FSE'09*, pages 91–100. ACM, 2009.

Efficient Re-resolution of SMT Specifications for Evolving Software Architectures

Kenneth Johnson
Computer and Mathematical Sciences
Auckland University of Technology
Auckland 1142, New Zealand
kenneth.johnson@aut.ac.nz

Radu Calinescu
Department of Computer Science
University of York
York, YO10 5GH, UK
radu.calinescu@york.ac.uk

ABSTRACT

We present a generic method for the efficient constraint re-resolution of a component-based software architecture after changes such as addition, removal and modification of components. Given a formal description of an evolving system as a constraint-specification problem, our method identifies and executes the re-resolution steps required to verify the system's compliance with constraints after each change. At each step, satisfiability modulo theory (SMT) techniques determine the satisfiability of component constraints expressed as logical formulae over suitably chosen theories of arithmetic, reusing results obtained in previous steps. We illustrate the application of the approach on a constraint-satisfaction problem arising from cloud-deployed software services. The incremental method is shown to re-resolve system constraints in a fraction of the time taken by standard SMT resolution.

Categories and Subject Descriptors

D.2.4 [**Software/Program Verification**]: Assertion checkers; D.2.11 [**Software Architectures**]: Languages

Keywords

Incremental Re-resolution; Domain-Specific Languages; Satisfiability Modulo Theory

1. INTRODUCTION

Software architectures are expected to evolve in response to changing business needs and processes [1, 2, 20]. New architectural paradigms enabled by emerging technologies such as cloud computing and wireless sensor networks require this evolution to take place on ever shorter time scales—often autonomously and at run time, while delivering uninterrupted service. Evolving software architectures in such scenarios is very challenging [6, 21]. In particular, existing methods and tools for identifying and evaluating suitable architectural changes were devised for use as part of off-line

Permission to make digital or hard copies of all or part of this work for personal or classroom use is granted without fee provided that copies are not made or distributed for profit or commercial advantage and that copies bear this notice and the full citation on the first page. Copyrights for components of this work owned by others than the author(s) must be honored. Abstracting with credit is permitted. To copy otherwise, or republish, to post on servers or to redistribute to lists, requires prior specific permission and/or a fee. Request permissions from permissions@acm.org.
CBSE'14, June 30–July 4, 2014, Marcq-en-Baroeul, France.
Copyright is held by the owner/author(s). Publication rights licensed to ACM.
ACM 978-1-4503-2577-6/14/06 ...$15.00.
http://dx.doi.org/10.1145/2602576.2602578

processes carried out manually by software architects, over longer time periods.

To address this challenge, the research community has recently advocated the use of lightweight variants of formal methods for the specification, development and verification of software architectures in fast-changing scenarios, including at run time [10, 22, 29]. As an example, *run-time quantitative verification* [8] has been used to ensure that service-based architectures [7, 9, 16] and cloud architectures [23] continue to comply with reliability, performance and other non-functional requirements as they are reconfigured dynamically. Likewise, [26] introduced a method for developing adaptive software architectures through predefining a set of system configurations, and using *aspect-oriented model reasoning* to select the most suitable of these configurations at run time. Similar results have been obtained through the rigorous use of architectural models as a guide for the software adaptation process [17, 21].

The *satisfiability modulo theory (SMT) re-resolution* method we introduce in this paper adds a powerful new tool to these results. Over the past decade, *SMT solvers* of constraint-satisfaction problems expressed in theories such as linear, non-linear and difference arithmetic have developed a strong track record of successfully addressing a wide range of real-world decision problems [3, 15], including in the area of software architecture analysis (e.g., [13, 19]).

Our SMT re-resolution method extends the applicability of SMT solvers to the analysis of rapidly evolving software architectures. To this end, we employ an *incremental* approach in which the re-resolution of a constraint-satisfaction problem reuses relevant partial results from the solution of the previous, unmodified version of the problem. The approach works well for component-based software architectures, whose constraint-satisfaction problems can be expressed as SMT specifications comprising interdependent parts that can be analysed in a *compositional* fashion. As illustrated by the first case study we apply our approach to, many of the typical changes within such systems affect individual components. Accordingly, the re-resolution of the associated SMT specification can be carried out efficiently through re-analysing only the parts associated with these affected components.

We envisage two important applications for our efficient SMT re-resolution method. First, the method can be used to ensure that architectural reconfigurations within a self-adaptive software system do not violate the constraints specified by the system requirements. The case study presented in the paper illustrate this application of the method. Second, efficient SMT re-resolution can be used to examine ranges of "what if" scenarios of architectural change for a software system. The ability to solve sets of related constraint-satisfaction problems efficiently can significantly speed up the analysis of the trade-offs between potentially large numbers of similar architectures—a common task in software development.

The main contributions of the paper are:

1. A method for the compositional resolution of constraint-satisfaction problems for component-based software architectures, and the incremental re-resolution of these problems after localised architectural changes.

2. Formal correctness proofs for the compositional and the incremental steps of our SMT re-resolution method.

3. An open-source Java prototype tool that implements the SMT re-resolution method on top of the state-of-the-art SMT solver Z3 [14].

4. An extensive evaluation of the effectiveness of SMT re-resolution in the context of cloud-deployed software systems.

The prototype SMT re-resolution tool and the SMT specifications for the two systems and detailed experimental results are freely available at http://www-users.cs.york.ac.uk/~raduc/IncrementalSMT.

The rest of the paper is organised as follows. Section 2 introduces the theoretical concepts underpinning the SMT re-resolution method. Section 3 describes a cloud-based software architecture used as a running example throughout the paper, as well as to evaluate our method within a case study. The incremental SMT re-resolution method is presented in Section 4, and its effectiveness is evaluated in Section 5 through a case study from the cloud computing application domain. The paper concludes with a discussion of related work in Section 6, and a summary of our contributions in Section 7.

2. PRELIMINARIES

In this section we provide a brief review of the mathematical tools used for modelling component-based systems and set the notation used throughout the paper. The reader is assumed to have a basic knowledge of universal algebra, logic and satisfiability-module theory techniques and is directed to the standard texts [25, 27] for detailed descriptions of these topics.

Signatures and Algebras

A signature Σ consists of a finite set S of sorts, a finite number of operation symbols $f : s_1 \times \cdots \times s_n \to s$ where $n \geq 0$ and $s_1, \ldots, s_n, s \in S$. Operation symbols of the form $c :\to s$ are constants and we assume that each sort $s \in S$ has at least one constant. We assume Σ possesses the sort $Bool$ and the constant symbols $true, false :\to Bool$ naming the Boolean truth values with logical operation symbols and, or and not. Operation symbols in Σ of the form $r : s_1 \times \ldots \times s_n \to Bool$ are called Σ-predicates and for each sort s there is an equality symbol $=: s^2 \to Bool$.

A Σ-algebra A is an interpretation of the signature Σ and consists of a non-empty carrier set A_s for each sort s in S. Each constant $c :\to s$ is interpreted by an element $c_A \in A_s$ and a total function $f_A : A_{s_1} \times A_{s_n} \to A_s$ models each operation symbol $f : s_1 \times \cdots \times s_n \to s$. The Boolean sort

$Bool$ is interpreted by the carrier $\mathbb{B} = \{\mathbf{t}, \mathbf{f}\}$ where $\mathbf{t}$ and $\mathbf{f}$ interpret the constant symbols $true$ and $false$ respectively, and each logical operation has the standard interpretation.

We describe a simple algebraic construction. Given a Σ-algebra A let u be an element not in any carrier of A. For each sort $s \in S$ we define the carrier $A_s^u = A_s \cup \{u\}$. For each operation $f_A : A_{s_1} \times A_{s_n} \to A_s$ we define a new operation $f^u(a_1, \ldots, a_n) = u$ if any operand $a_i = u$, for $1 \leq i \leq n$ and $f(a_1, \ldots, a_n)$ otherwise. We similarly extend each of the operations in the algebra $\mathbb{B}$. The algebraic constructions involving the value u will be helpful in raising errors and exceptions when evaluating the satisfiability of system component requirements. We assume throughout the paper that each algebra has been constructed in this manner.

Terms

Let Σ be a signature and variables $Z = (Z_s)$ be pairwise disjoint sets for $s \in S$. We define Σ-terms of sort s as follows:

- every variable $z \in Z_s$ is a term of sort s
- every Σ-constant $c :\to s$ is a term of sort s
- if $f : s_1 \times \cdots \times s_n \to s$ is a Σ-operation and $t_1, \ldots, t_n$ are Σ-terms of sorts $s_1, \ldots, s_n$ respectively then $f(t_1, \ldots, t_n)$ is a term of sort s,
- if $r : s_1 \times \cdots \times s_n \to Bool$ is a Σ-predicate and $t_1, \ldots, t_n$ are Σ-terms of sorts $s_1, \ldots, s_n$ respectively then $r(t_1, \ldots, t_n)$ is a term of sort $Bool$.

We define the function $var : T(\Sigma, Z) \to 2^Z$ such that $var(t)$ is the set of all variables appearing in the Σ-term t. The Σ-terms that have no variables are called $closed\ terms$.

Term Evaluation

Given a Σ-algebra A and an assignment $a \in [Z \to A]$ mapping values to the variables, we define the $term\ evaluation$ mapping $[\![-]\!] : T(\Sigma, Z) \times [Z \to A] \to A$ that works out a value for each Σ-term t by substituting the value $a(z)$ for each variable z in t. Term evaluation is defined by structural induction over the set $T(\Sigma, Z)$:

- $[\![c]\!](a) = c_A$,
- $[\![z]\!](a) = a(z)$,
- $[\![f_i(t_1, \ldots, t_n)]\!](a) = f_{i_A}([\![t_1]\!](a), \ldots, [\![t_n]\!](a))$,
- $[\![r(t_1, \ldots, t_n)]\!](a) = r_{\mathbb{B}}([\![t_1]\!](a), \ldots, [\![t_n]\!](a))$.

Quantifier-Free First Order Formulae

The set $F(\Sigma, Z)$ of quantifier-free first order formulae over the signature Σ is defined inductively by the rules

$$\alpha ::= t_1 = t_2 \mid r_1(t_1, \ldots, t_{n_1}) \mid \cdots \mid r_m(t_1, \ldots, t_{n_m}) \mid$$
$$\neg \alpha_1 \mid \alpha_1 \wedge \alpha_2 \mid \alpha_1 \vee \alpha_2,$$

where t_1 and t_2 are terms and α_1 and α_2 are quantifier-free first order formulae. When working with specific applications it is often convenient to display the variables in a formula. We write $\alpha(\mathbf{z})$ to mean the formula α contains at least one instance of the variables in the tuple $\mathbf{z} = (z_1, \ldots, z_p)$. Term evaluation is extended to Σ-formulae and we write $[\![\alpha(\mathbf{z})]\!](a)$ to mean that each $z_i \in \mathbf{z}$ for $1 \leq i \leq p$ is evaluated by setting $[\![z_i]\!] = a(z_i)$. The satisfiability relation $\models$ over A is defined as

$$a \models \alpha(\mathbf{z}) \iff [\![\alpha(\mathbf{z})]\!](a) = \mathbf{t}$$

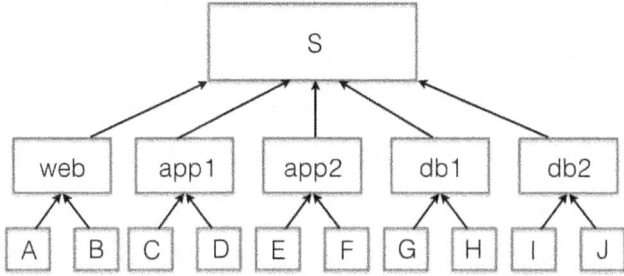

Figure 1: Multi-tiered service to be deployed on cloud infrastructure

by substituting the value $a(z)$ for each variable z in the formula $\alpha(\mathbf{z})$. In this case, we say that a is a *satisfiable assignment* of the formula $\alpha(\mathbf{z})$, where the satisfiability relationship $\models$ is defined inductively over the structure of the formulas in $F(\Sigma, Z)$ [27].

3. CASE STUDY

We introduce a case study from the domain of cloud computing technology to illustrate the theory underpinning our compositional SMT approach. Figure 1 presents a service **S** comprised of the following components:

- a website component **web**,
- two application components **app₁** and **app₂**, and
- two database components **db₁** and **db₂**.

Each component in **S** has two sub-components, and these sub-components are labelled alphabetically from **A** to **J**.

To take advantage of the elasticity of cloud computing infrastructure and to improve the reliability of the service, multiple instances of the sub-components **A** - **J** are deployed on virtual machines hosted on cloud data centres called *cloud availability zones*. As an example, at the time of writing the public infrastructure of major cloud resource provider Amazon EC2 is organised into 22 availability zones distributed across six regions worldwide and characterised by independent power supply, network infrastructure, physical protection, etc. In line with the best industry practice of distributing critical services across multiple availability zones, we assume that service **S** is to be distributed over zones numbered from 1 to p, where $p \geq 2$, and according to the following high-level requirements:

R1 components **A** - **J** have between 1 and 20 instances

R2 **A** has exactly 10 instances

R3 **B** cannot be deployed on zone 2

R4 **D** must be deployed on zone 1

R5 the two sub-components of **app1** have the same number of instances

R6 **db1** instances are deployed over at least two zones

R7 **app2** and **db2** must be identically distributed

4. INCREMENTAL RE-RESOLUTION

This section formalises the mathematical description of our incremental SMT approach to resolve component requirements after system changes. We consider how system architecture requirements can be decomposed into smaller, independent formulae to be solved in isolation and show how previous resolution analysis steps may be used to re-resolve requirements after changes.

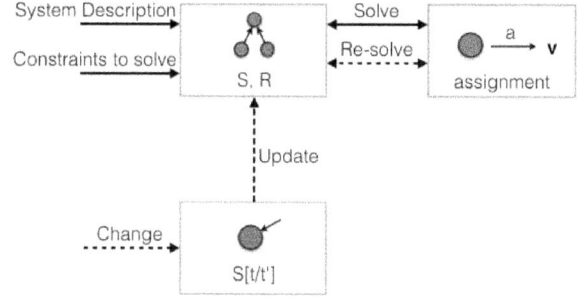

Figure 2: Incremental SMT re-resolution workflow

4.1 Overview

Our approach (Figure 2) comprises two stages:

1. In the *compositional stage*, the system is analysed for the first time. An algebraic description S of the system is expressed in terms of a component signature Σ. To each system component of S we associate a finite set of variables which model specific aspects of the component we wish to reason about. Our choice of variables and their meaning is dependent on the specific application domain and problem under consideration. Each component of S is associated with requirements expressed as formulae constructed from a *requirements signature* Γ over variables contained in the component's model. We define a Γ-algebra A which interprets the terms and formulae. The algebra A is extended to include an *unsatisfiable* element u. Compositional SMT resolution is performed on S and each component requirement is associated with an assignment a mapping the values in A to variables in Z. The actions associated with this stage are depicted by solid lines in Figure 2.

2. In the *incremental stage*, a component t of the system is affected by a change. In response, the system's algebraic description S is updated by substitution of the term t with a new term t' representing the modified component. The requirements of the components affected by the change are re-resolved using incremental SMT to ensure the system's continued compliance with its requirements. The actions associated with this stage are depicted by dashed lines in Figure 2.

4.2 Specifying Component-Based Architectures

A *component signature* Σ is a finite set C of component sorts that represent the parts of a system and a set $\{f_1, \ldots, f_n\}$ of operations that are performed on components. By choosing some basic components (e.g. constants in Σ) and applying a sequence of operations we form a representation of a component-based system as a high-level syntactic *component term* S, defined as a closed term. The terms describe the hierarchical structure of a component-based system by defining the *calculations* carried out in the construction of the system description, and specifying the *order* in which the operations on components are applied. Component algebras organise the operations we define and form the basis for domain specific languages. The inductive properties of terms provide a natural data structure for defining an incremental verification algorithm.

Example 1. **Specification of a Cloud Deployed System.** We define the component signature Σ for the specification of a component-based system $\mathbf{S}$ depicted in Figure 1. Let the sort of components be denoted C. We specify constants $\mathbf{A}, \ldots, \mathbf{J}$ in C that represent the sub-components of the system and define a single operation symbol $c : C \times C \to C$ which combines components to construct the algebraic expression of the system based on the interdependencies represented by the arrows in Figure 1. We have the term

$$\mathbf{S} \equiv c(\mathbf{web}, c(\mathbf{app_1}, c(\mathbf{app_2}, c(\mathbf{db_1}, \mathbf{db_2})))) \quad (1)$$

where specification of sub-components are given by $\mathbf{web} \equiv c(\mathbf{A}, \mathbf{B})$, $\mathbf{app_1} \equiv c(\mathbf{C}, \mathbf{D})$, $\mathbf{app_2} \equiv c(\mathbf{E}, \mathbf{F})$, $\mathbf{db_1} \equiv c(\mathbf{G}, \mathbf{H})$, $\mathbf{db_2} \equiv c(\mathbf{I}, \mathbf{J})$.

Component Models

We associate each component t in the component term S with a finite subset Z_t of variables from the set Z. We say that Z_t *models* the component t. We have the following

DEFINITION 4.1 (COMPONENT MODELS). *Let Z be a set of variables. We define the model $Z_t \subset Z$ of component term t by structural induction on component terms*
Base case: $Z_{c_i} \in \mathbb{P}(Z)$, *for each basic component term c_i such that models are pairwise disjoint: $Z_{c_i} \cap Z_{c_j} = \varnothing$ for $i \neq j$.*
Inductive step: $Z_{f(t_1, \ldots, t_m)} = \bigcup_{i=1}^m Z_{t_i}$, *for each operation $f \in \Sigma$ and subterms $t_1, \ldots, t_m$.*

Example 2. **Cloud Deployment Models.** The choice of model for components in the system depends on the kinds of problems the user of our approach wishes to analyse. In order to employ SMT techniques to analyse component requirements, we suppose that each sub-components $\mathbf{A}$ to $\mathbf{J}$ of the cloud deployed service (1) is modelled by a finite set of p integer-typed variables, according to the number of availability zones p that the component is to be distributed across. For example, we model sub-component $\mathbf{A}$ as the set $Z_{\mathbf{A}} = \{\mathbf{A}z_1, \ldots, \mathbf{A}z_p\}$ of integer-typed variables $\mathbf{A}z_i$ such that the assignment $\mathbf{A}z_i = n$ of a value $n \in \mathbb{Z}$ to the variable $\mathbf{A}z_i$ corresponds to the scenario in which n instances of $\mathbf{A}$ are deployed on the ith availability zone.

Now, according to Definition 4.1, the models for each component t of the system $\mathbf{S}$ is the union of its sub-components. For example, the component term $\mathbf{web} \equiv comp(\mathbf{A}, \mathbf{B})$ has the component model $Z_{\mathbf{web}} = Z_{\mathbf{A}} \cup Z_{\mathbf{B}}$. Thus, we have the following union of component models

$$Z_{\mathbf{S}} = Z_{\mathbf{web}} \cup Z_{\mathbf{app1}} \cup Z_{\mathbf{app2}} \cup Z_{\mathbf{db1}} \cup Z_{\mathbf{db2}},$$
$$= Z_{\mathbf{A}} \cup \cdots \cup Z_{\mathbf{J}}$$

derived from the system architecture of $\mathbf{S}$ defined in (1).

Component Requirements

Component requirements are expressed in terms of a language specific to the sorts of component properties we wish to reason with. We define this language by specifying a *requirements signature* Γ. The set of *component requirements* F is defined to be $F(\Gamma, Z)$, the formulae over the variables in Z used in Definition 4.1 for modelling the system components. Each component term is associated with a formula from F and contains variables from the component model $Z_t \subset Z$:

DEFINITION 4.2 (REQUIREMENT MAP). *We define the requirement map as a mapping $\phi : C \to F$ such that $\phi(t)$ is a logical formula in F associated with the component term t with the property $var(\phi(t)) \subseteq Z_t$, for all $t \in C$.*

For simplicity, we sometimes write the requirements $\phi(t)$ of component term t in subscript notation, ϕ_t.

The formula associated with a component may express multiple requirements, all of which must be met if the component is deemed compliant. For convenience, we assume that each requirement $\phi(t)$ is in conjunctive normal form

$$\phi(t) = \alpha_1 \wedge \cdots \wedge \alpha_n, \quad (2)$$

for component term $t \in C$. When no requirements are needed for t we set $\phi(t) = \epsilon$ where ϵ is the empty formula, satisfiable by all assignment mappings.

Example 3. **Cloud Deployment Requirements.** The high-level requirements (R1) to (R7) for the cloud-deployed software architecture described in Section 3 are formalised as logical formulae over integer-type variables in the model of $\mathbf{S}$. Let Γ be a signature comprising sorts for integers and Booleans, and symbols for arithmetical operations, equality and inequality predicates. We define the requirement map $\phi : C \to F$ for $\mathbf{S}$. First, Requirement (R1) sets the range of deployed instances for each sub-component of $\mathbf{S}$ between 1 and 20, and a negative number of instances cannot be deployed on any zone. This requirement is expressed as the formula

$$\alpha_{\mathbf{A}} := \bigwedge_{i=1}^p \mathbf{A}z_i \geq 0 \wedge \sum_{i=1}^p \mathbf{A}z_i \geq 1 \wedge \sum_{i=1}^p \mathbf{A}z_i \leq 20$$

for component $\mathbf{A}$, and using similar formulae $\alpha_{\mathbf{B}}, \ldots, \alpha_{\mathbf{J}}$ for sub-components $\mathbf{B}$ to $\mathbf{J}$.

In addition to this basic requirement, requirements (R2) to (R7) add further constraints to the deployment configuration of the case study system $\mathbf{S}$. We have

$$\phi_{\mathbf{A}} := \alpha_{\mathbf{A}} \wedge \overbrace{\sum_{i=1}^p \mathbf{A}z_i = 10}^{(R2)}$$

adding (R2) to the previous formula corresponding to Requirement (R1) for $\mathbf{A}$. For the components $\mathbf{B}$ and $\mathbf{D}$ we have the formulae

$$\phi_{\mathbf{B}} := \alpha_{\mathbf{B}} \wedge \overbrace{\mathbf{B}z_2 = 0}^{(R3)} \text{ and } \phi_{\mathbf{D}} := \alpha_{\mathbf{D}} \wedge \overbrace{\mathbf{D}z_1 > 0}^{(R4)}$$

respectively. Requirement (R6) is partitioned into two separate formulae involving the sub-components $\mathbf{G}$ and $\mathbf{H}$ of $\mathbf{db_1}$, yielding

$$\phi_{\mathbf{G}} := \alpha_{\mathbf{G}} \wedge \overbrace{\sum_{i=1}^p nz(\mathbf{G}z_i) \geq 2}^{(R6.1)} \text{ and } \phi_{\mathbf{H}} := \alpha_{\mathbf{H}} \wedge \overbrace{\sum_{i=1}^p nz(\mathbf{H}z_i) \geq 2}^{(R6.2)},$$

where $nz(n) = 1$ if $n \neq 0$ and $nz(n) = 0$ otherwise for $n \in \mathbb{Z}$. At the component level, we have Requirement (R5) which stipulates that the sub-components $\mathbf{C}$ and $\mathbf{D}$ of $\mathbf{app_1}$ must have the same number of instances deployed over the cloud infrastructure. Thus, we set

$$\phi_{\mathbf{app_1}} := \sum_{i=1}^p \mathbf{C}z_i = \sum_{i=1}^p \mathbf{D}z_i.$$

Lastly, at the topmost level of the service $\mathbf{S}$, we express Requirement (R7) as the formula and set

$$\phi_{\mathbf{S}} := \bigwedge_{i=1}^p (\mathbf{E}z_i = \mathbf{F}z_i) \wedge (\mathbf{I}z_i = \mathbf{J}z_i) \wedge (\mathbf{E}z_i = \mathbf{I}z_i).$$

The remaining components $\mathbf{db_1}$, $\mathbf{db_2}$, and $\mathbf{app_2}$ have no specific cloud deployment requirements and the map ϕ associates them with the empty formula ϵ.

4.3 Component Requirements Resolution

Satisfiability modulo theories (SMTs) represent a class of theoretical techniques and practical tools that determine the satisfiability of formulae expressed in a logical theory. An SMT technique computes and returns an assignment of values to variables that satisfy the formula. For formulae over variables from Z we model an SMT decision procedure as a total function $smt : F \to [Z \to A]$ such that $smt(\alpha(\mathbf{z})) \models \alpha(\mathbf{z})$ if $\alpha(\mathbf{z})$ is satisfiable in A. Otherwise, the unsatisfiable assignment $\mathbf{u} : Z \to A$ is returned where $\mathbf{u}(z) = u$, for all $z \in \mathbf{z}$, where $u \in A$. We wish to apply the SMT decision procedure smt to determine compliance of a component-based system to its requirements. Mathematically, this involves determining the satisfiability of the logical conjunction of all formulae associated with the system components. To this end, we have the following definition.

Definition 4.3 (Monolithic Requirements). *Let $\phi : C \to F$ be a requirement map. We define the function $\rho : C \times [C \to F] \to F$ over the inductive structure of component terms constructed from the signature Σ:*
Base case: *$\rho(c_i, \phi) = \phi(c_i)$, for each basic component c_i,*
Inductive step:
$\rho(f(t_1, \dots, t_n), \phi) = \phi(f(t_1, \dots, t_n)) \wedge (\wedge_{i=1}^n \rho(t_i, \phi))$, for each operation symbol f in Σ and terms $t_1, \dots, t_n$ in C.

Example 4. Applying Definition 4.3 to the case study system architecture $\mathbf{S}$ and requirement map ϕ, we construct the monolithic requirements as

$$\rho(\mathbf{S}, \phi) = \alpha_\mathbf{A} \wedge \alpha_\mathbf{B} \wedge \alpha_\mathbf{C} \wedge \alpha_\mathbf{D} \wedge \alpha_\mathbf{E} \wedge \alpha_\mathbf{F}$$
$$\wedge \, \alpha_\mathbf{G} \wedge \alpha_\mathbf{H} \wedge \alpha_\mathbf{I} \wedge \alpha_\mathbf{J} \wedge \alpha_\mathbf{app_1} \wedge \alpha_\mathbf{S} \quad (3)$$

where components associated with the empty formula have been omitted.

Definition 4.4 (Satisfiability). *The component term S satisfies requirements ϕ if, and only if, there exists an assignment $a : Z \to A$ such that $a \models \rho(S, \phi)$, for $S \in C$ and $\phi : C \to F$.*

The smt decision procedure can be used in a straightforward way to determine requirement satisfiability for any component term in C. We have

Definition 4.5 (Monolithic Analysis). *The function $mono : C \times [C \to F] \to [Z \to A]$ is defined as $mono(S, \phi) = smt(\rho(S, \phi))$ for component term S and requirement map ϕ.*

Example 5. **Monolithic Analysis of S.** We apply Definition 4.5 to compute a cloud deployment configuration for the system $\mathbf{S}$ over two availability zones. Mathematically, each sub-component is modelled by a set of two variables from Z, e.g. $Z_\mathbf{A} = \{\mathbf{A}z_1, \mathbf{A}z_2\}$, for the sub-component $\mathbf{A}$. Monolithic analysis yields the following assignment:

	A	B	C	D	E	F	G	H	I	J
z_1	10	1	0	1	0	0	1	1	0	0
z_2	0	0	1	0	1	1	1	1	1	1

of integer values to component model variables in $Z_\mathbf{S} = \{\mathbf{A}z_1, \mathbf{A}z_2, \dots, \mathbf{J}z_1, \mathbf{J}z_2\}$ satisfying Formula 3.

4.4 Compositional Resolution

Since modern software systems comprise large numbers of components, the monolithic approach to determining requirement compliance often involves analysing huge constraint-satisfaction problems. In this section we introduce a new *compositional* approach to component based system requirements resolution.

Proof Sequences

Our compositional approach is based on the observation that requirements can be syntactically deconstructed into a sequence of independent formulae resolvable in separate SMT analysis steps. The combined results form a solution for the entire system.

Definition 4.6 (Independent Formulae). *The formulae $\alpha(\mathbf{z})$ and $\beta(\mathbf{y})$ in F are independent if, and only if, $var(\alpha(\mathbf{z})) \cap var(\beta(\mathbf{y})) = \emptyset$ such that $\mathbf{z}$ and $\mathbf{y}$ are tuples of variables in the set Z.*

Formulae that share common variables are *dependent*.

To make use of this definition, we describe a procedure in which a formula in conjunctive normal form (2) is partitioned into a sequence of independent sub-formulae. We denote the set of finite sequences of formula as Seq, where σ_i denotes the ith element of σ in Seq.

Let $\pi : F \to Seq$ be a function that partitions the set of numbers $\{1, \dots, n\}$ corresponding to indices of formulae in the supplied input conjunction $\alpha = \alpha_1 \wedge \dots \wedge \alpha_n$ into the family $P = \{P_1, \dots, P_m\}$ of partition sets. The partition P is constructed with the property $var(P_i) \cap var(P_j) = \emptyset$ for $i \neq j$ where $var(P_i) = \cup_{k \in P_i} var(\alpha_k)$ is an extension of the variable set notation introduced for formulae. We define the elements of the sequence $\pi(\alpha)$ as $\pi_i(\alpha) = \wedge_{k \in P_i} \alpha_k$ for $1 \leq i \leq m$. Clearly, since each k belongs to precisely one partition and $\{1, \dots, n\} = \cup_{i=1}^m P_i$, we have

$$\wedge_{i=1}^m \pi_i(\alpha) = \alpha. \quad (4)$$

Definition 4.7 (Proof Sequence). *We define the sequence $\pi(\alpha)$ to be the proof sequence of the conjunction $\alpha = \alpha_1 \wedge \dots \wedge \alpha_n$ of n formulae.*

We extend proof sequence notation to construct independent formulae of requirement maps, setting $\pi(\phi) = \pi(\rho(S, \phi))$ for $\phi : C \to F$ for component term S.

Example 6. **Cloud Deployment Proof Sequence.** We construct the proof sequence comprising six formulae from the requirement map ϕ specified for $\mathbf{S}$:

$$\pi(\phi) = (\phi_\mathbf{S} \wedge \phi_\mathbf{E} \wedge \phi_\mathbf{F} \wedge \phi_\mathbf{I} \wedge \phi_\mathbf{J},$$
$$\phi_\mathbf{A}, \phi_\mathbf{B}, \phi_\mathbf{C} \wedge \phi_\mathbf{D} \wedge \phi_\mathbf{app_1}, \phi_\mathbf{G}, \phi_\mathbf{H}).$$

Proof Sequence Analysis

Independent formulas $\alpha(\mathbf{z})$ and $\beta(\mathbf{y})$ from Definition 4.6 can be solved in separate SMT resolution steps to obtain two satisfiable assignments a and b respectively. The assignments are combined using a *composition operation* $\oplus : [Z \to A]^2 \to [Z \to A]$ to build a new variable assignment satisfying the conjunction of the formulae. We have the definition

$$a \oplus b = \begin{cases} a(z) & \text{if } z \in dom(a), \\ b(z) & \text{otherwise,} \end{cases}$$

where z is a variable in Z. We note $dom(a \oplus b) = dom(a) \cup dom(b)$ and $a \oplus \eta = a$ and $\eta \oplus b = b$ for the null function η such that the domain and range of η are the empty set $\emptyset$.

LEMMA 4.1 (ONE-STEP). *If $a \models \alpha(\mathbf{z})$ and $b \models \beta(\mathbf{y})$ then $a \oplus b \models \alpha(\mathbf{z}) \wedge \beta(\mathbf{y})$, where $\alpha(\mathbf{z})$ and $\beta(\mathbf{y})$ are independent formulae.*

PROOF. Suppose $a \models \alpha(\mathbf{z})$ and $b \models \beta(\mathbf{y})$ and $\alpha(\mathbf{z})$ and $\beta(\mathbf{y})$ are independent. We show $a \oplus b \models \alpha(\mathbf{z}) \wedge \beta(\mathbf{y})$ by calculating

$$[\![\alpha(\mathbf{z}) \wedge \beta(\mathbf{y})]\!]_A(a \oplus b) = [\![\alpha(\mathbf{z})]\!]_A(a \oplus b) \wedge_\mathbb{B} [\![\beta(\mathbf{y})]\!]_A(a \oplus b).$$

Calculation of the LHS yields

$$\begin{aligned} [\![\alpha(\mathbf{z})]\!]_A(a \oplus b) &= \alpha_A([\![\mathbf{z}]\!]_A(a \oplus b)) \\ &= \alpha_A(a \oplus b)(\mathbf{z}) \\ &= \alpha_A(a)(\mathbf{z}) \text{ since } \mathbf{z} \in dom(a) \\ &= \mathbf{t} \text{ since } a \models \alpha(\mathbf{z}). \end{aligned}$$

It can be shown for the RHS that $a \oplus b \models \beta(\mathbf{y})$ following a similar calculation. Thus the evaluation $[\![\alpha(\mathbf{z}) \wedge \beta(\mathbf{y})]\!]_A(a \oplus b)$ yields $\mathbf{t} \wedge_\mathbb{B} \mathbf{t}$ and the result follows by the standard interpretation of the logical operation $\wedge_\mathbb{B}$. $\square$

DEFINITION 4.8 (COMPOSITIONAL ANALYSIS). *The function $comp : Seq \times [Z \to A] \to [Z \to A]$ is defined by induction over sequences. Let a be an assignment in $[Z \to A]$.*
Base case: $comp((\alpha), a) = a \oplus smt(\alpha)$
Structural Induction: $comp(\sigma \frown (\alpha), a) = comp(\sigma, a) \oplus smt(\alpha)$, for $a \in V$, $\alpha \in F(\Gamma, Z)$ and $\sigma \in Seq$.

We can now prove that function $comp$ returns a satisfiable assignment for a proof sequence.

THEOREM 4.1. *Let $\sigma = (\alpha_1, \ldots, \alpha_n)$ be a finite sequence of independent formulae. If $\wedge_{i=1}^n \alpha_i$ is satisfiable then*

$$comp(\sigma, \eta) \models \wedge_{i=1}^n \alpha_i.$$

PROOF. We prove the result by an inductive argument on the length of sequences. We have
Base case: For the sequence (α_1) containing the satisfiable formula α_1 we have

$$\begin{aligned} comp((\alpha_1), \eta) &= \eta \oplus smt(\alpha_1) \text{ by Definition 4.8} \\ &= smt(\alpha_1) \text{ since } dom(\eta) = \emptyset \end{aligned}$$

yielding a satisfiable assignment.
Inductive Assumption: Let $\sigma = (\alpha_1, \ldots, \alpha_k)$ be a sequence of independent formulae such that $\wedge_{i=1}^k \alpha_i$ is satisfiable and suppose $comp(\sigma, \eta) \models \wedge_{i=1}^k \alpha_i$.
Inductive Step: If α_{k+1} is a satisfiable formula then

$$comp(\sigma \frown (\alpha_{k+1}), \eta) = comp(\sigma, \eta) \oplus smt(\alpha_{k+1})$$

by Definition 4.8. But by the inductive assumption $\wedge_{i=1}^k \alpha_i$ is satisfiable and since α_{k+1} is a satisfiable we apply Lemma 4.1 to obtain

$$\begin{aligned} comp(\sigma, \eta) \oplus smt(\alpha_{k+1}) &\models \wedge_{i=1}^k \alpha_i \wedge \alpha_{k+1} \\ &= \wedge_{i=1}^{k+1} \alpha_i \end{aligned}$$

proving the result for the inductive step. $\square$

We have the following result which shows the equivalence of the compositional analysis approach with the monolithic approach given by Definition 4.5.

COROLLARY 4.1. *If t is ϕ satisfiable then*

$$comp(\pi(\rho(t, \phi)), \eta) \models \rho(t, \phi)$$

for component term t in C and requirement map $\alpha : C \to F$.

PROOF. Partitioning component t's requirement map yields a sequence $\pi(\rho(t, \phi))$ of independent formulae. We have

$$\begin{aligned} comp(\pi(\rho(t, \alpha)), \eta) &\models \wedge \pi_i(\rho(t, \phi)) \text{ by Theorem 4.1} \\ &= \rho(t, \phi) \text{ by Property (4) of partitions} \end{aligned}$$

proving the result. $\square$

Example 7. **Compositional Analysis of S**
We apply the compositional analysis Theorem 4.1 to the proof sequence of **S** from Example 6. The function $comp$ carries out six analysis steps to obtain $a_1 \models \phi_\mathbf{H}$, $a_2 \models \phi_\mathbf{G}$ $a_3 \models \phi_\mathbf{C} \wedge \phi_\mathbf{D} \wedge \phi_{\mathbf{app_1}}$, $a_4 \models \phi_\mathbf{B}$, $a_5 \models \phi_\mathbf{A}$, and $a_6 \models \phi_\mathbf{S} \wedge \phi_\mathbf{E} \wedge \phi_\mathbf{F} \wedge \phi_\mathbf{I} \wedge \phi_\mathbf{J}$. The compositional operation is used to form the assignment $a_1 \oplus \cdots \oplus a_6$ from the six individual results which satisfies the monolithic specification $\rho(S, \phi)$ by Corollary 4.1.

4.5 Incremental Re-resolution

Despite the speed up obtained by applying compositional SMT resolution to large component-based systems, it is still unfeasible to re-resolve every component within a software architecture after each of the frequent updates that characterise a growing number of systems. To address this limitation, we formulate an incremental approach that performs only the necessary SMT analysis steps to re-resolve system compliance after changes in

1. the system architecture S arising from the addition or removal of components, and
2. the system requirements ϕ arising from the addition, removal or update of component requirements.

We model change as a transformation T such that

$$(S, \phi) \overset{T}{\to} (S', \phi')$$

transforms the component term S and its requirement map ϕ to an updated component term S' and requirement map ϕ'. The transformation T of t comprises $t' \in C$ and $\tau : C \to F$ and is carried out in two steps:

1. The term substitution $S' = S[t/t']$ is performed, substituting all instances of t with the new component term t' in S,
2. The requirement substitution $\phi' = \phi[\tau]$, is performed, substituting a formula $\phi(t_i)$ with a new formula $\tau(t_i)$ for $t_i \in dom(\tau)$.

Example 8. **Sub-Component Addition.** Suppose that a new sub-component **K** is added to $\mathbf{app_2}$ in **S**. Also, assume that five instances of **K** must be deployed across the cloud infrastructure, and that Requirement (R7), which requires all sub-components of $\mathbf{app_2}$ and $\mathbf{db_2}$ to be identically distributed, must be maintained. We model this change scenario mathematically as the transformation T, comprising a term substitution $\mathbf{S}' \equiv S[c(\mathbf{E}, \mathbf{F})/c(\mathbf{K}, c(\mathbf{E}, \mathbf{F}))]$ and requirement map $\tau : \{\mathbf{K}, \mathbf{S}\} \to F$ such that

$$\tau(\mathbf{K}) = \alpha_\mathbf{K} \wedge \sum_{i=1}^p \mathbf{K}z = 5$$

$$\tau(\mathbf{S}) = \phi(\mathbf{S}) \wedge_{i=1}^p (\mathbf{K}z_i = \mathbf{E}z_i),$$

where $\alpha_{\mathbf{K}}$ specifies the basic requirements of $\mathbf{K}$, as defined for Requirement (R1) in Example 3.

Re-resolution Sequences

In response to a change at component t, a transformation T is carried out on the component term S and its requirement map ϕ. The transformation T comprises a component term t' and updated requirements in the requirement map $\tau : C \to F$. By inspecting the domain $dom(\tau) = \{t_1, \ldots, t_k\}$ of τ we are able to make an important observation on the proof sequence of the new system (S', ϕ'). We define the *characteristic set*

$$U = \bigcup_{t_i \in dom(\tau)} var(\tau(t_i)), \text{ for } 1 \le i \le k \quad (5)$$

which characterises the set of variables whose formulae have been affected by τ. By comparing formulae appearing in the proof sequence $\pi(\phi')$ of the new system S' to the set U, we split $\pi(\phi') = \mu \frown \sigma$ into two disjoint sequences such that

$$\alpha \in \sigma \iff var(\alpha) \cap U = \emptyset$$
$$\alpha \in \mu \iff var(\alpha) \cap U \ne \emptyset$$

for each $\alpha \in \pi(\phi')$. Furthermore, we note the sequence σ of unmodified formulae is a subsequence of the proof sequence $\pi(\phi)$ of the original system, and μ is a subsequence of the proof sequence $\pi(\phi')$ in the updated system. To summarise:

OBSERVATION 4.1. *The characteristic set U of τ specifies disjoint sequences σ and μ such that $\pi(\phi') = \mu \frown \sigma$, where σ is a subsequence of $\pi(\phi)$ and μ is a subsequence of $\pi(\phi')$.*

We call the proof sequence μ obtained from the characteristic set the *re-resolution sequence* of T.

Example 9. **Sub-component Addition Re-resolution Sequence.** In the sub-component addition transformation described in Example 8, the domain of τ comprised the component terms $\mathbf{K}$ and $\mathbf{S}$. Computing the characteristic set of τ from Equation 5 yields the set $U = \{\mathbf{E}z_i, \mathbf{F}z_i, \mathbf{I}z_i, \mathbf{J}z_i, \mathbf{K}z_i\}$ of variables for $1 \le i \le p$. By Observation 4.1, we split the proof sequence

$$\pi(\phi') = (\alpha_{\mathbf{S}} \wedge \alpha_{\mathbf{E}} \wedge \alpha_{\mathbf{F}} \wedge \alpha_{\mathbf{I}} \wedge \alpha_{\mathbf{J}} \wedge \alpha_{\mathbf{K}},$$
$$\alpha_{\mathbf{A}}, \alpha_{\mathbf{B}}, \alpha_{\mathbf{C}} \wedge \alpha_{\mathbf{D}} \wedge \alpha_{\mathbf{app_1}}, \alpha_{\mathbf{G}}, \alpha_{\mathbf{H}}).$$

into subsequences

$$\sigma = (\alpha_{\mathbf{A}}, \alpha_{\mathbf{B}}, \alpha_{\mathbf{C}} \wedge \alpha_{\mathbf{D}} \wedge \alpha_{\mathbf{app_1}}, \alpha_{\mathbf{G}}, \alpha_{\mathbf{H}}) \subseteq \pi(\phi)$$
$$\mu = (\phi_{\mathbf{S}} \wedge \phi_{\mathbf{E}} \wedge \phi_{\mathbf{F}} \wedge \phi_{\mathbf{I}} \wedge \phi_{\mathbf{J}} \wedge \phi_{\mathbf{K}}) \subseteq \pi(\phi').$$

We can now prove the following theorem.

THEOREM 4.2 (INCREMENTAL RE-RESOLUTION). *Let T be a transformation $(S, \phi) \xrightarrow{T} (S', \phi')$. If $a \models \rho(S, \phi)$ and S' is ϕ' satisfiable then $comp(\mu, \eta) \oplus a \models \rho(S', \phi')$, for the re-resolution sequence μ of T.*

PROOF. Let U be the characteristic set of the requirement map τ of T. By Observation 4.1, the proof sequence of S' is partitioned such that $\pi(\phi') = \mu \frown \sigma$. Since $a \models \rho(S, \phi)$, we have by Theorem 4.1 $a \models \wedge\pi(\phi)$, the conjunction of all independent formulae comprising the proof sequence of the original system S. It follows that $a \models \wedge\sigma_i$, since σ is a subsequence of $\pi(\phi)$. A similar argument holds for the proof sequence μ, since it is a subsequence of $\pi(\phi')$ of the updated

system S'. We therefore have by Theorem 4.1 $comp(\mu, \eta) \models \wedge\mu_i$. Application of Lemma 4.1 yields

$$comp(\mu, \eta) \oplus a \models (\wedge\mu_i) \wedge (\wedge\sigma_i) \quad (6)$$
$$= \pi(\alpha') = \rho(S', \alpha')$$

completing the proof $\square$

This theorem demonstrates that an analysis of an incremental re-resolution sequence μ combined with a previous resolution step is equivalent to re-resolving the entire system from scratch. We note the order in which the operands are applied to the composition operation $\oplus$. If the domains of a and b do not intersect, then $a \oplus b = b \oplus a$. In (6) the satisfiable assignment's domain $dom(comp(\mu, \eta))$ potentially intersects with a, and intuitively, replaces any assignment values obtained in previous resolution steps with the new ones obtained from analysing μ.

Example 10. **Incremental Re-resolution of Sub-component Addition.** We use Theorem 4.2 to re-resolve the cloud deployed system $\mathbf{S}'$ after the addition of sub-component $\mathbf{K}$. Observing the characteristic set, the incremental re-resolution is specified in Example 9 as $\mu = (\phi_{\mathbf{S}} \wedge \phi_{\mathbf{E}} \wedge \phi_{\mathbf{F}} \wedge \phi_{\mathbf{I}} \wedge \phi_{\mathbf{J}} \wedge \phi_{\mathbf{K}})$. The application of monolithic analysis on the system $\mathbf{S}$ in Example 5 yields an assignment such that $a \models \rho(S, \phi)$. Applying Theorem 4.2 we carry out compositional analysis $comp(\mu, \eta)$ using the Z3 SMT solver, and obtain the assignment

$$a' = \begin{array}{c|ccccc} & \mathbf{E} & \mathbf{F} & \mathbf{I} & \mathbf{J} & \mathbf{K} \\ \hline z_1 & 2 & 2 & 2 & 2 & 2 \\ z_2 & 3 & 3 & 3 & 3 & 3 \end{array} .$$

We note that the values of variables for the existing sub-components $\mathbf{E}, \mathbf{F}, \mathbf{G}, \mathbf{H}, \mathbf{I}$ have been appropriately updated by the composition operation $\oplus$ to maintain Requirement (R7) of the system.

Example 11. **Web Component Removal.** We observe that the removal of components in a system results in an update to the system architecture, but does not require re-resolution since the existing solution always satisfies the weaker constraints as a result of removing components and their requirements.

We demonstrate this fact by applying our incremental re-resolution approach to a change scenario in which the component **web** fails and is removed from $\mathbf{S}$. We model the scenario as a transformation involving term substitution whereby $\mathbf{S}' \equiv [\mathbf{S}/c(\mathbf{app_1}, c(\mathbf{app_2}, c(\mathbf{db_1}, \mathbf{db_2})))]$. Since no new requirements are added we specify $\tau : \emptyset \to F$. As a result, the characteristic set U is the empty set, so there are no steps in the re-resolution sequence μ and the original solution satisfies $\mathbf{S}'$.

We note the operations needed during re-resolution and their ordering are determined by the architectural structure of the system. When working with applications, stricter ordering conditions may be advantageous.

5. IMPLEMENTATION & EXPERIMENTS

We developed a general, re-useable prototype tool based on the theoretical results of Section 4, implementing the incremental re-resolution approach as an open-source Java application that realises the workflow in Figure 2. The core

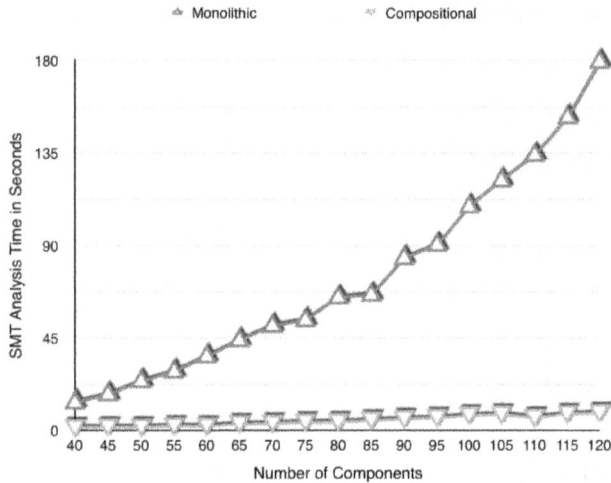

Figure 3: Experimental results comparing performance of monolithic and compositional resolution

component of our implementation is the general Java class `Z3Engine` that carries out SMT analysis on component models using the Z3 SMT solver. The models are specified in the `Z3Model` class comprising a set of component variables and formulae specifying constraints on the range of value assignments to the variables. Formulae are automatically generated by the `Requirement` class, which translates requirements expressed in a high-level domain specific language into assertions in the Z3 language.

The `Z3Engine` features the following methods for analysing requirements on component models:

- `monolithicSolve()`, which outputs a satisfiable assignment by performing SMT analysis on the model's monolithic specification (Definitions 4.3 and 4.5),
- `compositionalSolve()` that outputs an assignment obtained from the compositional analysis of a model's proof sequence (Definitions 4.7 and 4.8), and
- `incrementalSolve()` that outputs an assignment obtained by incremental re-resolution in response to a transformation, using previous resolution steps (Theorem 4.2).

To analyse cloud deployment configurations of the case study system **S**, we designed special `Z3Model` and `Requirement` classes for use with our `Z3Engine` class, and specific to the domain-specific language in which we expressed the requirements (R1) to (R7). Our prototype incremental SMT re-resolution tool is freely available to download from `http://www-users.cs.york.ac.uk/~raduc/IncrementalSMT`.

5.1 Monolithic & Compositional Experiments

To compare performances between monolithic and compositional resolution approaches we ran a range of experiments based on the cloud deployed system **S**. The experiments were conducted on a standard 2.3 GHz Intel Core i7 MacBook Pro computer with 16GB of memory, and we compared the execution times of the monolithic and compositional approaches to analysing the deployment of **S** over 20 availability zones. A quarter of components had requirements on their sub-components and a global constraint affected a tenth of the components in the system. Our experiment was performed on a range of system sizes, starting with a system architecture comprising ten components each

with nine sub-components. We increased the system size by adding five components at each step, corresponding to an increase of 450 variables in the Z3 specification. The results of the comparison are presented in Figure 3. Despite very large system sizes, the compositional approach benefits from the fact that most of the sub-components in the system are autonomous, and never exceeds 9 seconds to perform a complete analysis. For the largest system size analysed in our experiments, this is below 5% of the time taken by the analysis of the monolithic Z3 specification.

5.2 Incremental & Compositional Experiments

Starting with a system comprising 15 components each with 9 sub-components, we compared the performance of incremental re-resolution and the compositional approach in response to three kinds of changes:

- In the experiment whose results are presented in the leftmost graph of Figure 4, a sub-component is added to the system. After each such addition, compositional and incremental re-resolution approaches are performed. The execution time for incremental re-resolution is substantially lower than the compositional approach since the re-resolution step involves analysis of only a small number of local requirements of the autonomous sub-component. After the addition of the 17-th component, the incremental re-resolution requires less than half the amount of time taken by the compositional analysis.

- The middle graph depicts the result of an experiment in which a sub-component is added to an existing component and whose requirements constrain all of its sub-components. Like the previous experiment, incremental re-resolution performed up to 40% better than compositional re-resolution, since again the change affects a small portion of the components in the system.

- The rightmost graph depicts the result of a change scenario that occurs far less often in practice than the two scenarios above, but which we include here for completeness. In this scenario, a component with nine sub-components is added to the system. An existing system involving a quarter of the components is updated to constrain the new component. While in all cases the incremental re-resolution approach took less time to complete in comparison with the compositional approach, the improvement was marginal. This is due to a much larger portion of the system's components and sub-components being affected by a system wide property.

We observe that the key factor in the effectivity of our approach is the *change ratio* associated with each change the system undergoes. This number is defined as the ratio between components affected by a change (and thus needing to be re-resolved) compared to the total number of components in the system's architecture. In the first experiment, the change ratio is less than 1% since only one autonomous sub-component was changed at each step and decreased further as the size of the system grew. In the second experiment, the change ratio begins high at over 6% since a component comprising 9 sub-components is added to the initial system architecture with 15 components. This ratio also decreases very rapidly as the size of the system increases. In the last experiment the change ratio is very high at over 18% since the addition of a component constrained by system-wide requirements involves at least one tenth of the other compo-

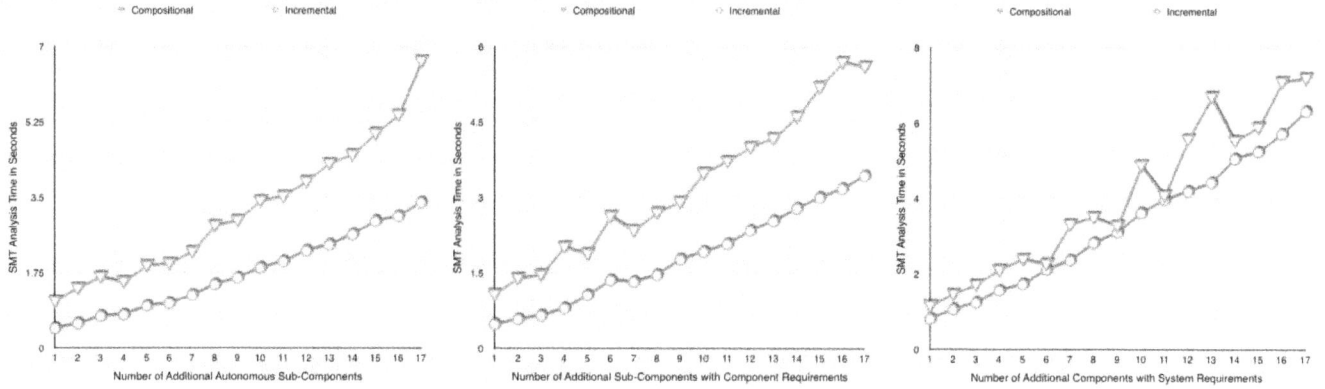

Figure 4: Experimental results comparing performance of incremental and compositional re-resolution

nents in the system architecture. Thus the change ratio stays around 10% for each subsequent change in the system, rather than tend to zero as the system size increases. The change ratio provides a simple metric that can be used to predict the effectiveness of our incremental SMT re-resolution approach for a given system. As the change ratio increases, the execution times taken by compositional and incremental re-resolution converge. Our experimental results and analysis provide heuristics indicating that

- architectures comprising a high number of autonomous components and sub-components, each governed by localised requirements, and
- architectures that are frequently affected by small changes to their components

are best suited to be re-resolved by our incremental approach, whenever a decomposition of their properties exists. These properties characterise a large class of real-world systems that operate in an environment of autonomous components. In most practical scenarios, changes involve a small fixed number of components and requirements, rather than more significant, system-wide changes.

6. RELATED WORK

Recent position papers and research agendas by researchers from the self-adaptive software community, including ourselves, have proposed incrementality as a potential approach for re-applying formal analysis and verification to rapidly evolving software architectures [6, 8, 22]. Nevertheless, to the best of our knowledge, no incremental approaches to the SMT resolution of constraint-satisfaction problems have been proposed so far.

The only related project we are aware of is the Ranger technique for parallelising the analysis of Alloy first-order logic models, which was recently proposed in [28]. This technique uses a divide and conquer method based on defining a linear ordering on the state space of candidate solutions for an Alloy model. This linear ordering allows the partition of the candidate solution space into ranges, and the analysis of Alloy models bounded to each range in parallel. The Ranger solution can be regarded as a compositional approach to solving a class of constraint-satisfaction problems. However, unlike our compositional SMT resolution method, Ranger requires that the models to be analysed have a finite solution space. Furthermore, although Ranger does not rely on specialised properties of the model structure for perfor-

mance improvements, there is no clear way in which it can be extended with incremental analysis capabilities.

Less related to the work presented in our paper are the ongoing efforts to develop incremental and compositional approaches for other formal modelling, analysis and verification techniques. This includes the recent results on incremental variants of probabilistic model checking described in [18, 24] and in our own work [23], and the significant body of work on compositional, assume-guarantee model checking (e.g., [4, 5, 11, 12]). Our incremental SMT re-resolution approach complements these results, as it enables the compositional and incremental analysis of constraint-satisfaction problems expressed as formulae over theories of arithmetic, and these problems cannot be typically encoded as probabilistic or traditional model checking problems.

7. CONCLUDING REMARKS

We presented a generic method for the effective SMT analysis of component-based systems after architectural changes such as component addition and removal. The theoretical framework at the core of our approach developed a new compositional resolution technique, enhanced with the ability to re-resolve components affected by change, reusing existing results when possible. A case study from the domain of cloud computing was modelled using the approach and its deployment requirements were formalised as logical formulae. Our experiments showed that carrying out incremental re-resolution in response to change performed consistently better than resolving the entire system, and demonstrated the effectiveness of the approach for a large software architecture evolving through a series of localised changes. Our approach was implemented as a prototype software package using an off-the-shelf SMT analysis tool Z3.

There are several directions in which we plan to extend our work. The theoretical results can be extended with a mechanism for the early termination of the SMT re-resolution process, through defining a comparison relation over the solution of the constraint-satisfaction problem. A standard stopping condition would be on the basis of an unsatisfiable outcome in one of the steps of the re-resolution process. However, in the context of our application domain, more elaborate comparison relations may be possible, e.g., by associating component deployment costs and/or levels of reliability with the cloud availability zones. In this way, deployment configurations can be compared according to relevant quality-of-service metrics. We also plan to extend the case study by developing a domain specific language and tool supporting the analysis of "what if" scenarios. This tool will allow cloud system administrators to analyse the quality-of-service properties of their cloud-deployed systems.

The extensions mention above will enable the integration of incremental SMT re-resolution with our existing INVEST incremental verification engine [23]. This integration supports our broader research theme to unify complementary formal modelling techniques into a single platform that can be readily employed by non-experts for the verification of evolving large-scale systems. Extending INVEST will involve developing SMT-specific instances of key components of its architecture, namely a domain-specific language acting as an adaptor interfaced with the component models defined in this paper, and augmenting the INVEST incremental verification engine with support for SMT proof sequences.

8. ACKNOWLEDGEMENTS

This work was partly supported by the UK Engineering and Physical Sciences Research Council grant EP/H042644/1.

9. REFERENCES

[1] O. Barais, A.-F. L. Meur, L. Duchien, and J. L. Lawall. Software architecture evolution. In T. Mens and S. Demeyer, editors, *Software Evolution*, pages 233–262. Springer, 2008.

[2] J. M. Barnes, A. Pandey, and D. Garlan. Automated planning for software architecture evolution. In *ASE'13*, pages 213–223, 2013.

[3] C. W. Barrett, R. Sebastiani, S. A. Seshia, and C. Tinelli. Satisfiability modulo theories. In A. Biere, M. Heule, H. van Maaren, and T. Walsh, editors, *Handbook of Satisfiability*, volume 185 of *Frontiers in Artificial Intelligence and Applications*, pages 825–885. IOS Press, 2009.

[4] S. Berezin, S. V. A. Campos, and E. M. Clarke. Compositional reasoning in model checking. COMPOS'97, pages 81–102. Springer-Verlag, 1998.

[5] C. Blundell, D. Giannakopoulou, and C. S. Pasareanu. Assume-guarantee testing. *ACM SIGSOFT Software Engineering Notes*, 31(2), 2006.

[6] R. Calinescu. Emerging techniques for the engineering of self-adaptive high-integrity software. In J. Camara et al., editors, *ASAS'13*, volume 7740 of *LNCS*, pages 297–310. Springer, 2013.

[7] R. Calinescu et al. Dynamic QoS management and optimization in service-based systems. *IEEE Trans. Soft. Eng.*, 37(3):387–409, 2011.

[8] R. Calinescu, C. Ghezzi, M. Kwiatkowska, and R. Mirandola. Self-adaptive software needs quantitative verification at runtime. *Comm. of the ACM*, 55(9):69–77, 2012.

[9] R. Calinescu, K. Johnson, and Y. Rafiq. Developing self-verifying service-based systems. In *ASE'13*, pages 734–737, 2013.

[10] R. Calinescu and S. Kikuchi. Formal methods @ runtime. In *Modeling, Development, and Verification of Adaptive Systems*, volume 6662 of *LNCS*, pages 122–135. Springer, 2011.

[11] E. Clarke, D. Long, and K. McMillan. Compositional model checking. In *Proc. 4th Intl. Symp. Logic in Computer Science*, pages 353–362, 1989.

[12] J. M. Cobleigh, D. Giannakopoulou, and C. S. Păsăreanu. Learning assumptions for compositional verification. TACAS'03, pages 331–346. Springer-Verlag, 2003.

[13] L. Cordeiro, B. Fischer, and J. Marques-Silva. SMT-based bounded model checking for embedded ANSI-C software. *Software Engineering, IEEE Transactions on*, 38(4):957–974, 2012.

[14] L. De Moura and N. Bjørner. Z3: an efficient SMT solver. In *TACAS'08*, pages 337–340. Springer-Verlag, 2008.

[15] L. De Moura and N. Bjørner. Satisfiability modulo theories: introduction and applications. *Comm. of the ACM*, 54(9):69–77, 2011.

[16] A. Filieri, C. Ghezzi, and G. Tamburrelli. A formal approach to adaptive software: continuous assurance of non-functional requirements. *Formal Asp. Comput.*, 24(2):163–186, 2012.

[17] J. Floch et al. Using architecture models for runtime adaptability. *IEEE Software*, 23:62–70, 2006.

[18] V. Forejt et al. Incremental runtime verification of probabilistic systems. In S. Qadeer and S. Tasiran, editors, *Runtime Verification*, volume 7687 of *Lecture Notes in Computer Science*, pages 314–319. Springer Berlin Heidelberg, 2013.

[19] H. Garavel, F. Lang, R. Mateescu, and W. Serwe. Cadp 2010: A toolbox for the construction and analysis of distributed processes. In P. Abdulla and K. Leino, editors, *TACAS'11*, volume 6605 of *LNCS*, pages 372–387. Springer Berlin Heidelberg, 2011.

[20] D. Garlan, J. M. Barnes, B. R. Schmerl, and O. Celiku. Evolution styles: Foundations and tool support for software architecture evolution. In *SA'09*, pages 131–140, 2009.

[21] D. Garlan and B. R. Schmerl. Using architectural models at runtime: Research challenges. In *EWSA'04*, volume 3047, pages 200–205, 2004.

[22] C. Ghezzi. Evolution, adaptation, and the quest for incrementality. In R. Calinescu and D. Garlan, editors, *LSCITS. Development, Operation and Management*, volume 7539 of *LNCS*, pages 369–379. Springer, 2012.

[23] K. Johnson, R. Calinescu, and S. Kikuchi. An incremental verification framework for component-based software systems. In *CBSE'13*, pages 33–42, 2013.

[24] M. Z. Kwiatkowska, D. Parker, and H. Qu. Incremental quantitative verification for Markov decision processes. In *DSN'11*, pages 359–370, 2011.

[25] K. Meinke and J. V. Tucker. Universal algebra. In *Handbook of logic in computer science*, volume 1, pages 189–368. Oxford University Press, 1992.

[26] B. Morin et al. Models@run.time to support dynamic adaptation. *Computer*, 42:44–51, 2009.

[27] W. Rautenberg. A concise introduction to mathematical logic. *Universitext Springer*, 2006.

[28] N. Rosner et al. Ranger: Parallel analysis of alloy models by range partitioning. In *ASE'13*, pages 147–157, 2013.

[29] J. M. Rushby. Runtime certification. In *RV'08*, pages 21–35, 2008.

Regression Verification of AADL Models through Slicing of System Dependence Graphs

Andreas Johnsen, Kristina Lundqvist, Paul Pettersson, Kaj Hänninen
School of Innovation, Design and Engineering
Mälardalen University
Västerås, Sweden
{andreas.johnsen,kristina.lundqvist,paul.pettersson,kaj.hanninen}@mdh.se

ABSTRACT

Design artifacts of embedded systems are subjected to a number of modifications during the development process. Verified artifacts that subsequently are modified must necessarily be re-verified to ensure that no faults have been introduced in response to the modification. We collectively call this type of verification as regression verification. In this paper, we contribute with a technique for selective regression verification of embedded systems modeled in the Architecture Analysis and Design Language (AADL). The technique can be used with any AADL-based verification technique to efficiently perform regression verification by only selecting verification sequences that cover parts that are affected by the modification for re-execution. This allows for the avoidance of unnecessary re-verification, and thereby unnecessary costs. The selection is based on the concept of specification slicing through system dependence graphs (SDGs) such that the effect of a modification can be identified.

Keywords

software architectures, AADL, regression verification, specification slicing, system dependence graph

1. INTRODUCTION

Software verification of embedded systems consumes a majority of the development cost [6]. Numerous research efforts have been devoted to the development of more efficient regression testing techniques as studies show that regression testing consumes up to one-third of the total development cost of a software system [5]. Although the efficiency of regression testing is highly important, empirical studies show that the majority of development faults are introduced by incorrect, incomplete, and inconsistent specifications and models (we use the terms "specification" and "model" interchangeably) [10]. Such artifacts are, in addition to a significant source of fault introduction, also often subjected to a large number of modifications. Hence, they are also subjected to regression verification activities in form of reviewing, inspection, simulation, model-checking, etc., which efficiency may be even more important than the efficiency of regression testing.

The techniques used to perform regression verification of specifications and models do seldom identify the effect the modification has on the artifact under analysis. A modification does not only affect the behavior of the part that explicitly has been modified, but also the behavior of any other part that is dependent on it. By contrast, a modification does typically not affect the complete artifact. As the effect of a modification is not analyzed, there is little understanding of which parts of the artifact that, directly or indirectly, are affected by the modification and must be re-verified. This type of problem is essential for selective (efficient) regression testing [5] and, logically, for selective regression verification of specifications and models as well. A rerun of all already existing and still valid verification sequences, in addition to possibly newly created sequences to cover possibly added parts, is in this case necessary to ensure that no new faults follow from a modification. A rerun-all approach may be significantly more time-consuming and costly, depending on the extent of unnecessary exercised parts, compared to a selective approach where only the necessary verification sequences are executed, i.e., where only parts that are affected by the modification are exercised.

The contribution of this paper is a technique for selective regression verification of embedded systems modeled in the Architecture Analysis and Design Language (AADL) [2] – an overview of AADL can be found in [8]. The technique uses the concepts of *specification slicing* [9] and *system dependence graphs* [7] to identify the parts of a modified AADL model that are directly or indirectly affected by the modification and must be covered by verification sequences in the regression verification process. It can therefor be used with any AADL-based verification technique to efficiently perform regression verification.

The approach originates from the regression testing technique proposed by Bates and Horwitz in [3] who used *program slicing* [14] algorithms on so called *program dependence graphs* [12] to determine which parts of a software program that are affected by a modification and need to be retested. Both specification slicing and system dependence graphs, which backgrounds are presented in Section 2, are extensions of these concepts and can be used for the same purpose as of the approach proposed by Bates and Horwitz. The concept of program slicing is to remove statements, instructions, and variables that do not have an effect on and are not af-

Permission to make digital or hard copies of all or part of this work for personal or classroom use is granted without fee provided that copies are not made or distributed for profit or commercial advantage and that copies bear this notice and the full citation on the first page. Copyrights for components of this work owned by others than ACM must be honored. Abstracting with credit is permitted. To copy otherwise, or republish, to post on servers or to redistribute to lists, requires prior specific permission and/or a fee. Request permissions from permissions@acm.org.

QoSA'14, June 30–July 4, 2014, Marcq-en-Baroeul, France
Copyright 2014 ACM 978-1-4503-2576-9/14/06 ...$15.00.
http://dx.doi.org/10.1145/2602576.2602589.

fected by the value of a variable at some program point (statement or instruction) referred to as the *slicing criterion*. Causal relationships to the value of a variable at some point are determined by the control and data dependencies of the system. These are commonly expressed through a directed graph [13], such as a program dependence graph or, the more expressive, system dependence graph. The parts that have causal relationships to the value of the variable are thus determined by computing the transitive closure of the dependence graph on the slicing criterion. The parts that do not have an effect on the value of the variable are removed by computing the backward (with respect to the directions of the arrows of the graph) transitive closure, known as backward-slicing. The parts that are not affected by the point are removed by computing the forward transitive closure, known as forward-slicing [13].

The technique we propose for selective regression verification comprises four main steps. The first step is to use the algorithms and rules presented in Section 4 to generate the system dependence graphs of an AADL model and its modified version. These algorithms and rules are defined upon an abstract syntax of AADL, presented in Section 3, that has been tailored for the purpose of slicing. The two graphs are then compared according to the criteria presented in Section 5 to precisely identify the modification in the graph of the modified AADL model. With the modification constituting the slicing criterion, backward- and forward-slicing techniques presented in Section 5 are used to identify the elements of the model that have an effect on and are affected by the modification. These must be covered by verification sequences in the regression verification process. Note that the behavior of elements included in the backward-slice but not in the forward-slice is not dependent on the slicing criterion and does not need to be re-verified. However, they are necessary to be executed in the regression verification process (for full coverage) since the behavior of the modified part is dependent on those elements. A running example of applying the technique is initiated by an AADL model presented in Section 3.

The proposed slicing technique is also a contribution to the AADL community as it can be used for comprehension, analysis, verification and validation, maintenance, vectorization and parallelization, integration, removal of unreachable/dead software, worst case execution time analysis, compilation and code generation, reuse, etc., as most other forward- and backward-capable slicing algorithms [13, 7]. There exist to our knowledge no such contribution. In Section 6, we elaborate on the limitations of our work and possibilities for future work and present some concluding remarks.

2. BACKGROUND

The idea of slicing specifications was first introduced by Oda and Araki [11]. The idea is based on the concept of *program slicing* through control and data flow analysis, originally defined by Weiser [14]. Ottenstein and Ottenstein [12] later showed how program slicing algorithms could be defined in terms of operations on so called *program dependence graphs* (PDG) – a method also used for effectively slicing specifications [9]. A PDG is a directed graph of different types of vertices (nodes) and edges (arcs), where vertices represent the statements and predicate expressions of a single monolithic program, and where edges represent control

and data dependencies among those vertices. Each PDG consists of a distinguished *entry* vertex representing the entry into the program. Essentially, a PDG is the union of a *control dependence graph* (CDG), where edges describe the control conditions on which the execution of vertices depends, and a *flow dependence graph* (FDG), where edges describe the data variables on which the operations of vertices depend [12]. Both graphs can be generated by analyzing the control flow graph (CFG) [1] of a program.

To be able to perform program slicing in the more general case where a program consists of multiple procedures, Horwitz et al. [7] introduced the so called *system dependence graph* (SDG). SDGs extend the expressiveness of PDGs such that procedure calls and parameter passing (by value) can be integrated.

3. PRELIMINARIES

In this section we present an example of an AADL model and an abstract syntax for AADL. Rules and algorithms for slicing AADL models through SDGs are then defined upon the abstract syntax in Section 4 and Section 5 while they are applied to the AADL example.

The AADL example, shown in Table 1 and Table 2, comprises an embedded system partly consisting of a process component *process.impl* that reads data produced by a dual modular redundant sensor and presents it to the operator through a display (sensors and display are not shown). *process.impl* has two periodically dispatched thread subcomponents, *thread_A* and *thread_B*, which are instances of *thread_1.impl* and *thread_2.impl* respectively. These threads provide the functionality together with three static (shared) data subcomponents, *sensorData_1*, *sensorData_2*, and *displayData_1*, whereby interactions with the sensors and the display are performed. The function of *thread_1.impl*, as described by its behavior specification, is simply to read the sensor data and to send it to *thread_2.impl* through the connected ports. The function of *thread_2.impl* is to compare the two received values and, if they are unequal, display the mean value or, if they are equal, display the value.

The abstract syntax for AADL is defined in terms of a tuple including constructs that determine the control and data dependencies of an AADL model. Let $part_1.part_2$ denote that $part_2$ is a set, sequence, or element of the set, sequence, or element $part_1$. An AADL model is a tuple:

$$\mathcal{AADLMDL} = \langle \mathcal{COMP}, \mathcal{THR}, \mathcal{DATA}, \mathcal{SUB}, \mathcal{C}, \mathcal{CALL} \rangle$$

$\mathcal{COMP} = \{comp_1, comp_2, \ldots, comp_n\}$ denotes the set of software components in the architecture, where $\mathcal{THR}$ denotes the subset of *thread components*, $\mathcal{DATA}$ denotes the subset of *data components*, and $\mathcal{SUB}$ denotes the subset of *subprogram components*. Let *thr*, *data*, and *sub* range over $\mathcal{THR}$, $\mathcal{DATA}$, and $\mathcal{SUB}$ respectively.

A thread $thr = \langle \mathcal{DATA\_S}, \mathcal{SUB\_S}, \mathcal{DP}, \mathcal{EP}, \mathcal{EDP}, \mathcal{DA}, \mathcal{SA}, \mathcal{MSM}, \mathcal{BM} \rangle$ has a set of *data subcomponents* $\mathcal{DATA\_S} \subseteq \mathcal{DATA}$; a set of *subprogram subcomponents* $\mathcal{SUB\_S} \subseteq \mathcal{SUB}$; a set of *data ports* $\mathcal{DP} = \{dp(data) \mid dp(data)$ is an in/out/in out *data port* of data type $data \in \mathcal{DATA}$ and of the form *port* (see Table 3)$\}$; a set of *event ports* $\mathcal{EP} = \{ep \mid ep$ is an in/out/in out *event port* and of the form *port*$\}$; a set of *event data ports* $\mathcal{EDP} = \{edp(data) \mid edp(data)$ is an in/out/in out *event data port* of data type $data \in \mathcal{DATA}$ and of the form *port*$\}$; a set of *data accesses* $\mathcal{DA} = \{da(data) \mid da(data)$ is a *data access* to shared data

data $\in \mathcal{DATA}$ and of the form *component_access*}; a set of subprogram accesses $\mathcal{SA} = \{sa(sub) \mid sa(sub)$ is a *subprogram access* to subprogram $sub \in \mathcal{SUB}$ and of the form *component_access*}; a *Mode State Machine* $\mathcal{MSM}$; and a *Behavioral Model* $\mathcal{BM}$.

Table 1: Running AADL example.

...
process implementation process.impl
  subcomponents
  thread_A: thread thread_1.impl;
  thread_B: thread thread_2.impl;
  sensorData_1 : data Base_Types::Integer;
  sensorData_2 : data Base_Types::Integer;
  displayData_1 : data Base_Types::Integer;
  connections
  Connection_1: data port thread_A.output_1 ->
  thread_B.input_1;
  Connection_2: data port thread_A.output_2 ->
  thread_B.input_2;
  Connection_3: access sensorData_1 ->
  thread_A.sensor_data_1;
  Connection_4: access sensorData_2 ->
  thread_A.sensor_data_2;
end process.impl;

thread thread_1
  features
  output_1: out data port Base_Types::Integer;
  output_2: out data port Base_Types::Integer;
  sensor_data_1 : requires data access sensorData_1;
  sensor_data_2 : requires data access sensorData_2;
end thread_1;

thread implementation thread_1.impl
  properties
  Dispatch_Protocol => Periodic; Period => 50ms;
  annex behavior_specification {**
  states
  s0: initial complete final state;
  transitions
  s0 -[on dispatch]->s0 { output_1 := sensor_data_1;
  output_2 := sensor_data_2 };
  **};
end thread_1.impl;

thread thread_2
  features
  input_1: in data port Base_Types::Integer;
  input_2: in data port Base_Types::Integer;
  display_data_1 : requires data access displayData_1;
end thread_2;

thread implementation thread_2.impl
  properties
  Dispatch_Protocol => Periodic; Period => 50ms;
  annex behavior_specification {**
  variables
  sensor_1, sensor_2, tmp: Base_Types::Integer;
  states
  s0: initial complete final state;
  s1: state;
  transitions
  s0 -[on dispatch]->s1 { sensor_1 := input_1;
  sensor_2 := input_2 };
  s1 [2] -[sensor_1 != sensor_2]->s0 { mean!(sensor_1,
  sensor_2,tmp); display_data := tmp };
  s1 [1] -[sensor_1 = sensor_2]->s0 { display_data
  := sensor_1 };
  **};
end thread_2.impl;
...

Table 2: Continuation of running example.

...
  subprogram mean
    features
    x : in parameter Base_Types::Integer;
    y : in parameter Base_Types::Integer;
    z : out parameter Base_Types::Integer;
  end mean;

  subprogram implementation mean.impl
    annex behavior_specification {**
    states
    s0: initial state;
    s1: final state;
    transitions
    s0 -[ ]->s1 { z := (x + y)/2 };
    **};
  end mean.impl;
...

A subprogram $sub = \langle \mathcal{DATA\_S}, \mathcal{SP}, \mathcal{EP}, \mathcal{EDP}, \mathcal{DA}, \mathcal{SA}, \mathcal{MSM}, \mathcal{BM} \rangle$ has a set of *data subcomponents* $\mathcal{DATA\_S} \subseteq \mathcal{DATA}$; a set of *subprogram parameters* $\mathcal{SP} = \{sp(data) \mid sp$ is an in/out/in out *parameter* of data type $data \in \mathcal{DATA}$ and of the form *parameter* }; a set of event ports $\mathcal{EP} = \{ep \mid ep$ is an out *event port* of data type $d \in \mathcal{DATA}\}$; a set of event data ports $\mathcal{EDP} = \{edp(data) \mid edp(data)$ is an out *event data port* of data type $data \in \mathcal{DATA}\}$; a set of data accesses $\mathcal{DA} = \{da(data) \mid da(data)$ is a *data access* to shared data $data \in \mathcal{DATA}\}$; a set of subprogram accesses $\mathcal{SA} = \{sa(sub) \mid sa(sub)$ is a *subprogram access* to subprogram $sub \in \mathcal{SUB}\}$; a *Mode State Machine* $\mathcal{MSM}$; and a *Behavioral Model* $\mathcal{BM}$.

Let $\mathcal{DP\_U}$, $\mathcal{EP\_U}$, $\mathcal{EDP\_U}$, $\mathcal{SP\_U}$, $\mathcal{DA\_U}$ and $\mathcal{SA\_U}$ denote the union of all sets of component data ports, event ports, event data ports, parameters, data accesses, and subprogam accesses respectively. $\mathcal{C}$ denotes the set of connections in the architecture, $\mathcal{C} = \{c(source, destination) \mid c$ is a *port connection* from $source \in \mathcal{DP\_U} \cup \mathcal{EP\_U} \cup \mathcal{EDP\_U}$ to $destination \in \mathcal{DP\_U} \cup \mathcal{EP\_U} \cup \mathcal{EDP\_U}$ of the form *port_connection*; or a *data access connection* (access to shared data) from $source \in \mathcal{DATA}$ to $destination \in \mathcal{DA\_U}$ of the form *data_access_connection*; or a *subprogram access connection* from $source \in \mathcal{SUB}$ to $destination \in \mathcal{SA\_U}$ of the form *subp_access_connection*; or a *parameter connection* from $source \in \mathcal{SP\_U} \cup \mathcal{DP\_U} \cup \mathcal{EDP\_U}$ to $destination \in \mathcal{SP\_U} \cup \mathcal{DP\_U} \cup \mathcal{EDP\_U}$ and $\langle source, destination \rangle \notin \mathcal{DP\_U} \times \mathcal{DP\_U} \cup \mathcal{DP\_U} \times \mathcal{EDP\_U} \cup \mathcal{EDP\_U} \times \mathcal{DP\_U}$ of the form *parameter_connection*}.

$\mathcal{CALL}$ denotes the set of subprogram calls in the architecture, $\mathcal{CALL} = \{call(sub) \mid call$ is a *subprogram call* to $sub \in \mathcal{SUB}$ of the form *subprogram_call*}.

A Behavioral Model $comp_i.\mathcal{BM} = \langle \mathcal{S}, s_o, \mathcal{CPL}, \mathcal{FIL}, \mathcal{VAR}, \mathcal{TR} \rangle$ has a set of *states* $\mathcal{S}$ of the form *state*; an *initial state* $s_0 \in \mathcal{S}$; a set of *complete states* $\mathcal{CPL} \subseteq \mathcal{S}$; a set of *final states* $\mathcal{FIL} \subseteq \mathcal{S}$; a set of *typed variables* $\mathcal{VAR}$ of the form *variable*; and a set of *state transitions* $\mathcal{TR} \subseteq \mathcal{S} \times \mathcal{PRI} \times \mathcal{G} \times \mathcal{ACT} \times \mathcal{S}$ of the form *state_transition*. A state $s \notin \mathcal{CPL} \cup \mathcal{FIL} \cup s_0$ is called an *execution state*. We shall use the denotation $s \xrightarrow{pri,g,act} s'$ iff $\langle s, pri, g, act, s' \rangle \in \mathcal{TR}$. $pri \in \mathbb{N}$ is the *priority* of the transition. g is a (possibly empty) set of *guards*, which are predicates (also known as *execute conditions*) over local variables, component ($comp_i$) in ports, component in parameters, subcomponent ($comp_i.sub\_s_j$) out ports, subcomponent out parameters, data subcomponents, or accesses to shared data components iff $s \notin \mathcal{CPL} \cup \mathcal{FIL}$; or predicates (also known as dispatch conditions) over (dispatch triggered by) event ports or event data ports (including receipt of a call) iff $s \in \mathcal{CPL}$. *act* is a (possibly empty) set of *actions* which are sequences (elements of a sequence are separated by ";" and executes in that order) and sets (separated by "&" and executes non-deterministically) of: subprogram calls with arguments of the form $sub!(list)$ where $sub \in \mathcal{SUB}$ and $list \in ARG \times ARG^*$ where ARG is the union of local variables, component ($comp_i$) in ports and parameters, subcomponent ($comp_i.sub\_s_j$) out ports and parameters, data subcomponents, and accesses to shared data components; of *assignments* of the form $target := expr$ where $target \in VAR \cup comp_i.DATA \cup comp_i.DA \cup comp_i.DP \cup comp_i.EP \cup comp_i.EDP$ where $expr$ is an arithmetic expression over local variables, component in ports and parameters, subcomponent out ports and parameters, data subcomponents, and accesses to shared data components; and of timed actions of the form **computation**(min .. max) which represent the use of the bounded CPU in terms of a duration between $min \in \mathbb{N}$ and $max \in \mathbb{N}$ time units.

A Mode State Machine $comp_i.\mathcal{MSM} = \langle \mathcal{M}, m_o, \mathcal{MTR} \rangle$ has a set of operational states (runtime configurations) called *modes* $\mathcal{M}$ of the form *mode*; an *initial mode* $m_0 \in \mathcal{S}$; and a set of *mode transitions* $\mathcal{MTR} \subseteq \mathcal{M} \times \mathcal{TRI} \times \mathcal{M}$ of the form *mode_transition*. We shall use the denotation $m \xrightarrow{tri} m'$ iff $\langle s, tri, s' \rangle \in \mathcal{MTR}$. $\mathcal{TRI}$ is a set of *triggers* which is the union of component ($comp_i$) in event and event data ports, and subcomponent ($comp_i.sub\_s_j$) out event and event data ports.

The complete semantics of the above abstract syntax is available in the AADL standard [2] and the Behavioral Annex [4].

4. SLICING THROUGH SYSTEM DEPENDENCE GRAPHS

Let $\mathcal{EXPR}$ be the set of possible expressions described by the abstract syntax. The slicing algorithm we propose builds on the general definition of program slicing originally discussed by Weiser [14]:

Definition 1. A backward slice of an AADL model with respect to slicing criterion $CRI = \langle comp, expr, var \rangle$, where $expr \in \mathcal{EXPR}$ is an expression within $comp$, and var is a variable or data component defined/assigned or used/read at $expr$, consists of all control flow and data flow determining expressions of the model that the value of var at $expr$ in $comp$ possibly depend on. A forward AADL slice with respect to slicing criterion $CRI = \langle comp, expr, var \rangle$ consists of all control flow and data flow determining expressions of the model that possible are dependent on the value of var at $expr$ in $comp$.

As usual, there exist two types of dependencies: control dependence and data dependence.

Definition 2. An AADL expression $expr_1 \in \mathcal{EXPR}$ is *control-dependent* on an AADL expression $expr_2 \in \mathcal{EXPR}$ if $expr_2$ possibly decides whether $expr_1$ will be executed or not. $expr_1$ is *data-dependent* on $expr_2$ if $expr_2$ defines a data variable possibly used by an execution of $expr_1$.

Control and data dependencies of an AADL model are represented by its SDG. A SDG is generated through a process of algorithms starting with the generation of the CFGs of the components representing concurrent units of sequential execution: thread and subprogram components. The control flow through such a component is determined by its behavioral model that represents its logical execution, i.e. the CFG of a component is generated based on its behavioral model. Algorithms can then be applied to the CFGs to determine the internal control and data dependencies of each component. The set of (internal) control dependencies and the set of (internal) data dependencies of a component yield the CDG and the FDG of a component, respectively. The PDG of each component is then formed by merging their corresponding CDG and FDG. PDGs do not, however, have the ability to describe interdependencies among components. AADL models express control and data flow interactions among components throughout the architecture, from sensors to actuators through software components. The possible interactions among software components are represented by four different types of connections: *port connections*, *data access connections*, *subprogram calls*, and *parameter connections*. These expressions explicitly yield control and data dependencies and are similar to the dependencies that can be represented in a SDG, but not in a PDG, i.e., calls and parameter (data) passing. In order to generate the SDG of an AADL model, the set of PDGs of an AADL model must be integrated with these interdependencies.

In Section 4.1, we describe how CFGs of an AADL model are generated. In Section 4.2, we describe how PDGs are generated by performing operations on the CFGs, and in Section 4.3, we describe how to generate the SDG of an AADL model from the set of PDGs, which can be sliced for the purpose of selective regression verification as described in Section 5.

4.1 Generating Control Flow Graphs

The set of CFGs of an AADL model is generated by mapping the behavioral model ($comp_i.\mathcal{BM}$) of each thread component and subprogram component to its corresponding CFG as described in Algorithm 1.

Definition 3. A control flow graph $CFG(comp_i.\mathcal{BM}) = \langle V, A \rangle$ of a (possibly concurrent) component of sequential execution $comp_i$ is a directed graph of a set of vertices $V = \{v \mid v \in \mathcal{EXPR} \cup \langle \text{"}ENTRY\text{"}, comp \rangle \cup \langle \text{"}REENTRY\text{"}, comp \rangle \cup \langle \text{"}EXIT\text{"}, comp \rangle \}$ representing AADL expressions, and a set of arcs $A \subseteq V \times V$ describing how control flows through the vertices. Vertex v_1 of an arc $\langle v_1, v_2 \rangle \in A$ is called a **predecessor** of v_2 whereas vertex v_2 is called a **successor** of v_1. A vertex can have zero, one, or two successors. Let $outdegree(v)$ be a function mapping the number of successors to a vertex v and $indegree(v)$ the number of predecessors. A vertex v with $outdegree(v) = 2$ represents a so called **control expression** including a Boolean condition. The two outgoing arcs of v are attributed with $\langle v, v_x \rangle_T$ ($TRUE$) and $\langle v, v_y \rangle_F$ ($FALSE$) and correspond to the control flow in response to the evaluation of the condition. The $\langle \text{"}ENTRY\text{"}, comp \rangle$ vertex represents the point of the component $comp$ through which control enters and $outdegree(\langle \text{"}ENTRY\text{"}, comp \rangle) = 1$. A $\langle \text{"}REENTRY\text{"}, comp \rangle$ vertex represents a point of the component $comp$ through which control suspends, and reenters when the component has been reactivated/dispatched after the suspension

Table 3: AADL Grammar in Backus-Naur Form (BNF)

port_connection	::=	identifier : (**data port** | **event port** | **event data port**) source_port_reference (− > | − >>)
		destination_port_reference
data_access_connection	::=	identifier : **data access** data_component_reference (− > | < − >) access_require_reference
subp_access_connection	::=	identifier : **subprogram access** subprogram_component_reference < − > access_require_reference
parameter_connection	::=	identifier : **parameter** source_parameter_reference − > destination_parameter_reference
subprogram_call	::=	identifier : **subprogram** subprogram_reference
port	::=	identifier : (**in** | **out** | **inout**) (**data port** | **event data port** | **event**) data_component_reference
component_access	::=	identifier : **requires** (**data access** | **subprogram access**) component_reference
parameter	::=	identifier : (**in** | **out** | **in out**) **parameter** [data_component_reference]
state	::=	state_identifier : [**initial**][**complete**][**final**] **state**
variable	::=	variable_declarator : data_component_reference
state_transition	::=	[identifier [priority] :] source_state_identifier −[guard]− > destination_state_identifier [action]
mode	::=	identifier : [**initial**] **mode**
mode_transition	::=	[identifier :] source_mode_identifier −[trigger]− > destination_mode_identifier

and $outdegree(\langle\text{"}ENTRY\text{"}, comp\rangle) = 1$. The $\langle\text{"}EXIT\text{"},$
$comp\rangle$ vertex represents the point of the component $comp$
through which control exits/stops and $outdegree(EXIT) =$
0. A **path** $P = v_1 v_2 \cdots v_n$ of CFG is a sequence of vertices
such that $n \geq 2$ and for $i = 1, 2, \ldots, n - 1$, $\langle v_i, v_{i+1}\rangle \in A$.
A path $P = v_1 v_2 \cdots v_n$ is called a **basic block** if $v_1 \neq$
$ENTRY \cup REENTRY$, $outdegree(v_1) = 1$, for $n > 2$ and
$i = 2, 3 \ldots, n - 1$, $indegree(v_i) = 1$ and $outdegree(v_i) = 1$,
and $indegree(v_n) = 1$ and $outdegree(v_n) \geq 2$.

For simplicity, we assume that a $comp_i.\mathcal{BM}$ only includes
deterministic behavior when defining the transformation to a
$CFG(comp_i.\mathcal{BM})$. The assumption restricts the behavioral
model (BM) such that actions of transitions cannot be of
sets (i.e. actions must be of sequences), multiple outgoing
edges from the same state must not have equivalent priorities
(which otherwise execute non-deterministically), and there
can only be one final state.

In a BM, the atomic expressions which define executable
operations are guards and actions of state transitions. Hence,
the vertices of $CFG(comp_i.\mathcal{BM})$ represent guards and actions of state transitions in $comp_i.\mathcal{BM}$. Each state transition yields a fixed execution order of operations: the guard
of the transitions is first computed, and if evaluated to the
Boolean value $TRUE$, the sequence of actions of the transition is executed according to the order of the sequence.
Consequently, each transition $s \xrightarrow{pri,g,act} s'$, where $act =$
$action_1; action_2; \ldots; action_n$ is a sequence of n actions (executes deterministically according to the sequence), maps
to a CFG construct of one vertex $v_1 = g$ representing the
guard of the state transition, a basic block of n vertices $v_2 =$
$action_1, v_3 = action_2, \ldots, v_{n+1} = action_n$ representing the
actions of the state transition, and n arcs $\langle v_1, v_2\rangle_T, \langle v_2, v_3\rangle,$
$\ldots, \langle v_n, v_{n+1}\rangle$ representing the control flow through the executable operations. Note that the arc from the guard to
the first action is attributed with a "T". Let $stateTrToV :$
$\mathcal{TR} \rightarrow \mathcal{P}(V)$ be a function mapping a state transition to a
set of vertices, and $stateTrToA : \mathcal{TR} \rightarrow \mathcal{P}(A)$ to a set of
arcs such that $stateTrToV(s \xrightarrow{pri,g,act} s') = \{v_1, v_2, v_3, \ldots,$
$v_{n+1}\}$ and $stateTrToA(s \xrightarrow{pri,g,act} s') = \{\langle v_1, v_2\rangle_T, \langle v_2, v_3\rangle,$
$\ldots, \langle v_n, v_{n+1}\rangle\}$ where $v_1 = g, v_2 = action_1, v_3 = action_2,$
$\ldots, v_{n+1} = action_n$. The fixed execution order of opera-
tions is repeated throughout the BM until a final state is
reached, regardless of the evaluation of the guard – and under the assumptions that the model is free from deadlocks.

If evaluated to the Boolean value $TRUE$, the actions are executed, resulting in the arrival of a new state s', whereupon
the transition going out from s' with the highest priority is
executed according to the fixed order. If the guard is evaluated to the Boolean value $FALSE$, another state transition
going out from s with the (next) highest priority is exe-
cuted in the fixed order. Let $guardVertex : \mathcal{TR} \rightarrow \mathcal{V}$ be
a function mapping a state transition $s \xrightarrow{pri,g,act} s'$ to the
vertex v_x representing the guard of the state transition. Let
$lastActionVertex : \mathcal{TR} \rightarrow \mathcal{V}$ be a function mapping a state
transition $s \xrightarrow{pri,g,act} s'$ to the vertex v_x representing the
last action of the state transition. Let $guardVertexPrio :$
$\mathcal{S} \times \mathbb{N} \rightarrow \mathcal{V} \cup \{FALSE\}$ be a function mapping a state s
to the vertex v_x representing the guard of the state tran-
sition going out from v and with the highest priority, or
with the highest priority but less than n if a natural number is given as argument, or $FALSE$ if there exist no such
vertex. In the case of an evaluation of a guard to $TRUE$,
the control flow from the last action of the transition to the
guard of the second transition with the highest priority is
simply represented by an arc $\langle lastActionVertex(s \xrightarrow{pri,g,act}$
$s'), guardVertexPrio(s')\rangle$. In case of an evaluation to
$FALSE$, the control flow to the guard with the (next) highest priority is represented by an $(FALSE\text{-})$arc $\langle guardVertex$
$(s \xrightarrow{pri,g,act} s'), guardVertexPrio(s, pri)\rangle_F$.

It should be mentioned that actions may be of **if**, **while**
and **for** constructs. Such an action comprises multiple vertices where control can leave the construct (action) from
several vertices rather than a single one. In such constructs
are predicates and nested actions also represented through
distinguished vertices. Assume that v_x represents a control
predicate expression of a loop or conditional, and v_y represents an action expression immediately nested within the
loop or condition. If v_x is the predicate of a conditional
expression the arc $\langle v_x, v_y\rangle$ is labeled with "T" or "F" according to weather v_y exists in the **then** branch, **elsif** or
else branch. If v_x is the predicate of a while- or for-loop,
the arc $\langle v_x, v_y\rangle$ is labeled with "T". In case a state transition
consists of an action sequence where the last action consists
of an **if** construct, each (nested) action ending the control
flow of the construct, including the current state transition,
must be connected to the subsequent transition guard vertex, $REENTRY$ vertex, or $EXIT$ vertex by an arc.

Algorithm 1 Algorithm for generating control flow graphs

Input: $comp_i.\mathcal{BM} = \langle \mathcal{S}, s_o, \mathcal{CPL}, \mathcal{FIL}, \mathcal{VAR}, \mathcal{TR} \rangle$ and $\mathcal{TR}_{rel} \subseteq \mathcal{TR}$

Output: $\mathcal{CFG}(comp_i) = \langle V, A \rangle$

1: $V \leftarrow \emptyset \cup \{\langle "ENTRY", comp_i \rangle, \langle "EXIT", comp_i \rangle\}$
2: $A \leftarrow \emptyset$
3: **for all** $s \xrightarrow{pri,g,act} s' \in \mathcal{TR}_{rel}$ **do** ▷ generate vertices and arcs for each relevant transition
4:     $V \leftarrow V \cup stateTrToV(s \xrightarrow{pri,g,act} s')$
5:     $A \leftarrow A \cup stateTrToA(s \xrightarrow{pri,g,act} s')$
6: **end for**
7: $A \leftarrow A \cup \{\langle\langle "ENTRY", comp_i\rangle, guardVertexPrio(firstState(comp_i.\mathcal{BM}))\rangle\}$ ▷ Generate the arc representing control flow from the $ENTRY$ vertex to the guard vertex with highest priority
8: **for all** $cpl_j \in \mathcal{CPL}$ **do** ▷ generate possible $REENTRY$ vertices
9:     **if** $\exists s \xrightarrow{pri,g,act} s' \in \mathcal{TR}_{rel}[s' = cpl_j]$ **then**
10:       $V \leftarrow V \cup \{"REENTRY_j"\}$
11:       $A \leftarrow A \cup \{\langle "REENTRY_j", guardVertexPrio(s')\rangle\}$ ▷ Any control flow to $"REENTRY_j"$ will successively flow to $guardVertexPrio(s')$
12:     **end if**
13: **end for**
14: **for all** $s \xrightarrow{pri,g,act} s' \in \mathcal{TR}_{rel}$ **do** ▷ Generate arcs to connect each transition representation to the subsequent guard, complete state (reentry) or final state representation
15:     **if** $s' \in \mathcal{CPL})$ **then**
16:       $A \leftarrow A \cup \{\langle lastActionVertex(s \xrightarrow{pri,g,act} s'), CPLState Vertex(s')\rangle\}$
17:     **else if** $s' \in \mathcal{FIL}$ **then**
18:       $A \leftarrow A \cup \{\langle lastActionVertex(s \xrightarrow{pri,g,act} s'), \langle "EXIT", comp_i\rangle\}$
19:     **else**$A \leftarrow A \cup \{\langle lastActionVertex(s \xrightarrow{pri,g,act} s'), guard VertexPrio(s')\rangle\}$
20:     **end if**
21:     **if** $guardVertexPrio(s, pri)$ **then** ▷ generate a false arc if a subsequent guard exists
22:       $A \leftarrow A \cup \{\langle guardVertex(s \xrightarrow{pri,g,act} s'), guard VertexPrio(s, pri)\rangle_F\}$
23:     **end if**
24: **end for**
25: **return** $\langle V, A \rangle$

The complete flow of control, i.e. the possible orders in which transitions are executed, is determined by the possible orders states can be visited through state transitions (the possible *paths* in the BM) and by the priorities of the state transitions. A BM of a subprogram component has: one initial state representing the starting point of a call; zero or more intermediate execution states representing the logical execution between start and completion of a call; and one final state representing the completion of a call. Thus, the initial state of a subprogram maps to an $ENTRY$ vertex whereas the final state maps to an $EXIT$ vertex. A BM of a thread component, on the other hand, has: one initial state representing the state (halted) of the thread before it is initialized; zero or more intermediate execution states representing the initialization steps (such as checking correctness of initial values of input and output ports) of the thread between the initial state and one, first, complete state (any path from the initial state will reach the same complete state before any other complete state); one or more complete states representing that the thread has suspended itself and is awaiting dispatch/reactivation (the first complete state reached from an initial state does also represent completion of initialization the first time it is reached); zero or more intermediate execution states representing logical execution between dispatches, that is, from and back to a complete

state or between complete states; and one final state representing completion of finalization.

Execution of a subprogram component is triggered by incoming calls where the transition out from the initial state with the highest priority (if several) and with valid execute conditions is executed. A thread component, on the other hand, must first be initialized by an initialize action triggered when the process containing the thread is completely loaded into its virtual address space before it can be executed. An initialize action triggers the transition out from the initial state eventually leading to one, first, complete state. A state transition to a complete state means that the thread is calling an "await dispatch" run-time service, whereupon the thread is suspended after the action of the state transition has been executed. A dispatch of the thread component is triggered according to the dispatch conditions of the transitions out from the current complete state and the specified scheduling protocol of the thread. Dispatches of a periodic thread are solely triggered by a clock and the time interval (period) specified with the thread. In this case, dispatch conditions (guards of transitions out from complete states) are left empty. Dispatches of aperiodic, sporadic, timed and hybrid threads are essentially triggered by the arrival of an event or an event data at an event or event data port of the thread, or a remote subprogram call arriving to a provides subprogram access feature of the thread. By default, any arrival of event, event data or subprogram call triggers a dispatch where dispatch conditions restrict the number of triggers if modeled. In either case, an input-

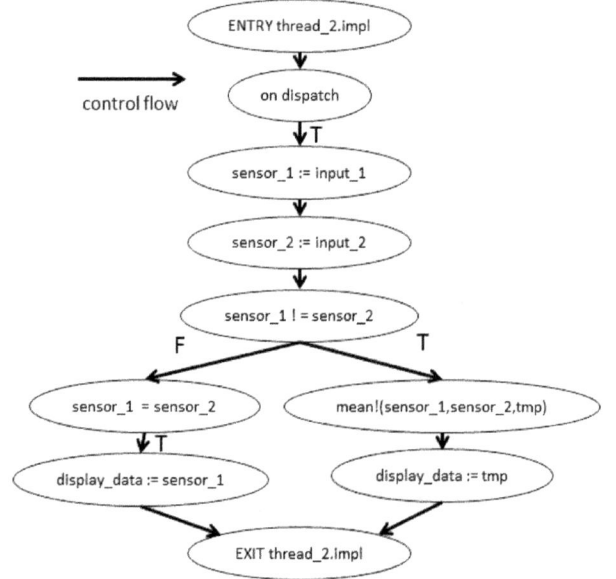

Figure 1: The CFG of thread_2.

compute-output model of execution is triggered. Input on in ports is frozen at the time of dispatch, where input from each port connection is read and assigned to a corresponding port variable which value (by default) is not affected by new arrivals for the remainder of the current dispatch. Output on out ports is transmitted through the connections at the time of completion, deadline or at specific output times according to an *Output_Time* property. For simplicity, we assume that the output is transmitted at completion. A state transition to a final state means that the thread completes and is calling a "finalize" run-time service, whereupon the thread terminates after the action of the state transition has been executed. Consequently, a BM of a thread component, in contrast to a BM of a subprogram component, expresses state transitions which are not relevant to the logical execution (such as initialization transitions).

The relevant set of state transitions includes each transition that exists on every path from every complete state in the BM. Each of these are either from a complete state to a complete state, execution state, or a final state; or from an execution state to a complete state, an execution state, or a final state. Thus, the first complete state reached from an initial state maps to an $ENTRY$ vertex, any subsequently reachable complete states, including the one first reached from an initial state, maps to a $REENTRY$ vertex. The final state maps to an $EXIT$ vertex. Let $firstState$: $\mathcal{P}(\mathcal{S}) \times S \times \mathcal{P}(\mathcal{S}) \times \mathcal{P}(\mathcal{S}) \times \mathcal{P}(\mathcal{VAR}) \times \mathcal{P}(\mathcal{TR}) \to \mathcal{CPL}$ be a function mapping a BM to the initial state if the BM is of a subprogram component, or the first complete state reachable from the initial state if the BM is of a thread component. Let $CPLStateVertex : \mathcal{CPL} \to \mathcal{V}$ be a function mapping a complete state to its corresponding $REENTRY$ vertex. Note that the first complete state is mapped to both an $ENTRY$ and an $REENTRY$ vertex if there exist a transition back to the state. However, there exist only one distinguished $ENTRY$ vertex, so there is no need to define a function to retrieve it. Let $\mathcal{TR}_{rel} \subseteq \mathcal{TR}$ be the relevant set of state transitions of a BM. If the BM is of a subprogram component, then $\mathcal{TR}_{rel} = \mathcal{TR}$. The transformation from a $comp_i.\mathcal{BM}$ to the corresponding $CFG(comp_i.\mathcal{BM})$ can then be calculated as shown in Algorithm 1. The result of applying the algorithm on $thread\_2.impl$ of the running example (Table 1) is shown in Figure 1.

Each state transition out from or to a complete state comprises interactions (of control, data, or both) with other components if the thread has in ports or out ports connected to them, respectively. These are relevant to the logical execution but not considered in the CFG, however, they are considered when constructing the SDG from PDGs as described in Section 4.3.

4.2 Generating Program Dependence Graphs

A $CDG(comp_i)$ or a $FDG(comp_i)$ of a component is a directed graph $\langle V, A \rangle$ of a set of CFG vertices V and arcs $A \subseteq V \times V$ of the form $\langle v, v' \rangle_c$ or $\langle v, v' \rangle_d$. An arc $\langle v_1, v_2 \rangle_c$ labeled with "c" represents that v_2 is control-dependent on v_1. An arc $\langle v_1, v_2 \rangle_d$ labeled with "d" represents that v_2 is data (flow) dependent on v_1.

A $PDG(comp_i)$ of a component is simply the union of $CDG(comp_i)$ and $FDG(comp_i)$. Control dependencies of a CFG are calculated by so called dominator vertices [12]. Assume that v_x, v_y and v_z are vertices of $CFG(comp_i.\mathcal{BM})$. A vertex v_x is *post-dominated* by a vertex v_y if every path from v_x to the EXIT vertex includes v_y. Control dependency is then defined as:

Definition 4. A vertex v_y is *control-dependent* $\langle v_x, v_y \rangle_c$ on a vertex v_x iff **1)** v_x is an $ENTRY$ or an $REENTRY$ vertex and v_y is not nested within any loop or conditional vertex, or **2)** there exists a path P from v_x to v_y such that any vertex v_z in P is post-dominated by v_y, and v_x is not post-dominated by v_y (v_x must be a control expression).

An algorithm to generate the corresponding CDG of a CFG, based on this definition of control dependency, can be found in [12]. The corresponding CDG of the CFG in Figure 1 is shown in Figure 2.

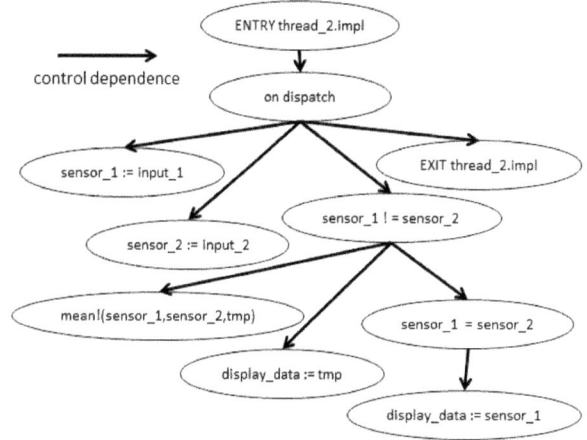

Figure 2: The CDG of thread_2.

Data dependencies of a CFG are calculated by so called *def-use pairs*. Assume that v_x is a vertex that defines/assigns variable var, and v_y is a vertex that uses/reads var. Flow-dependency is then defined as:

Definition 5. A vertex v_y is *data-dependent* $\langle v_x, v_y \rangle_d$ on a vertex v_x iff v_x defines/assigns a variable var that is used/read by v_y, and there exists a path P from v_x to v_y such that any vertex v_z in P does not define/assign var.

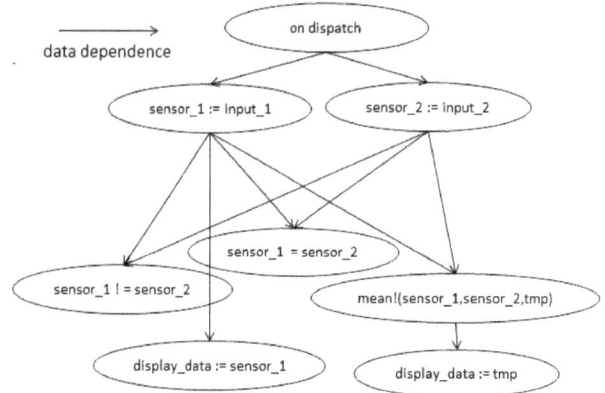

Figure 3: The FDG of thread_2.

Since each thread dispatch and subprogram activation includes assignments to input port and parameter variables if the component has such connections, a control flow from an $ENTRY$ and $REENTRY$ vertex includes assignment which are not represented in a CFG. Interactions between components are considered when constructing the SDG, however, to calculate all possible data dependencies it is assumed that all necessary initial assignments occur in the $ENTRY$ vertex of a subprogram, and in the dispatch condition vertices of $ENTRY$ and $REENTRY$ vertices of a thread. In addition, a vertex including a subprogram call includes assignment of return values to in data ports connected with the out parameters of the called subprogram. Such assignments are assumed to occur in the vertex including the call. The corresponding FDG of the CFG in Figure 1 is shown in Figure 3.

4.3 Generating the System Dependence Graph

SDGs, as originally defined in [7], extend the expressiveness of PDGs such that procedure calls and parameter (data) passing (by value) can be integrated. The extension consists of five distinguished types of vertices to accurately represent the semantics of procedure calls and parameter passing: *call* vertices ($subprogram(arg_0, arg_1, \ldots, arg_m, var_0, var_1, \ldots, var_n)$ where $m, n \in \mathbb{N}$), representing call sites; *actual-in* vertices ($\{temp_i\_in = arg_i \mid i \in \mathbb{N} \text{ and } 0 \le i \le m\}$), representing assignments that copy the values of the actual arguments of call sites to temporary "in" variables; *formal-in* vertices ($\{parameter_i = temp_i\_in \mid i \in \mathbb{N} \text{ and } 0 \le i \le m\}$), representing assignments that copy the values of temporary "in" variables to the formal parameters of procedures; *formal-out* vertices ($\{temp_i\_out = return_i \mid i \in \mathbb{N} \text{ and } 0 \le i \le n\}$), representing assignments that copy the values of return variables of procedures to temporary "out" variables; and *actual-out* vertices ($\{var_i = temp_i\_out \mid i \in \mathbb{N} \text{ and } 0 \le i \le n\}$), representing assignments that copy the values of temporary "out" variables to the variables assigned by the calls. Actual-in and actual-out vertices are control-dependent on the call vertex, whereas formal-in and formal-out vertices are control-dependent on the entry vertex (of the called subprogram). In addition, the extension includes three distinguished types of dependence edges, which also maintain a clear structure of the system: *call* edges, representing the control dependence between a call site and the entry of the called procedure; *parameter-in edges*, representing the data dependence between an actual-in vertex and the corresponding formal-in vertex; *parameter-out* edges, representing the data dependence between a formal-out vertex and the corresponding actual-out vertex. A SDG is basically formed by: 1) representing each procedure of a program by a PDG extended with vertices for procedure calls and parameter passing; 2) connecting call vertices of PDGs to the entries of the corresponding called PDGs through call edges; and connecting actual-in vertices to formal-in vertices and formal-out vertices to actual-out vertices through parameter-in and parameter-out edges respectively. In AADL, however, there are additional types of interdependencies than procedure calls and parameter passing. The original definition of a SDG must therefore be extended to be applicable to AADL models.

A $SDG(\mathcal{AADLMDL})$ of an AADL model is a directed graph $\langle V, A \rangle$ of a set of CFG vertices V and arcs $A \subseteq V \times V$ of the form $\langle v, v' \rangle_c$, $\langle v, v' \rangle_d$, $\langle v, v' \rangle_{call}$, $\langle v, v' \rangle_{p-in}$, $\langle v, v' \rangle_{p-out}$, and $\langle v, v' \rangle_{mode}$ representing control, data, call and event, data passing by value and reference, and mode dependencies. A SDG of an AADL model is formed by generating the set of PDGs, and annotating them to include interdependencies between the set of PDGs, such as shown in Figure 4 where the SDG of our running example is presented. The possible interactions among components are represented by four different types of connections: *port connections*, *data access connections*, *subprogram calls*, and

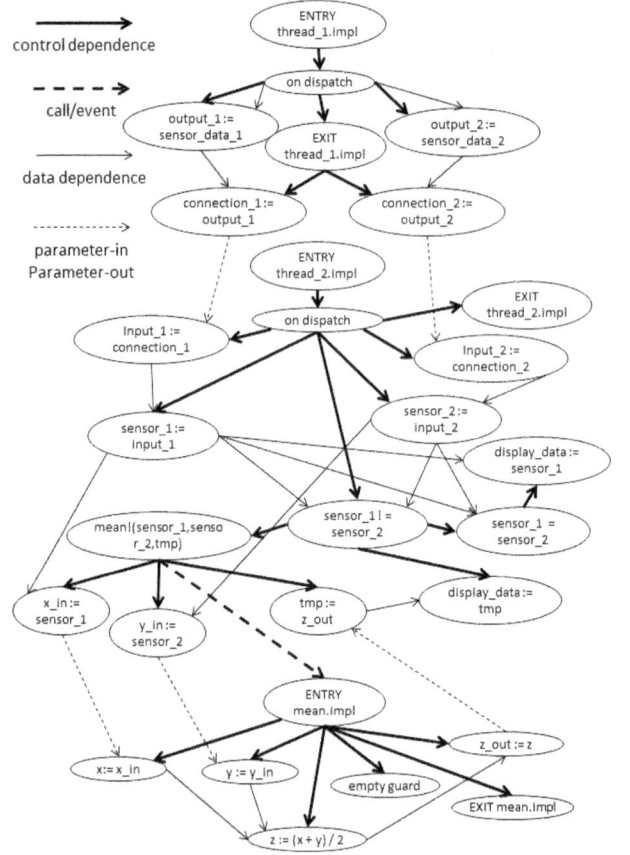

Figure 4: The SDG of the AADL example.

parameter connections. Ports, parameters, and data components are accessible as typed data variables.

Port connections represent transfers of data (by value), control, or both, depending on the type of interconnected interfaces: data ports, event ports, or event data ports. A data port connection can be accurately represented by an unidirectional variant of SDG parameter passing including an actual-in vertex $connection_i\_temp = outdataport\_var$ and a formal-in vertex $indataport\_var = connection_i\_temp$ interconnected through a parameter-in (data dependence) arc denoted $\langle connection_i\_temp = outdataport\_var, indataport\_var = connection_i\_temp \rangle_{p-in}$. The actual-in vertex is control dependent on each $REENTRY$ vertex and the $EXIT$ vertex of the sending thread (since we assume transfer of output at completion). The formal-in vertex is control-dependent on the dispatch condition vertices of the receiving thread. E.g., data port connection $Connection\_1$ in the AADL example (Table 1) maps to the actual-in vertex "$connection\_1 := output\_1$" and the formal-in vertex "$Input\_1 := connection\_1$" in Figure 4. An event port connection can be accurately represented by an event port "call" vertex $outeventport\_var!$ (an exclamation mark denotes the triggering of an event in AADL) and a target event port variable vertex $ineventport\_var$ interconnected through a call (control dependence) arc denoted $\langle outeventport\_var!, ineventport\_var \rangle_{call}$. The dispatch condition vertices of the receiving thread is control-dependent on the event port variable vertex. Event data port connections can be represented through an actual-in vertex $connection_i\_temp = outevent$

dataport_var and a formal-in vertex *ineventdataport_var* = *connection_i_temp* interconnected through both a parameter in arc and a call arc, where actual-in and formal-in vertices are control-dependent on the sending and receiving thread according to the union of data and event port connections.

Subprogram calls represent transfers of control whereas *parameter connections* represent transfers of data (by value). Control and data dependencies of subprogram calls with parameter connections can be represented as originally defined in a SDG [7], however, where actual-in, formal-in, formal-out, and actual-out vertices operates on port and parameter variables. E.g., the subprogram call *mean!(sensor_1,sensor_2,tmp)* in the AADL example (Table 1) maps to actual-in vertices "*x_in := sensor_1*" and "*y_in := sensor_2*", formal-in vertices "*x := x_in*" and "*y := y_in*", formal-out vertex "*z_out := z*", and actual-out vertex "*tmp := z_out*" in Figure 4.

Data access connections to a common data component may represent transfers of data (by reference) if there exist both write-right (a component is able to write data) and read-right (a component is able to read data) access connections. In case this condition holds, data dependence between a write-right (*connection_i*) and a read-right (*connection_j*) data access connection can be represented through a variant of SDG parameter passing including an actual-in vertex *connection_{i-j}_temp = datacomp_var*, representing the write-right connection, and an inverting formal-in vertex *datacomp_var = connection_{i-j}_temp*, representing the read-right connection, interconnected through a parameter-in arc. We assume that a thread or a subprogram gets the data source upon dispatch, and releases it upon a completion. There are thereby no data dependencies among components on the data component during the execution of a thread or subprogram. Consequently, the actual-in vertex is control-dependent on each *REENTRY* vertex and the *EXIT* vertex of the sending thread, or the *EXIT* vertex of the sending subprogram. The formal-in vertex is control-dependent on the dispatch condition vertices of the receiving thread, or the *ENTRY* vertex of the receiving subprogram.

The runtime configuration of subcomponents and their interactions within a component may change if it is specified with *modes*. For each mode, it is possible to set the active components and connections, mode-specific subprogram calls, and mode-specific properties. Modes essentially determine if complete components and interactions between components will be executed or not and therefore express control dependencies. Hence, entry vertices of components and vertices involved with dependencies between components may be control-dependent on modes. To accurately represent the SDG of an AADL model, we extend the expressiveness of a SDG with a *mode* and a *mode trigger* vertex type representing modes and mode triggers, and a *mode dependence* arc type representing control dependence due to modes. Each mode, except for the initial mode, in a mode state machine is control-dependent on the previous mode and the mode transition triggers of the mode transitions to the mode. Hence, for each mode transition $m \xrightarrow{tri} m'$ of each $comp_i.\mathcal{MSM}$, the following vertices and dependence arcs are generated:$\langle$"*MODE*"$, m \rangle \in V$, $\langle$"*MODETRI*"$, tri \rangle \in V$, $\langle$"*MODE*"$, m' \rangle \in V$, $\langle \langle$"*MODE*"$, m \rangle, \langle$"*MODE*"$, m' \rangle \rangle_{mode} \in A$, and $\langle \langle$"*MODETRI*"$, tri \rangle, \langle$"*MODE*"$, m' \rangle \rangle_{mode} \in A$.

To complete the interdependencies between a set of PDGs to form the SDG, a dependence construct according to above description must be generated for each connection and mode state machine. The constructs and PDGs are completely integrated by adding a control, data, and/or a call dependence edge for each definition, use, event call, and event call retrieval of a port, parameter, or data component variable of each PDG that yields a data or control dependency with the added set of vertices. E.g., vertex "*output_1 := sensor_data_1*" yields a data dependency with the added actual-in vertex "*connection_1 := output_1*" in Figure 4 and must be connected with a data dependence edge as shown. Since we assume that output is sent on the time of completion, an actual-in or a formal-out vertex is only data-dependent on the corresponding final definitions of the out data port, out event data port, out parameter, or data component variable of each thread dispatch or subprogram activation. Note that a *CFG* with multiple paths between dispatches may include multiple final definitions. An actual-in vertex, of an event data port connection, or an event port call vertex is control-dependent on the corresponding final definitions and event calls. In addition, entry, actual-in, formal-in, formal-out, and actual-out vertices that are dependent on modes are connected to the corresponding mode vertices through mode-dependence arcs.

Note that in the construction of a *PDG*, it is assumed that initial assignments of in data or event data ports, in parameters, and accessed data components variables, and of return values of subprogram calls to in data ports occur in *ENTRY* vertices of subprograms, dispatch vertices of threads, and vertices including subprogram calls. In a *SDG* are these assignments explicitly represented in formal-in and actual-out vertices. Any data dependence on such vertices is substituted with a data dependence on the corresponding formal-in or actual-out vertex. E.g., vertex "*sensor_1 := input_1*" is data-dependent on formal-in vertex "*Input_1 := connection_1*" in Figure 4, rather than on the dispatch vertex as in Figure 3. The corresponding SDG of the running example according to the rules defined in this section is presented in Figure 4.

5. SLICING AND SELECTION

Through comparison of SDGs generated from the architecture model and its modified version, the modifications can be identified and their effects on the system architecture can be traced by slicing the modified model with respect to the variables assigned or used in the modifications. A modification is defined as an added or changed vertex, or a vertex which dependency on another vertex has been removed, added or changed. Verification sequences which do not cover modified or affected vertices, i.e., the sliced model, can then be disregarded to generate a more efficient subset for regression verification.

A backward-slice of an AADL model with respect to slicing criterion $CRI = \langle comp, expr, var \rangle$ and a $SDG = \langle V, A \rangle$ is simply the subset of vertices $V_{b-slice} \subseteq V$ that are backwards reachable (through arcs) from vertex $expr \in V$ (including $expr \in V$). A forward-slice, on the other hand, is simply the subset of vertices $V_{f-slice} \subseteq V$ that are forward reachable (through arcs) from vertex $expr \in V$ (including $expr \in V$).

As an example, consider the SDG of our running example and assume that there exist a prior SDG of a prior version of the AADL model in Table 1 and Table 2. Further assume that according to a comparison between the two SDGs, the vertex "$z := (x + y)/2$" is a changed vertex and constitutes the modification and therefore also the slicing criterion. The forward-slice $V_{f-slice} = \{$ "$z := (x + y)/2$", "$z\_out := z$", "$tmp := z\_out$", "$display\_data := tmp$" $\}$ includes the set of elements of the AADL model that may exhibit a different behavior with respect to the prior version and thus must be re-verified. Any previous verification sequence covering any of these vertices should therefore be re-executed since it may generate a different result. The backward slice includes all vertices that may affect the behavior of the modification and, depending on the verification technique (e.g. unit- or system-level verification) and the coverage criteria (e.g. statement, condition, or path coverage), can be used to guide the selection process. There are two extremes: 1) if the technique has the ability to directly execute the modification (e.g. directly call a modified subprogram rather than stimulating the system with input that eventually causes a call to the modified subprogram) and the coverage criteria allow it, none of the vertices in the backward slice except for the modification and vertices also included in the forward-slice may be covered, and 2) if the coverage criteria require all possible scenarios in which the modification may be executed to be covered, all vertices of the backward slice must be covered (in fact, all paths of the backward slice must be covered for full coverage). Despite verification technique and coverage criteria, vertices that are not included in the forward nor backward transitive closure $\{$ "$sensor\_1 = sensor\_2$", "$display\_data := sensor\_1$" $\}$ can, with respect to the modification, be confidentially disregarded in the regression verification process. With auxiliary vertices (ENTRY and EXIT) excluded, this constitutes a $2/23 \approx 9\%$ to $19/23 \approx 83\%$ reduction of exercised elements.

6. CONCLUSIONS

In this paper we presented a technique for selective regression verification of AADL models through slicing. We showed how it can be applied to reduce the scope of re-verification due to modifications. The technique allows for a more efficient regression verification process and could therefore result in significant cost and time savings.

In the current form, the technique may however introduce a slight overestimation of the data and control dependencies between concurrently executed tasks, by not taking into account dynamic properties such as patterns of (timed) scheduling and concurrency protocols for access to shared memory (critical regions). These properties may, in a complex manner, constrain the possible flows of control and data between concurrent tasks and, thus, the possible number of dependencies. A future area of improvement is an inclusion of such dynamic properties to generate more precise dependencies. The overestimation however makes interdependences between tasks easy and fast to compute, which advocate the overhead a selective approach yields compared to a rerun-all approach. The downside is that some elements may still be unnecessarily exercised in the regression verification process, which delimits the return on the investment. The possible return in terms of time-efficiency with respect to a non-selective approach is a subject for future research. In the running example of this paper, the technique resulted in a 9% to 83% reduction of exercised elements. As slicing

of SDGs can be performed in linear time [7], such results indicate a beneficial use.

7. REFERENCES

[1] F. E. Allen. Control flow analysis. *SIGPLAN Not.*, 5(7):1–19, July 1970.

[2] As-2 Embedded Computing Systems Committee SAE. Architecture Analysis & Design Language (AADL). SAE Standards n° AS5506A, 2009.

[3] S. Bates and S. Horwitz. Incremental Program Testing Using Program Dependence Graphs. In *Proceedings of the 20th ACM SIGPLAN-SIGACT Symposium on Principles of Programming Languages*, POPL '93, pages 384–396, New York, NY, USA, 1993. ACM.

[4] R. B. Franca, J.-P. Bodeveix, M. Filali, J.-F. Rolland, D. Chemouil, and D. Thomas. The AADL behaviour annex – experiments and roadmap. In *ICECCS '07: Proceedings of the 12th IEEE International Conference on Engineering Complex Computer Systems*, pages 377–382, Washington, DC, USA, 2007. IEEE Computer Society.

[5] R. Gupta, M. Jean, M. J. Harrold, and M. L. Soffa. An Approach to Regression Testing using Slicing. In *In Proceedings of the Conference on Software Maintenance*, pages 299–308. IEEE Computer Society Press, 1992.

[6] M. J. Harrold. Testing: A Roadmap. In *In The Future of Software Engineering*, pages 61–72. ACM Press, 2000.

[7] S. Horwitz, T. Reps, and D. Binkley. Interprocedural slicing using dependence graphs. In *Proceedings of the ACM SIGPLAN 1988 conference on Programming Language design and Implementation*, PLDI '88, pages 35–46, New York, NY, USA, 1988. ACM.

[8] A. Johnsen, K. Lundqvist, P. Pettersson, and O. Jaradat. Automated Verification of AADL-Specifications Using UPPAAL. *Ninth IEEE International Symposium on High-Assurance Systems Engineering (HASE'05)*, 0:130–138, 2012.

[9] Juei Chang and Debra J. Richardson. Static and Dynamic Specification Slicing. In *In Proceedings of the Fourth Irvine Software Symposium*, 1994.

[10] N. G. Leveson. *Safeware: system safety and computers*. ACM, New York, NY, USA, 1995.

[11] T. Oda and K. Araki. Specification slicing in formal methods of software development. In *Proceedings of the 17th annual International computer software and applications conference (COMPSAC'93)*, pages 313–319, 1993.

[12] K. J. Ottenstein and L. M. Ottenstein. The program dependence graph in a software development environment. *SIGPLAN Not.*, 19(5):177–184, Apr. 1984.

[13] J. Silva. A Vocabulary of Program Slicing-based Techniques. *ACM Comput. Surv.*, 44(3):12:1–12:41, June 2012.

[14] M. Weiser. Program slicing. In *Proceedings of the 5th international conference on Software engineering*, ICSE '81, pages 439–449, Piscataway, NJ, USA, 1981. IEEE Press.

Evaluation of a Static Architectural Conformance Checking Method in a Line of Computer Games

Tobias Olsson, Daniel Toll,
Anna Wingkvist
Dept. of Computer Science
Linnaeus University
Kalmar, Sweden
tobias.ohlsson|daniel.toll|anna.wingkvist@lnu.se

Morgan Ericsson
Dept. of Computer Science and Engineering
Chalmers University of Technology and
University of Gothenburg
Gothenburg, Sweden
morgan@cse.gu.se

ABSTRACT

We present an evaluation of a simple method to find architectural problems in a product line of computer games. The method uses dependencies (direct, indirect, or no) to automatically classify types in the implementation to high-level components in the product line architecture. We use a commercially available tool to analyse dependencies in the source code. The automatic classification of types is compared to a manual classification by the developer, and all mismatches are reported. To evaluate the method, we inspect the source code and look for a pre-defined set of architectural problems in all types. We compare the set of types that contained problems to the set of types where the manual and automatic classification disagreed to determine precision and recall. We also investigate what changes are needed to correct the found mismatches by either designing and implementing changes in the source code or refining the automatic classification. Our evaluation shows that the simple method is effective at detecting architectural problems in a product line of four games. The method is lightweight, customisable and easy to implement early in the development cycle.

Categories and Subject Descriptors

D.2.11 [**Software Engineering**]: Software Architectures—*patterns*

Keywords

Model-View-Controller, MVC, Computer Game, Product Line Architecture, Static Conformance Checking

1. INTRODUCTION

The use of patterns is a popular approach to software architecture. The patterns allow architects and developers to benefit from documented knowledge and serve as a base that enable different characteristics, e.g., Client-Server pattern or Layers pattern [2, 6].

Since the patterns are abstract and general it can be unclear how to best implement them. Misconceptions and discrepancies in how the pattern is interpreted by different developers can result in architectural erosion.

Two of the authors of this paper have experience from the computer game industry where they developed a number of games. These games all had similar basic requirements, used the same iterative development process, the same game engine, and an architecture based on the Model-View-Controller (MVC) pattern. Their experience show how difficult it can be to understand and implement a pattern properly. The implementation (process) of their games show that the MVC pattern was not clearly understood and that the interpretation changed over time and between games. In many cases mistakes or misunderstandings accumulated to the point where parts of the source code had to be refactored or even abandoned.

A method that help architects and developers find mistakes and misunderstandings in early stages of architectural erosion can save both time and effort. When we investigate the games and how they use the MVC pattern, we find that a key dependency in the pattern can be used to automatically classify types in the implementation to high-level components defined by the pattern. This classification can be compared to the developers' intentions captured by, e.g., name spaces or type names, and any difference may suggest a mistake or a misunderstanding, i.e., an architectural problem. We investigate four games to determine how many architectural problems we can find with this method. In two of the games we also investigate and implement the changes needed to conform to the intended architecture to determine what type of problems we can detect and if the classification can be customized to remove found false positives.

The remainder of the paper is organised as follows; first we introduce software architecture in computer games. We then present our research questions and study design. After that we present our results, our analysis, validity issues and related work. We end with conclusions and future directions.

2. COMPUTER GAME ARCHITECTURE

Most computer games are real-time, interactive computer simulations; they collect input from the user, execute a simulation step and render a representation of the current simulation state. This is done as fast as possible to maintain

Permission to make digital or hard copies of all or part of this work for personal or classroom use is granted without fee provided that copies are not made or distributed for profit or commercial advantage and that copies bear this notice and the full citation on the first page. Copyrights for components of this work owned by others than ACM must be honored. Abstracting with credit is permitted. To copy otherwise, or republish, to post on servers or to redistribute to lists, requires prior specific permission and/or a fee. Request permissions from permissions@acm.org.
QoSA'14, June 30–July 4, 2014, Marcq-en-Baroeul, France.
Copyright 2014 ACM 978-1-4503-2576-9/14/06 ...$15.00.
http://dx.doi.org/10.1145/2602576.2602590 .

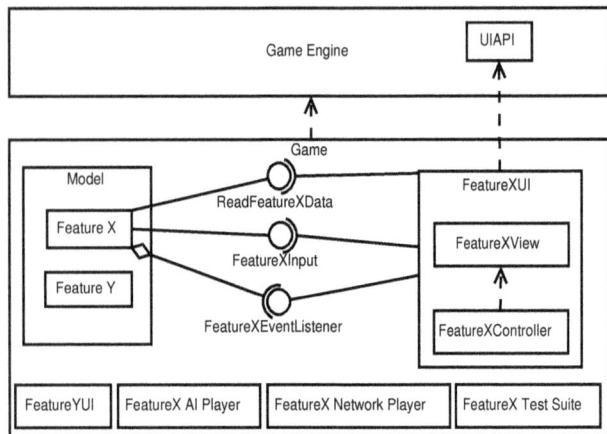

Figure 1: A Model-View-Controller Style Architecture for Computer Games

suspension of disbelief [17, 14] and provide smooth user interaction.

The software architecture in games is traditionally based on an Entity architecture where a central base concept, an *Entity*, is extended via inheritance or composition [14]. For example, Doom 3 uses an Entity inheritance hierarchy where the AI and player classes are both actors, which in turn are animated entities and so on all up to the base entity class [7]. Entities are typically plugged into a game engine that handles many of the cumbersome algorithms and structures related to games in general and real-time rendering in particular. An Entity architecture implemented using inheritance produces cumbersome and top-heavy inheritance structures that are deep and difficult to extend or reuse [14, 9]. The combination of game rules, input, and visualisation is difficult to model in a single inheritance structure, but domain knowledge is present in the code-base by class names, abstractions and explicit relations [9]. In recent years composition has been favoured over inheritance. Composition improves reuse, but does not capture domain knowledge and explicit dependencies between behaviours. Composition also relies on a message passing policy rather than method calls, which can decrease performance [1, 9]. Both Entity architecture variants (inheritance and composition) are highly dependent on the underlying game engine. The use of a game engine provides many advantages but it can also become a liability, since changes to the game engine affects the entire game [1].

An architecture based on the MVC pattern should be a good match for a computer game, since the basic tasks of input, simulation, and rendering intuitively map to the high-level components of MVC. The *Model* represents game rules and simulation, the *Controller* collects and maintains state information related to user interaction, and the *View* is responsible for rendering. An appropriate structure of entities can be constructed within the Model without the need to manage responsibilities of platform-dependent tasks, e.g., input and rendering. MVC brings the following benefits [2, 4, 5] to game development:

Domain Specific Model. Game rules and game data can be specific and allowing for easier change, better testability and a high degree of game engine independence. More

specific structures and algorithms give the opportunity for application specific optimisations and thus better performance.

Feature Focus. The Model can be divided into several high-level features that represent major usage scenarios, e.g., playing the game or editing some aspects of the game. More fine grained responsibilities increase portability and make development easier; there may for instance be no need to port some game editing features of the Model to a mobile platform.

Portability. Different platforms can have different Views with radically different visualisations and data. The game to be ported to platforms with different performance requirements with no change to the Model or Controller components.

Multiple User Interfaces. There can be several different user interfaces (Controller and View) in the same application, e.g., interfaces for editing, testing, and debugging. Developers can implement their tools inside the game and not in separate editors to allow fast tweak-test cycles.

AI and Multiplayer. Input to a feature need not come from and events need not be sent to a user interface controlled by a human player. Input and events can be generated and used by components representing AI-players or players available over a network.

Rendering Independence. If the rendering engine is changed or replaced, only types in the view should be affected. This allows both Model and Controller to be more easily maintained as the rendering engine evolve.

Figure 1 summarises a computer game architecture based on MVC that uses View and Controller components according to the Supervising Controller-variant proposed by Fowler [5]. The User Interface API (UIAPI) is provided by reusable game engine that supplies rendering, audio, and input APIs. Access to these APIs are isolated to the View types. The Model is divided into high-level features that represent major usage scenarios, e.g., playing or editing some aspects of the game. Each feature has its own interfaces for input, event, and data access.

3. STUDY DEFINITION AND DESIGN

We suggest a method that automatically classifies types in an implementation to high-level components defined by an architectural pattern based on dependencies. In order to determine how effective this method is at finding problems and what types of problems it can detect, we design a study that address the following research questions:

RQ1. How effective is the method at finding architectural problems in a line of products that use an architecture based on the MVC pattern?

RQ2. What types of changes are required to correct mismatches detected by the method?

To answer the questions we need to: 1) perform an automatic type classification based on dependencies in the pattern, 2) perform a manual type classification based on the developers' intentions, and 3) compare the two. Our hypothesis is that a difference between the two classifications indicates an architectural problem. To test this hypothesis we need to 4) manually inspect every type and record any problems found. We use the comparison and inspection to 5) determine the *precision* and *recall* of our method. Finally, we should 6) find and implement changes to any architectural problems we find and 7) rerun the method to verify that we solved the problem.

We rely on the MVC pattern variant depicted by Figure 1 to define a method for automatic type classification in Step 1. We compute a dependency graph over a game to measure the distance between each type and the UIAPI. Based on the distance we classify types as follows:

- Types that do not use the UIAPI are classified as Model classes.

- Types that indirectly use the UIAPI are classified as Controller classes.

- Types that directly use the UIAPI are classified as View classes.

The manual classification in Step 2 is done by inspection. We study naming conventions, use of namespaces, IDE specific organisation, and if the type is responsible for maintaining state for user interaction, rendering or game rules. If the automatic and manual classification disagree (Step 3), we investigate further to determine if there is an architectural problem (Step 4). We record a true positive (TP) if the automatic classification found a problem and a false positive (FP) otherwise. If the two classifications agree we investigate this further and record of false negative (FN) if there were no architectural problems. We compute precision (P) and recall (R) of the method in Step 5 according to Equations 1 and 2. High precision indicates that any reported problem is likely to be an actual problem and high recall indicates that we find most of the problems.

$$P = TP/(TP + FP) \qquad (1)$$

$$R = TP/(TP + FN) \qquad (2)$$

The architectural problems we specifically look for in Step 4 are based on the intended responsibilities and relations of components in the MVC pattern [2, 5] as well as problems we have encountered:

- A Model type depends on a type in the View, Controller, or UIAPI.

- A Controller type directly depends on the UIAPI.

- There are game rules in a Controller or View type.

- A Model type is adapted to a specific type of a View or Controller.

- There is user interface specific data in a Model type (data is not used in the Model itself, only in the View or Controller).

- A painted type is used to hide a dependency, i.e., a primitive type is used instead of a class, for example a 32-bit int instead of a Color class.

- Incohesive Model types, e.g., a Model type supports multiple high-level Controllers.

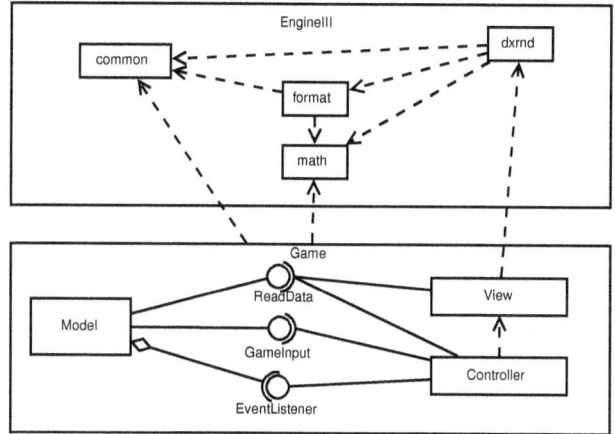

Figure 2: The Product Line Architecture. Note that dxrnd is the UIAPI.

- A type is contained in the wrong component, i.e., a type does not fulfill the responsibilities of the component as defined in the pattern or it has a mix of responsibilities.

To answer the second question we inspect the source problems of mismatches (TP or FP) found during Step 3 and suggest appropriate and realistic changes. We then implement these (Step 6) and rerun the method to check for architectural compliance (Step 7).

4. RESULTS

We selected four games that use the MVC pattern. They were selected with respect to age, genre, and maturity (in terms of readiness for commercial realease). All games were developed in C++ using the Visual Studio IDE. They use the same game engine for rendering (using the DirectX API) and common functionality. Table 1 provides basic information about the projects. We measure Lines of Code (LoC) as the number of lines of code in C++ source and header files using Cloc v. 1.60 [3]. Type metrics are measured by CPPDepend v. 3.1.0.6445 Professional Edition [19]. Figure 2 depicts the games' architecture and the UIAPI (**dxrnd**) used by the View. Note that some components in the game engine and other domain specific components have been left out to reduce the complexity of Figure 2.

We use CPPDepend to construct dependency graphs for each of the games and LINQ to construct a generic query. CPPDepend handles common types of dependencies such as inheritance, declarations, type definitions, and references. We use the same query on all projects without any modification (except the project name). The query string is constructed as follows:

```
from t in Application.Types where
t.ParentProject.Name == "ProjectName"
let d = t.DepthOfIsUsing("dxrnd")
select new { t, d }
```

The query measures the depth of calls from a type to the **dxrnd** name space. A type with a direct dependency (distance = 1) to the UIAPI name space is classified as a View type, a type with an indirect dependency (distance > 1) is

Table 1: Project Size and Genre

Project	LoC	Types	Genre
EngineIII	46,390	225	Game engine
GoL	5,362	56	3d platform
Pirate Quest	12,046	68	2d puzzle
Hero	21,639	167	2.5d role playing
TWTPB	14,212	137	2d action

Table 2: TP: True Positive, FP: False Positive, P: Precision, and R: Recall

Project	TP	FP	FN	P	R
GoL	10	1	6	0.909	0.625
Pirate Quest	15	3	2	0.833	0.882
Hero	28	9	8	0.757	0.778
TWTPB	23	5	9	0.821	0.719
Total	76	18	25	0.809	0.753

Table 3: Project Refactorings

Refactoring	GoL	TWTPB
Split Type	0	3
Move Type	6	6
Move Function	0	4
Move Variable	3	0
Encapsulate Type	1	10
Refine Rule	1	5

classified as a Controller type, and a type no dependency (distance = 0) is classified as Model type.

We inspected the implementation of each type and looked at naming, organisation and responsibility of the types. We found Model types to be well encapsulated within a name space in general. In some cases an in-depth inspection was required to classify Controller and View types. During inspection, some types where decided to not be included in the MVC part of the architecture, e.g., types related to copy protection and automatic testing.

We then compared the automatic and manual classifications to find architectural problems. The results as well as precision and recall are depicted by Table 2. To determine whether a detected problem was an actual problem we performed a manual inspection of the four games. The inspection took approximately 180 person hours divided over the course of six weeks. Of the problems the method did not find (FN), three major problems stood out. In PirateQuest, a sub-game with game rules was implemented entirely in the user interface. In Hero, audio was sent directly from the Model to the types representing the user interface in the form of integer identifiers. In GoL, the type representing the game world implemented functionality for both playing and editing the game.

All mismatches (TP and FP) were further investigated and resolved in two games. In most cases a refactoring of source code was required. Many of these refactorings were substantial, especially those related to the Split Type refactoring. An overview of changes made is shown in table 3. The changes are ordered by amount of effort required. A *Split Type* refactoring is when a type needs to be thoroughly refactored due to mixed responsibilities. A *Move Type* refactoring is when a type should be moved to the correct component and possibly reused in the game engine. *Move Function* and *Move Variable* refactorings are when a function or variable should be relocated to an existing type of the correct classification. A *Encapsulate Type* refactoring is when a type, often a simple struct or enumeration, should be encapsulated by another type of the correct classification. A *Refine Rule* refactoring is when the rule (implemented in LINQ) needs to be improved.

5. DISCUSSION

The results show that a high-level architectural rule can be constructed based on the MVC pattern. The rule proved reusable across several games in the same product line without modification and revealed points of architectural erosion. This suggests that patterns can be used as the basis for rules to check conformance and that rules are reusable without modification in product lines.

Using the method post development resulted in significant refactorings. If the method was integrating early in the development cycle these problems could be avoided or at least promptly handled. We suggest that defining such rules up-front will force architects to make more informed decisions. The rules could then be refined and used throughout a project. The architects work is not done after the initial architecture is decided, he or she should monitor and help developers make decisions in unforeseen situations, find rules for the decisions, and then use these rules for conformance checking.

Conformance checking a line of products provided insight to common problems and typical errors. We found that developers in these projects have succeeded in isolating the Model component from the View and Controller, but not managed to isolate the Controller components from the UI-API to a high degree. The detected problems are mainly located to the View and Controller components where the aforementioned confusion about what a Controller should be responsible for is a common source of architectural problems [2]. A surprising result is that we found several types that should be reused, e.g., a set of types for geometrical constructs suitable for reuse in a geometry/math library and a type hierarchy representing input devices.

Table 3 shows that the smaller project GoL has not been as affected by architectural erosion. The larger and more mature project TWTPB has an increased number of severe problems. This is in line with the idea that small violations accumulate and become problems [12, 20, 10]. First violating variables are introduced, then these variables are used in methods, the methods and variables become interdependent, and finally the type as a whole is affected. It is possible that one violation triggers the introduction of more violations as developers may think of the previous violation as a valid construct, or possibly consider the type a lost cause where (yet) another violation will not make a big difference.

Further analysis of the problems that were not detected (FN) by the metod revealed problems in Hero and PirateQuest that could be traced to architectural violations in the `GameInput` and `EventListener` interfaces respectively. A suspicious construct in the `GameInput` interface of PirateQuest made it possible for Controllers to add a score to the player directly. This mistake effectively opened up the

Model so that any game rule that affected the player's score could be implemented in the Controller or View.

In Hero the `EventListener` interface used an integer value to represent a sound in the View that should be played when an event triggered. The game rules have an implicit dependency on the sounds available in the View, which makes the code harder to understand, maintain, port, and reuse. If the correct type, in this case a sound type, was used the problem could be automatically detected and raise suspicion during development. The use of an integer was most likely an active choice to avoid an explicit dependency that would be an obvious violation of the architecture. The developer instead thought that by using a generic integer this would be fine, when in reality the dependency is still there, only harder to detect. In GoL the problem was more subtle and detected by inspecting which Controller types used what functions in the Model. A subset of the editing functions were mixed with a subset of functions used by the game rules for playing the game. While it can be considered good practice to group functionality that use the same data in the same type, it can cause problems if the game is ported and the editing functionality is not required. This case cannot be detected by our method, but a project specific dependency analysis could find these types of problems.

It was easy to perform the analysis required for our method using commercially off the shelf tools. We found architectural violations that traced to architectural problems in the implementation. The precision and recall of our method are acceptable but might improve if the rule was customised to each project and used throughout the development cycle. A combination of the rule and some mechanism for developers to clearly describe what component they are working in (e.g., more consistent use of name spaces) could allow a fully automatic and possibly integrated method for architectural compliance checking.

Our method should generalise well to architectures based on the Layers pattern because of the transitive dependencies between components. It should therefore be possible to use a similar rule to classify types to different layers.

6. VALIDITY ISSUES

Finding the right dependency to use to classify types is an important part of our method. Other dependencies than the one used might give different results. We base our selection on the known liabilities of the MVC pattern [2] and our own experience from using it.

The method is only as good as the tools are at accurately detecting dependencies in the source code. Pruijt et al. [16] compare several tools to check dependency in Java source code and on average 74% of the tested dependencies were detected. Low accuracy could affect the result in our study by increasing the number of false positives and negatives which reduces the precision and recall. Some of the false negatives we found were indeed caused by undetected dependencies. There is also risk of implicit dependencies in the code, which are difficult to detect with static analysis.

Manual inspection of source code is hard, time consuming, and prone to errors; there is always the risk that something is overlooked. In this particular case the number of false negatives might be too low and which would inflate the recall. We put extra effort in investigating types that did not seem to contain any architectural problems.

7. RELATED WORK

Knodel and Popescu [8] gives an overview of three popular methods for static architectural conformance checking; reflection models, relation conformance rules and component access rules. Passos et al. [15] present an overview of Dependency-Structure Matrices (DSM) and Source Code Query Languages (SCQL), as well as reflection models. They point to the expressiveness of SCQLs but the lack of visual architectural overview. Reflection models focus on helping developers to sufficiently understand a software system to solve a software development task. The developer provides her view over a system and a mapping of relevant source components to this view. The reflection model is then computed to provide the developer with information about where her view and the actual implementation converges and diverges. While reflection models can be used to check design conformance the method is a more general approach aimed at providing software developers with a method of iteratively understanding the implementation to solve a problem [13]. Our method focus on architectural conformance checking and work in the opposite way; we automatically classify the type and check if this conforms to the classification in the implementation using rules for dependencies found in the implementation. This has the advantage of less expert involvement as the developer essentially just need to decide if she agrees with the automatic classification or not. In reflection models the developer needs to understand the entirety of the model and provide a comprehensive mapping schema to perform architectural conformance checking.

Sangal et al. [18] propose a method for using dependencies to both capture an architecture and to provide support for architectural analysis and architectural rules. In their approach they use a DSM as the main tool. They also present the appearance of some basic patterns like Layers in these DSMs. Our work expands on this and investigates a transitive relationship that can be hard to spot in a DSM. We also present the precision and recall of a dependency-based conformance checking method, thus giving some insight on the general effectiveness of such approaches. Macia et al. [10] investigate how automatically detected code smells are related to architectural problems. They did not find this approach to be effective in detecting architectural problems with recall and precision values falling well below 0.60 for most smells. Maffort et al. [11] present the tool ArchLint that use static and historical code analysis to automatically detect architectural problems. This approach is promising and has the apparent advantage of working using the source code and its history only, there is no need for any added models or rules. They report precision values ranging from 0.48 to 0.89 and 0.16 to 0.96. ArchLint seem to be prone to producing false positives which is a drawback.

8. CONCLUSIONS AND FUTURE WORK

We studied how effective a dependency rule derived from a common architectural pattern is at finding architectural problems in a product line. We also investigated how problems found should be handled. Our method can easily be extended to provide support for automatic type mapping using, e.g., name spaces or other naming conventions rather than to rely on experts for mapping and thus provide a fully automatic approach to conformance checking.

Our work builds on reflection models, source code queries and dependency models in the sense that types in an implementation are mapped to components in a high-level architectural description. The advantage of our method is that it can easily be used by developers to perform continuous architectural conformance checks during development.

We evaluated our method using a variation of the MVC pattern defined in a product line architecture. We found it to be effective (Precision = 0.809, Recall = 0.753) at finding architectural problems in four games and that the method can find types to refactor and reuse. A initial set of rules could be included in the product line architecture and then reused and refined throughout the development process to give better results for specific projects. Our particular rule could be used as a starting point for any project using an MVC pattern, e.g., web applications.

Our evaluation is focused on a single line of games from one developer, so there is no guarantee that the method will work for other lines of products. The results are promising and the method is based on a documented liability of MVC [2]. We plan to validate the method on other applications and domains, e.g., web-based systems that often use an architecture based on the Layers pattern [2]. We consider exploring the use of dependencies to model sets of features, to enable a more natural division of major components. Another interesting area is to evaluate the quality of the architecture itself using its ability to unambiguously map types in the implementation to components in the architecture.

9. REFERENCES

[1] A. BinSubaih and S. Maddock. Game portability using a service-oriented approach. *Int. J. Comput. Games Technol.*, pages 3:1–3:7, Jan. 2008.

[2] F. Buschmann, R. Meunier, H. Rohnert, P. Sommerlad, and M. Stal. *Pattern-Oriented Software Architecture, Volume 1: A System of Patterns.* Wiley, Chichester, UK, 1996.

[3] A. Danial. Cloc v. 160. URL http://cloc.sourceforge.net/.

[4] M. Fowler. Gui architectures, 2006. URL http://www.martinfowler.com/eaaDev/uiArchs.html.

[5] M. Fowler. Supervising controller, 2006. URL http://www.martinfowler.com/eaaDev/SupervisingPresenter.html.

[6] E. Gamma, R. Helm, R. Johnson, and J. Vlissides. *Design patterns: elements of reusable object-oriented software.* Addison-Wesley Longman Publishing Co., Inc., 1995.

[7] Id Software. Making doom 3 mods: The code, 2004. http://www.iddevnet.com/doom3/code.php/.

[8] J. Knodel and D. Popescu. A comparison of static architecture compliance checking approaches. In *The Working IEEE/IFIP Conference on Software Architecture*, pages 12–12, Jan 2007.

[9] D. Llansó, M. A. Gómez-Martín, P. P. Gómez-Martín, and P. A. González-Calero. Explicit domain modelling in video games. In *Proceedings of the 6th International Conference on Foundations of Digital Games*, pages 99–106, 2011.

[10] I. Macia, J. Garcia, D. Popescu, A. Garcia, N. Medvidovic, and A. von Staa. Are automatically-detected code anomalies relevant to architectural modularity?: An exploratory analysis of evolving systems. In *Proceedings of the 11th Annual International Conference on Aspect-oriented Software Development*, pages 167–178, 2012.

[11] C. Maffort, M. Valente, M. Bigonha, N. Anquetil, and A. Hora. Heuristics for discovering architectural violations. In *Reverse Engineering (WCRE), 2013 20th Working Conference on*, pages 222–231, Oct 2013.

[12] B. Merkle. Stop the software architecture erosion: Building better software systems. In *Proceedings of the ACM International Conference Companion on Object Oriented Programming Systems Languages and Applications Companion*, SPLASH '10, pages 129–138, New York, NY, USA, 2010. ACM.

[13] G. C. Murphy, D. Notkin, and K. Sullivan. Software reflexion models: Bridging the gap between source and high-level models. *SIGSOFT Softw. Eng. Notes*, 20(4): 18–28, Oct. 1995.

[14] E. B. Passos, J. W. S. Sousa, E. W. G. Clua, A. Montenegro, and L. Murta. Smart composition of game objects using dependency injection. *Comput. Entertain.*, 7(4):53:1–53:15, Jan. 2010.

[15] L. Passos, R. Terra, M. Valente, R. Diniz, and N. Mendonça. Static architecture-conformance checking: An illustrative overview. *IEEE Software*, 27 (5):82–89, Sept 2010.

[16] L. Pruijt, C. Koppe, and S. Brinkkemper. On the accuracy of architecture compliance checking support accuracy of dependency analysis and violation reporting. In *IEEE 21st International Conference on Program Comprehension*, pages 172–181, May 2013.

[17] D. Sanchez-Crespo. *Core Techniques and Algorithms in Game Programming.* New Riders Games, 2003.

[18] N. Sangal, E. Jordan, V. Sinha, and D. Jackson. Using dependency models to manage complex software architecture. In *Proceedings of the 20th Annual ACM SIGPLAN Conference on Object-oriented Programming, Systems, Languages, and Applications*, pages 167–176, 2005.

[19] SMACCHIA.COM. Cppdepend v. 3.1.0.6445 professional edition. URL http://www.cppdepend.com.

[20] R. Terra, M. Valente, K. Czarnecki, and R. Bigonha. Recommending refactorings to reverse software architecture erosion. In *16th European Conference on Software Maintenance and Reengineering (CSMR)*, pages 335–340, March 2012.

An Empirical Investigation of Modularity Metrics for Indicating Architectural Technical Debt

Zengyang Li
Department of Mathematics and
Computer Science
University of Groningen
Nijenborgh 9, 9747 AG
Groningen, The Netherlands
(+31) 50 363 7127
zengyang.li@rug.nl

Peng Liang
State Key Lab of Software
Engineering, School of Computer
Wuhan University
Luojiasha 430072
Wuhan, China
(+86) 27 6877 6137
liangp@whu.edu.cn

Paris Avgeriou
Department of Mathematics and
Computer Science
University of Groningen
Nijenborgh 9, 9747 AG
Groningen, The Netherlands
(+31) 50 363 7057
paris@cs.rug.nl

Nicolas Guelfi
Computer Science and
Communications Research Unit
University of Luxembourg
6, rue Richard Coudenhove-Kalergi
L-1359 Luxembourg, Luxembourg
(+352) 46 66 44 5251
nicolas.guelfi@uni.lu

Apostolos Ampatzoglou
Department of Mathematics and
Computer Science
University of Groningen
Nijenborgh 9, 9747 AG
Groningen, The Netherlands
(+31) 50 363 5181
a.ampatzoglou@rug.nl

ABSTRACT

Architectural technical debt (ATD) is incurred by design decisions that consciously or unconsciously compromise system-wide quality attributes, particularly maintainability and evolvability. ATD needs to be identified and measured, so that it can be monitored and eventually repaid, when appropriate. In practice, ATD is difficult to identify and measure, since ATD does not yield observable behaviors to end users. One indicator of ATD, is the average number of modified components per commit (ANMCC): a higher ANMCC indicates more ATD in a software system. However, it is difficult and sometimes impossible to calculate ANMCC, because the data (i.e., the log of commits) are not always available. In this work, we propose to use software modularity metrics, which can be directly calculated based on source code, as a substitute of ANMCC to indicate ATD. We validate the correlation between ANMCC and modularity metrics through a holistic multiple case study on thirteen open source software projects. The results of this study suggest that two modularity metrics, namely Index of Package Changing Impact (IPCI) and Index of Package Goal Focus (IPGF), have significant correlation with ANMCC, and therefore can be used as alternative ATD indicators.

Permission to make digital or hard copies of all or part of this work for personal or classroom use is granted without fee provided that copies are not made or distributed for profit or commercial advantage and that copies bear this notice and the full citation on the first page. Copyrights for components of this work owned by others than ACM must be honored. Abstracting with credit is permitted. To copy otherwise, or republish, to post on servers or to redistribute to lists, requires prior specific permission and/or a fee. Request permissions from Permissions@acm.org.

QoSA'14, June 30 - July 04 2014, Marcq-en-Bareul, France
Copyright 2014 ACM 978-1-4503-2576-9/14/06...$15.00.
http://dx.doi.org/10.1145/2602576.2602581

Categories and Subject Descriptors

D.2.8 [**Software Engineering**]: Metrics- *Product metrics*; D.2.11 [**Software Engineering**]: Software Architectures - *languages*

General Terms

Measurement, Experimentation

Keywords

Architectural technical debt; modularity metric; commit; software architecture

1. INTRODUCTION

Technical debt has been increasingly gaining attention from researchers in the software engineering domain and from practitioners in the software industry in the past years [3; 9; 16]. The concept of technical debt was coined by Ward Cunningham to describe immature work in coding that can yield short-term benefit (e.g., fast delivery), but will lead to high maintenance and evolution cost in the long term [4]. Technical debt can span all phases of the software development lifecycle, including requirements analysis, architecture design, detailed design, testing etc. [8]. More generally, technical debt refers to immature work in a software system that takes compromises in one dimension to meet urgent needs in some other dimension [3]. In this work, we focus on the technical debt at architecture level [11], i.e., architectural technical debt (ATD).

ATD is caused by design decisions that consciously or unconsciously compromise system-wide quality attributes (QAs), especially maintainability and evolvability [8; 10]. Typical ATD includes violations of best architecture practices and breakages of the consistency and integrity of software architectures. An example of ATD is the creation of architecture dependencies that violate the strict layered architectural pattern, i.e., a higher layer having direct dependencies to layers other than the one directly below it. ATD may also include the adoption of immature architecture techniques. Another ATD example is the use of an immature web application framework, which might require significant modifications, and therefore extra effort, to adapt in the developed web application.

By taking into account the negative impact on the long-term health of a software system, ATD needs to be effectively managed to keep its amount under a reasonable level. Management of ATD entails identifying and measuring it, so that it can be monitored and eventually repaid [10]. However, in practice ATD is difficult to identify and measure, since ATD does not yield observable behaviors to end users [3; 10; 16]. One solution is to define ATD *indicators* that denote the presence and relative amount of ATD. One such indicator is the average number of modified components per commit (further referred as ANMCC). A commit, also called a revision, is a unit of modification to the source code of a software system. ANMCC indicates the presence of ATD as follows:

- ANMCC reflects the complexity and difficulty of making changes to a software system. A high ANMCC means that in a specific revision, and in order to perform a maintenance task (e.g., debugging or implementing a new feature) many components had to be modified. This fact indicates a difficulty in performing maintenance activities, due to high coupling between components, and intensive ripple effects.

- The increase of the complexity and difficulty of making changes to a software system is the consequence of accumulated ATD. If not repaid, ATD will continuously accumulate interest, which makes the system more complex and difficult to implement changes later on [3; 4].

- A higher ANMCC entails an increase in the complexity and difficulty to change, thus implying potential increase in ATD.

However, it is hard and sometimes even impossible to calculate ANMCC, because the commit records (i.e., history data of source code changes) are not always available. For instance, a legacy system may not have commit history data; or a system that is built based on reused components from different projects has no complete commit history data. To address this issue, we try to find a substitute for ANMCC indicator that can be calculated based on source code; such a substitute should be accurate (ground truth representation of the system) and available.

In order to identify such a substitute we look into *modularity metrics*. According to ISO/IEC 25010 standard [7], modularity is one of the sub-characteristics of maintainability, which is one of the QAs compromised by ATD. Modularity is defined as the *"degree to which a system or computer program is composed of discrete components such that a change to one component has minimal impact on other components [7]"*. A snapshot of the source code of a project is the result of previous changes (commits). The modularity metrics of a snapshot of the project source code can, to a certain extent, reflect the development difficulty of changes to this project in the near future [19]. Specifically, as the modularity of a software system increases, the ANMCC of this software system is expected to decrease. Consequently, system modularity, to a certain degree, can also substitute ANMCC in terms of indicating ATD.

In this work, we empirically investigate the ability of existing modularity metrics to substitute ANMCC as ATD indicators, through a holistic multiple case study on thirteen open source projects. The main contribution of this work is the empirical evidence supporting that two of the investigated modularity metrics, i.e., Index of Package Changing Impact (IPCI) and Index of Package Goal Focus (IPGF), have significant negative correlations with ANMCC – the ATD indicator. Thus, the two software modularity metrics (IPCI and IPGF) can be used as indicators of ATD of a system. The merit of using IPCI and IPGF as ATD indicators is that they can be automatically calculated using a single version of source code, while the calculation of ANMCC requires commit history information of a project which is not always available.

The remainder of this paper is organized as follows: we discuss related work on technical debt measurement, especially ATD measurement in Section 2. The case study design is illustrated in Section 3. Section 4 describes the results of the case study and Section 5 discusses the study results and their implications. The threats to the validity of the case study are identified in Section 6. We conclude this work with future work directions in Section 7.

2. RELATED WORK

Technical debt measurement is considered as an important step in the technical debt management process [18]. Although technical debt is not easy to measure [3], there have already been some attempts trying to estimate it at various levels (e.g., code level, architecture level) and from different perspectives.

In [3], Brown et al. proposed to aggregate individual technical measures of technical debt in three aspects similarly to financial debt: principal, interest probability, and interest amount. The total technical debt is the sum of the principal, and the product of interest probability and interest amount. Seaman and Guo measured these three aspects of a technical debt item by assigning them values of high, medium, or low [18]. They suggested that these coarse-grained estimates should be sufficient for tracking technical debt items and making preliminary decisions on technical debt management. When more required information (e.g., historical effort data) is available, fine-grained estimations can be made upon that information for refined management decision-making.

Curtis et al. estimated technical debt by calculating the cost of fixing different types of violations (e.g., code smells) that were identified through automatic static analysis of source code against rules of good architecture and coding practice [5]. They analyzed millions of lines of source code of business applications collected from various companies in different application domains. These collected applications were written in 28 programming languages. The principal of technical debt can be calculated through the following formula [5]:

*Principal =
((Σ high-severity violations) × (percentage to be fixed) ×
(average hours needed to fix) × ($ per hour)) +
((Σ medium-severity violations) × (percentage to be fixed) ×
(average hours needed to fix) × ($ per hour)) +
((Σ low-severity violations) × (percentage to be fixed)
× (average hours needed to fix) × ($ per hour)).*

When the percentages of high-, medium-, and low-severity violations to be fixed are 50%, 25%, and 10%, respectively, fixing each violation takes one hour and the labor cost is 75 US dollar per hour, the average estimated technical debt principal is 3.61 US dollar per line of code in the aforementioned collected source code. The technical debt principal per line of source code differs among programming languages. However, there are some issues with estimating the technical debt of a concrete software system with fixed value (i.e., 3.61 US dollar per line of code). Usually, architectural violations are much more difficult to fix compared with the design-level and code-level violations. In addition, the cost of fixing the same type of violations differs largely in different contexts of various software projects.

Marinescu proposed an approach to identify and measure technical debt of object-oriented software systems by detecting and assessing specific types of design flaws through object-oriented metrics [12]. The approach is composed of four steps: (1) choose a set of concerned design flaws, (2) define rules for detecting the selected design flaws, (3) measure the negative impact of each instance of the design flaws, and, finally, (4) calculate an overall score based on all detected design flaws to indicate the design quality of a system. The accuracy of the technical debt measurement in this approach depends on the ability of the design flaws detection. This approach can only identify and measure technical debt at detailed design level, while our investigation focuses on technical debt at architecture level.

Nord et al. defined a metric for managing ATD [15]. The value of this metric, calculated for each release, is the total cost of the implementation of new architectural elements introduced in this release, and the rework of pre-existing elements in previous releases. They considered architectural rework as the necessary adaption work for adding new architectural elements to the existing architecture of a software system. The rework cost is calculated based on the analysis of the changing dependencies from existing adapted architectural elements to the new introduced elements. This metric can be used to calculate the relative amount of ATD incurred in different software evolution paths, i.e., release plans. Suppose that there are two release plans RP1 and RP2, in which the same features are implemented, i.e., they generate the same amount of business value. The relative amount of ATD is the difference between the values of metric calculated on RP1 and RP2. Thus, this metric can facilitate architecture decision-making in ATD management. The main limitation of this approach is the accuracy of the estimation of implementing new features and rework, especially the latter. Each software evolution path involves several releases, which implies that the estimation of rework and new implementations of later releases is based on the estimation of the earlier releases. This may pose a significant threat to the accuracy of ATD estimation.

In our work, we consider that the estimation of ATD should be calculated on real data (i.e., source code), and the estimation makes more sense within a relative short term, e.g., between two releases. That is, the estimation of the next release is based on the real data of this implemented release.

3. CASE STUDY DESIGN
In order to investigate the ability of modularity metrics to substitute the average number of modified components per commit (ANMCC), and thus act as alternative indicators of system's ATD, we performed a holistic multiple case study on thirteen C# open source software (OSS) projects provided by GitHub[1]. The main reason for conducting a case study is that, through using OSS projects, and more specifically their source code and commit information, we examine the phenomenon in its real-life context, since both factors, i.e., modularity and ANMCC, cannot be monitored in isolation, and their environment cannot be controlled. In this section we describe the case study, which was designed and reported according to the guidelines proposed by Runeson and Host [17].

3.1 Objective and Research Questions
The goal of this study, described using the Goal-Question-Metric (GQM) approach [2], is: *to analyze modularity metrics for the purpose of evaluation with respect to their ability to act as substitutes of ANMCC, for indicating ATD, from the point of view of software architects in the context of OSS evolution.*

Based on the abovementioned goal, we have extracted two research questions (RQs):

RQ1: Are there modularity metrics that correlate with ANMCC?

RQ2: Which modularity metrics have the most accurate correlation with ANMCC?

3.2 Case and Unit Analysis
According to [17], case studies can be characterized based on the way they define their cases and units of analysis. This study is a holistic multiple case study, in the sense that we investigate multiple OSS projects, i.e., cases, and from each case we extract a single unit of analysis. In this study, as unit of analysis we use the pair of two selected releases of an OSS project.

3.3 Case Selection
In this study, we only investigate C# OSS projects, since we make use of the functionalities provided by Microsoft Visual Studio 2012 (MS VS2012). Specifically, the functionality of code map generation can create detailed and complete reports on the structure of a software system, and the reports on the software structure can be used to calculate modularity metrics.

For selecting cases (OSS projects) included in our study, we apply the following criteria:

1. Each selected project should have at least 6 releases, so that we can choose two neighboring releases that meet the release selection rules that are defined in the later part of this section. If a project has only two releases, it may still be in very early development stages, leading to tremendous changes between two neighboring releases. Thus, any estimation for the second release based on the first release is not likely to be reliable.

2. Each release of a selected project should have at least 5 components. With this criterion, the modularity concept for a software system makes sense, in the sense that a system with less than five components is either not modular, or small in terms of size.

3. The full list of commit records of the selected project can be automatically extracted using the TortoiseSVN[2] client. The TortoiseSVN client is a user-friendly tool that can automatically export the complete commit records of a project from most SVN servers.

The source code of the selected project should be successfully compiled, which is the prerequisite of generating code maps using MS VS2012. The code maps generated by VS2012 are used as input for the modularity metrics calculation.

Since a unit of analysis is the pair of two selected releases of the OSS, we need to set rules to ensure that the selected releases are reasonable. The rules are defined as follows:

1. The difference between the numbers of components of the two selected releases is relatively small (<=2).

---

[1] https://github.com/

[2] http://tortoisesvn.tigris.org

2. The difference between the numbers of types (e.g., classes, interfaces) of the two selected releases should not be too small (>=10);

3. The number of commits between the two selected releases should not be too small (>=15).

The first two rules ensure that the OSS project did not dramatically change, but still changed significantly, and the third rule helps to reduce the unevenness of changes over commits.

3.4 Data Collection

3.4.1 Dataset

For each unit of analysis, we have recorded seven variables, six modularity metrics (V1-V6) and the ANMCC value, i.e., the ATD indicator (V7), as follows:

V1. **Index of Inter-Package Usage (IIPU)** is the ratio of the number of *Use* dependencies between classes within a local package against the total number of *Use* dependencies between classes of the whole software system [1].

V2. **Index of Inter-Package Extending (IIPE)** is the ratio of the number of *Extend* dependencies between classes within a local package against the total number of *Extend* dependencies between classes of the whole software system. The *Extend* dependency here can be the inheritance relationship between two classes or the implementation relationship between a class and an interface [1].

V3. **Index of Package Changing Impact (IPCI)** is the percentage of the number of the non-dependency package pairs against the total number of all possible package pairs. This metric measures the strength of the independency of packages [1].

V4. **Index of Inter-Package Usage Diversion (IIPUD)** is the average extent of how diverse the classes used by a specific package distribute in different packages [1].

V5. **Index of Inter-Package Extending Diversion (IIPED)** is the average extent of how diverse the classes extended by a specific package distribute in different packages [1].

V6. **Index of Package Goal Focus (IPGF)** is the average extent of the overlap between the different service sets provided by the same component to other different components in a software system [1]. IPGF indicates the average extent that the services of a specific package serve for the same goal.

V7. **Average Number of Modified Components per Commit (ANMCC)** is the average number of components that are modified during each commit (i.e., revision) in the studied period.

The value of each modularity metrics falls in the range [0, 1]. A greater value of a modularity metric indicates that the software system is better modularized. Finally, in order to mitigate the influence of project size on the ANMCC value, for data analysis, we have used the normalized value of ANMCC. We normalize the ANMCC value by dividing ANMCC with the number of the components (as a representation of project size) of the early release in the two selected releases. All the modularity metrics are calculated by the *ModularityCalculator* tool, while the ANMCC is calculated by the *CommitAnalyer* tool. Both tools are developed by the authors and publicly available[3].

---

[3] http://www.cs.rug.nl/search/uploads/Resources/ATDAnalysis Tools.zip

Note that in this study we define a component as an assembly[4] in C# software projects.

3.4.2 Data collection method

Figure 1 shows the data collection method of this case study. More specifically, for each selected C# OSS project, we need to collect its full list of commit records and the source code of a set of releases. The former is used to calculate the ANMCC, and the latter is used to calculate the modularity metrics of releases. A commit record is the log information of changes to the source code repository during this commit.

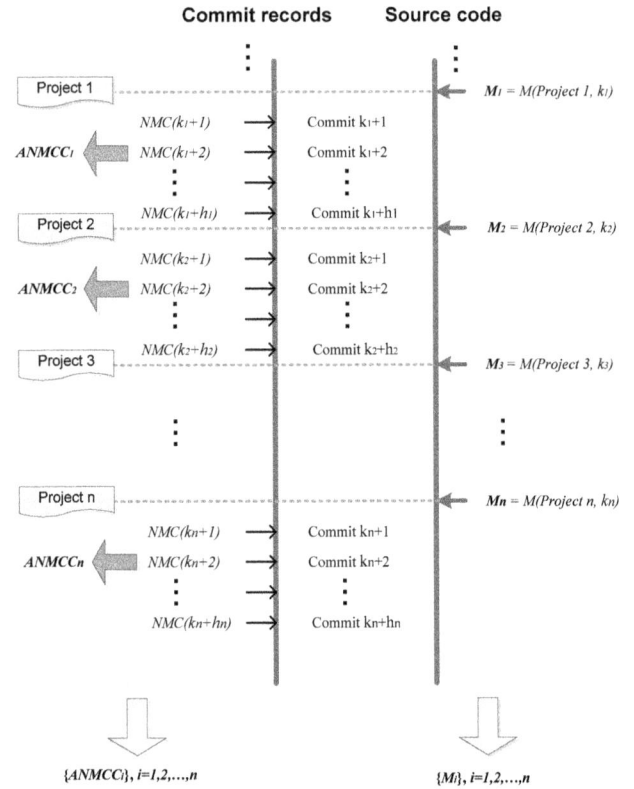

Figure 1. The method to collect the data for calculating ANMCC and modularity metric M.

Suppose that there are n OSS projects. For project i, the two selected releases are releases i_1 and i_2, k_i is the total number of commits of the first i_1 releases, and release i_2 has h_i commit records. In Figure 1, $NMC(k_i+j)$ denotes the number of modified components in commit k_i+j of project i, and $ANMCC_i$ denotes the value of ANMCC during release i_2 (i.e., between releases i_1 and i_2) of project i. Thus, we use formula (1) to calculate $ANMCC_i$:

$$ANMCC_i = (\textstyle\sum_{j=1}^{h_i} NMC(k_i + j))/h_i \qquad (1)$$

M_i denotes the value of the modularity metric M of release i_1 of project i. M_i is calculated based on the source code of release i, i.e., the commit k_i.

---

[4] In C# (or generally in .NET) "*an assembly is a collection of types and resources that forms a logical unit of functionality* [13]."

3.4.3 Data collection procedure for modularity metrics

The task of data collection for modularity metrics calculation is performed in four steps that are described below:

(1) **Source code download**. The source code of each release of a selected OSS project can be downloaded and stored locally using the TortoiseSVN client for further analysis.

(2) **Code map generation**. The goal of this step is to get the structure data of the selected OSS projects. The code map of a version of the source code of a C# OSS project is an XML file that contains the structure data of all the software elements (e.g., assembly, class, and method) and links between them. We generate the code maps for all releases of the selected C# OSS projects using VS2012. For an OSS project, there are two types of code that should be filtered out when generating the code maps: 1) test code (e.g., unit tests, integration tests) and 2) code of examples that show how to use the functions and APIs provided by the functional part. The reasons for excluding these two types of code are that: test code will not be delivered to users, and code of examples is not related to the internal quality of the OSS. But both types of code are tightly coupled with the functional code and can seriously reduce the modularity of software systems, and consequently should be removed from modularity metrics calculation.

(3) **Code map parsing**. Since the code maps generated by VS2012 are too complicated to understand and use, we use our tool *CodeMapParser* to parse the generated code map into a simplified and clean format that is easier to handle than the original format. This *CodeMapParser* tool is available together with the other two tools used in this work[5].

(4) **Modularity metrics calculation**. We use the tool *ModularityCalculator* to calculate the modularity metrics (V1-V6) presented in Section 3.4.1 based on the simplified form of the code map data generated in the previous step. For each selected OSS project, this tool can generate a report in Microsoft Excel format, which contains the modularity metrics of all releases of the project.

3.4.4 Data collection procedure for ANMCC

The goal of this task is to calculate the average number of the components that are modified in each commit (i.e., ANMCC, the ATD indicator) in the selected projects. For each project, we need to extract all the commit records and to identify the component that each modified source code file belongs to in every commit. The detailed steps of the data collection procedure for ANMCC are described as follows:

(1) **Commit records download**. The commit records of the selected OSS projects can be downloaded using the TortoiseSVN client, which can automatically extract a complete list of commit records of a project. With the TortoiseSVN client, we can extract commit records from standard SVN servers and any code repositories supporting Subversion, such as GitHub.

(2) **Commit records parsing**. We need to parse the commit records to extract needed data items for ANMCC calculation. This step can be performed using our developed tool *CommitAnalyzer*. The extracted data items include the start and end commit numbers of each release and the list of files modified in each commit.

(3) **Commit records filtering**. Some data in commit records are invalid for the ANMCC calculation and therefore need to be filtered out. First, the data on the test code files should be removed, and second, the data on the code files of examples should also be removed for the same reasons we presented in Section 3.4.3. The tool *CommitAnalyzer* can semi-automate the commit records filtering with human intervention to confirm which source code directories contain the invalid data.

(4) **ANMCC calculation**. In order to calculate the ANMCC, we need to identify the component that a modified source code file belongs to in every commit, and the release that each commit record belongs to. The tool *CommitAnalyzer* also provides the functionality for calculating ANMCC.

3.5 Data Analysis

In order to explore the research questions, set in section 3.1, we will investigate the correlations between the modularity metrics and ANMCC. Intuitively, we expect that there are negative correlations between modularity metrics and ANMCC. There are two candidate correlation tests, i.e., the Pearson correlation coefficient and Spearman's rho [6]. Pearson correlation coefficient is a parametric test, used to measure the strength of a linear association between two variables. Spearman's rho is a non-parametric test used to measure the strength of monotonic association between two variables. The values of both Pearson correlation coefficient and Spearman's rho range in [-1, 1], where the value 1 means a perfect positive correlation, and the value -1 means a perfect negative correlation. Using the Pearson correlation coefficient requires that two variables for the correlation calculation follow normal distributions, while using the Spearman' rho does not have such a requirement. To select the appropriate correlation calculation method, we need to check the normality of the variables (i.e.,V1-V7), through a Shapiro-Wilk's test [6].

Concerning RQ1, we choose the appropriate correlation test according to the results of the Shapiro-Wilk's tests. We use the correlation coefficient value of the selected correlation test and the level of statistical significance, for each correlation. Next, concerning RQ2, we use the Hoteling-Williams test [6], in order to test possible differences among the predictive ability of different modularity metrics, which appear to be significantly correlated to ANMCC, in RQ1.

All statistical tests will be performed with Matlab by one author, and will be validated with SPSS by another author.

4. CASE STUDY RESULTS

We analyzed thirteen OSS projects by following the case study design presented in Section 3. The list of the selected OSS projects along with demographic information is shown in Table 1, where: "#Release" is the number of all the releases of the project, "#Component" is the number of the components of the latest release of the project, "#Type" is the number of the types of the latest release of the project, and "#Commit" is the number of all the commits of the project. The data of the aforementioned four columns describe the sizes and change frequency of the selected OSS projects.

The rest of this section presents the collected dataset and the results of the correlation tests between the modularity metrics and ANMCC.

4.1 Collected Dataset

The selected releases and their demographic information of the thirteen selected OSS projects are shown in Table 2, where: the

---

[5]http://www.cs.rug.nl/search/uploads/Resources/ATDAnalysis Tools.zip

column "Release 1" is the early release of the corresponding project; the column "Release 2" is the later release; the columns "#Component" and "#Type" are the number of components and the number of Types of Release 1, respectively; the column "#Commit" is the number of commits during the period between Release 1 and Release 2; and the "Δ(#Component)" and "Δ(#Type)" are the difference of the numbers of components and types between Release 1 and Release 2, respectively.

As shown in Table 3, the dataset has thirteen data rows, and each data row is collected from a different C# OSS project. A data row in Table 3 includes two parts: the modularity metrics and (normalized) ANMCC. The former is calculated based on the source code of an early release (i.e., release 1 in Table 2), and the latter is calculated based on the commit records that occurred during the period between the early release and later one (i.e., release 2 in Table 2).

Table 1. Selected OSS projects in the case study

#	Name	#Release	#Component	#Type [a]	#Commit	Duration	URL
1	Cassette	8	13	398	2022	1.5 years	github.com/andrewdavey/cassette
2	CastleCore	12	6	569	6744	9.0 years	github.com/castleproject/Core
3	CCNET	28	14	1093	6359	10.5 years	github.com/ccnet/CruiseControl.NET
4	ILSpy	7	14	2641	1706	6.0 years	github.com/icsharpcode/ILSpy
5	MassTransit	20	17	960	4165	6.0 years	github.com/phatboyg/MassTransit
6	Nancy	25	20	493	3471	4.5 years	github.com/NancyFx/Nancy
7	NSpec	38	5	162	644	2.5 years	github.com/mattflo/NSpec
8	NUnit	20	20	861	3723	10.0 years	github.com/nunit/nunitv2
9	Rebus	87	18	304	1257	2.0 years	github.com/rebus-org/Rebus
10	Scriptcs	9	5	120	842	0.5 year	github.com/scriptcs/scriptcs
11	SignalR	23	18	598	18978	2.5 years	github.com/SignalR/SignalR
12	SimpleData	21	9	307	774	3.0 years	github.com/markrendle/Simple.Data
13	SolrNet	11	9	301	1782	6.0 years	github.com/mausch/SolrNet

[a] A Type in C# can be a Class, Interface, Enum, Delegate, or Struct

Table 2. Selected releases and their demographic information

#	Project	Release 1	#Component	#Type	#Commit	Release 2	Δ(#Component)	Δ(#Type)
1	Cassette	v2.0.0	12	327	134	v2.1.0	1	71
2	CastleCore	v3.0.0	6	558	44	v3.1.0	0	10
3	CCNET	v1.3.0	8	547	239	v1.4.1	0	52
4	ILSpy	v1.0.0-M3	8	1772	179	v1.0.0-Beta	1	68
5	MassTransit	v1.x.eol	18	564	107	v2.0b1	-1	70
6	Nancy	v0.7.1	12	241	155	v0.8.1	0	32
7	NSpec	v0.9.61	5	150	76	v0.9.64	0	10
8	NUnit	v2.5.9	22	767	194	v2.6.0	0	28
9	Rebus	v0.27.0	16	232	20	v0.28.0	0	36
10	Scriptcs	v0.7.0	5	109	55	v0.8.0	0	10
11	SignalR	v1.0.0a2	17	377	423	v1.1.0beta	2	25
12	SimpleData	V1.0.0-beta3	9	285	68	v0.18.1	0	22
13	SolrNet	v0.2.3	6	166	191	v0.3.0b1	1	62

Table 3. Dataset of modularity metrics and ANMCC.

#	Project	IIPU	IIPE	IPCI	IIPUD	IIPED	IPGF	ANMCC	Normalized ANMCC
1	Cassette	0.7444	0.7128	0.8939	0.8676	0.9444	0.9379	1.8284	0.1524
2	CastleCore	0.9837	0.9612	0.8667	0.9063	1.0000	0.9343	1.6136	0.2689
3	CCNET	0.8032	0.9419	0.8214	0.763	0.9028	0.8473	1.1297	0.1412
4	ILSpy	0.9017	0.9733	0.7500	0.7334	0.8311	0.7516	2.6983	0.3373
5	MassTransit	0.7930	0.8991	0.9118	0.8333	0.9259	0.9527	3.7757	0.2098
6	Nancy	0.7367	0.7755	0.9167	1.0000	1.0000	0.9355	1.6387	0.1366
7	NSpec	0.4937	0.5923	0.8500	1.0000	1.0000	0.8952	1.4737	0.2947
8	NUnit	0.5143	0.7593	0.9113	0.6640	0.8526	0.8563	2.6804	0.1218
9	Rebus	0.7943	0.7213	0.9333	0.9346	1.0000	0.9501	1.7500	0.1094
10	Scriptcs	0.3936	0.5882	0.6000	0.6493	0.8933	0.7804	2.1636	0.4327
11	SignalR	0.8702	0.8015	0.9265	0.7658	0.8822	0.9093	2.0047	0.1179
12	SimpleData	0.8043	0.7368	0.8333	0.7382	0.9306	0.8494	2.3529	0.2614
13	SolrNet	0.7691	1.0000	0.8333	1.0000	1.0000	0.8927	1.8063	0.3011

Table 4. Results of Shapiro-Wilk Test

	IIPU	IIPE	IPCI	IIPUD	IIPED	IPGF	Normalized ANMCC
W	0.899	0.925	0.803	0.917	0.880	0.891	0.903
p-value	0.096	0.296	0.007	0.231	0.072	0.101	0.145

4.2 Correlation Coefficient Results

As described in Section 3.5, we performed Shapiro-Wilk's tests on the modularity metrics and the normalized ANMCC to check their normality. The results of the Shapiro-Wilk's tests are shown in Table 4, where only the IPCI does not follow a normal distribution, with p-value <0.05 (the corresponding column is marked with gray background); the normalized ANMCC and other modularity metrics (i.e., IIPU, IIPE, IIPUD, IIPUE, and IPGF) follow normal distributions. Thus, we cannot use Pearson correlation test to calculate the correlation between the IPCI and normalized ANMCC. However, since we need to run the Hotelling-Williams' test on the correlation coefficients between the modularity metrics and normalized ANMCC, the correlation coefficients should be calculated by the same test. In order to use a uniform test for all correlations, we selected to use the Spearman's correlation test. As presented in the Introduction section, an increase of modularity indicates a decrease of ANMCC. This is a directional hypothesis for the correlation tests between the modularity metrics and normalized ANMCC, thus we use one-tailed test. In this Section, we answer the research questions stated in Section 3.1.

RQ1: Are there modularity metrics that correlate with ANMCC?

The results of Spearman's correlation tests between the six modularity metrics and the normalized ANMCC are shown in Table 5. The second and third columns present the resulting correlation coefficient using Spearman's rho test (shortly, *rho*) and its *p-value*, respectively.

Table 5. Correlation coefficients between modularity metrics and normalized ANMCC.

	rho	p-value
IIPU	-0.099	0.3741
IIPE	-0.104	0.3671
IPCI	**-0.828**	**0.0001**
IIPUD	-0.138	0.3261
IIPED	-0.028	0.4631
IPGF	**-0.522**	**0.0341**

As shown in Table 5, concerning IPCI the Spearman's rho is -0.828 with *p-value* 0.0001 < α=0.05, which means the IPCI has a significant negative correlation with the normalized ANMCC. In addition, the IPGF also has a significant negative correlation with the normalized ANMCC, because the Spearman's rho is -0.522, and its *p-value* is 0.0341 (less than 0.05).

The modularity metrics IIPU, IIPE, IIPUD, and IIPED, do not significantly correlate with the normalized ANMCC, since the value of the Spearman's rho of each modularity metric is close to zero and the *p-value* is way bigger than 0.05.

RQ2: Which modularity metrics have the most accurate correlation with ANMCC?

We used the Hotelling-Williams test to explore the possible difference in the predictive ability of IPCI and IPGF. The test result shows that IPCI and ANMCC are more highly correlated than IPGF and ANMCC. To obtain this result, we first calculated the rho between IPCI and IPGF and the resulting rho is 0.831 with *p-value*=0.0001 < α=0.05. Then, with the three *rhos* (i.e., the rho between IPCI and IPGF, rho between IPCI and ANMCC, and rho between IPGF and ANMCC), we conducted the Hotelling-Williams test, which is used to investigate if there is significant difference between two dependent correlations. We got $t = -3.4838$, p-value $= 0.0059$, i.e., $|t| > 1.771$ (α=0.05) => p-value < 0.05. Thus, we can reject the null hypothesis, i.e., equality between two dependent correlations, which means that there is significant difference between the rho values of IPCI and IPGF. In addition, the rho value of IPCI is greater than the rho value of IPGF, therefore, IPCI has a significantly stronger correlation with ANMCC than IPGF. That means IPCI is more accurate than IPGF as an alternative indicator of ANMCC.

5. DISCUSSION

In this section, we interpret the case study results and discuss their implications for researchers and practitioners in this section.

5.1 Explanation of Obtained Results

The results of the correlations between modularity metrics and ANMCC show that the modularity metrics IPCI and IPGF have a significant negative correlation with the normalized ANMCC, while the other modularity metrics (i.e., IIPU, IIPE, IIPUD, and IIPED) do not. Although the main objective of this work is not to investigate the casual relationship between modularity metrics and ANMCC, we still try to explore the potential reasons for the aforementioned correlation results.

To understand the potential reasons for the significant negative correlation between IPCI, IPGF and ANMCC, we examined the definitions of IPCI and IPGF. First, according to [1], ICPI is defined as the percentage of the number of non-dependency component pairs against the number of all possible component pairs. This metric measures to what extent other components will **not** be impacted by changes to a specific component. Intuitively, a higher ICPI indicates a smaller change propagation influence. In other words, a higher ICPI indicates that a smaller number of components will be modified in each commit (which directly links to ANMCC). Second, IPGF is defined as the extent of the overlap between the different service sets provided by the same component to other different components in the software system. IPGF indicates to what extent the services of a specific component serve the same goal. A larger value of IPGF of a software system indicates that services of components focus more on the logical goals provided by the components. Thus, to a certain degree, each component is more stable and provides services to relatively fewer client components. Therefore, the components will undergo relatively fewer modifications, and the value of ANMCC of the software system will decrease.

The results of the correlation analysis have also shown that the other four modularity metrics (i.e., IIPU, IIPE, IIPUD, and IIPED) do not have significant correlations with the ANMCC value. The potential reason for these insignificant correlations is that the calculation of the four modularity metrics does not take into account both *Use* and *Extend* dependencies at the same time. Thus, some of the dependencies are ignored in the calculation of these four modularity metrics. In these four modularity metrics, IIPU and IIPUD are defined based on the *Use* dependencies among classes, while IIPE and IIPED are defined based on the *Extend* dependencies (i.e., implementing an interface or inheriting from a class) among classes. In contrast, both *Use* and *Extend* dependencies are used in the calculation of the modularity metrics IPCI and IPGF which are in significant negative correlations with ANMCC. The ANMCC value of a software system is calculated based on all the commits occurring during the later release in the two selected releases, i.e., all the changes made during this release, and these changes can involve any one of the *Use* and *Extend*

dependencies between classes. In this sense, the exclusion of either the *Use* or *Extend* dependencies in the calculation of a modularity metric can lead to a weak and insignificant correlation between this metric and ANMCC.

The result of the Hotelling-Williams test has shown that the modularity metric IPCI has a stronger correlation with the normalized ANMCC than the modularity metric IPGF. The potential reason leading to this fact is: the calculation of the ICPI metric takes into consideration the influence of all the types (e.g., interfaces) acting as services to the client components, while the calculation of the IPGF metric does not. A change to any service of a specific component may lead to the change(s) of its client component(s). When calculating the ICPI metric of a software system, the influence of all the services (e.g., interfaces) in every component on its client components has been taken into account. The IPGF metric calculates the average percentage of the overlap between the service (e.g., interface) sets that each component provides to its client components. Thus, the IPGF metric emphasizes the influence of part of the services in a component out of all services provided to its client components, i.e., the intersection of the service sets that the component provides to its client components. However, the changes of the rest services can also lead to the modifications of their client components, which is not taken into consideration in the calculation of the IPGF metric. Thus, the IPGF metric may lose some ability of correlating to the ANMCC, compared to the IPCI metric, i.e., the IPGF metric is less accurate than the IPCI metric in terms of substituting the ANMCC.

5.2 Implications for Researchers

The results of this work imply that the modularity metrics defined purely based either on the *Use* dependencies or on the *Extend* dependencies among classes may not effectively reflect the complexity and difficulty of making changes to a software system (and thus potentially ATD). We should take into account both the *Use* and *Extend* dependencies (i.e., all kinds of dependencies in a software system) when considering modularity metrics in relation to ATD.

The architecture of a software system is in a higher level and more abstract than the source code of the system, and consequently the architecture quality is harder to measure than source code. A feasible way to measure architecture quality is to relate architecture quality to software metrics based on source code; the architecture quality can then be estimated if the source code-based software metrics have a significant correlation with the architecture quality. In our case, modularity metrics are calculated based on the source code, but some of these metrics (e.g., IPCI and IPGF) can still indicate architecture-level phenomena such as ATD.

5.3 Implications for Practitioners

Based on the results of this study, we can conclude to a number of implications for practitioners. First, the modularity metrics IPCI and IPGF can be used to indicate ATD. We have provided evidence about the significant negative correlation between IPCI, IPGF and ANMCC, which means that a greater IPCI or IPGF is linked to a smaller ANMCC (indicator of the amount of ATD). Like ANMCC, IPCI and IPGF are also not absolute quantifiable measures of ATD, but they can be used to relatively suggest whether one version of a software system has more or less ATD than another version [10]. This way, architects and project managers can get informed about the potential ATD of the software system. Consequently, IPCI and IPGF can be considered as ATD indicators. A higher IPCI or IPGF indicate less ATD.

Second, IPCI and IPGF can be used to estimate the needed effort for software development in the near future (e.g., next release). The ANMCC reflects the degree of the difficulty and complexity to maintain and evolve a project, thus, it can facilitate the estimation of the needed effort of software development in the near future. Due to the significant negative correlations between IPCI, IPGF and ANMCC, the values of IPCI and IPGF can also be used to estimate effort needed of software development. Furthermore, as presented in Section 4.2, IPCI has a significantly stronger negative correlation with ANMCC than IPGF, thus, IPCI is preferable than IPGF when both metrics can be calculated with similar effort.

Third, modularity metrics can be calculated based on source code. Therefore, it is an opportunity for Integrated Development Environment (IDE) vendors to integrate such kind of ATD indicators (e.g., IPCI and IPGF) into IDE tools based on source code, which is directly available in IDE tools, for practical use. This can facilitate the ATD management in the daily work of architects and project managers as well as provide ATD indication information to developers, since they can measure and monitor ATD easily and take appropriate actions timely to prevent the situation when too much ATD is accumulated.

6. THREATS TO VALIDITY
There are several threats to the validity of the study results. We discuss these threats according to the guidelines in [17]. We note that internal validity is not discussed, because we do not investigate causal relationships.

6.1 Construct Validity
Construct validity is related to whether we can correctly use modularity metrics as substitutes for ANMCC. Both ANMCC and modularity metrics of a software system will change due to the evolution of the system. The modularity metrics of a software system at some specific point of development time can only be used to substitute ANMCC in a relatively short period after that point of time (e.g., a release of a project in this work), in which not too many commits occur. If the period is too long and too many commits happen, and the software system evolves dramatically, the modularity metrics may not be appropriate to be used to substitute ANMCC. To mitigate this threat, we have proposed three rules for release selection for each OSS project in Section 3.3 to ensure that the software system did not dramatically change but still significantly changed, and to reduce the unevenness of changes over commits.

6.2 External Validity
External validity is concerned with the generalization of the case study results. This is related to the representativeness of the selected OSS projects used in the case study. The rules for OSS project selection described in Section 3.3 may affect the representativeness of the selected projects. However, to a large extent, the project selection is random and representative. We searched OSS projects in GitHub, which is one of the largest OSS repositories. For each retrieved project, we checked if it meets all the project selection rules defined in Section 3.3. During the OSS searching and selecting process, we prevented introducing any personal preference or bias on the OSS selection. Furthermore, the selected OSS projects come from different application domains, and the projects have significantly different size and development duration. This also improves the representativeness of the selected OSS projects.

In this case study, only C# OSS projects were selected and used to validate the correlation between modularity metrics and ANMCC.

Consequently, the conclusion drawn is only valid for C# projects. There is a need of conducting more studies for the projects written in other object-oriented languages, such as Java.

6.3 Conclusion Validity
Conclusion validity concerns the statistical significance of the study. In the data analysis of the case study, we carefully checked if the variables meet the prerequisites of using different statistical tests and in order not to use the wrong tests. For example, when selecting the appropriate correlation test, we checked the normality of variables (V1-V7), and then we found the variable V3 is not normally distributed. Thus, we choose the Spearman analysis rather than Pearson analysis. When conducting the Hotelling-Williams test, we used the correlation coefficients calculated by the same correlation test, i.e., the Spearman's rho test, as source data. To make sure the correctness of the statistical results, two authors separately used different tools (i.e., Matlab and SPSS) running the statistical tests and got the same results. We believe that the aforementioned actions mitigate the threats to conclusion validity.

7. CONCLUSION AND FUTURE WORK
In this paper, we provided evidence that the modularity metrics IPCI and IPGF have significant negative correlations with ANMCC – an ATD indicator. Therefore, we can consider the IPCI and IPGF metrics as alternative indicators of ATD. The advantage of using the modularity metrics IPCI and IPGF as ATD indicators is that these modularity metrics can be automatically calculated based on source code (i.e., the update-to-date and accurate structure data of a software system), while ANMCC should be calculated based on commit records that are not always available, and ANMCC calculation is hard to be performed automatically. Moreover, the modularity metric IPCI is more strongly correlated with ANMCC than IPGF, which means that IPCI is a more accurate substitute ATD indicator to ANMCC than IPGF.

Based on the results and findings of this work, we plan to do further research in the following directions. First, we intend to validate the correlation between modularity metrics and ANMCC with Java projects. Second, it will be interesting to define new system-wide modularity metrics or adapt existing modularity metrics defined in other perspectives (e.g., complex networks [14]), and investigate the correlation between the metrics and ATD indicators. We expect that the new modularity metrics can improve the accuracy or take less effort of predicting ANMCC. Third, it is practically valuable to develop plugins to calculate the modularity metrics IPCI and IPGF for IDE tools (e.g., in VS2012 or Eclipse).

8. ACKNOWLEDGMENTS
This work is partially supported by AFR-Luxembourg under the contract No. 895528 and the NSFC under the grant No. 61170025. Thanks to Can Menekse for his contribution to the tool *CodeMapParser* during his internship at the University of Groningen.

9. REFERENCES
[1] Abdeen, H., Ducasse, S., and Sahraoui, H., 2011. Modularization Metrics: Assessing Package Organization in Legacy Large Object-Oriented Software. In *Proceedings of the Proceedings of the 2011 18th Working Conference on Reverse Engineering* (2011), IEEE Computer Society, 2086275, 394-398. DOI= http://dx.doi.org/10.1109/wcre.2011.55.

[2] Basili, V.R., 1992. *Software modeling and measurement: the Goal/Question/Metric paradigm.* University of Maryland at College Park.

[3] Brown, N., Cai, Y., Guo, Y., Kazman, R., Kim, M., Kruchten, P., Lim, E., Maccormack, A., Nord, R., Ozkaya, I., Sangwan, R., Seaman, C., Sullivan, K., and Zazworka, N., 2010. Managing technical debt in software-reliant systems. In *Proceedings of the Proceedings of the FSE/SDP workshop on Future of software engineering research (FoSER'10)* (Santa Fe, New Mexico, USA2010), ACM, 1882373, 47-52. DOI= http://dx.doi.org/10.1145/1882362.1882373.

[4] Cunningham, W., 1992. The WyCash portfolio management system. In *Proceedings of the Addendum to the proceedings on Object-oriented programming systems, languages, and applications (Addendum)* (Vancouver, British Columbia, Canada1992), ACM, 157715, 29-30. DOI= http://dx.doi.org/10.1145/157709.157715.

[5] Curtis, B., Sappidi, J., and Szynkarski, A., 2012. Estimating the size, cost, and types of Technical Debt. In *Proceedings of the 3rd International Workshop on Managing Technical Debt (MTD '12)*, 49-53. DOI= http://dx.doi.org/10.1109/mtd.2012.6226000.

[6] Field, A., 2013. *Discovering Statistics using IBM SPSS Statistics.* SAGE Publications Ltd.

[7] ISO/IEC, 2011. Systems and software engineering — Systems and software Quality Requirements and Evaluation (SQuaRE) — System and software quality models. In *ISO/IEC FDIS 25010:2011*, 1-34.

[8] Kruchten, P., Nord, R.L., and Ozkaya, I., 2012. Technical Debt: From Metaphor to Theory and Practice. *IEEE Software 29*, 6, 18-21. DOI= http://dx.doi.org/10.1109/MS.2012.167.

[9] Kruchten, P., Nord, R.L., and Ozkaya, I., 2013. 4th International workshop on managing technical debt (MTD 2013). In *Software Engineering (ICSE), 2013 35th International Conference on*, 1535-1536. DOI= http://dx.doi.org/10.1109/ICSE.2013.6606774.

[10] Li, Z., Liang, P., and Avgeriou, P., 2014. Architectural debt management in value-oriented architecting. In *Econimics-driven software architecture* Elsevier, In press.

[11] Li, Z., Liang, P., Avgeriou, P., Guelfi, N., and Chen, Y., 2014. A systematic mapping study on technical debt and its management. In *Under submission*.

[12] Marinescu, R., 2012. Assessing technical debt by identifying design flaws in software systems. *IBM Journal of Research and Development 56*, 5, 9:1-9:13. DOI= http://dx.doi.org/10.1147/JRD.2012.2204512.

[13] Microsoft, 2002. Understanding and Using Assemblies and Namespaces in .NET. DOI= http://dx.doi.org/http://msdn.microsoft.com/en-us/library/ms973231.aspx.

[14] Newman, M.E., 2003. The structure and function of complex networks. *SIAM review 45*, 2, 167-256. DOI= http://dx.doi.org/doi:10.1137/S003614450342480.

[15] Nord, R.L., Ozkaya, I., Kruchten, P., and Gonzalez-Rojas, M., 2012. In search of a metric for managing architectural technical debt. In *Proceedings of the 10th Working IEEE/IFIP Conference on Software Architecture (WICSA '12)* IEEE Computer Society, Helsinki, Finland.

[16] Ozkaya, I., Kruchten, P., Nord, R., and Brown, N., 2011. Second international workshop on managing technical debt (MTD 2011). In *Proceedings of the Proceedings of the 33rd International Conference on Software Engineering (ICSE '11)* (Waikiki, Honolulu, HI, USA2011), ACM, 1986051, 1212-1213. DOI= http://dx.doi.org/10.1145/1985793.1986051.

[17] Runeson, P. and Höst, M., 2009. Guidelines for conducting and reporting case study research in software engineering. *Empirical Software Engineering 14*, 2 (2009/04/01), 131-164. DOI= http://dx.doi.org/10.1007/s10664-008-9102-8.

[18] Seaman, C. and Guo, Y., 2011. Measuring and Monitoring Technical Debt. In *Advances in Computers*, M. Zelkowitz Ed. Elsevier Science, 25-45.

[19] Sethi, K., Yuanfang, C., Wong, S., Garcia, A., and Sant'anna, C., 2009. From retrospect to prospect: Assessing modularity and stability from software architecture. In *Software Architecture, 2009 & European Conference on Software Architecture. WICSA/ECSA 2009. Joint Working IEEE/IFIP Conference on*, 269-272. DOI= http://dx.doi.org/10.1109/WICSA.2009.5290817.

Formalizing Correspondence Rules for Automotive Architecture Views

Yanja Dajsuren, Christine M. Gerpheide, Alexander Serebrenik,
Anton Wijs, Bogdan Vasilescu, Mark G. J. van den Brand
Eindhoven University of Technology
5612 AZ Eindhoven, The Netherlands
y.dajsuren@tue.nl, c.m.gerpheide@student.tue.nl, a.serebrenik@tue.nl
{a.j.wijs | b.n.vasilescu | m.g.j.v.d.brand}@tue.nl

ABSTRACT

Architecture views have long been used in software industry to systematically model complex systems by representing them from the perspective of related stakeholder concerns. However, consensus has not been reached for the architecture views between automotive architecture description languages and automotive architecture frameworks. Therefore, this paper presents the automotive architecture views based on an elaborate study of existing automotive architecture description techniques. Furthermore, we propose a method to formalize correspondence rules between architecture views to enforce consistency between architecture views. The approach was implemented in a Java plugin for IBM Rational Rhapsody and evaluated in a case study based on the Adaptive Cruise Control system. The outcome of the evaluation is considered to be a useful approach for formalizing correspondences between different views and a useful tool for automotive architects.

Categories and Subject Descriptors

D.2.11 [**Software Engineering**]: Software architectures

Keywords

automotive architecture; architecture framework; architecture view; correspondence rule

1. INTRODUCTION

An architecture framework provides conventions, principles and practices for the description of architectures within a specific domain and/or community of stakeholders [23]. The benefits of existing architecture frameworks such as Kruchten's 4+1 View Model [27], MODAF [32], TOGAF [1], and RM-ODP [22] drive the creation of an architecture framework for the automotive industry, which faces the challenge of tackling increasing complexity and cost of automotive electronic and software components. Currently, an

Permission to make digital or hard copies of all or part of this work for personal or classroom use is granted without fee provided that copies are not made or distributed for profit or commercial advantage and that copies bear this notice and the full citation on the first page. Copyrights for components of this work owned by others than the author(s) must be honored. Abstracting with credit is permitted. To copy otherwise, or republish, to post on servers or to redistribute to lists, requires prior specific permission and/or a fee. Request permissions from permissions@acm.org.

QoSA'14, June 30–July 4, 2014, Marcq-en-Baroeul, France.
Copyright is held by the owner/author(s). Publication rights licensed to ACM.
ACM 978-1-4503-2576-9/14/06 ...$15.00.
http://dx.doi.org/10.1145/2602576.2602588.

automotive architecture framework [5] and an architecture design framework [19] are being defined with the goal of establishing a standard architecture framework for the automotive industry. However, in these frameworks, the definition of architectural elements including architecture viewpoints, views, and correspondences have not been tackled consistently with automotive Architecture Description Languages (ADLs). Furthermore, the architecture frameworks remain still closed, i.e. difficult to extend with new stakeholder concerns, viewpoints, and views.

1.1 Automotive Architectural Challenges

There are a number of issues which make the development of automotive architecture framework challenging:

- Automotive embedded systems are categorized into vehicle-centric functional domains (including powertrain control, chassis control, and active/passive safety systems) and passenger-centric functional domains (covering multimedia/telematics, body/comfort, and human machine interface (HMI)) [30]. Although each functional domains need to tackle different system concerns (e.g. the power train control enables the vehicle longitudinal propulsion of the vehicle, body domain supports airbag, wiper, lighting etc. for the vehicle users), all the integrated functionalities must not jeopardize the key vehicle requirements, e.g. a safe and efficient way of transporting.

- ADLs like EAST-ADL [7], AADL [18], and AML [3] have been defined for the automotive industry. According to the ISO/IEC/IEEE-42010 or ISO-42010 [23], an ADL provides one or more model kinds (data flow diagrams, class diagrams, state diagrams etc.) as a means to frame some concerns for its stakeholders. An ADL can consist of model kinds, which may be organized into architecture views. Architectural elements e.g. architecture viewpoints, views, and correspondences of the automotive ADLs are not explicitly defined. This results in the loose relation between automotive ADLs and architecture frameworks (which can be improved by refining the definition of the architecture elements of automotive ADLs and architecture frameworks as defined in ISO-42010 standard [23]).

- The automotive industry is vertically organized [4], which facilitates independent development of vehicle parts. An automobile manufacturer (called an "original equipment manufacturer", or OEM) creates the functional architecture and distributes the development of the functional components to the suppliers, who implement and deliver the software models and/or hardware [4]. (Software models for each functional component or subsystem can be developed in different ADLs or programming languages, which may make the integration process at the OEM more cumbersome.) This process requires common architecture frameworks between OEMs and suppliers or at least better formalization of architecture views and consistency between them.

1.2 Motivation

For the software architecture community, the consistency checking for architecture views and architectural models has been researched vigorously. Specifically, consistency checking for UML diagram types is a well researched area. However, for the automotive architecture field, the issues discussed in the previous section and lack of standard ADL [10] require the consistent definition of architectural elements such as viewpoint, view, correspondence, and correspondence rule. Therefore, we define the automotive architectural elements as part of an Architecture Framework for Automotive Systems (AFAS) and formalize the correspondence between the views extending the expression language.

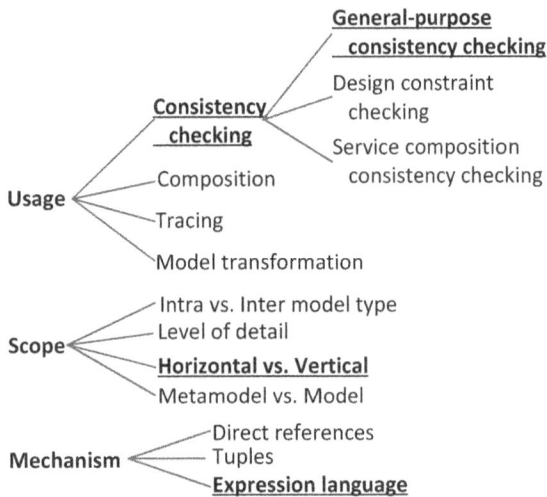

Figure 1: Framework characterizing relations between viewpoints.

In Figure 1, we illustrate a framework, which comprises three dimensions (Usage, Scope, and Mechanism) to characterize relations between views [2]. From four main use cases i.e. consistency checking, composition, tracing, and model transformation, the consistency checking is the focus of this paper. Consistency checking can be used to determine if the information in several views does not conflict with each other [2]. From three example uses of consistency checking relations i.e. general-purpose consistency checking approaches include inconsistency checking of UML diagrams [31]. The scope criteria in Figure 1 defines the range of view relations. From four criteria for the scope, we focus on the horizontal vs. vertical relations. Horizontal relation is used for relations between views at the same abstraction level and the vertical relation is used either relations between views at

different abstraction levels or relations between other representations as requirements, detailed design, or implementation [2]. In this paper, our specific scope is in vertical relations i.e. consistency checking between different abstraction levels (e.g. refinement relation). Our approach is based on a language-neutral approach that checks consistency between horizontal and vertical view relations [29]. The mechanism, the third criteria of the framework in Figure 1, categorizes constructs in the architecture description to represent view relations. Our approach extends the existing approach on expression language [25, 29].

1.3 Main Contributions and Outline

This research aims to refine existing automotive architecture frameworks and to formalize the correspondence rules between automotive architecture views. Specifically we focus on the refinement of the structural views, leaving the other views and correspondences for future research. The resulting conformance checking builds upon the hierarchical reflexion model [25] and employs a notion of abstraction similar to that used in the consistency checking approach [29]. As input, the consistency definition requires only a *strength ordering* of the connectors offered by the specific ADL used. In this way the consistency checking approach presented here is applicable to many automotive ADLs. The second contribution of this research is a prototype consistency checking tool in the form of an IBM Rational Rhapsody plugin. Specifically the plugin was developed for SysML [33] structural diagrams.

The remainder of the paper is structured as follows. Section 2 presents the architectural elements of the Architectural Framework for Automotive Systems (AFAS) and architecture views that we have defined based on existing architecture description methods. The scope of the paper is consistency issues between automotive structural views, in particular between functional and software views. These views are presented in the following section. Section 3 describes the ISO-42010 compliant correspondence rules between the functional and software views. Sections 4, 5, and 6 present the consistency semantics, consistency definitions, and tool development, respectively. We evaluate the approach in Section 7 and discuss related work in Section 8. Finally, Section 9 summarizes our contributions and discusses directions for future work.

2. AUTOMOTIVE ARCHITECTURAL FRAMEWORK AND ITS VIEWS

Although automotive architectural frameworks have not been standardized in automotive industry, different types of architecture viewpoints and views as part of automotive architectural frameworks have been introduced recently. The Automotive Architecture Framework (AAF) was defined to describe the entire vehicle system across all functional and engineering domains [5]. This is the first architecture framework for the automotive industry to pave the foundation of a standardized architecture description. The AAF proposes two sets of architectural viewpoints: mandatory or general viewpoints and optional viewpoints. The mandatory viewpoints and their respective views include *Functional viewpoint*, *Technical viewpoint*, *Technical viewpoint*, *Information viewpoint*, *Driver/vehicle operations viewpoint*, and *value net viewpoint*. Optional viewpoints suggested by the

AAF are *safety, security, quality and RAS* (reliability, availability, serviceability), *energy, cost, NVH* (noise, vibration, harshness), and *weight* viewpoints. The general viewpoints are intended to be closer to the already proven frameworks in other manufacturing industries e.g. RASDS[1] and RM-ODP[2]. Since the concepts are introduced in the first draft of the AAF, there needs to be further research to identify automotive specific architectural elements.

An Architectural Design Framework (ADF) is defined to support the construction of an architecture framework for the automotive industry [19]. The ADF supports only the system design process ("Technical processes") of the ISO/IEC 15288 standard[3] and derived from the SAGACE method [19]. The ADF includes *operational, functional, constructional,* and *requirements* viewpoints. Although the AAF and ADF are defined to provide the basis for the architecture framework for the automotive industry, architectural viewpoints and views are extracted from architecture frameworks from other industries. Therefore, we defined an Architectural Framework for Automotive Systems (AFAS) as illustrated in Figure 2 based on the study of proprietary automotive architectural models and practices, draft automotive architecture frameworks as AAF and ADF, and automotive ADLs like EAST-ADL [7], AADL [18], AML [3], and TADL [38]. The AFAS framework thus contains architectural viewpoints and views complementary to automotive ADLs.

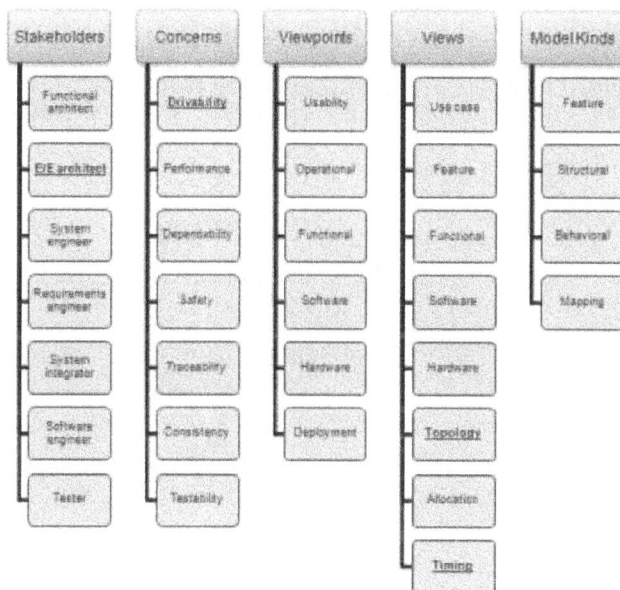

Figure 2: AFAS overview.

- *Use case view* shows the interaction between users and the system.

- *Feature view* captures the vehicle product line features, such as cruise control or bluetooth telephone connection, which can be configured for a product or a specific vehicle.

[1] Reference Architecture for Space Data Systems: http://public.ccsds.org/publications/
[2] Reference Model of Open Distributed Processing: http://www.rm-odp.net
[3] ISO/IEC 15288: http://www.15288.com/

- *Functional view* specifies a structural model that contains a number of functions or subsystems realizing features.

- *Software view* represents the software architecture, where detailed descriptions and implementation of a function is realized in software components or blocks.

- *Hardware view* represents the electrical/electronical (E/E) hardware architecture. The hardware architecture typically consists of electronic control units (ECUs), sensors, actuators and Controller Area Network (CAN) busses.

- *Topology view* specifies the connections (buses e.g. CAN, Local Interconnect Network (LIN) and wires etc.,) between ECUs, sensors, and actuators.

- *Allocation view* describes the mapping between software components to ECUs.

- *Timing view* specifies timing analysis such as bus schedulability analysis and CPU response time analysis views of the system.

In Figure 2, the architectural elements of the AFAS are similar to other architectural framework elements. Only E/E architect, Driveability, Topology and Timing views are specific for automotive domain. Although Functional and Software views exist in other frameworks, the correspondences between these views are specific to the automotive domain. As mentioned in the Introduction, functional decomposition is carried out by the OEMs and the functional models are delivered to the supplier, who elaborates the model in the software view and delivers back the functionality in the ECU. The elaboration of the functionality in software view may take several iterations e.g. the feedback to the functional model of the OEM or changes in the functional model need to be propagated into the supplier's software models. This process is currently rather document-centric and error-prone [19]. Therefore, improving consistency between these views is a step towards a semantic consistency of architectural modeling between OEMs and suppliers.

3. ARCHITECTURE CORRESPONDENCE

Consistency between views is one of the key problems in functional and software architectures [17]. Although software consistency has been a focus of the research community for many years, it has not been fully addressed in the automotive architecture views. Since more than a decade automotive ADLs have been developed and automotive architecture frameworks have been created recently. However, there is no standard ADL and architecture framework for the automotive industry yet. The architecture views and correspondences between them are not explicitly defined, which hinders semantic consistency of architectural modeling between OEMs and suppliers. Therefore, in this section we define the notion of correspondence and correspondence rules between functional and software views with the purpose of expressing and enforcing consistency among these views. Although OEMs and suppliers may use different ADLs, for illustrating the correspondences, functional and software models are represented in SysML structural diagrams.

In the ISO-42010 standard [23], a *correspondence* defines a relation between architecture description (AD) elements,

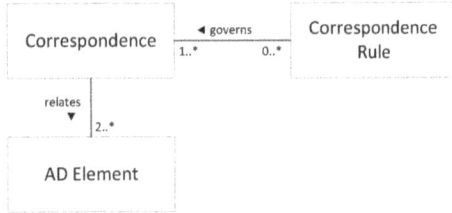

Figure 3: AD elements and correspondences [23].

which in the context of this paper is called the architecture view. Architecture relations can be, e.g. *refinement, composition, consistency,* and *traceability* [23]. Correspondences can be governed by *correspondence rules* as depicted in Figure 3. We specify below the correspondences, which define a refinement relation between functional and software views. Although the ISO-42010 standard does not specify a format for correspondences, they can be defined as relations and tables [16]. The following correspondence and correspondence rule are defined based on the refinement relation between architecture views (functional and software view) as illustrated in Figure 4.

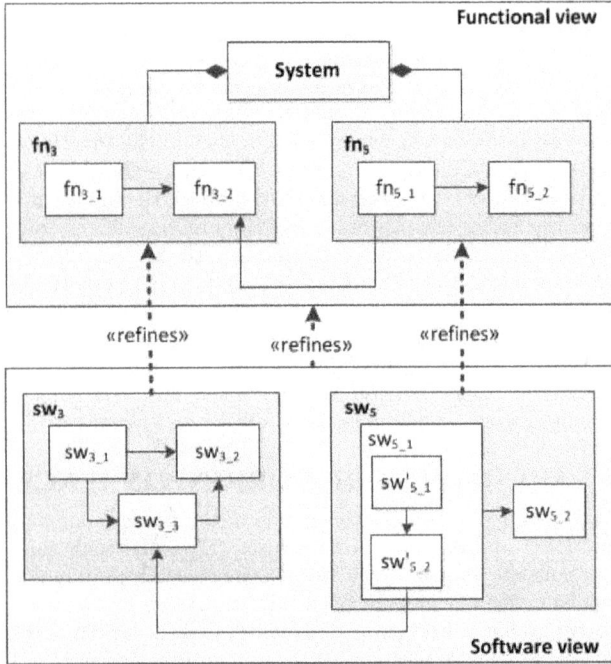

Figure 4: Example of functional and software views.

Consider functional and software views of a system S as a functional view, $FN(S)$, and a software view, $SW(S)$. Given that $FN(S)$ includes functional components, $fn_1, \ldots, fn_n$ and $SW(S)$ has software components, $sw_1, \ldots, sw_r$, a correspondence expressing which functional components are refined by which software components is specified in Table 1.

The correspondence rule for the refinement correspondence between functional and software views is:

R1: Every functional component, fn, defined by the functional view $FN(S)$, needs to be refined by one or more

Table 1 Refinement correspondence.

$SW(S)$ refines $FN(S)$ See rule: R1	
sw_3	fn_3
sw_5	fn_5

software components, sw, as defined by the software view $SW(S)$ of a system S.

In Figure 4 and Table 1, we have for example sw_3 *refines* fn_3 , and sw_5 *refines* fn_5.

4. CONSISTENCY SEMANTICS

Checking the consistency between the functional view and the software view involves checking the refinement correspondence between a high-level model and a low-level model. To perform this check, it suffices to perform a model transformation of the refined model into a model with the same level of abstraction as the high-level model. In the hierarchical reflexion model [25], this transformation is referred to as a *lifting* operation. Lifting abstracts from the details inserted into the refinement, leaving only information relevant for comparison with the high-level model. In terms of static models, this requires that for every entity present in the high-level model, the relationship present in the low-level model must be derived. The high-level model can then be directly compared with the lifted model. Possible inconsistencies are relations which exist in the high-level model but not in the lifted model, or relations which exist in the lifted model but not in the high-level model. These inconsistencies are referred to as *absences* and *divergences*, respectively, as depicted in Figure 5.

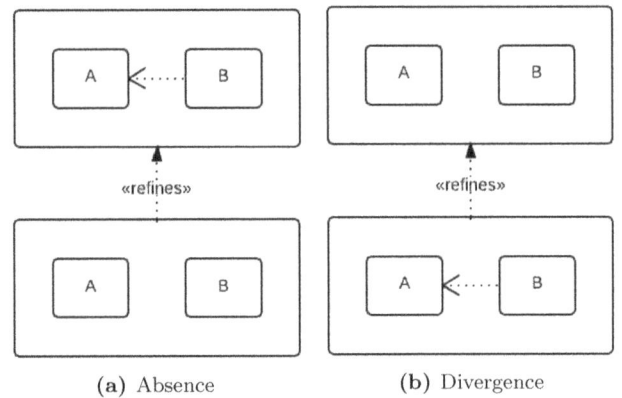

(a) Absence   **(b)** Divergence

Figure 5: Absence and divergence inconsistencies

To perform the lifting operation, we first generalize the hierarchical reflexion model. This generalization is necessary because the ADLs used in the automotive industry are more expressive than what can be accommodated by the reflexion model itself, where only *partof* (e.g. composition) and *reference* (e.g. dependency) relation types are considered. Specifically, rather than distinguishing relations, we impose a strength ordering on ADL connectors. This not only generalizes the vocabulary of the model, but also allows an extended role of transitivity in the model to more connector types than that used in the reflexion model, therefore substantially increasing the expressiveness of the consistency definition.

To illustrate the role of connector strength, Figure 6 depicts two similar functional models in SysML, each with two possible software refinements. Figure 6a shows a functional model with a dependency relation. In the left-hand refinement of Figure 6a, a wrapper entity was inserted. Semantically this still indicates that `Driveline` makes an (indirect) call to `BrakeLights`. Therefore the derived relationship between `Driveline` and `BrakeLights` is a dependency relationship, and should be considered consistent with the functional model. In the right-hand refinement, the entity `DriveLine` was refined to specify that in fact a child entity `LightingSystem` makes a call to `BrakeLights`. In this case clearly the derived relationship is again dependency. Therefore, regardless of whether the dependency relationship preceded, the derived relationship when combined with composition was still semantically a dependency. This suggests that connectors can in fact be arranged in an *ordering* according to their relative strengths. The lifting operation then involves transitively applying the ordering to allow stronger connectors to override weaker ones.

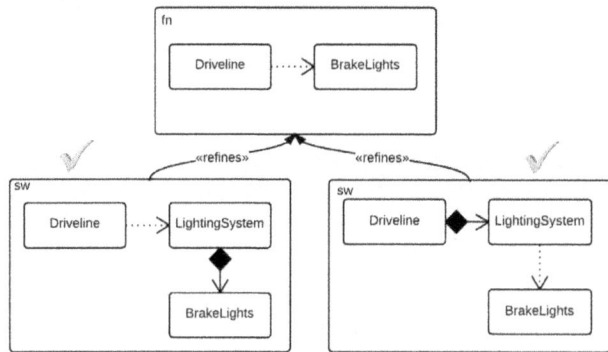

(a) Consistent dependency refinements

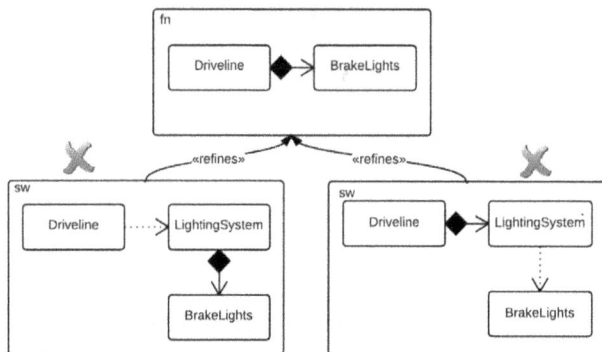

(b) Inconsistent composition refinements

Figure 6: Semantic differences between dependency and composition refinements

In Figure 6b, the same refinements are now refining a composition relation in the functional model. However, an automotive architect would not consider either proposed refinement to be consistent, since splitting up a composite entity into two entities which communicate via function calls was not intended by the architect. Therefore, applying the

connector ordering (which again derives only implicit dependencies in the refinements), again correctly yields an inconsistency. It is essential however to note that the high-level model must be taken into account when performing the lifting operation on the low level model. The original hierarchical reflexion model, due to its use of the full transitive closure in composition, simply extracts *all* implicit relationships between all elements in the low-level model, and then performs a comparison with the high-level model. However, this approach would yield many false positives due to the loss of information incurred during the transformation. This problem is illustrated in Figure 7. There, if a full transitive closure is taken to extract all implicit (lifted) dependencies, the two low-level models cannot be distinguished. However, it is clear that the left-hand refinement should be consistent with the functional model, while the right-hand refinement should not, in that case because the refinement is violating the layering specified by the high-level model. Therefore, it is essential that the lifting operation does not use a full transitive closure to derive the lifted relationships from the refinement. Instead, the strength ordering should only be applied transitively until an entity also present in the high-level model is encountered.

5. CONSISTENCY DEFINITION

In this section, we formalize the inconsistency checking approach explained in the previous section.

Let $REL = \{rel_1, \ldots, rel_k\}$ be an ordered set of relations available in the automotive ADL, where rel_1 is the weakest relation and rel_k is the strongest one. For the SysML examples provided in Section 4, $REL = \{composition, dependency\}$.

Next we introduce two new operations, which we term the *right-lifting* and *left-lifting* operations on the low-level model (i.e. software model), denoted as $\overrightarrow{R_i}$ and $\overleftarrow{R_i}$ in Equations 1 and 2, respectively. These relations are defined for each connector $rel_i \in REL$. Below, FN represents the functional model, SW is the software model, $rel_i(A, B)$ is a direct relation of type rel_i between entities A and B in FN, and $\widetilde{rel_i}(A, B)$ is a direct relation of type rel_i in SW. The lifting operation is carried out on the software model.

$$\overrightarrow{R_i}(X,Y) \quad \Leftrightarrow \quad \bigvee_{j \leq i} \widetilde{rel_j}(X,Y) \wedge Y \notin FN \qquad (1)$$

$$\overleftarrow{R_i}(X,Y) \quad \Leftrightarrow \quad \bigvee_{j \leq i} \widetilde{rel_j}(X,Y) \wedge X \notin FN \qquad (2)$$

Note that $\overrightarrow{R_i}^+(X,Y)$ and $\overleftarrow{R_i}^+(X,Y)$ are the irreflexive transitive closures of $\overrightarrow{R_i}(X,Y)$ and $\overleftarrow{R_i}(X,Y)$, respectively. The right-lifting operation represents a series of elements in the software model connected by relations, where (at least) the target entities of each relation exist only in the software model, and connectors are equal or weaker in strength to rel_i. The same intuition holds for the left-lifting operation, except the restriction there is that at least all relation *sources* only exist in SW. As illustrated in examples from Figure 6 and 7, incorporating the entities present in the high-level model while performing the lifting operation clearly distinguishes our method from previous research utilizing hierarchical reflexion.

In the Equation 3, we redefine the *lifted relation* between two model entities, denoted $\widetilde{rel_i}^\uparrow$, incorporating the left- and right-lifting operations. This new definition takes into

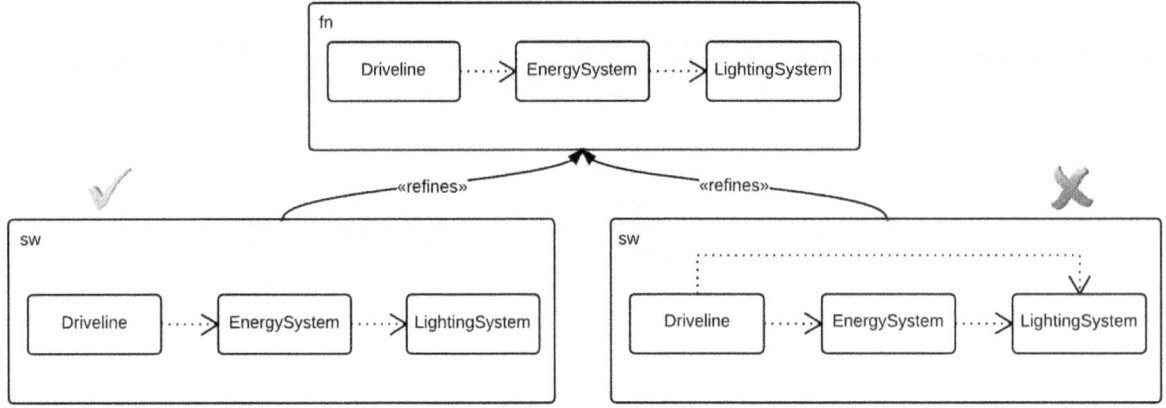

Figure 7: Inadequacy of using full transitive closure to extract relations in refinements

account the cases where either two entities are directly connected by relation rel_i, or there exist one or more intermediary entities in between which appear only in SW and are connected by relations which are equal or weaker than rel_i. A and B are functional and software model entities.

$$\widetilde{rel_i}^{\uparrow}(A,B) \Leftrightarrow \widetilde{rel_i}(A,B) \vee \exists C, D \in SW \backslash FN :$$
$$\left(\overrightarrow{R_i}^+(A,C) \wedge \widetilde{rel_i}^*(C,D) \wedge \overleftarrow{R_i}^+(D,B) \right) \qquad (3)$$

where $\widetilde{rel_i}^*$ is the reflexive transitive closure of $\widetilde{rel_i}$.

The lifting operation should then be performed on SW using all entity pairs A,B that appear in FN, resulting in a lifted low-level model. The lifted model can then be straightforwardly compared to the high-level model to check for absent and divergent relations for each relation type, presented in Equations 4 and 5.

$$absence_{rel_i}(A,B) \Leftrightarrow rel_i^+(A,B) \wedge \neg\widetilde{rel_i}^{\uparrow}(A,B) \qquad (4)$$

$$divergence_{rel_i}(A,B) \Leftrightarrow \neg rel_i^+(A,B) \wedge \widetilde{rel_i}^{\uparrow}(A,B) \qquad (5)$$

6. TOOL DEVELOPMENT

In the following sub-sections, the algorithm for checking inconsistencies based on the definitions in the previous section, the details for the tool implementation, and a description of using the tool are presented.

6.1 Checking Algorithm

The lifted model that is calculated by applying the Equations 4 and 5 results in a low-level model, e.g. software model, that has been abstracted from all details not already present in the high-level model, e.g. functional model. Comparing this lifted model to the high-level model then fulfills the intuition of consistency described initially by Dijkman et al [12]. Furthermore, calculating a lifted model and then applying consistency checks for *absence* and *divergence*, rather than working directly on the low-level model, has been seen to significantly improve the scalability and maintainability of consistency checking algorithms in practice [14].

The implementation of the consistency checking algorithm is described below. Note that in addition to the *absence* and *divergence* checks, an additional check is run to make sure

that all blocks from the high-level model exist in the low-level model; if not, an *absentBlock* error is reported.

Algorithm *CheckConsistency*($\boldsymbol{FN}, \boldsymbol{SW}$)
Input: FN is the high-level functional model, and SW is the low-level software model
Output: A(possibly empty) set of consistency errors
1. Encode FN and SW as directed graphs, where edges are annotated with the relation type (*dependency* or *composition*)
2. Let $\tilde{SW}$ be a new, empty graph to contain the lifted model of SW
3.
(∗ Populate the lifted model of SW ∗)
4.   **for** all elements $A, B \in FN$
5.   **do**
6.   **if** $\widetilde{rel_{dep}}^{\uparrow}(A,B)$ is **true**
7.   **then** Add an edge from A to B to $\tilde{SW}$ annotated with *dependency*
8.   **if** $\widetilde{rel_{comp}}^{\uparrow}(A,B)$ is **true**
9.   **then** Add an edge from A to B to $\tilde{SW}$ annotated with *composition*
10.
(∗ Check for absence ∗)
11.   **for** each edge $e = (A, B) \in FN$
12.   **do**
13.   **if** $A \notin \tilde{SW}$ (or $B \notin \tilde{SW}$)
14.   **then** Report error *absentBlock*(A) (or
15.   *absentBlock*(B), respectively)
16.   **if** e is annotated with *dependency* $\wedge$
17.   *absence_{dep}*(A, B) is **true**
18.   **then** Report error *absentDependency*(A, B)
19.   **if** e is annotated with *composition* $\wedge$
20.   *absence_{comp}*(A, B) is **true**
21.   **then** Report error *absentComposition*(A, B)
22.
(∗ Check for divergence ∗)
23.   **for** each edge $e = (A, B) \in \tilde{SW}$
24.   **do**
25.   **if** e is annotated with *dependency* $\wedge$
26.   *divergence_{dep}*(A, B) is **true**
27.   **then** Report error
28.   *divergentDependency*(A, B)
29.   **if** e is annotated with *composition* $\wedge$

```
30.              divergence_comp(A, B) is true
31.         then Report error
32.              divergentComposition(A, B)
```

While there are many parts of the algorithm which could be optimized for a faster running time, they are left out here to improve readability. Furthermore, although the algorithm accepts only two models as input, it can be used to check deeper models (i.e. where a high-level model is refined by another model, which in turn refined by yet another model), simply by running the *CheckConsistency* algorithm for each pair of parent-child models.

6.2 Tool Implementation

A prototype tool was implemented as a Java plugin integrated into the IBM Rational Rhapsody for SysML structural diagrams, i.e., Block Definition Diagram (BDD) and Internal Block Diagram (IBD). The reason for this choice is three-fold: First, IBM Rational Rhapsody is a well-established, enterprise modeling tool for designing complex software products including automotive software systems [21]. In addition to support for SysML, Rational Rhapsody also supports UML and some domain-specific languages (DSLs). So, a plugin developed for use with SysML is easily convertible to a tool for other supported languages. Second, it is important for the tool to be integrated directly into the development environment. This not only increases usability by allowing architects to work with a tool they already understand, but also increases the likelihood that consistency checks are run often. This integration is possible in Rational Rhapsody because it offers a comprehensive Java API for plugin development. Finally, IBM Rational Rhapsody is well-documented and has an active developer community, making it a low-risk choice for development.

In addition to the Rational Rhapsody API functions, the Java Universal Network/Graph (JUNG) library was used for encoding the graphs required to represent the high-level, low-level, and lifted low-level models. Using a third-party, comprehensive graph library greatly reduced the complexity required to implement the checking algorithm. As output, the tool notifies the user of all absences and divergences encountered inside the error pane.

6.3 Using the Tool

The consistency checking plugin expects a project to have at least two SysML Package elements: a high-level package and a low-level package. A top-level element of Package was chosen to separate the high-level from the lower-level models because it was seen that some automotive companies already organize their models this way.

Each Package should contain exactly one SysML BDD, which describes the Blocks relevant for that Package together with their dependency and composition relationships. Then there should be another diagram, which we term Overview, which specifies which Packages refine which other Packages. A refinement is specified by adding a Dependency relation between the Packages in the Overview diagram with the «refine» stereotype.

The consistency check tool can run on the Overview diagram by selecting the *Tools > Check Model* command. The plugin will then find all refinements described in the Overview diagram. For each refinement relation, it will retrieve the high-level and low-level models (in this case Block Definition Diagrams) and run the plugin's *CheckConsistency* al-

gorithm. When errors are found, a new bottom frame opens with a list of all the errors, noting exactly which diagram, relation, and specific offending elements caused the consistency error, according to the list of failed elements generated during plugin execution. After performing this check, the architect can resolve the errors or alert another architect that there are errors, and then rerun the check.

7. EVALUATION

In this section we evaluate the tool implemented for the inconsistency checking as presented in Section 6. We applied the tool to an Adaptive Cruise Control (ACC) system. ACC, Figure 8, is a cruise control system with enhanced functionality assisting the driver to keep a safe distance to other traffic ahead and alerting her if manual intervention is required [8]. In our evaluation of the prototype inconsis-

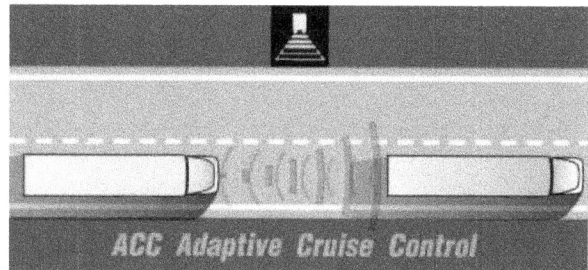

Figure 8: Adaptive cruise control [8].

tency checking tool, two student teams emulated an OEM and a supplier. The students follow a Master of Science in Automotive Technology, therefore they have experience in modeling automotive systems. The "OEM" team created a functional architecture for a truck and handed in a functional model of the ACC (Figure 9a) to the "supplier" team. The "supplier" team elaborated the ACC software model (Figure 9b) and created a running ACC prototype. In the real life automotive modeling case, at this phase the supplier software would be integrated the ACC by the OEM and tested thoroughly.

Although ACC subsystem works correctly according to the OEM specification, the ACC software model created by the "supplier" team is inconsistent with the functional model provided by the "OEM" team. Indeed, using the prototype inconsistency checking tool with *Tools > Check Model*, the divergence relations between ACC_Controller and ACC_UI, and Driveline and Radar are detected. These relations are missing in the functional view shown in Figure 9a.

Early inconsistency detection by the prototype tool was considered useful by both teams. The team members appreciated that the consistency checks are executed only when specifically invoked by the architect. This is in sharp contrast with a recommendation of Rosik, Buckley and Ali Babar [36] that argue that consistency errors should be reported continuously during development.

8. RELATED WORK

MEGAF (MEGamodeling Architecture Frameworks) infrastructure is developed to enable reusable architecture frameworks [20]. Due to the limitation of the MEGAF tool support for extracting the architectural elements from the

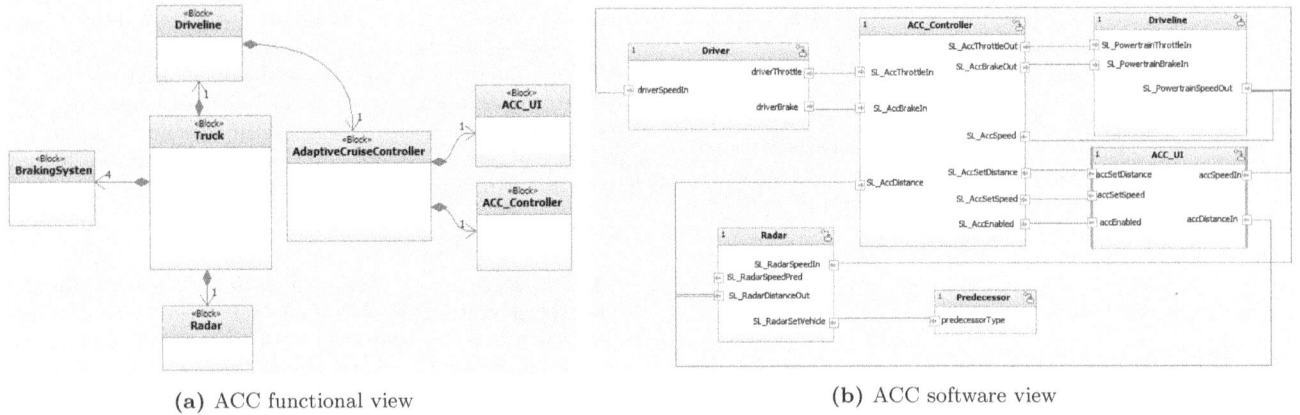

(a) ACC functional view   (b) ACC software view

Figure 9: Consistency checking between functional and software views of the ACC system

automotive ADLs and architecture frameworks, we defined the AFAS manually by analyzing state-of-the-art architecture description mechanisms. Our approach is based on the hierarchical reflexion model [25, 29]. Specifying correspondences between viewpoints has been introduced in [35] [34]. OCL is used for implementing the correspondence rules in this approach. However, in this approach, views are expressed as UML models which are not widely used in the automotive architectural modeling. Our approach extends this approach by enabling a technique to specify intentional correspondences for automotive architecture modeling.

In their overview of UML consistency management, Elaasar and Briand [15] describe viewpoint unification to transform one UML view to another. Since different UML diagram types contain different sorts of information, this process often resulted in lost information and furthermore only appropriate for certain diagram pairs. Such transformation-based consistency approaches are employed by many authors [28] [6] [37]. However, the desire of the researchers to keep the operation generic for many domains and diagram types results in only basic consistency rules. For example, a rule may guarantee that classes with a certain name exists. Since we consider only the refinement correspondence, more powerful rules can be formulated.

In the UML Analyzer tool [13], Egyed presents a rule-based approach to abstract from entities and relations which exist in a refinement model, resulting in a scalable consistency checking tool [14]. Furthermore it was found to be beneficial for both performance and usability to separate the transformation (abstraction) phase from the consistency checking phase. However, the rules are limited to UML, making them not directly applicable to automotive ADLs. Furthermore, the rule format does not lend itself to generalization, in contrast to a generic mathematical definition for consistency. Some authors choose to translate architectural diagrams to an intermediate language, for example XMI [39] [26], to take advantage of the existing power for expressing consistency rules available in those languages. Such representations are however considerably less intuitive, whereas using a graph representation can already maintain the structure and information present in most automotive ADLs while requiring a less radical model transformation.

In the hierarchical reflexion model [25], relations that exist in a parent model are checked to exist in a *lifted* model which

has been derived from source code. This approach is useful since it can equally be applied to checking two hierarchical models against each other. It is also highly intuitive and results in few false positives [24]. Previous work in automotive ADL consistency has adapted the reflexion model to the automotive domain [10]. There, multiple levels of automotive models are considered. Furthermore, the research presented here extends [10] by providing more sound consistency rules for the functional and software views.

9. CONCLUSION AND FUTURE WORK

In this paper, first we presented architecture description elements including architecture views of the AFAS framework based on the study of state-of-the-art architecture description mechanisms for automotive systems. To further revise the framework, we plan to use the MEGAF approach [20], since the MEGAF is built upon the ISO/IEC/IEEE-42010 standard and enables the definition of a reusable and open architecture framework. Although consistency issues between architecture viewpoints and views were tackled before in the software industry, there is still a need to develop a method to enforce the consistency between different views of OEMs and suppliers.

Therefore, in this paper we also proposed an inconsistency detection approach based on correspondence rules between automotive architecture views. We focus on the refinement relationship between functional and software views, where the functional models are refined by adding more details in the software view. The revised definition for consistency proposed here requires only that an ordering be imposed on the connector types available in a given ADL, allowing it easily to be used with many automotive ADLs. Then a prototype tool was developed for IBM Rational Rhapsody which can perform this consistency checking between different architecture views. The inconsistency checking approach and the prototype tool were evaluated in the scope of an Adaptive Cruise Control modeling among two separate teams emulating an OEM and automotive supplier. The early inconsistency detection by the prototype tool was considered useful by both teams.

The future work will be improving the prototype tool after carrying out a comprehensive case study in an industrial setting by extending the consistency rules and overall usability of the tool. The end result is expected to be a powerful consistency checking approach and useful tool for automotive system and software architectures. The preliminary demonstration of the prototype has already attracted the attention of potential users and received some insightful feedback. Support for consistency checking between the other automotive views identified in Section 2 is also planned. This will be integrated into the automotive-specific quality framework that comprises quality specification, measurement, and evaluation methods targeting both architectural and design models [11] [9].

10. ACKNOWLEDGEMENT

Yanja Dajsuren, Alexander Serebrenik and Mark G.J. van den Brand are supported by the Dutch Automotive Innovation Programme (HTAS) project (HTASI10002). Bogdan Vasilescu gratefully acknowledges support from the Dutch Science Foundation (NWO) through the project NWO 600. 065.120.10N235.

11. REFERENCES

[1] The Open Group Architectural Framework (TOGAF). http://www.opengroup.org/togaf/.

[2] N. Boucké, D. Weyns, R. Hilliard, T. Holvoet, and A. Helleboogh. Characterizing relations between architectural views. In R. Morrison, D. Balasubramaniam, and K. Falkner, editors, *Software Architecture*, volume 5292 of *Lecture Notes in Computer Science*, pages 66–81. Springer Berlin Heidelberg, 2008.

[3] P. Braun and M. Rappl. A model-based approach for automotive software development. In P. Hofmann and A. Schürr, editors, *OMER*, volume 5 of *LNI*, pages 100–105. GI, 2001.

[4] M. Broy. Challenges in automotive software engineering. In *Proceedings of the 28th international conference on Software engineering*, pages 33–42. ACM, 2006.

[5] M. Broy, M. Gleirscher, S. Merenda, D. Wild, P. Kluge, and W. Krenzer. Toward a holistic and standardized automotive architecture description. *Computer*, 42(12):98–101, 2009.

[6] R. Buhr. Use case maps as architectural entities for complex systems. *Software Engineering, IEEE Transactions on*, 24(12):1131–1155, 1998.

[7] P. Cuenot, P. Frey, R. Johansson, H. Lönn, Y. Papadopoulos, M. Reiser, A. Sandberg, D. Servat, R. T. Kolagari, M. Törngren, and M. Weber. The EAST-ADL Architecture Description Language for Automotive Embedded Software. In *Model-Based Engineering of Embedded Real-Time Systems*, pages 297–307. Springer Verlag, 2011.

[8] DAF Trucks N.V. Adaptive Cruise Control. http://www.daf.com/SiteCollectionDocuments/Products/Safety_and_comfort_systems/DAF-ACC-EN.pdf, 2013.

[9] Y. Dajsuren, A. Serebrenik, R. Huisman, and M. G. J. van den Brand. A quality framework for evaluating automotive architecture. In *Proceedings of the FISITA World Automotive Congress*, 2014.

[10] Y. Dajsuren, M. G. J. van den Brand, A. Serebrenik, and R. Huisman. Automotive ADLs: a study on enforcing consistency through multiple architectural

[11] Y. Dajsuren, M. G. J. van den Brand, A. Serebrenik, and S. Roubtsov. Simulink models are also software: Modularity assessment. In *Proceedings of the 9th international ACM Sigsoft conference on Quality of software architectures*, pages 99–106. ACM, 2013.

[12] R. Dijkman, D. Quartel, and M. van Sinderen. Consistency in multi-viewpoint design of enterprise information systems. *Information and Software Technology*, 50(7):737–752, 2008.

[13] A. Egyed. Automatically validating model consistency during refinement. In *23rd International Conference on Software Engineering (ICSE 2001), Toronto, Ontario, Canada*, pages 12–19, 2000.

[14] A. Egyed. Scalable consistency checking between diagrams - The VIEWINTEGRA approach. In *Automated Software Engineering, 2001.(ASE 2001). Proceedings. 16th Annual International Conference on*, pages 387–390. IEEE, 2001.

[15] M. Elaasar and L. Briand. An overview of UML consistency management. *Carleton University, Canada, Technical Report SCE-04-18*, 2004.

[16] D. Emery and R. Hilliard. Every architecture description needs a framework: Expressing architecture frameworks using ISO/IEC 42010. In *Software Architecture, 2009 European Conference on Software Architecture. WICSA/ECSA 2009. Joint Working IEEE/IFIP Conference on*, pages 31 –40, 2009.

[17] G. Fairbanks and D. Garlan. *Just Enough Software Architecture: A Risk-Driven Approach*. Marshall & Brainerd, 2010.

[18] P. Feiler, D. Gluch, and J. Hudak. The architecture analysis & design language (AADL): An introduction. Technical Report CMU/SEI-2006-TN-011, Software Engineering Institute, Carnegie Mellon University, 2006.

[19] H. Góngora, T. Gaudré, and S. Tucci-Piergiovanni. Towards an architectural design framework for automotive systems development. In M. Aiguier, Y. Caseau, D. Krob, and A. Rauzy, editors, *Complex Systems Design and Management*, pages 241–258. Springer Berlin Heidelberg, 2013.

[20] R. Hilliard, I. Malavolta, H. Muccini, and P. Pelliccione. On the composition and reuse of viewpoints across architecture frameworks. In *Proceedings of the 2012 Joint Working IEEE/IFIP Conference on Software Architecture and European Conference on Software Architecture*, WICSA-ECSA '12, pages 131–140, Washington, DC, USA, 2012. IEEE Computer Society.

[21] IBM. Rational Rhapsody Designer for systems engineers. http://www.ibm.com/software/products/.

[22] ISO. ISO/IEC 10746-1 Information technology – Open Distributed Processing – Reference Model: Overview. December 1998.

[23] ISO/IEC/IEEE 42010:2011. Systems and software engineering—architecture description. http://www.iso.org/iso/catalogue_detail.htm?csnumber=50508, 2011.

[24] J. Knodel and D. Popescu. A comparison of static architecture compliance checking approaches. In *Software Architecture, 2007. WICSA'07. The Working IEEE/IFIP Conference on*, pages 12–12. IEEE, 2007.

[25] R. Koschke and D. Simon. Hierarchical reflexion models. In *Proceedings of the 10th Working Conference on Reverse Engineering*, page 36. IEEE Computer Society, 2003.

[26] Y. Kotb and T. Katayama. Consistency checking of UML model diagrams using the xml semantics approach. In *Special interest tracks and posters of the 14th international conference on World Wide Web*, pages 982–983. ACM, 2005.

[27] P. B. Kruchten. The 4+1 View Model of architecture. *Software, IEEE*, 12(6):42–50, Nov. 1995.

[28] D. Liu, K. Subramaniam, B. Far, and A. Eberlein. Automating transition from use-cases to class model. In *Electrical and Computer Engineering, 2003. IEEE CCECE 2003. Canadian Conference on*, volume 2, pages 831–834. IEEE, 2003.

[29] J. Muskens, R. Bril, and M. R. V. Chaudron. Generalizing consistency checking between software views. In *Software Architecture, 2005. WICSA 2005. 5th Working IEEE/IFIP Conference on*, pages 169–180, 2005.

[30] N. Navet and F. Simonot-Lion. *Automotive Embedded Systems Handbook*. CRC Press, Inc., USA, 2009.

[31] C. Nentwich, L. Capra, W. Emmerich, and A. Finkelsteiin. xlinkit: A consistency checking and smart link generation service. *ACM Transactions on Internet Technology (TOIT)*, 2(2):151–185, 2002.

[32] B. M. of Defence. MOD Architecture Framework. http://www.modaf.org.uk/.

[33] OMG. Systems Modeling Language (SysML) Specification version 1.2. http://www.sysml.org/specs, 2010.

[34] J. Romero, J. Jaen, and A. Vallecillo. Realizing correspondences in multi-viewpoint specifications. In *Enterprise Distributed Object Computing Conference, 2009. EDOC '09. IEEE International*, pages 163–172, 2009.

[35] J. Romero and A. Vallecillo. Well-formed rules for viewpoint correspondences specification. In *Enterprise Distributed Object Computing Conference Workshops, 2008 12th*, pages 441–443, 2008.

[36] J. Rosik, J. Buckley, and M. Ali Babar. Design requirements for an architecture consistency tool. In *21st Annual Psychology of Programming Interest Group Conference*, pages 1–15, 2009.

[37] B. Shishkov, Z. Xie, K. Lui, and J. Dietz. Using norm analysis to derive use case from business processes. In *5th Workshop on Organizations semiotics. June*, pages 14–15, 2002.

[38] The TIMMO Consortium. TADL: Timing Augmented Description Language version 2. http://www.timmo-2-use.org/timmo/index.htm.

[39] C. Zapata, G. González, and A. Gelbukh. A rule-based system for assessing consistency between UML models. *MICAI 2007: Advances in Artificial Intelligence*, pages 215–224, 2007.

SRMP: A Software Pattern for Deadlocks Prevention in Real-Time Concurrency Models

Rania Mzid
CES Laboratory, National
school of engineers of Sfax
Sfax, Tunisia
rania.mzid@gmail.com

Chokri Mraidha
CEA, LIST, Laboratory of
model driven engineering for
embedded systems
91191 Gif-sur-Yvette, France
chokri.mraidha@cea.fr

Jean-Philippe Babau
Lab-STICC, UBO, UEB
Brest, France
Jean-
Philippe.Babau@univ-
brest.fr

Mohamed Abid
CES Laboratory, National
school of engineers of Sfax
Sfax, Tunisia
Mohamed.Abid@enis.rnu.tn

ABSTRACT

Model-based approaches for the development of software intensive real-time embedded systems allow early verification of timing properties at the design phase. At this phase, the Real-Time Operating System (RTOS) may not be chosen, hence some assumptions on the software platform are made to achieve timing verifications such as schedulability analysis of tasks describing the application. Among these assumptions, the synchronization protocol which is used to manage the concurrent access to resources that are shared between tasks. A classical solution is to consider the Priority Ceiling Protocol (PCP) synchronization protocol to avoid deadlocks. However, when this protocol is not provided by the target RTOS on which the application will be deployed, the concurrency model becomes not *implementable* and a new synchronization protocol must be considered. In this paper, we propose the Shared Resource Merge Pattern (SRMP) which aims to prevent deadlocks when the use of PCP protocol is not allowed by the target RTOS. The application of this pattern on the concurrency model must guarantee that the timing properties of the real-time application are still met.

Categories and Subject Descriptors

D.2.7 [**Software Engineering**]: Distribution, Maintenance, and Enhancement—*Portability*; D.2.11 [**Software Engineering**]: Software Architectures —*Patterns*

General Terms

Design, Verification

Permission to make digital or hard copies of all or part of this work for personal or classroom use is granted without fee provided that copies are not made or distributed for profit or commercial advantage and that copies bear this notice and the full citation on the first page. Copyrights for components of this work owned by others than ACM must be honored. Abstracting with credit is permitted. To copy otherwise, or republish, to post on servers or to redistribute to lists, requires prior specific permission and/or a fee. Request permissions from Permissions@acm.org.
QoSA'14, June 30 - July 04 2014, Marcq-en-Bareul, France
Copyright 2014 ACM 978-1-4503-2576-9/14/06ÂÉ:.$15.00.
http://dx.doi.org/10.1145/2602576.2602591.

Keywords

Real-Time Embedded Systems, MDA, Real-Time Verification, Deadlock, Software Pattern

1. INTRODUCTION

In order to increase productivity and reduce the time-to-market of Real-Time Embedded Systems (RTES), Model-Driven Development (MDD) [15] proposes the use of models (which are abstractions of the real system) that are refined through several levels of abstractions from requirements specification to the binary code. These models allow verification activities at each level of abstraction to ensure that the refined model is preserving properties of the upper level. In that context, Model-Driven Architecture(MDA) [14] standardized by the Object Management Group (OMG), recommends system development following the branches of the Y-Chart approach [8]. Thus, the real-time application is described in a concurrency model (called also design model) independent from any particular RTOS (i.e. PIM: Platform Independent Model). Then, this concurrency model is deployed onto a RTOS (i.e. PM: Platform Model) to produce the RTOS-specific model (i.e.PSM: Platform Specific Model).

Schedulability analysis based on the computation of an upper bound of the response time of the different tasks constituting the concurrency model aims to verify whether these tasks complete their computations within the time limit specified by the real-time application i.e. the deadline. This verification requires an abstraction of the underlying hardware platform. To this end, at this level, execution nodes and communication media are supposed to be known. In this paper, we consider only *single-processor* platforms. In addition *software assumptions* related to the target RTOS are considered in order to keep RTOS-independence at this level. Among these assumptions, the synchronization protocol used to protect the access to the critical sections in the concurrency model.

A classical solution [10], is to consider the Priority Ceiling protocol (PCP) [6] as a synchronization protocol in order to avoid deadlocks at the implementation level. Indeed, this protocol prevents the incorrect handling of resources which may lead to deadlocks by ensuring that no higher-priority task could be blocked by more than one lower-priority task. However, due to the variety of RTOS, it is not always guaranteed that the target RTOS provides this synchronization protocol (i.e. PCP). MicroC-OS/II [2] and VRTX [1] are some examples of real-time operating systems belonging to this RTOS family. In that case, a deployment problem is detected and the concurrency model is said to be not "implementable" on that RTOS.

In previous works [13] [11] [12], we have proposed an approach to guide the refinement of the concurrency model satisfying the real-time constraints to a RTOS-specific model. The proposed approach introduces a *refactoring phase* which aims to advise solutions for the designer when the input concurrency model is not "implementable". This refactoring phase is based on a set of software patterns. Each pattern defines a way to change the original concurrency model with the aim to solve the deployment problem. A timing verification of the refactored concurrency model resulting from patterns application is required in order to verify whether the real-time properties of the application are still met. Figure 1 gives an overview of this phase.

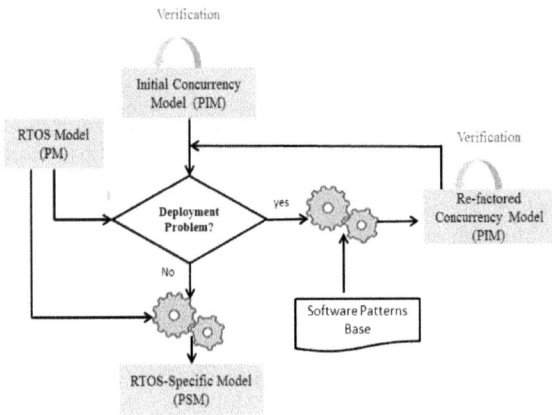

Figure 1: *Overview of the refactoring phase*

In this paper, we focus on a particular deployment problem related to the synchronization protocol used to implement the critical sections in the concurrency model. Indeed, when the PCP protocol is not provided by the target RTOS, an alternative synchronization protocol must to be considered. Nevertheless, when the concurrency model presents in addition a potential situation of deadlock (i.e. the concurrency model consists of tasks that share more than one resource at the same time), we propose the Shared Resource Merge Pattern (SRMP). This pattern aims to prevent deadlocks at the implementation level by merging the different resources leading to such problem.The resulting concurrency model after applying this pattern must respect the timing properties of the application.

This paper is organized as follows. In section 2, we briefly introduce some real-time verification concepts and explain the deadlock problem. Section 3 describes the proposed pattern (SRMP). In section 4, an example illustrating the application of the SRMP pattern is given. Finally, section 5 presents some related work and section 6 concludes the paper and sketches some future work.

2. BACKGROUND

In this section, we give a formal description of the concurrency model describing the real-time application at the design level and we introduce some real-time verification concepts. Then, we explain the deadlock problem.

2.1 Real-Time Verification at the Design Level

We define a concurrency model C (describing the real-time application) by $C = \{M, R\}$ where M is a set of tasks and R a set of software resources that can be shared between several tasks.

$M = \{T_1, T_2, \ldots, T_m\}$ represents m *periodic* tasks running on a *single-processor* hardware platform. Each task T_i is characterized by its priority p_i, its execution time c_i , its activation period P_i and its deadline D_i that represents the time limit in which a task must complete its execution.

$R = \{R_1, R_2, \ldots, R_\ell\}$ is a set of software resources that can be used by one or several tasks (e.g. a mutex to access a critical section). We denote by $Used(T_i)$ the set of resources used by the task T_i. In addition, c_{R_i, T_j} denotes the *lock time* of the resource R_i by the task T_j which represents the worst-case time for the task T_j to acquire and release the lock of the resource R_i in case of no contention. Let us remark that c_{R_i, T_j} is considered as an input and that $c_{R_i, T_j} \leq c_j$. Due to the presence of shared resources, a task is also characterized by a blocking time B_i. The blocking time accounts for the time a higher-priority task has to wait, before acquiring the lock, since a lower-priority task owns this lock. The computation of this term depends on the synchronization protocol used to implement the access to the shared resource. The expression used to compute the blocking time for the *PCP* synchronization protocol, for example, is given just below:

$$B_i = \max_{T_j \in HP, R_k \in R} \{c_{R_k, T_j} : p_j < p_i \text{ and } \pi_k \geq p_i\} \quad (1)$$

In this protocol each resource R_i is assigned a priority ceiling π_i, which is a priority equal to the highest priority of any task which may lock the resource.

We perform Rate-Monotonic (RM) response time analysis [9]. The analysis results correspond to the computation of the response time Rep_i of the different tasks in the model. The model satisfies its timing constraints if and only if $\forall i \in \{1..m\}$ $Rep_i \leq D_i$. The expression used to compute Rep_i is given just below, where HP_j represents the set of tasks with priority higher than priority of T_j.

$$Rep_i = c_i + B_i + \sum_{T_j \in HP_j} \left\lceil \frac{Rep_i}{P_j} \right\rceil * c_j \quad (2)$$

2.2 The Deadlock Problem

In a real-time context, deadlocks arise when tasks which hold resources are blocked indefinitely from access to resources held by other tasks within the concurrency model. The simplest illustration of these conditions involves two tasks, each holding, for exclusive access, a different resource and each requesting access to the resource held by the other which results in a *circular wait*.

An example of such situation is given in Figure 2. The figure shows a timing diagram, with a class diagram showing the structure of the concurrency model. In this example, the concurrency model consists of two tasks T_1 and T_2, the priority of the task T_1 is higher than that of the task T_2. In addition, there are two resources, R_1 and

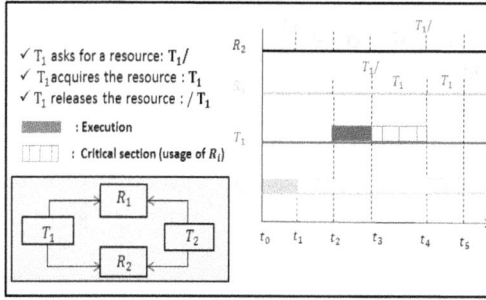

Figure 2: Deadlock Example

Situation 1 | Situation 2 | Situation 3
//code | //code | //code
$P(R_n)$ | $P(R_n)$ | $P(R_n)$
//sc1 | //sc1 | //sc1
$P(R_m)$ | $P(R_m)$ | $V(R_n)$
//sc2 | //sc2 | $P(R_m)$
$V(R_m)$ | $V(R_n)$ | //sc2
$V(R_n)$ | $V(R_m)$ | $V(R_m)$

Figure 3: *The three possible implementation strategies of a task T_i to access to the resources R_n and R_m*

R_2, shared between both tasks. The problem of deadlock occurs if the tasks lock the resources in reverse order and T_1 preempts T_2 in a critical section.

Thus, at *the design level*, the concurrency model presents a possible situation for deadlock when it consists of tasks that share more than one resource at the same time. In that case, merging the different resources in a single resource may be a potential solution which guarantees an *ordered access* to the different resources and prevents thus deadlocks occurrence at the implementation level. In the next section, we present in details this solution by describing the Shared Resource Merge Pattern (SRMP).

3. SRMP DESCRIPTION

In this section, we explain the problem related to the Shared Resource Merge Pattern (SRMP). Then, we describe the proposed solution and we give a structural description of the pattern.

3.1 Problem Statement

In order to enable timing verification, the PCP protocol is assumed to be used as a synchronization protocol to protect the access to the different critical sections (i.e. shared resources) defined in the concurrency model. On the other hand, the target RTOS on which the application (i.e. the PIM) will be deployed, does not provide this protocol. In that case, if the concurrency model consists of at least two tasks that share more than one resource at the same time, a deadlock may occur at the implementation level. Therefore, this pattern must be applied to prevent this risk.

3.2 Solution Description

Let's consider an initial concurrency model M which consists of m tasks $\{T_1, T_2, ., T_m\}$ and p resources $\{R_1, R_2, ., R_p\}$ that can be used by one or several tasks. Let's consider also two tasks T_i and $T_j \in \{T_1, T_2, ., T_m\}$ such as these two tasks share two resources R_n and $R_m \in \{R_1, R_2, ., R_p\}$ at the same time.

In order to enable timing verification of this concurrency model at the design level, we assume that the *PCP* protocol is used to implement all the shared resources in this model. Thus, based on the lock time of the different resources by the tasks (c_{R_i,T_j}) and some other parameters of tasks such as priority, period, computation time, etc. the corresponding analysis test computes the blocking time B_i and the response time Rep_i of the different tasks.

If the selected RTOS does not support PCP protocol to implement the shared resources, three implementations are possible for T_i (respectively for T_j) to access to the resources R_n and R_m. These situations are described in Figure 3.

In fact, at the implementation level, the deadlock may occur when T_i and T_j access to the resources R_n and R_m in a nested way. Consequently the situations 1 and 2 correspond to potential situations for deadlock. For the first situation, the access and release of the resource R_m is done during the critical section of the resource R_n. However in the second situation, the access to the resource R_m is done during the critical section of the resource R_n and the release is done just after the release of the resource R_n.

At the design level these implementation details are abstracted (i.e. we have no idea about how these resources are implemented). Thus, when the concurrency model consists of tasks that share more than one resources at the same time, this pattern supposes that a deadlock may occur and proposes to merge these resources in order to prevent the deadlock. Considering this solution, the resources R_n and R_m previously mentioned will be merged to a resource R'_n ($R'_n = R_n \cup R_m$). The critical section of the resulting resource corresponds to the critical section of R_n and R_m.

The application of this pattern corresponds to the generation of *a re-factored concurrency model* which consists of *p-1* resources. The tasks T_i and T_j in the resulting model share only R'_n instead of R_n and R_m. However, as already mentioned, the re-factored model after applying the SRMP pattern must fulfill the timing properties of the real-time application. Hence, a new timing verification of the resulting model in mandatory. To enable this verification, some input parameters for the analysis test have to be re-computed. These parameters are to: (1) $c_{R'_n,T_i}$: the lock time of the resource R'_n by the task T_i and (2) $c_{R'_n,T_j}$: the lock time of the resource R'_n by the task T_j.

Table 1: Computation of the new lock time depending on the critical sections implementation strategies

Situation 1	The lock time of the resulting resource R'_n by T_i (respectively by t_j) will be equal to the maximum between the lock time of the resource R_n and R_m by the task T_i (i.e. $c_{R'_n,T_i} = max(c_{R_n,T_i}, c_{R_n,T_j})$)
Situation 2	The lock time of the resulting resource R'_n by T_i (respectively by t_j) will be equal to the sum of the lock time of the resource R_n and R_m by the task T_i (i.e. $c_{R'_n,T_i} = c_{R_n,T_i} + c_{R_n,T_j}$).

Figure 4: *Merging the resources R_n and R_m following the SRMP pattern*

As illustrated in Table 1, the computation of these parameters depends on how the tasks access to the resources at the implementation level (i.e. situation 1 or situation 2).

As already mentioned, at the design level we have no idea about the implementation details and consequently we consider always the *worst case* (for the analysis) which corresponds to the second situation (i.e. the sum).

From these considerations, the solution considered by this pattern is the merge of all the resources in the case where they are shared by more than one task at the same time. The critical section of the resulting resource corresponds to the set of critical sections of the initial resources and the lock times of the resulting resource by the tasks will be equal to the sum of the lock times of the different resources by the same tasks. For the previous example the solution is defined as follow:

In the case where a third task T_q uses one of these resources R_n and R_m, we have to update also the lock time of the resulting resource by this task. Consequently, expression 3 gives the general formula used to compute the lock times of the different tasks sharing at least one of the merged resources.

$$c_{R'_n,T_i} = \sum_{R_j \in Used(T_i) \cap R'_n} c_{R_j,T_i}, \forall T_i \in M_{concurrency} \quad (3)$$

In this expression, the term $Used(T_i)$ corresponds to the set of resources used by the task T_i. Therefore, we compute the lock time of this new resource by all the tasks that share one of the resources which constitute this resulting resource (i.e. R_j in $Used(T_i) \cap R'_n$).

3.3 Pattern Structure

Gamma et al. [5] promote the utilization of the UML class diagram to describe the pattern structure involving the different classes participating in the considered pattern. Figure 5 gives the structure of the SRMP pattern. Indeed, in this figure, the concurrency model is represented by an UML class called *ConcurrencyModel*. This class is composed of tasks (class *Task*) and resources (class *Resource*) and defines an *update* method used to produce the re-factored concurrency model after merging resources. The lock time of a resource by a task is represented by an association class called *LockTime* defined by its *value* and an *update* method. The class *Resource* defines the *merge* method which serves to produce the resource resulting from the merge of the resources leading to a potential deadlock.

The client that use the SRMP pattern (represented by the *SRMPClient* class in this figure) must update the initial concurrency model with the resource resulting from the merge to produce the re-factored concurrency model (invokes the *update* method of the *ConcurrencyModel* class) from one side. From the other side, this client must update the lock

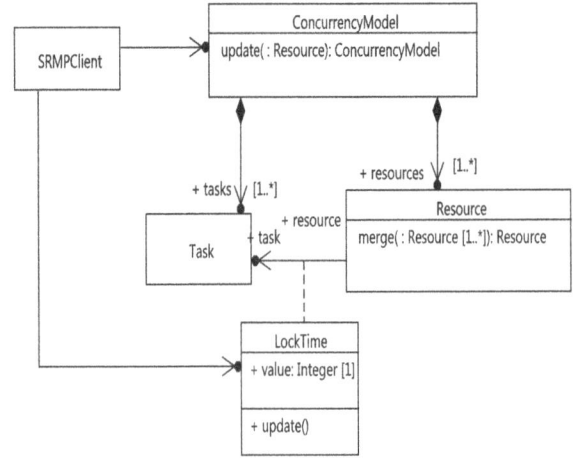

Figure 5: *SRMP Structure*

times of the different tasks using the new resource (invokes the *update* method of the *LockTime* association class).

4. EVALUATION

In this section, the proposed pattern is illustrated through a case study. We give an example of an initial concurrency model describing a real-time application. This model should satisfy the real-time constraints of the application, thus software assumptions are fixed and analysis results are presented. Then, we illustrate the application of the proposed pattern on the considered concurrency model and we discuss the obtained results.

4.1 Initial concurrency model

Figure 6 shows a schematic description of an initial concurrency model describing a real-time application. This model consists of four tasks T_1, T_2, T_3 and T_4 and three resources R_1, R_2 and R_3 shared between the different tasks.

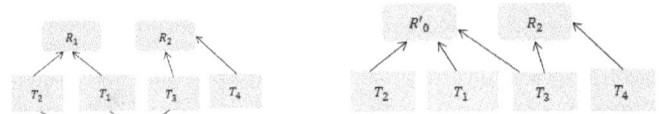

Figure 6: An initial Concurrency Model

Figure 7: Refactored concurrency model resulting from SRMP application

To fulfill the MDA principals, this concurrency model is independent from any particular RTOS. Thus, in order to enable timing verification using schedulability analysis techniques, some software assumptions on the target RTOS must to be considered. So that, we assume:(1) *fixed-priority scheduler* is used to schedule the different tasks in this model. Hence, each task is characterized by a fixed priority value, (2) the priority order is *increasing* i.e. 0 is the lowest priority level and (3) the *PCP protocol* is used as a synchronization protocol to implement the different resources in the model.

Table 2 gives a tabular description of the initial concurrency model (Figure 6) showing the different parameters required to perform schedulability analysis.

Table 2: Initial concurrency model: schedulability analysis parameters

	priority (p_i)	period (P_i)	deadline (D_i)	time Budget (c_i)	Resources Usage (c_{R_i,T_j})
T_1	4	100	100	13	$c_{R_0,T_1}=4$, $c_{R_1,T_1}=7$
T_2	3	100	100	14	$c_{R_0,T_2}=4$, $c_{R_1,T_2}=7$
T_3	2	200	200	8	$c_{R_0,T_3}=4$, $c_{R_2,T_3}=3$
T_4	1	200	200	9	$c_{R_2,T_4}=3$

Consequently, a schedulability analysis test can be carried out on this model (table 2). Such test calculates the worst case response times of the different tasks Rep_i. Note that the worst-case response time includes the blocking time B_i calculated by the test (the computation of the term B_i depends on the synchronization protocol used to implement the shared resource). The different analysis results are given in table 3.

Table 3: Initial concurrency model: schedulability analysis results

	T_1	T_2	T_3	T_4
blocking Time (B_i)	7	4	3	0
Response Time (Rep_i)	20	31	38	44

The response times of different tasks in the initial concurrency model are lower than their deadlines. Thus, this models satisfies the timing constraints.

4.2 SRMP application

The designer aims to deploy the initial concurrency model presented in Figure 6 on the VRTX [1] operating system. In terms of synchronization protocols, this RTOS provides just the Priority Inheritance Protocol (PIP) [17]. From the other side, the initial concurrency model presents a potential situation of deadlock since the tasks T_1 et T_2 in this model share the resources R_0 and R_1 at the same time (i.e. Shared(T_1,T_2)= $\{R_0, R_1\}$). Consequently, in that case, the SRMP pattern must be applied to prevent deadlocks at the implementation level.

4.2.1 Re-factored concurrency model

A schematic description of the re-factored concurrency model resulting from SRMP application on the initial concurrency model (Figure 6) is given in Figure 7.

In this model, the resources R_0 and R_1 are merged into a single resource R'_0. Consequently, the tasks T_1 and T_2 share only R'_0 instead of R_0 and R_1. In addition, the task T_3 shares R'_0 with T_1, T_2 instead of R_0 and shares R_2 with T_4.

After applying the SRMP pattern, it is important to verify whether the re-factored concurrency model still satisfying the timing requirements of the application. In terms of scheduling parameters, only the lock times of the new resource R'_0 by the different tasks that share it, must be updated flowing expression 3. Table 4 gives a tabular description of the re-factored concurrency model (Figure 7) showing the different parameters required to perform schedulability analysis.

Table 4: Re-factored concurrency model: schedulability analysis parameters

	priority (p_i)	period (P_i)	deadline (D_i)	time Budget (c_i)	Resources Usage (c_{R_i,T_j})
T_1	4	100	100	13	$c_{R'_0,T_1}=11$
T_2	3	100	100	14	$c_{R'_0,T_2}=11$
T_3	2	200	200	8	$c_{R'_0,T_3}=4$, $c_{R_2,T_3}=3$
T_4	1	200	200	9	$c_{R_2,T_4}=3$

Analysis results carried out on the re-factored concurrency model are given in table 5. Note that the computation of the blocking term assumes that the *PIP protocol* is used to protect the access to the shared resources in this model. This table shows that the response times of the different tasks in the re-factored concurrency model are lower than their deadlines. Hence, this model respects timing properties of the application.

Table 5: Re-factored concurrency model: schedulability analysis results

	T_1	T_2	T_3	T_4
blocking Time (B_i)	11	4	3	0
response Time (Rep_i)	24	31	38	44

4.2.2 Discussion

The analysis results, given in table 5, show that the response time of the task T_1 increases after applying the SRMP pattern. Indeed, the purpose behind pattern application in our approach is to prevent deployment problems. This is achieved by performing architectural refactorings at early stages of the Model-based development flow (at the design level before the effective deployment), even at the expense of some performance loss. This bring us to define the deployment cost of a real-time application, in a model-driven approach, on a given *RTOS family not allowing the use of PCP synchronization protocol*.

$$Cost_{deployment} = 1 - \frac{\sum_{T_i \in M_{initial}} Rep_{T_i}}{\sum_{T_i \in M_{refactored}} Rep_{T_i}} \quad (4)$$

The formula expressing this *Cost* is given in expression 4. The deployment cost for the considered example is equal to 0.03. This means that the application of the SRMP pattern for this example leads to 3 % of performance degradation.

Note that this deployment cost strongly depends on the real-time application. Indeed, this cost is all the more important since the number of shared resources leading to a potential deadlock is more important.

5. RELATED WORK

Several works have proposed patterns in the real-time and embedded domains. For instance, in [16], the authors propose a set of patterns for the development of Distributed Real-Time (DRE) applications with the aim to satisfy the real-time needs of these applications. The general context of the proposed patterns in this paper [16] is DRE applications based on the real-time CORBA standard [7]. In [4], the author propose C-based design patterns for embedded systems. In particular, the author defines two patterns for deadlocks avoidance (Simultaneous Locking Pattern and Ordered Locking) for embedded systems based on C language. Nevertheless, these patterns correspond to platform-specific solutions and can not be applied at the design level of a model-based flow.

In a model-driven context, the development of real-time embedded systems promotes timing verification from the design level. In that context, model-based approaches consider assumptions on the underlying software platform to keep RTOS-independence from one side and to enable timing verification of the concurrency model from the other side [10] [3]. These approaches assume that the target software platform is an ideal one and they do not focus on implementation issues. Consequently, many problems may appear after deployment which requires architectural refactorings in order to find an "implementable" solution. In that context we have proposed in previous work [13] an approach to detect these problems before the effective deployment and to perform the refactoring of the concurrency model if necessary (i.e. if a deployment problem appears) based on a set of patterns. We have also proposed, in this previous work, the Distinct Priority Merge Pattern (DPMP) which aims to solve a deployment problem related to the number of distinct priority levels. The present work is a step toward enriching our pattern base by proposing the Shared Resource Merge Pattern (SRMP) dealing with a new deployment problem related to the synchronization protocol used to implement a critical section in the concurrency model.

6. CONCLUSIONS AND FUTURE WORK

In this paper, we have proposed a software real-time pattern called Shared Resource Merge Pattern(SRMP).This pattern aims to prevent deadlocks in a model-driven approach, from the design level, when the PCP protocol is not provided by the target Real-Time Operating System (RTOS) on which the real-time application will be deployed. The application of this pattern on the initial concurrency model corresponds to the generation of the refactored real-time concurrency model.The resulting model must in turn meet the timing constraints of the real-time application. We have shown, in this paper, that the purpose behind proposing this pattern is to solve a particular deployment problem of a real-time application even at the expense of some performance loss. Such approach provides a guideline for the designer to find an "implementable" concurrency model describing a real-time application for a given RTOS family witout a complete re-design of the application.

As perspective of this work, we aim at considering other real-time software patterns to enrich the pattern base and to tackle other deployment problems (deployment problems related to the priority concept or communication mechanisms for example).

7. REFERENCES

[1] VRTX, "VRTX Real-Time Operating System". http://www.mentorgraphics.com/embedded/vrtxos/.

[2] MicroC/OS-II. http://micrium.com/rtos/ucosii/overview/, 2012.

[3] C. Bartolini, G. Lipari, and M. Di Natale. From functional blocks to the synthesis of the architectural model in embedded real-time applications. In Real Time and Embedded Technology and Applications Symposium, 2005. RTAS 2005. 11th IEEE, pages 458–467. IEEE, 2005.

[4] B. P. Douglass. Design Patterns for Embedded Systems in C: An Embedded Software Engineering Toolkit. Elsevier, 2010.

[5] G. Erich, H. Richard, J. Ralph, and V. John. Design patterns: elements of reusable object-oriented software. Reading: Addison Wesley Publishing Company, 1995.

[6] J. B. Goodenough and L. Sha. The priority ceiling protocol: A method for minimizing the blocking of high priority Ada tasks, volume 8. ACM, 1988.

[7] O. M. Group. The Common Object Request Broker (CORBA): Architecture and Specification. Object Management Group, 1995.

[8] B. Kienhuis, E. F. Deprettere, P. van der Wolf, and K. Vissers. A methodology to design programmable embedded systems. In Embedded processor design challenges, pages 18–37. Springer, 2002.

[9] M. H. Klein, T. Ralya, B. Pollak, R. Obenza, and M. G. Harbour. A practitioner's handbook for real-time analysis. Kluwer Academic Publishers, 1993.

[10] C. Mraidha, S. Tucci-Piergiovanni, and S. Gerard. Optimum: a marte-based methodology for schedulability analysis at early design stages. ACM SIGSOFT Software Engineering Notes, 36(1):1–8, 2011.

[11] R. Mzid, C. Mraidha, J.-P. Babau, and M. Abid. A mdd approach for rtos integration on valid real-time design model. In Software Engineering and Advanced Applications (SEAA), 2012 38th EUROMICRO Conference on, pages 9–16. IEEE, 2012.

[12] R. Mzid, C. Mraidha, J.-P. Babau, and M. Abid. Real-time design models to rtos-specific models refinement verification. In Proceedings of the 5th International Workshop on Model Based Architecting and Construction of Embedded Systems, pages 25–30. ACM, 2012.

[13] R. Mzid, C. Mraidha, A. Mehiaoui, S. Tucci-Piergiovanni, J.-P. Babau, and M. Abid. Dpmp: a software pattern for real-time tasks merge. In Modelling Foundations and Applications, pages 101–117. Springer, 2013.

[14] OMG. MDA Guide Version 1.0.1. OMG omg/2003-06-01, June 2003.

[15] B. Schätz, A. Pretschner, F. Huber, and J. Philipps. Model-based development of embedded systems. In Advances in Object-Oriented Information Systems, pages 298–311. Springer, 2002.

[16] D. C. Schmidt and C. OâĂŹRyan. Patterns and performance of distributed real-time and embedded publisher/subscriber architectures. Journal of Systems and Software, 66(3):213–223, 2003.

[17] L. Sha, R. Rajkumar, and J. P. Lehoczky. Priority inheritance protocols: An approach to real-time synchronization. Computers, IEEE Transactions on, 39(9):1175–1185, 1990.

Software QoS Enhancement through Self-adaptation and Formal Models

Raffaela Mirandola
Politecnico di Milano
Dipartimento di Elettronica, Informazione e
Bioingegneria
Milano, Italy
raffaela.mirandola@polimi.it

Diego Perez-Palacin
Politecnico di Milano
Dipartimento di Elettronica, Informazione e
Bioingegneria
Milano, Italy
diego.perez@polimi.it

1. ABSTRACT

Modern software operates in highly dynamic and often unpredictable environments that can degrade its quality of service. Therefore, it is increasingly important having systems able to adapt their behavior to the environment where they execute at any moment. Nevertheless, software with self-adaptive capabilities is difficult to develop. To make easier its development, different architectural frameworks have been proposed during the last years. A shared characteristic among most frameworks is that they define applications that make an internal use of models, which are analyzed to discover the configurations that better fit in the changing environments.

In this context, this tutorial presents the current research advances on architectural frameworks for building self-adaptive software that meets its Quality of Service (QoS). We discuss architectures that use self-adaption to improve the QoS and whose adaptations are planned as a result of the analysis of formal models. We also describe a set of current research challenges that are still preventing the complete automatic control of dependable self-adaptive software.

Categories and Subject Descriptors

D.2.9 [**Software Engineering**]: [Software quality assurance (SQA)];
D.2.11 [**Software Engineering**]: [Software Architectures]

Keywords

Quality of Service; Self-adaptive software; Models;

2. OVERVIEW

The success in the marketplace of a software application, nowadays, is often conditioned by its offered QoS. However, a satisfactory QoS is not always easy to achieve and, this difficulty can be exacerbated when the application execution environments are dynamic or even unknown at design time. In the worst case, it may be even impossible to develop a static application that meets its required QoS in every potential environment.

The development of software that autonomously manages and changes its behavior at runtime has been proposed as a possible so-lution to deal with these situations. To make easier the development of this type of software, the Software Engineering research community has proposed architectural methodologies and frameworks [9, 5, 11, 7, 10]. In the following, we use the term *self-adaptive software* to refer to this kind of systems. In this tutorial we introduce these architectural approaches and then we concentrate on a deeper description and usage of one of them, the three-layer architecture presented in [10]. A common step of all of these methodologies is that self-adaptive software needs to plan its adaptations, which is usually a complex and time consuming task that requires some analysis and deliberations. For doing its adaptation planning, software uses models of its execution environment and of its internal behavior and characteristics. These models are analyzed to obtain results of the software configuration that can better deal with environment changes. To obtain reliable results from the analysis of the models, formal methods can be used [1]. In this manner, self-adaptive software can take advantage of the expertise of the formal methods community on accurate model analysis to plan the best configuration and the corresponding adaptation activities.

In this tutorial we explain some techniques and research advances for QoS enhancement using formal methods for the adaptation planning (i.e., what to adapt) and adaptation decision (i.e., when to adapt) activities of self-adaptive software [20, 4, 13, 12, 14, 16, 18]. The QoS and non-functional properties that will be illustrated are: service performance, availability, energy consumption of software and running cost.

This tutorial describes the current trends, research achievements and research challenges on the satisfaction of the QoS requirements of software systems using self-adaptation.

3. DETAILED OUTLINE

The tutorial consists of the following parts:

Part 1: QoS assurance under requirements tradeoffs.

We start the tutorial describing the importance for software systems to execute with an appropriate QoS and we provide an introduction of model-based software analysis for QoS assessment in static systems. Then, we briefly introduce some of the analysis approaches based on formal methods. We then discuss the limitations of static software to execute with good QoS in dynamic environments.

Part 2: Self-adaptation and Software architectures.

We proceed by describing the main aspects of self-adaptive systems. We describe several proposed methodologies to build self-adaptive software and we explain in depth one of them: an architectural methodology based on a three-layer architecture [10]. We describe approaches for self-adaptive software where adaptations are intended to improve the QoS [2, 3, 6, 4] and we detail the in-

Permission to make digital or hard copies of part or all of this work for personal or classroom use is granted without fee provided that copies are not made or distributed for profit or commercial advantage, and that copies bear this notice and the full citation on the first page. Copyrights for third-party components of this work must be honored. For all other uses, contact the owner/author(s). Copyright is held by the author/owner(s).

QoSA'14, June 30–July 4, 2014, Marcq-en-Baroeul, France.
ACM 978-1-4503-2576-9/14/06.
http://dx.doi.org/10.1145/2602576.2611459 .

stantiation of the three-layer architecture with the QoS enhancement goal.

Part 3: Formal methods for self-adaptive software planning activity.

We detail the research advances on the activity of planning adaptations of self-adaptive software. We focus on research advances that use formal methods at runtime to evaluate the software behavior, plan adaptations and decide when to adapt [12, 8, 13]. These techniques use the previous knowledge on QoS evaluation (e.g., performance or availability evaluation) of static software systems using formal methods.

One of the aspect of the dynamic contexts that requires an accurate modeling is the workload the application has to execute. Indeed, many proposals for the development of self-adaptive software systems were conceived for solving the problem of QoS satisfaction of software systems that operate on the Internet under variable workload.

Part 4: Research challenges for self-adaptive software

We conclude the tutorial by presenting some of the current research challenges to make self-adaptive software a reality broadly adopted by software application developers. At the current state of the art in the research in self-adaptive software, many concerns are still a challenge and there is not a solution to enable software to behave autonomously, correctly and showing high dependability. Currently, some aspects of self-adaptive software still need to be guided by engineers, domain experts or sysadmins to allow appropriate adaptation decisions. For example:

- The inclusion of a human in the loop to reason about the achievability of QoS requirements. We present an approach based on adaptability metrics to guide the system in its finding potentially suitable architectures for obtaining the pursued QoS [17, 19].

- Uncertainties in the models managed by self-adaptive software that are used to reason about adaptations [15].

4. INTENDED AUDIENCE

The tutorial will highlight challenges of building software with a required QoS that can be only achieved through self-adaptation. The tutorial covers the areas of software architectures, quality of service and architectures of self-adaptive systems. There are not specific pre-requisites for this tutorial but basic knowledge of software engineering principles and interest in the software QoS.

5. REFERENCES

[1] R. Calinescu, C. Ghezzi, M. Z. Kwiatkowska, and R. Mirandola. Self-adaptive software needs quantitative verification at runtime. *Commun. ACM*, 55(9):69–77, 2012.

[2] R. Calinescu, L. Grunske, M. Z. Kwiatkowska, R. Mirandola, and G. Tamburrelli. Dynamic QoS management and optimization in service-based systems. *IEEE Trans. on Software Engineering*, 37(3):387–409, 2011.

[3] V. Cardellini *et al.*. MOSES: A framework for QoS driven runtime adaptation of service-oriented systems. *IEEE Trans. on Software Engineering*, 38(5):1138–1159, 2012.

[4] V. Cardellini, E. Casalicchio, V. Grassi, F. Lo Presti, and R. Mirandola. QoS-driven runtime adaptation of service oriented architectures. In *Procs. of the the 7th Joint Meeting of the European Software Engineering Conference and the ACM SIGSOFT Symposium on The Foundations of Software Engineering*, ESEC/FSE '09, pages 131–140, New York, NY, USA, 2009. ACM.

[5] S. Dobson *et al.*. A survey of autonomic communications. *ACM Trans. on Auton. and Adap. Syst.*, 1(2):223–259, 2006.

[6] I. Epifani, C. Ghezzi, R. Mirandola, and G. Tamburrelli. Model evolution by run-time parameter adaptation. In *Procs. of the 31st Int. Conference on Software Engineering*, ICSE '09, pages 111–121. IEEE, 2009.

[7] D. Garlan, S.-W. Cheng, A.-C. Huang, B. Schmerl, and P. Steenkiste. Rainbow: architecture-based self-adaptation with reusable infrastructure. *Computer*, 37(10):46–54, 2004.

[8] C. Ghezzi, A. Motta, V. Panzica La Manna, and G. Tamburrelli. QoS driven dynamic binding in-the-many. In *Research into Practice - Reality and Gaps*, volume 6093 of *LNCS*, pages 68–83. Springer Berlin Heidelberg, 2010.

[9] J. Kephart and D. Chess. The vision of autonomic computing. *Computer*, 36(1):41–50, 2003.

[10] J. Kramer and J. Magee. Self-managed systems: An architectural challenge. In *2007 Future of Software Engineering*, FOSE '07, pages 259–268, Washington, DC, USA, 2007. IEEE Computer Society.

[11] P. Oreizy *et al.*. An architecture-based approach to self-adaptive software. *IEEE Intelligent Systems*, 14(3):54–62, 1999.

[12] D. Perez-Palacin and J. Merseguer. Performance sensitive self-adaptive service-oriented software using hidden markov models. In *Procs. of the 2nd ACM/SPEC Int. Conference on Performance Engineering*, ICPE '11, pages 201–206, New York, NY, USA, 2011. ACM.

[13] D. Perez-Palacin, J. Merseguer, and S. Bernardi. Performance aware open-world software in a 3-layer architecture. In *Procs. of the First Int. Conference on Performance Engineering*, WOSP/SIPEW '10, pages 49–56, New York, NY, USA, 2010. ACM.

[14] D. Perez-Palacin, J. Merseguer, and R. Mirandola. Analysis of bursty workload-aware self-adaptive systems. In *Procs. of the 3rd ACM/SPEC Int. Conf. on Performance Engineering*, ICPE '12, pages 75–84, New York, NY, USA, 2012. ACM.

[15] D. Perez-Palacin and R. Mirandola. Uncertainties in the modeling of self-adaptive systems: A taxonomy and an example of availability evaluation. In *Procs. of the 5th ACM/SPEC Int. Conference on Performance Engineering*, ICPE '14, pages 3–14, New York, NY, USA, 2014. ACM.

[16] D. Perez-Palacin, R. Mirandola, and J. Merseguer. Enhancing a QoS-based self-adaptive framework with energy management capabilities. In *Procs. of the 7th Int. Conference on Quality of Software Architectures*, QoSA'11, pages 165–170, New York, NY, USA, 2011. ACM.

[17] D. Perez-Palacin, R. Mirandola, and J. Merseguer. Software architecture adaptability metrics for QoS-based self-adaptation. In *Procs. of the 7th Int. Conference on Quality of Software Architectures*, QoSA'11, pages 171–176, New York, NY, USA, 2011. ACM.

[18] D. Perez-Palacin, R. Mirandola, and J. Merseguer. QoS and energy management with petri nets: A self-adaptive framework. *Journal of Syst. Soft.*, 85(12):2796–2811, 2012.

[19] D. Perez-Palacin, R. Mirandola, and J. Merseguer. On the relationships between QoS and software adaptability at the architectural level. *Journal of Syst. Soft.*, 87:1–17, 2014.

[20] D. Sykes, W. Heaven, J. Magee, and J. Kramer. Exploiting non-functional preferences in architectural adaptation for self-managed systems. In *Procs. of the 2010 ACM Symposium on Applied Computing*, SAC '10, pages 431–438, New York, NY, USA, 2010. ACM.

Designing and Evolving Distributed Architecture using Kevoree

François Fouquet
Grégory Nain
Interdisciplinary Center for
Security Reliability and Trust
(SnT)
University of Luxembourg

Erwan Daubert
Johann Bourcier
Olivier Barais
Noel Plouzeau
University of Rennes 1, IRISA
INRIA Centre Rennes, France

Brice Morin
SINTEF ICT
Oslo, Norway

ABSTRACT

Modern software applications are distributed and often operate in dynamic contexts, where requirements, assumptions about the environment, and usage profiles continuously change. These changes are difficult to predict and to anticipate at design time. The running software system should thus be able to react on its own, by dynamically adapting its behavior, in order to sustain a required quality of service. A key challenge is to provide the system with the necessary flexibility to perform self-adaptation, without compromising dependability. Models@Runtime is an emerging paradigm aiming at transferring traditional modeling activities (focusing on quality, verification, and so on) performed by humans, to the running system. In this trend, Kevoree provides a models@ runtime platform to design heterogeneous, distributed and adaptive applications based on the component based software engineering paradigm. At the end of this tutorial, applicants will be able to develop and assemble new components and communication channel to design complex self- adaptable distributed architectures by reusing existing piece of code.

1. PRESENTERS

Dr François Fouquet is Research Associate at SnT Luxembourg. He holds a Master degree in Software Engineering at the University of Rennes 1 in 2009 and he obtained his PhD thesis from the Triskell research group in Rennes in 2013. His main activities are related to Model-Driven Engineering, Dynamically Adaptable Cyber Physical Systems and Search-based and evolutionary algorithms. As main contributor of the Kevoree project, he namely contributes to apply it to drive Cyber Physical Systems and massive distributed systems such as Cloud computing. Today he is involved in the SmartGrid project for the Luxembourg City, trying to make Smart Cities more sustainable using sensors values.

Dr Olivier Barais (http://goo.gl/fQOF7) is an Associate Professor at the University of Rennes 1, member of the Triskell INRIA research team. He received an engineering degree from the Ecole des Mines

de Douai, France in 2002 and a PhD in computer science from the University of Lille 1, France in 2005. After having been a PhD student in the Jacquard INRIA research team, he is currently associate professor at University of Rennes 1 and a member of the Triskell INRIA group. His research interests include Component Based Software Design, Model-Driven Engineering and Aspect Oriented Modeling. Olivier Barais has co-authored 8 journals, 36 international conference papers, 2 book chapters and 26 workshop papers in conferences and journals such as SoSyM, IEEE Computer, ICSE, MoDELS, SPLC and CBSE.

Dr. Grégory Nain is Research Associate at SnT in Luxembourg. As head of the Internet of Things Laboratory Infrastructure of the SnT, his main activities focus on supporting research activities related to the Internet of Things domain and Cyber Physical Systems, by providing help for the realization of tests, experimentations and validations of IoT-related software systems. He is also participating to the Kevoree project effort, and uses this development platform and Model-Driven Engineering approaches to implement the IoT Lab base software system.

2. DURATION

The workshop duration is half a day (4 hours). The type of tutorial will be a hands-on tutorial. This tutorial requires a room with wireless access for participants. We expect 15-20 participants.

3. SCOPE

The intended audience is both software engineers/researchers and PhD students. The attendants must have a laptop with Virtual Box installed or a laptop with a JDK 1.8 and a recent Java IDE. The attendants must be familiar with Java or any Object Oriented Technology. Academics and practitioners alike will benefit from the tutorial. We expect that the presentation is of particular interest for builders of distributed tools and algorithms, both academics and practitioners, who would like to have abstractions to deal with heterogeneous and distributed adaptive applications.

4. GOAL AND OBJECTIVES

The goal of this tutorial is to provide the fundamentals of the Kevoree framework language for designing heterogeneous and distributed adaptive applications.

The goal of this tutorial is to present Kevoree through a practical session to a wide number of Software Engineering practitioners. This event would be a great venue for people to learn-by-example about dynamic adaptations, distribution and continuous design in a reliable environment. This tutorial is also intended to be a privi-

Permission to make digital or hard copies of part or all of this work for personal or classroom use is granted without fee provided that copies are not made or distributed for profit or commercial advantage, and that copies bear this notice and the full citation on the first page. Copyrights for third-party components of this work must be honored. For all other uses, contact the owner/author(s). Copyright is held by the author/owner(s).

QoSA'14, June 30–July 4, 2014, Marcq-en-Baroeul, France.
ACM 978-1-4503-2576-9/14/06.
http://dx.doi.org/10.1145/2602576.2611461.

leged moment to collect comments and feedback on our approach and realizations.

This overall goal can be broken down into several concrete sub-objectives:

1. Component development Use the Kevoree Annotation API to create component types, then use a Kevoree Maven plugin to extract the components' models at compile time.

2. Assembly (graphical & script) Use editor to assemble an application through a graphical DSL or through the use of a Kevoree Script.

3. Deployment on (single & multiple) node Experiment the simple deployment on single vs multiple execution nodes.

4. Continuous Design Experiment the continuous design facilities of Kevoree that shorten the development cycles.

5. Development of Self-Adaptive system Design and create a self-adaptive system, through the development of a simple ECA reactive system.

6. Cloud infrastructure management Deployment of an application in a private Cloud, and perform cross-layer adaptations using the Kevoree abstraction.

5. OVERVIEW OF THE TUTORIAL

The tutorial divides into four main parts here described.

5.1 Part 0 - Introduction (20 min talk - 20 min Prerequisites)

Presentation This first part introduces models@runtime and the Kevoree Framework. After a bit of history, some facts, and examples of realizations, the participants prepare their machines with the necessary tools for the following parts.

Prerequisites The practical session of this part ensures that a JDK and a JavaIDE are available.

Material http://kevoree.org/doc/

5.2 Part 1 - The basics (20 min talk - 30 min hands-on)

Presentation In this part, the different basic features manipulated in Kevoree are presented. Participants get familiar with the Domain Specific language used in Kevoree to deal with distributed systems.

Practical The participants discover the Kevoree Editor and During and Runtime in this practice. They have to create a first application, deploy it and run it.

Material http://kevoree.org/practices/level0/

5.3 Part 2 - Do-It-Yourself (20 min talk - 30 min hands-on)

Presentation The presentation of this session describes how to create a Kevoree Component Type. It introduces the Annotation API, used to describe the component type in the code, and the Compilation Chain to extract the component model at compile time, and create the component library.

Practical In this session, attendees complete and change a sample Producer/Consumer component code. They then go through the entire chain from development to deployment and experience the continuous design abilities of Kevoree. Through this session, they will also discover the Kevoree development plugins within Eclipse or IntelliJ.

Material http://kevoree.org/practices/level1/

5.4 Part 3 - Self-Adaptation@Runtime (15 min talk - 45min hands-on)

Presentation Finally, we present the principle of using Models@Runtime to develop self-adaptive systems, that can autonomously adapt at runtime.

Practical Participants have to two kinds of reasonning engine. (i) a simple Event-Condition-Action reasoner that modifies the model of the running system and ask for an adaptation at runtime. (ii) an advanced reasonning engine that uses genetic algorithms to explore the architectural solution space to find a suitable architecture on a multi-criteria decision challenge.

Material http://kevoree.org/practices/level2/

5.5 Part 4 - Cloud adaptation using Kevoree (10 min talk - 30 min hands-on))

Presentation This part presents how the abstractions provided by Kevoree can be used to drive a cross-layer cloud adaptation).

Practical Participants have to design a simple architecture to drive several system virtual machines (built on top of LXC (https://github.com/lxc/lxc)).

Material http://kevoree.org/practices/level3/

6. RESOURCES

Resources about Kevoree are available at http://www.kevoree.org. The source code is available on Github. Some talks given about Kevoree are proposed online along with video tutorials. This tutorial was delivered during the Middleware conference in 2013. (http://2013.middleware-conference.org/tutorial.html)

Acknowledgments

This project is partially funded by the European Commission under the Seventh (FP7 - 2007-2013) Framework Programme for Research and Technological Development in the context of the Heads project. The research activities were also conducted in the context of ITEA2-MERgE (Multi-Concerns Interactions System Engineering, ITEA2 11011), a European collaborative project with a focus on safety and security.

7. REFERENCES

[1] Gordon S. Blair, Nelly Bencomo, and Robert B. France. Models@runtime. *IEEE Computer*, 42(10):22–27, 2009.

[2] François Fouquet, Olivier Barais, Noël Plouzeau, Jean-Marc Jézéquel, Brice Morin, and Franck Fleurey. A Dynamic Component Model for Cyber Physical Systems. In *15th International ACM SIGSOFT Symposium on Component Based Software Engineering*, Bertinoro, Italie, July 2012.

[3] Francois Fouquet, Erwan Daubert, Noel Plouzeau, Olivier Barais, Johann Bourcier, and Arnaud Blouin. Kevoree : une approche model@runtime pour les systemes ubiquitaires. In *UbiMob2012*, Anglet, France, June 2012.

[4] François Fouquet, Erwan Daubert, Noël Plouzeau, Olivier Barais, Johann Bourcier, and Jean-Marc Jézéquel. Dissemination of reconfiguration policies on mesh networks. In *DAIS 2012*, Stockholm, Suède, June 2012.

[5] François Fouquet, Grégory Nain, Brice Morin, Erwan Daubert, Olivier Barais, Noël Plouzeau, and Jean-Marc Jézéquel. An Eclipse Modelling Framework Alternative to Meet the Models@Runtime Requirements. In *Models 2012*, Innsbruck, Autriche, October 2012.

[6] B. Morin, O. Barais, J-M. Jézéquel, F. Fleurey, and A. Solberg. Models@ run.time to support dynamic adaptation. *Computer*, 42(10):44–51, 2009.

[7] Brice Morin, Olivier Barais, Gregory Nain, and Jean-Marc Jezequel. Taming Dynamically Adaptive Systems with Models and Aspects. In *ICSE'09: 31st International Conference on Software Engineering*, Vancouver, Canada, May 2009.

Author Index

www.ingramcontent.com/pod-product-compliance
Lightning Source LLC
Chambersburg PA
CBHW081539220326
41598CB00036B/6484